NORTH CAROLINA GUIDE TO ANIMAL SERVICES LAW

Aimee Wall and Christopher Tyner

UNC | SCHOOL OF GOVERNMENT

The School of Government at the University of North Carolina at Chapel Hill works to improve the lives of North Carolinians by engaging in practical scholarship that helps public officials and citizens understand and improve state and local government. Established in 1931 as the Institute of Government, the School provides educational, advisory, and research services for state and local governments. The School of Government is also home to a nationally ranked Master of Public Administration program, the North Carolina Judicial College, and specialized centers focused on community and economic development, information technology, and environmental finance.

As the largest university-based local government training, advisory, and research organization in the United States, the School of Government offers up to 200 courses, webinars, and specialized conferences for more than 12,000 public officials each year. In addition, faculty members annually publish approximately 50 books, manuals, reports, articles, bulletins, and other print and online content related to state and local government. The School also produces the *Daily Bulletin Online* each day the General Assembly is in session, reporting on activities for members of the legislature and others who need to follow the course of legislation.

Operating support for the School of Government's programs and activities comes from many sources, including state appropriations, local government membership dues, private contributions, publication sales, course fees, and service contracts.

Visit sog.unc.edu or call 919.966.5381 for more information on the School's courses, publications, programs, and services.

Michael R. Smith, DEAN
Thomas H. Thornburg, SENIOR ASSOCIATE DEAN
Jen Willis, ASSOCIATE DEAN FOR DEVELOPMENT
Michael Vollmer, ASSOCIATE DEAN FOR ADMINISTRATION

FACULTY

Whitney Afonso
Trey Allen
Gregory S. Allison
David N. Ammons
Ann M. Anderson
Maureen Berner
Mark F. Botts
Anita R. Brown-Graham
Peg Carlson
Leisha DeHart-Davis
Shea Riggsbee Denning
Sara DePasquale
James C. Drennan
Richard D. Ducker
Jacquelyn Greene

Norma Houston
Cheryl Daniels Howell
Jeffrey A. Hughes
Willow S. Jacobson
Robert P. Joyce
Diane M. Juffras
Dona G. Lewandowski
Adam Lovelady
James M. Markham
Christopher B. McLaughlin
Kara A. Millonzi
Jill D. Moore
Jonathan Q. Morgan
Ricardo S. Morse
C. Tyler Mulligan

Kimberly L. Nelson
David W. Owens
William C. Rivenbark
Dale J. Roenigk
John Rubin
Jessica Smith
Meredith Smith
Carl W. Stenberg III
John B. Stephens
Charles Szypszak
Shannon H. Tufts
Aimee N. Wall
Jeffrey B. Welty
Richard B. Whisnant

The animals featured on the cover and in the pages of this book are family members of School of Government faculty and staff.

Printed in the United States of America

22 21 20 19 18   1 2 3 4 5

ISBN 978-1-56011-937-1

Contents

Acknowledgments

I am delighted to provide this revised and updated version of the 2008 book, *A North Carolina Guide to Animal Control Law*, and I am extremely grateful to have had the opportunity to work with such a fantastic collaborator this time around. This update never would have happened without Chris's patience, persistence, and outstanding scholarship. It is also essential to recognize our School of Government predecessors who paved the way with many earlier animal-related publications, including Patrice Solberg, L. Poindexter Watts, and Ben Loeb, Jr.

I also want to thank the local and state officials who assisted with reviews and feedback throughout the revision process, including Bob Marotto from Orange County Animal Services, Erica Berl from the North Carolina Division of Public Health, and Michael Smallwood from the North Carolina Wildlife Resources Commission. Finally, a big thank you to the School of Government community (and my kids!) for sharing photos for the publication. Special congratulations go to my colleague Cindy Lee, whose dog Moby won our pet photo contest and is featured on the book's cover.

Aimee Wall
Chapel Hill, September 2018

I join in Aimee's delight regarding the release of this book and am grateful for her good-humored collaboration. Her significant experience with the wide variety of animal services issues that arise in North Carolina and her extensive scholarly writings on the subject are the foundation of this publication.

Along with our School of Government predecessors and the state and local officials who contributed to this work, we also want to thank our current colleagues for their invaluable assistance with this publication. Kevin Justice supervised the publication process; Dan Soileau, Emily Hinkle, and Robby Poore provided the book's visual design; Mary Judge coordinated the marketing process; and Melissa Twomey provided a careful editorial review that significantly strengthened this final product. Our thanks to all.

Christopher Tyner
Chapel Hill, September 2018

Chapter 1

Introduction: Framework for Animal Services Law

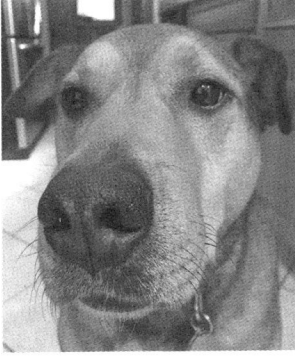

Local governments in North Carolina take the lead in traditional animal services activities, ranging from rabies control to dangerous dogs to animal cruelty. Much of this work is discretionary. The only activities local governments are required to undertake are in the fields of rabies control and dangerous dogs. Many local governments, however, have elected to offer more comprehensive animal services programs as a general public service. This book is designed to provide an overview of the laws that apply in many of the key animal services areas.[1] While it includes a significant amount of legal detail and citations in some areas, the book is not intended to be a resource only for legal professionals. Rather, the goal is to provide information that is accessible and useful for all local government officials interested in and involved with animal services as well as for the general public.

This chapter offers some preliminary background on animal services programs in North Carolina and then provides a general overview of fundamental legal principles that permeate animal services law in North Carolina.

Administrative Responsibility

Perhaps because of the flexibility provided to local governments under state law, there is not really an animal services "system" in North Carolina but, rather, a relatively fragmented set of local government programs, agencies, and staff. In some areas, the county is responsible for many or all functions while in others, the municipalities develop independent programs that run parallel to or complement a county program. Elected boards in some municipalities have, for example, adopted resolutions agreeing to have some or all of the county animal services ordinance apply within the municipality.[2] Some local governments have entered into interlocal agreements related to staffing and service provision within the different jurisdictions.

---

1. An earlier edition of this book uses the term "animal control" rather than "animal services." Several state laws also use the term "animal control." The authors elected to adopt this new, more expansive term to reflect a shift in how many local governments across the state are referring to the agencies that perform these governmental functions.

2. The general rule is that a county ordinance applies only within the unincorporated areas of a county. Chapter 153A, Section 122 of the North Carolina General Statutes (hereinafter G.S.). State law allows municipalities to unilaterally "opt-in" to a county ordinance. G.S. 153A-122(b) ("The governing board of a city may by resolution permit a county ordinance adopted pursuant to this Article to be applicable within the city. . . . The city may by resolution withdraw its permission to such an ordinance. If it does so, the city shall give written notice to the county of its withdrawal of permission; 30 days after the day the county receives this notice the county ordinance ceases to be applicable within the city.").

Within the local government framework, various local government agencies, offices, and departments assume responsibility for providing animal services.[3] County health departments often house county animal services programs because their health directors have several statutorily mandated duties related to rabies control. Other local governments have elected to make animal services a function of law enforcement agencies or public safety departments. Having law enforcement officers available to enforce animal laws can be advantageous when it becomes necessary to conduct a search or make an arrest. Some local governments have placed animal services responsibilities directly in the manager's office or in a separate department. Finally, some have contracted with private nonprofit agencies to manage some animal services functions. Many local governments have also established citizen advisory boards to support animal services.[4] This patchwork "system" can be difficult to navigate for the public and for the state and local government officials who are responsible for administering animal services programs.

Primary responsibility for enforcing animal services laws and running related programs typically rests with animal services employees, although in some jurisdictions, law enforcement officers take the lead. The state's rabies law defines the term "animal control officer" to mean

> [a] city or county employee whose responsibility includes animal control. The term "Animal Services Official" also includes agents of a private organization that is operating an animal shelter under contract with a city or county whenever those agents are performing animal control functions at the shelter.[5]

Because there are so many different administrative homes for animal services programs, these officials may have very different training and backgrounds. State law imposes training and certification requirements in two areas—rabies vaccinators and euthanasia

---

3. Aimee N. Wall, *Animal Control: Who Is Responsible?*, Coates' Canons: NC Loc. Gov't L. blog (UNC School of Government, Feb. 26, 2013), https://canons.sog.unc.edu/animal-control-who-is-responsible-2/.

4. Onslow County, for example, has established an Animal Services Advisory Board (http://www.onslowcountync.gov/1294/Animal-Services-Advisory-Board), and Forsyth County has set up an Animal Control Advisory Board (www.forsyth.cc/animalcontrol/advisory_board.aspx).

5. G.S. 130A-184(1). While the statutes reference "animal control officers," the authors will use the term "animal services officials" when not quoting from the law. (See note 1, *supra*). *See also id.* § 67-30 (authorizing counties to appoint animal services officials). At one time, many counties relied on "dog wardens," officials who were authorized to enforce laws related to dogs. *Id.* § 67-31. Some counties have entertained the idea of appointing dog wardens because G.S. 67-31 grants wardens the power of arrest. The statute is misleading, though, because wardens would be able to exercise the power of arrest only if they were also sworn law enforcement officers. *Id.* § 17C-11 (prohibiting persons from making arrests if they fail to satisfy the standards and requirements established by the North Carolina Criminal Justice Education and Training Standards Commission).

technicians.[6] In all other areas, local governments have flexibility to develop their own training programs or seek out opportunities available from national organizations, community colleges, and others.

Services and Scope

Because of the flexibility provided to local governments under the law and due to resource allocation decisions made at the local level, there is some variety across jurisdictions in the type of services offered as well as the complexity or intensity of those services. The key areas that many programs address are rabies control, dangerous dogs, animal cruelty, stray and nuisance animals, and shelter management. Some local governments also offer other programs and services, such as exotic animal regulation, trap-neuter-release programs to address pet overpopulation concerns, and animal licensing programs.

This book addresses many of these core animal services functions. Note that some significant animal-related topics are largely outside the scope of this book. Hunting, fishing, and other activities involving wildlife fall under the jurisdiction of the state Wildlife Resources Commission and, for the most part, its officers enforce statewide laws. Farm and other animals raised to be commercially processed as food fall under the jurisdiction of the North Carolina Department of Agriculture and Consumer Services. There are some limited areas of overlap between these fields and local government animal services programs, but for the most part they fall outside the scope of this book.

Fundamental Legal Principles

Laws about animals exist at the federal, state, and local levels and are animated by a spectrum of concerns, including protection of individual interests, protection of the public health, and protection of animals themselves. Despite the breadth of the subject, certain fundamental legal principles and relationships spin a common thread that runs through much of the content of this book. The rest of this chapter provides background information about these general principles that may help the reader better understand the detailed discussions of specific areas of law found throughout the rest of the book.

Sources of Law

Each chapter in this book includes summaries and analyses of laws at all three levels of government: federal, state, and local. Federal law is relatively limited in most areas, but there are significant bodies of both state and local animal law. In some areas, such

---

6. G.S. 130A-186 (certified rabies vaccinators); 19A-24 (certified euthanasia technicians).

as rabies, state law dominates the legal landscape. In other areas, such as nuisances, local law will be the primary source of authority. Some of the laws are legislative, which means they were adopted by an elected body, such as the U.S. Congress, the North Carolina General Assembly, a board of county commissioners, or a town council. Other laws are regulatory, which means they were adopted by an administrative or rulemaking body, such as a federal agency, the North Carolina Board of Agriculture, the North Carolina Commission for Public Health, or a local board of health.[7] Some of the legal issues discussed in this book draw heavily on court opinions that have interpreted statutes, regulations, or traditional common law.[8] Some of these court opinions are binding law and others simply provide guidance. Whenever possible, this book tries to highlight the most important laws that apply in any given area, recognizing that other laws may be implicated or involved.

Criminal and Civil Law

It is not unusual for a single incident involving an animal to implicate both criminal and civil law. For example, if a person treats an animal cruelly, he or she may be subject to criminal prosecution under Chapter 14 of the North Carolina General Statutes (hereinafter G.S.) and also subject to a civil action under G.S. Chapter 19A. Though a single act may give rise to both a criminal prosecution and a civil lawsuit, the civil and criminal actions are mostly distinct from each other as a matter of legal substance and procedure. That is why this book discusses criminal animal cruelty and civil animal cruelty in separate chapters. While using this book, a reader should remain mindful of the fact that criminal and civil law are distinct areas of law while also remaining aware that a single practical issue involving an animal may implicate both.

Apart from the fundamental distinction between civil and criminal law, a reader should know that North Carolina, like other states, has a robust law of torts which may impose civil liability upon a person for a wrongful act involving an animal.[9] A substantial amount of tort law is based on common law principles that are not codified in statute. In some cases, the General Statutes explicitly acknowledge the connection between certain animal activities and the law of torts. For example, in addition to establishing a framework that regulates dangerous dogs, Article 1A of G.S. Chapter 67 provides that the owner of a dangerous dog is "strictly liable in civil damages" for any injuries or property damage the dog inflicts.[10] In many other cases, however,

---

7. While technically distinct from a *law*, a *regulation*, in that it is adopted under statutorily granted authority, has the force of law.

8. *Common law* is the "body of law derived from judicial decisions, rather than from statutes or constitutions." BLACK'S LAW DICTIONARY 334 (10th ed. 2014).

9. *See, e.g.,* CHARLES E. DAYE & MARK W. MORRIS, NORTH CAROLINA LAW OF TORTS 412 (2d ed. 1999) (describing animal trespass law in North Carolina in the nineteenth century).

10. G.S. 67-4.4.

the law of torts lurks in the background of the animal issue at hand and any statute that may address the animal issue directly. Here is an example: North Carolina has no statewide leash law or nuisance statute dealing directly with stray animals, but some local governments have enacted leash laws and animal-specific nuisance ordinances. Regardless of the absence of statutory law at the state level and the existence of relevant ordinances in certain localities, the law of torts potentially is applicable to many situations involving at-large or nuisance animals. If a person's dog causes a motor vehicle wreck while at large, the driver may decide to sue the dog's owner in a civil tort action and the presence or absence of an applicable state statute or local ordinance may bear upon the suit only incidentally.

Local Government Authority

Local governments have long had the authority to regulate the treatment and keeping of animals. For the most part, the powers and duties that comprise this authority are permissive rather than mandatory.[11] That is, a local government may choose to regulate animals by ordinance, but a local government is not required to do so. Though North Carolina local governments commonly choose to regulate animals by ordinance, the extent of regulation varies greatly among jurisdictions. Violations of local ordinances are often punishable as misdemeanors. Some jurisdictions also use such civil law remedies as monetary fines, injunctions, or other forms of equitable relief as alternative mechanisms for addressing ordinance violations.[12] A general overview of local government ordinance-making authority follows.

G.S. Chapter 160A delegates certain ordinance-making powers to North Carolina cities. Some ordinance authority speaks directly to issues involving animals while other authority is more general. With regard to animal-specific authority, Chapter 160A explicitly allows cities to

- define and prohibit the abuse of animals;[13]
- regulate, restrict, or prohibit the keeping, running, or going at large of any domestic animals, including dogs and cats;[14]

---

11. Aimee N. Wall, *Mandates in Animal Control: What MUST Local Governments Do?*, COATES' CANONS: NC LOC. GOV'T L. blog (UNC School of Government, Nov. 23, 2009), https://canons.sog.unc.edu/mandates-in-animal-control-what-must-local-governments-do/ (identifying mandates related to dangerous dogs and rabies). See also *infra* chapter 7, "Animal Shelters," discussing minimum holding periods and other requirements that apply if a local government operates an animal shelter.

12. *See* Trey Allen, *Ordinance Enforcement Basics*, COATES' CANONS: NC LOC. GOV'T L. blog (UNC School of Government, Feb. 1, 2016), https://canons.sog.unc.edu/ordinance-enforcement-basics/.

13. G.S. 160A-182.

14. G.S. 160A-186. Ordinances enacted pursuant to this statute often are referred to as "leash laws." *See also* BEN F. LOEB, JR., ANIMAL CONTROL LAW FOR NORTH CAROLINA LOCAL

- regulate, restrict, or prohibit the possession or harboring of animals which are dangerous to persons or property;[15]
- establish a bird sanctuary within city limits;[16]
- levy an annual license tax on the privilege of keeping any domestic animal, including dogs and cats, within the city;[17] and
- establish, equip, operate, and maintain an animal shelter or contribute to the support of an animal shelter.[18]

Cities also have general ordinance-making power pursuant to G.S. 160A-174, which states that "a city may by ordinance define, prohibit, regulate, or abate acts, omissions, or conditions, detrimental to the health, safety, or welfare of its citizens and the peace and dignity of the city, and may define and abate nuisances."[19] This broad authority is often referred to as a city's "police power," and, in conjunction with the animal-specific provisions outlined above, provides North Carolina cities with substantial authority to regulate animals and their owners.[20]

Like cities, North Carolina counties have specific authority to regulate animals by ordinance and also have general ordinance-making power. With respect to specific authority to regulate animals, G.S. Chapter 153A explicitly authorizes counties to

- define and prohibit the abuse of animals;[21]
- regulate, restrict, or prohibit the possession or harboring of animals that are dangerous to persons or property;[22]
- levy an annual license tax on the privilege of keeping dogs and other pets within the county;[23] and

---

Governments 3 (UNC School of Government, 3d ed. 1997).

15. G.S. 160A-187. The statute provides that no ordinance regulating, restricting, or prohibiting the possession or harboring of dangerous animals shall have an effect which conflicts with regulations of the state Wildlife Resources Commission.

16. G.S. 160A-188.

17. G.S. 160A-212.

18. G.S. 160A-493.

19. G.S. 160A-174(a).

20. *See, e.g.,* State v. Maynard, 195 N.C. App. 757, 758–59 (2009) (identifying both G.S. 160-186 and 160A-174 as sources for town's authority to enact ordinance which limited the number of dogs that could be kept on property within town limits and holding the ordinance constitutional).

21. G.S. 153A-127.

22. G.S. 153A-131. As is the case with the analogous authority of cities, the statute provides that no ordinance regulating, restricting, or prohibiting the possession or harboring of dangerous animals shall have an effect which conflicts with regulations of the Wildlife Resources Commission.

23. G.S. 153A-153.

- establish, equip, operate, and maintain an animal shelter or contribute to the support of an animal shelter.[24]

The general ordinance-making power of counties is found in G.S. 153A-121, which states that "[a] county may by ordinance define, regulate, prohibit, or abate acts, omissions, or conditions detrimental to the health, safety, or welfare of its citizens and the peace and dignity of the county; and may define and abate nuisances."[25] Just as with cities, this broad police power, in conjunction with the animal-specific provisions listed above, provides counties with substantial regulatory authority.

Relationship between State Laws and Local Ordinances

While local governments have relatively broad authority to regulate the treatment and keeping of animals by ordinance, this authority is not without limits. Specifically, a local ordinance must not

- infringe a liberty guaranteed to the people by the state or federal constitution;
- make unlawful an act, omission, or condition that is expressly made lawful by state or federal law;
- make lawful an act, omission, or condition that is expressly made unlawful by state or federal law;
- purport to regulate a subject that local governments are expressly forbidden to regulate by state or federal law;
- purport to regulate a field for which a state or federal statute clearly reflects a legislative intention to provide a complete and integrated regulatory scheme exclusive of local regulation; or
- define the elements of an offense in a way that is identical to the elements of an offense defined by state or federal law.[26]

In short, a local ordinance may regulate the same conduct as a state or federal law, but it must not duplicate or undermine the other law. Rather, it should impose higher standards or expectations within the jurisdiction. Given the broad scope of state and federal animal-related laws, local government officials drafting local ordinances need to be familiar with these laws to ensure that they do not run afoul of the restrictions described above.[27] An example of a local ordinance that appropriately builds on state law is Asheville's ordinance that prohibits leaving animals in motor vehicles under

---

24. G.S. 153A-442.

25. G.S. 153A-121(a).

26. G.S. 160A-174(b). While these limitations are named only in the law governing munici-palities, the courts have consistently applied them to counties as well. *See* State v. Tenore, 280 N.C. 238, 248 (1972).

27. *See* G.S. 153A-121 (general ordinance-making power of counties); 160A-174 (general ordinance-making power of cities).

conditions that would endanger their health or well-being.[28] While leaving an animal confined in a hot car could be considered cruelty under the state's criminal cruelty statute, singling out this action in a local ordinance is a reasonable means of addressing a specific local concern without risking explicit duplication of state law.

Challenges to Local Authority

When enacting an animal ordinance and crafting its specific provisions, a local government must consider whether the ordinance can be successfully challenged by a citizen who is opposed to or feels aggrieved by the ordinance. Challenges to the fundamental authority of local governments to regulate animals have seldom been successful. As a general proposition, challenges to local government animal regulation authority take two forms. Sometimes a challenger asserts that a local government lacks authority to implement a particular type of animal regulation. For example, in *State v. Lutterloah*, the defendant argued, unsuccessfully, that the Town of Carolina Beach had no authority to deem it "unlawful to ride, lead, or drive any animal [in certain places] within the corporate limits."[29]

Other times, a challenger does not take issue with a local government's authority to implement a type of regulation but, rather, argues that a specific regulation, though an allowable type, is constitutionally deficient. For example, in *State v. Maynard*, the defendant argued that a town ordinance limiting to no more than three the number of dogs that could be kept on property inside town limits was unconstitutional because it was arbitrary and lacked a rational basis.[30] In other words, the *Maynard* defendant did not contest the town's authority to regulate the keeping of dogs but, rather, contested the town's manner of exercising that authority—the decision to allow for the keeping of no more than three dogs. The paragraphs that follow examine challenges to ordinances in more detail.

North Carolina local governments commonly regulate, through ordinances, animal behavior as well as the manner of care and keeping of animals; depending on the circumstance, a local government may rely on its police power or its animal-specific regulatory authority to enact such ordinances. The North Carolina Supreme Court has

---

28. ASHEVILLE, N.C., CODE OF ORDINANCES, § 3-12(e) ("It shall be unlawful for any person to place or confine an animal or allow an animal to be placed or confined in a motor vehicle under such conditions or for such a period of time as to endanger the health or well-being of such animal due to temperature, lack of food or drink, or such other conditions as may reasonably be expected to cause suffering, disability, or death. After making a reasonable effort to find the driver of a vehicle in which an animal is confined, the animal services official, in the presence of a law enforcement officer, may use the least intrusive means to enter the vehicle if necessary to remove the animal, where reasonable cause exists to believe the animal may die if not immediately removed.").

29. 171 N.C. App. 516 (2005) (unpublished) (rejecting this argument).

30. 195 N.C. App. 757 (2009) (rejecting this argument).

repeatedly found that local governments may regulate the keeping of animals pursuant to this authority, regardless of the animals' behavior. In *State v. Harrell*, for example, the court recognized that "ordinances regulating dogs and requiring them to be registered and licensed, and at times muzzled . . . are within the police powers usually conferred upon the local corporation."[31] In *State v. Stowe*, Charlotte's authority to enact an ordinance that prohibited the keeping of cows within certain areas of the city was sufficiently obvious to the parties such that the city's power to enact it was conceded, though the validity of its terms was disputed.[32] In a later case involving a restriction on keeping animals other than housepets within city limits, *Town of Atlantic Beach v. Young*, the court had no trouble concluding that the restriction fell within a municipal corporation's "power to regulate domestic animals within its corporate limits."[33] In *Maynard*, a 2009 case, as noted above, the court of appeals upheld a town ordinance that limited the number of dogs that could be kept on a parcel of land within town limits, noting that the town had the police power to enact such an ordinance.[34]

Ordinances regulating animal behavior also have been deemed valid. In *Gray v. Clark*, the court of appeals determined that it was within Charlotte's municipal police power to prohibit the keeping of a dog "which habitually or repeatedly chases, snaps at, attacks or barks at pedestrians, bicycles or vehicles or turns over garbage pails or damages gardens, flowers or vegetables, or conducts itself so as to be a public nuisance."[35] In *State v. Taylor*, the court upheld a county ordinance that prohibited the keeping of any animal that "habitually or repeatedly makes excessive noises that tend to annoy, disturb, or frighten [county] citizens."[36] In *Pharo v. Pearson*, the court found that the city of Kinston was authorized to enact an ordinance that prohibited allowing dogs to run at large.[37] As these cases indicate, North Carolina courts consistently have taken the view that local governments have the authority to enact ordinances that regulate the keeping of animals generally, as well as ordinances that regulate animal behavior.

Given that North Carolina courts typically find that local governments have the power to enact ordinances that regulate animals, challengers tend to attack the validity of specific provisions of ordinances using constitutional arguments rather than attack the validity of the enactment of ordinances using arguments about local government

---

31. 203 N.C. 210, 215 (1932) (internal quotation marks omitted) (citation omitted).
32. 190 N.C. 79 (1925).
33. 307 N.C. 422, 427 (1983).
34. 195 N.C. App. 757.
35. 9 N.C. App. 319, 321 (1970).
36. 128 N.C. App. 616, 618 (1998).
37. 28 N.C. App. 171, 174 (1975). Earlier cases also recognized the validity of such ordinances. *See, e.g.*, State v. Tweedy, 115 N.C. 704 (1894) (holding that a person could not be convicted of killing livestock running at large when the livestock was running at large in violation of a valid local ordinance); Jones v. Duncan, 127 N.C. 118 (1900) (confirming that the city had the authority to adopt an ordinance prohibiting livestock from running at large).

ordinance-making authority. As the court of appeals has said, "it is . . . necessary that in using its powers [to regulate animals], the constitutional rights and guarantees of [the local government's] citizens are not infringed upon."[38] Common constitutional arguments leveled against animal ordinances include the following: (1) the ordinance is unconstitutionally vague, (2) the jurisdiction does not have a rational basis for implementing the ordinance as constructed, and (3) the ordinance violates equal protection rights.[39] The challenger bears the burden of establishing the unconstitutionality of an ordinance, and courts approach constitutional challenges with the presumption that the ordinance is constitutional.[40]

An argument that an ordinance is unconstitutionally vague involves the assertion that the challenged ordinance does not sufficiently inform an ordinary person as to what constitutes a violation of the ordinance. Ordinances targeting animal noise provide a good example of challenges based upon vagueness. Despite the relatively general standards and language used in many noise laws, they consistently have been upheld by the courts. For example, Martin County's animal noise ordinance provides that "[i]t shall be unlawful for any person to own, keep, or have within the county an animal that habitually or repeatedly makes excessive noises that tend to annoy, disturb, or frighten its citizens."[41] The court of appeals rejected a claim that the ordinance is unconstitutionally vague, or indefinite. It explained that while the terms used in the ordinance are general in nature, they have "commonly accepted meanings and are sufficiently certain to inform persons of ordinary intelligence as to what constitutes a violation."[42] The court further noted that such ordinances must be enforced and reviewed "based upon an objective standard" that considers the common meanings of the terms used in the law.[43]

The argument that a local government does not have a rational basis for implementing an ordinance, an argument grounded in constitutional principles of due process, often involves an allegation that the ordinance is arbitrary and unreasonable. In order to pass constitutional muster, an ordinance must be reasonably related to the accomplish-

---

38. *Taylor*, 128 N.C. App. at 618.

39. *See, e.g.*, Town of Atl. Beach v. Young, 307 N.C. 422 (1983) (challenger advanced these arguments).

40. *Id.*

41. Martin County, N.C., Code of Ordinances, § 4-6.

42. *Taylor*, 128 N.C. App. at 619.

43. *Id.* at 620. *See also* State v. Dorsett, 3 N.C. App 331, 335–36 (1968) (upholding a Greensboro noise ordinance that prohibited "unreasonably loud, disturbing and unnecessary noise in the city"); State v. Garren, 117 N.C. App. 393, 397–98 (1994) (upholding a provision of a Jackson County noise ordinance prohibiting "loud, raucous and disturbing noise," which was defined as any sound that "annoys, disturbs, injures or endangers the comfort, health, peace or safety of reasonable persons of ordinary sensibilities").

ment of a legitimate government objective.[44] As an example of this sort of challenge, the legitimate state objective that commonly animates animal nuisance ordinances is the exercise of a local government's police power. Thus, the legal question presented by this sort of challenge is whether the provisions of an ordinance are reasonably related to the health and welfare of the local government's citizens.[45] By way of example, North Carolina courts confronting this constitutional argument have upheld ordinances prohibiting the keeping of certain types[46] or certain numbers[47] of animals within a jurisdiction.

An argument that an ordinance violates the constitutional guarantee of equal protection generally involves an allegation that the ordinance impermissibly classifies certain persons and subjects them to unfavorable treatment compared to others. If a classification set out in a local government ordinance is "suspect," meaning that it consists of individuals historically subject to discrimination, courts will apply "strict scrutiny" to the ordinance and require the local government to demonstrate that it is necessary to promote a compelling state interest.[48] Regardless of whether a classification is "suspect," ordinances that classify persons "in terms of their ability to exercise a fundamental right" also are subjected to strict scrutiny.[49] In contrast, if a classification is not "suspect" and does not implicate a fundamental right, courts apply "rational basis scrutiny" to the ordinance and a local government merely has to demonstrate that it bears "some rational relationship to a legitimate state interest."[50] For example, in considering an equal protection challenge to an ordinance prohibiting the keeping of certain types of animals within city limits, the North Carolina Supreme Court decided that the classification based upon ownership of a type of animal was not a suspect classification and that there was not a fundamental right to keep certain types of animals within city limits. Thus, the court applied rational basis scrutiny and found that the ordinance did not violate principles of equal protection because it was rationally related to the local government's interest in protecting the health and welfare of its citizens.[51]

It is clear that courts often uphold local governments' authority to regulate animals, but it is important to be mindful of the scope of that authority when crafting and enforcing ordinances.

---

44. *See, e.g., Young*, 307 N.C. at 428 (explaining this analysis).

45. *Id.*

46. *Id.* (ordinance prohibited the keeping of animals other than housepets within city limits).

47. State v. Maynard, 195 N.C. App. 757 (2009) (ordinance limited number of dogs that could be kept within city limits).

48. *Young*, 307 N.C. at 429 (explaining this analysis).

49. Texfi Indus., Inc. v. City of Fayetteville, 301 N.C. 1, 11 (1980).

50. *Young*, 307 N.C. at 429.

51. *Id.*

Boards of Health

In some counties, animal services programs are administered in whole or in part by local health departments,[52] and each of these departments has a governing board referred to as a *local board of health*.[53] Local boards of health have the authority to adopt local laws called "rules."[54] These rules apply throughout the entire county, including within the municipalities. Violations of board of health rules are punishable as misdemeanors.[55] In addition, a health director may also seek an injunction if a person fails to comply with a rule.[56]

The rule-making authority of boards of health is more limited than the ordinance-making authority addressed above. Under state law, a board of health may only adopt rules that are necessary to "protect and promote the public health."[57] The term "public health" usually refers to issues affecting *human* health.[58] Therefore, while a board of health may appropriately adopt a rule governing rabies (provided it does not conflict with or duplicate state law), it may not be appropriate for the board to adopt rules on animal issues unrelated to human health, such as cruelty or nuisance animals.

Conclusion

With this foundation in the framework and legal landscape for animal services in place, the rest of the book will delve more deeply into the core areas of local government animal services law in North Carolina. After the publication date for this book, it may be useful for readers to periodically visit *Coates' Canons*, the UNC School of Government's local government law blog, to learn about changes to the law that may impact practice.

---

52. *See* Wall, *supra* note 3.

53. The type of governing board varies from county to county. A county may have a single-county board of health or a consolidated human services board. It may be part of a district or a multi-county health department with a district board of health as the governing board. Alternatively, the board of county commissioners may have abolished the governing board and assumed its powers and duties pursuant to G.S. 153A-77. For more details, see JILL D. MOORE, *Public Health, in* COUNTY AND MUNICIPAL GOVERNMENT IN NORTH CAROLINA (UNC School of Government, Frayda S. Bluestein ed., 2d ed. 2014).

54. G.S. 130A-39.

55. G.S. 130A-25.

56. G.S. 130A-18.7.

57. G.S. 130A-39(a).

58. G.S. 130A-39. *See also* INST. OF MED., COMM. FOR THE STUDY OF THE FUTURE OF PUB. HEALTH, THE FUTURE OF PUBLIC HEALTH 7 (1988) (characterizing public health's mission as "fulfilling society's interest in assuring conditions in which people can be healthy").

Chapter 2
Criminal Cruelty

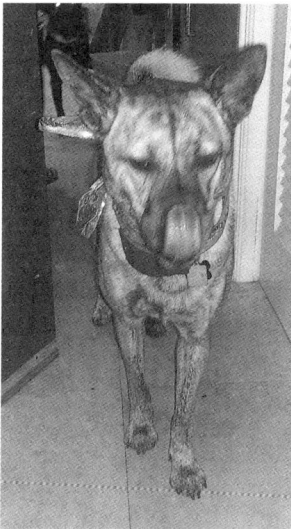

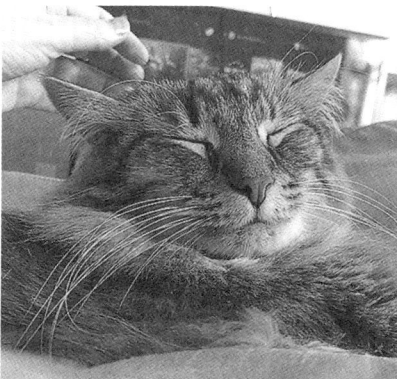

A variety of legal tools are available at the federal, state, and local levels to address the abuse, neglect, or otherwise cruel treatment of animals. Under federal law, a few specific activities, such as animal fighting, are subject to criminal penalties. At the state level, North Carolina law includes both criminal and civil remedies for animal cruelty. The criminal laws target general acts of cruelty as well as such specific activities as animal fighting.[1] The civil remedy allows any person to ask a court to enjoin another person from cruelly treating an animal.[2] Many cities and counties have also adopted ordinances that supplement the remedies available under federal and state law.[3]

This chapter—the first of two addressing animal cruelty laws—reviews the state's criminal cruelty laws in detail and discusses some of the court decisions that have shaped this area of the law. It also briefly discusses federal laws on animal cruelty. Chapter 3 addresses the state's civil remedies, local governments' authority to appoint animal cruelty investigators, and the laws governing those investigators. Neither chapter deals with the law governing an animal owner's ability to sue another person for money damages related to the loss or injury of an animal.

General Cruelty

The earliest state criminal statutes governing animal cruelty were passed in the late nineteenth century. Many of those enacted by the General Assembly as far back as 1881 remain in force today, although amended a good bit over time. The cornerstone of the criminal cruelty laws is the prohibition on cruelty found in Chapter 14, Section 360 of the North Carolina General Statutes (hereinafter G.S.). This provision defines a misdemeanor crime of cruelty to animals as well as a felony, with the primary difference between the misdemeanor and the felony being the defendant's state of mind[4] and, to a lesser extent, the manner of harming the animal. The crimes defined by the statute are discussed in more detail below.

---

1. Article 47 of Chapter 14 of the North Carolina General Statutes (hereinafter G.S.) is entitled "Cruelty to Animals" and contains most of the criminal statutes discussed in this chapter.

2. Article 1 of G.S. Chapter 19A is entitled "Civil Remedy for Protection of Animals" and describes the civil remedy referred to in the text. The civil remedy is discussed in detail in the next chapter of this book.

3. As noted in Chapter 1, the General Assembly has granted cities and counties specific statutory authority to "define and prohibit the abuse of animals." *See* G.S. 153A-127 (counties); 160A-182 (cities).

4. *See, e.g.*, State v. Wilson, ___ N.C. App. ___, 794 S.E.2d 921 (2016) (unpublished) (not paginated on Westlaw) ("[T]he distinguishing factor between the felony and misdemeanor offenses is the presence of malice."), *aff'd per curiam*, 370 N.C. 269 (2017).

Misdemeanor Cruelty

A person is guilty of a Class 1 misdemeanor if he or she

(1) intentionally

(2) (a) overdrives,

    (b) overloads,

    (c) wounds,

    (d) injures,

    (e) torments,

    (f) kills, *or*

    (g) deprives of necessary sustenance

(3) any animal.[5]

A person who causes or procures an act resulting in one of the seven types of cruelty identified above (elements (2)(a)–(g)) also is guilty of misdemeanor cruelty to animals.[6] For example, if Person A persuades Person B to intentionally injure an animal, both Person A and Person B can be charged as principals with misdemeanor cruelty to animals.

For the purposes of misdemeanor cruelty to animals, the term "animal" is defined by statute to include "every living vertebrate in the classes Amphibia, Reptilia, Aves, and Mammalia except human beings."[7] The term does not include fish or insects.[8]

To understand the parameters of misdemeanor cruelty, it is important to take a closer look at the state of mind required by the law. As mentioned above, misdemeanor

---

5. G.S. 14-360(a). For ease of discussion, the authors refer to subsection (a) of G.S. 14-360 as "misdemeanor cruelty" and subsections (a1) and (b) as "felony cruelty" throughout this chapter. Note that these shorthand references apply only in the context of the general animal cruelty law, G.S. 14-360. Other laws related to specific types of cruelty, such as animal fighting and abandonment, are discussed separately.

6. G.S. 14-360(a).

7. G.S. 14-360(c).

8. The categories of animals protected under the law have changed over time. In 1881 the law applied to "any useful beast, fowl, or animal," and "animal" was defined to include "every living creature." N.C. Code §§ 2482, 2490 (1883). The language related to useful beasts was later dropped, but the general category of "every living creature" remained in the law until 1998, when it was changed to "every living vertebrate except human beings." S.L. 1998-212, § 17.16(c). In 1999 the definition took its current form. S.L. 1999-209, § 8.

The same definition is also used in the context of civil animal cruelty cases. *See* G.S. 19A-1(1). One scholar suggests that the definition should be expanded because of its omission of fish. *See* William A. Reppy Jr., *Citizen Standing to Enforce Anti-Cruelty Laws by Obtaining Injunctions: The North Carolina Experience*, 11 Animal L. 39, 45–46 (2005) (advocating a return to the more expansive definition).

cruelty requires that the defendant act "intentionally." According to G.S. 14-360(c), an act is intentional if it is committed

- knowingly and
- without justifiable excuse.[9]

As is the case with each element of the crime, the State bears the burden of proving that a defendant acted intentionally. The two statutory components of the term "intentionally" merit further discussion, in part because it is relatively uncommon for a North Carolina criminal statute to provide a substantive definition of a mental state and in part because the substantive definition combines several criminal law concepts in a somewhat unusual manner. As a general matter, a person must act with a particular state of mind to be guilty of a criminal offense.[10] Different states of mind are required for different offenses in North Carolina; among the various states of mind commonly found in our state's criminal laws are that a defendant act intentionally, that a defendant act knowingly, and that a defendant act willfully (a term generally understood to mean that the defendant acted without excuse or justification).[11] The statutory definition for the term "intentionally" in the context of the animal cruelty law combines these often distinct states of mind in a manner that can be confusing.

The term "knowingly" is not defined in the statute but has been interpreted by the courts in the context of other criminal laws to mean that the person is aware or conscious of what he or she is doing.[12] If, for example, a pet starved to death after the pet's owner suffered a medical emergency and was incapacitated for an extended period of time, the owner likely could not be convicted of misdemeanor cruelty because the owner did not consciously deprive the animal of food and water. As a point of contrast, in *State v. Coble*, the North Carolina Court of Appeals concluded that there was sufficient evidence that the defendant knowingly deprived her dogs of necessary sustenance where the emaciated dogs were discovered at the defendant's house, despite the defendant's contention that a relative was supposed to feed the dogs.[13] The court explained

---

9. G.S. 14-360(c). Note that the Class 1 misdemeanor cruelty charge does not require evidence that the person acted maliciously or with evil intent.

10. *See generally* Jessica Smith, North Carolina Crimes: A Guidebook on the Elements of Crime 3 (UNC School of Government, 7th ed. 2012).

11. *Id.* Acting with malice also is a common state of mind and is discussed in more detail below in the context of felony cruelty to animals.

12. Smith, *supra* note 10, at 6 ("[A] person acts (or fails to act) 'knowingly' when the person is aware of what he or she is doing. . . . [A] person has knowledge of a condition . . . when he or she has actual information concerning the condition. The fact that the circumstances would cause a reasonable person to believe a fact is insufficient to establish that the defendant acted knowingly; to establish this mental state, the person must actually have knowledge of the fact." (internal citations omitted)).

13. 163 N.C. App. 335, 338–39 (2004).

that evidence which tended to show that the defendant knew the dogs were at her house and knew that they were emaciated, yet did not feed or water them, demonstrated that the defendant knowingly deprived the dogs of necessary sustenance.[14]

Whether an act was done without a justifiable excuse[15] is often in dispute. In *State v. Gerberding*, a felony cruelty to animals case involving a defendant who killed her dog after the dog bit her finger, the jury asked the trial court for clarification on the concept of justifiable excuse.[16] Noting that the defendant would not be guilty of either felony or misdemeanor cruelty to animals if the defendant had a justifiable excuse for killing the dog, the trial court explained the concept as follows:

> A justification or excuse is a circumstance, that if it exists, excuses the defendant's actions and the defendant. Even if he or she did the act charged, it would be not guilty because there was a reason for committing the act that the law recognizes as an excuse or valid justification.[17]

In misdemeanor and felony cruelty prosecutions, in order to establish that a defendant acted "intentionally" the State bears the burden of proving that a defendant *did not* have a justifiable excuse for his or her action.[18] Though not an exhaustive list, common examples of justifications or excuses for otherwise criminal conduct include self-defense, defense of others, defense of property, necessity, and duress.[19] The court of appeals also has suggested that punishing an animal in a good faith effort at training could serve as a justification or excuse in some cases,[20] and this suggestion is in accord with the notion that a parent or teacher sometimes may, by virtue of domestic authority, impose moderate punishment to correct a child without criminal liability.[21]

---

14. *Id.*

15. A distinction sometimes is drawn between "excuse" defenses and "justification" defenses in criminal law. The term "justifiable excuse" seems to be a conflation of the two concepts, but neither the distinction nor the conflation have a meaningful impact on this discussion. *Cf.* SMITH, *supra* note 10, at 18 (explaining that whether necessity and duress are "excuse" defenses or "justification" defenses is an academic question).

16. 237 N.C. App. 502, 504–05 (2014).

17. *Id.* at 505.

18. *See, e.g.*, N.C.P.I.—CRIM. 247.10 (in misdemeanor cruelty prosecutions State must prove beyond reasonable doubt that defendant acted without justification or excuse, though pattern instruction suggests that defendant must first assert a justification or excuse in order for jury to be instructed that State must prove that defendant was without such justification or excuse); *id.* § 247.10A (same as to felony cruelty prosecutions); State v. Coble, 163 N.C. App. 335, 338 (2004) (in misdemeanor cruelty case court stated that "the State was required to present substantial evidence that defendant knowingly, and without justifiable excuse, deprived the dogs . . . of necessary sustenance").

19. *See, e.g.*, SMITH, *supra* note 10, at 18. The examples in the text are not an exhaustive list of justifications or excuses.

20. *See* State v. Fowler, 22 N.C. App. 144, 147 (1974).

21. SMITH, *supra* note 10, at 20.

While many of the common justifications or excuses for criminal conduct have not been explicitly considered by North Carolina courts in the context of animal cruelty prosecutions, the courts have long recognized self-defense or defense of others as justifications for acts that otherwise would constitute misdemeanor cruelty.[22] Our courts also have indicated that it may be necessary in some circumstances for a person to kill or injure an animal in order to protect his or her own animal.[23] However, the courts have been careful to narrowly limit the availability of this justification. For example, in 2006 the court of appeals issued an unpublished opinion, *State v. Dockery*, rejecting a defendant's argument that he was justified in killing a dog that was fighting with his dog.[24] In that case, the defendant had stopped the fight but after doing so shot and killed the other dog.[25] The court recognized that (1) neither dog appeared to be the aggressor, (2) the dog killed had no history of aggression, (3) no animals or people were at risk after the fight was interrupted, and (4) the defendant was easily able to stop the fight.[26] Taken together, the court held that these findings supported the State's argument that deadly force was not necessary to protect the defendant's dog or other people and that, therefore, the killing was not justified.

Numerous other cases dating back to the late nineteenth century address the issue of justification. North Carolina courts have found that the following are not legally sufficient justifications for acts of cruelty:

- A person's "desire for amusement and sport"[27]

---

22. *See* State v. Simmons, 36 N.C. App. 354, 355 (1978).

23. *See* Parrott v. Hartsfield, 20 N.C. 242, 244 (1838) ("The law authorizes the act of killing a dog found on a man's premises in the act of attempting to destroy his sheep, calves, coneys [rabbits] in a warren, deer in a park, or other reclaimed animals used for human food and unable to defend themselves. . . . The law is different where the dog is chasing animals *feræ naturæ,* such as hares or deer in a wild state, or combating with another dog."); State v. Dickens, 215 N.C. 303, 305 (1939) ("There was here no evidence offered that the dog of the prosecuting witness, at the time he was killed, was attempting to attack any animal or person, or threatening injury to property, so as to reasonably lead the defendant to believe that it was necessary to kill in order to protect the property of his employer."); *see also* State v. Smith, 156 N.C. 628, 634 (1911) ("If the danger to the animal, whose injury or destruction is threatened, be imminent or his safety presently menaced, in the sense that a man of ordinary prudence would be reasonably led to believe that it is necessary for him to kill, in order to protect his property, and to act at once, he may defend it, even unto the death of the dog, or other animal, which is about to attack it.").

24. 179 N.C. App. 652 (2006) (unpublished) (not paginated on Westlaw).

25. *Id.*

26. *Id.*

27. State v. Porter, 112 N.C. 887, 887 (1893) ("Since [the enactment of the cruelty statute,] it has been unlawful in this state for a man to gratify his angry passions or his love for amusement and sport at the cost of wounds and death to any useful creature over which he has control.").

- A person's "impulse of anger"[28]
- An animal's previous offense, such as trespassing[29]
- An animal's act of damaging crops[30]

Although rather old, the cases cited interpret and apply statutes that are quite similar to North Carolina's current cruelty statute.[31] Thus, they provide useful guidance in determining what constitutes a legally defensible justification. It is worth noting that in very limited circumstances G.S. 67-3 provides specific authority for any person to kill a dog that has killed sheep, other domestic animals, or a human being.[32] After a judicial determination that the dog committed such a killing and notice to the dog's owner or keeper of the situation, the dog may be killed by anyone if discovered at large.[33] The owner of such a dog may also be charged with a Class 3 misdemeanor. In addition, G.S. 67-4 creates an unusual form of civil liability for the owner or keeper of a dog that has been bitten by a "mad dog" (i.e., a rabid dog) if the owner or keeper refuses or neglects to kill the bitten dog.[34] Each of these statutes is fairly antiquated[35] but potentially could serve as a defense to a charge of animal cruelty in some limited situations.

---

28. *Id. See also* State v. Neal, 120 N.C. 613, 619 (1897) (rejecting the defendant's claim that killing chickens out of an "impulse of anger" was legally justified and therefore did not constitute cruelty).

29. State v. Dickens, 215 N.C. 303, 305 (1939) ("The right to slay him cannot be justified by [the dog's] previous act of bursting in through a door, or by the fact that his body emitted an odor peculiar to dogs, but is founded only on the right to protect person or property.").

30. *Neal*, 120 N.C. 613; *see also* State v. Butts, 92 N.C. 784, 787 (1885) ("It never was the law that a man might shoot and kill his neighbor's horses and cows for a trespass upon his crops.").

31. Until 1998 the statute did not specifically state that the act must be without justification. Instead, it provided that the act needed to have been done willfully. *See* S.L. 1998-212, § 17.16(c) (replacing the term "willfully" with "intentionally" and amending the statute to provide the current definition of the term "intentionally"). Earlier, courts interpreted the term "willfully" to require a showing that the act was done "without just cause, excuse, or justification." *Dickens*, 215 N.C. at 305 (quoting State v. Yelverton, 196 N.C. 64, 66 (1928)).

32. G.S. 67-3.

33. *Id.*

34. *See* G.S. 67-4 (providing that such an owner or keeper "shall forfeit and pay the sum of fifty dollars ($50.00) to him who will sue therefor").

35. G.S. 67-4 dates back to 1862 but was amended as recently as 1993 to address the penalties applicable to the dog owner. S.L. 1993-539, § 530 (classifying the misdemeanor and removing language authorizing a $50 fine or imprisonment of no more than 30 days).

Felony Cruelty

G.S. 14-360(a1) and (b) together define the crime of felony cruelty to animals. Felony cruelty to animals is distinguishable from the misdemeanor in two significant ways. First, it requires that a defendant act not only intentionally, as that term is defined by statute, but also with malice. Second, the felony covers several specific acts of cruelty that arguably are more brutal, such as torture, mutilation, and poisoning, than the acts which constitute misdemeanor cruelty to animals.

A person is guilty of a Class H felony if he or she

(1) maliciously
(2) (a) tortures,
    (b) mutilates,
    (c) maims,
    (d) cruelly beats,
    (e) disfigures,
    (f) poisons,
    (g) kills, *or*
    (h) kills by deprivation of necessary sustenance
(3) any animal.[36]

As is the case with misdemeanor cruelty to animals, the statute specifically provides that a person who causes or procures an act which constitutes felony cruelty to animals may be convicted of the crime and punished as a principal.[37]

What Is Malice?

According to G.S. 14-360, an act is committed "maliciously" if it is done (1) intentionally and (2) with malice or bad motive.[38] Because the definition of "maliciously" incorporates the term "intentionally," the statutory definitions of both terms are relevant. "Intentionally" is defined as "knowingly and without justifiable excuse." Taking both definitions together, an act of cruelty is done maliciously if it is committed

- knowingly (with awareness of or consciousness of what one is doing),
- without a justifiable excuse, and
- with malice or bad motive.[39]

The first two concepts are discussed above in the context of misdemeanor cruelty, but the third concept—malice or bad motive—applies only to felony cruelty. While the term "malice" is often used and interpreted in criminal cases involving human victims, it

---

36. G.S. 14-360(a1), (b).
37. *Id.*
38. G.S. 14-360(c).
39. *Id.*

has been subject to little examination by the courts in cases involving felony cruelty to animals.

In homicide cases, North Carolina courts have recognized three meanings for the term "malice":[40]

- the killing is done with express ill will, hatred, or spite (sometimes called *actual*, *express*, or *particular* malice);[41]
- the act that causes death is inherently dangerous to human life and is done so recklessly or wantonly that it reflects disregard of life and social duty; or
- the killing is done intentionally and without just cause, excuse, or justification (or *implied* malice).

While developed in homicide cases, the three-pronged formulation of malice has been applied outside of the homicide context,[42] including in felony animal cruelty cases.[43] Of the three, the first formulation probably has the clearest connection to the felony cruelty to animals statute because the statutory definition of "maliciously" refers to acts committed with "bad motive."[44]

The second formulation focuses on an act that is inherently dangerous, a concept that could arguably translate from acts endangering humans to those endangering animals. Currently, the pattern jury instruction used in felonious animal cruelty cases has not incorporated the "inherently dangerous" concept and no court has directly addressed it in the context of animal cruelty. It is conceivable that a case could involve facts that trigger consideration of this definition of malice in an animal cruelty case.

The third formulation—often referred to as "implied malice"—can be confusing to consider in the context of animal cruelty because language used to express the concept of implied malice in homicide cases overlaps substantially with the statutory definition of "intentionally" in the cruelty law. Table 2.1, below, compares the two concepts.

Table 2.1. Comparison of "Implied Malice" and "Intentionally"

State of Mind	Crime	The Act Is . . .
Implied malice	Homicide	. . . done intentionally and without just cause, excuse, or justification
Intentionally	Animal cruelty	. . . committed knowingly and without justifiable excuse

---

40. *See* SMITH, *supra* note 10, at 7; *see also* State v. Reynolds, 307 N.C. 184, 191 (1982) (discussing the three types of malice).

41. *See* State v. Conrad, 275 N.C. 342, 352 (1969) (explaining that the term "malicious" in the context of a statute criminalizing property damage "connotes a feeling of animosity, hatred or ill will toward the owner, the possessor, or the occupant").

42. SMITH, *supra* note 10, at 7.

43. *See* State v. Gerberding, 237 N.C. App. 502 (2014).

44. G.S. 14-360(c).

The state court of appeals addressed this overlap in 2014 in *State v. Gerberding*.[45] In that case, the defendant was convicted of felony animal cruelty based on killing a dog. During the trial, the judge provided the jury with instructions taken directly from the pattern jury instructions:

> For you to find the Defendant guilty of [felony animal abuse], the State must prove three things beyond a reasonable doubt.
>
> First, that the Defendant killed the dog.
>
> Second, that the Defendant acted intentionally; that is knowingly and without justification or excuse.
>
> And third, that the Defendant acted with malice. Malice means not only hatred, ill will or spite, as it is ordinarily understood -- to be sure, that is malice -- but it also means the condition of mind which prompts a person to intentionally inflict serious bodily harm which proximately results in injury to an animal without just cause, excuse or justification.
>
> . . .
>
> Non-felonious cruelty to animals differs from felonious cruelty to animals in that the State is not required to prove the Defendant acted with malice. Thus, if you find . . . Defendant acted intentionally, that is, knowingly and without justification or excuse -- killed a dog, it would be your duty to return a verdict of non-felonious cruelty to animals.[46]

On appeal, the defendant argued that the court should not have provided an instruction that incorporated the concept of implied malice because the language that described the concept, lifted from the homicide context and incorporated into the pattern jury instructions, overlapped so closely with the statutory definition of "intentionally" that is specific to animal cruelty. The majority dismissed this argument, explaining:

> The mere fact that the lesser-included offense of misdemeanor cruelty to animals defines the element of "intent" as "knowingly and without justification or excuse" (terms also used in the implied malice definition) does not render the jury instruction concerning implied malice invalid. The jury was free to convict defendant of either the felony or misdemeanor offense. Accordingly, we conclude that the trial court's instruction was proper.[47]

In a concurring opinion, Judge Ervin disagreed with the majority's conclusion that the instruction related to implied malice was acceptable. He explained that the court should not have relied on the common law definition of malice used in homicide cases because

---

45. 237 N.C. App. 502.

46. *Id.* at 507. *See also* State v. Sexton, 357 N.C. 235, 238 (2003) (affirming lower court's use of a similar jury instruction in a case alleging malicious burning of an occupied dwelling when there was no statutory definition of malice).

47. *Gerberding*, 237 N.C. App. at 508.

the animal cruelty statute includes a definition.[48] Judge Ervin ultimately concurred in the result because, based on the facts, he did not think the outcome would have been different if the jury instruction had omitted the information about implied malice. As the tension between the majority and dissenting opinions in *Gerberding* suggests, importing the concept of implied malice from homicide law into the context of felony cruelty to animals is somewhat awkward. Nevertheless, the majority found no error in charging the jury using the pattern jury instructions and there has been no further North Carolina case law on the issue.

For the sake of clarity, it is worth briefly discussing the distinction between implied malice, a legal term of art describing a very specific state of mind, and the principle that actual malice may be proved by circumstantial evidence, a principle upon which both the majority and the dissent in *Gerberding* explicitly agreed. North Carolina courts frequently explain that because malice is a state of mind, it is "seldom proven by direct evidence" and, instead, "is ordinarily proven by circumstantial evidence from which it may be inferred."[49] Regardless of their differences with respect to the propriety of the jury instructions, both the majority and the dissent in *Gerberding* explicitly agreed that it was possible for the jury to infer from the defendant's act of killing the dog by stabbing it to death that the defendant in fact acted maliciously. While the distinction between implied malice and inferring actual malice based on circumstantial evidence can be confusing for anyone who does not frequently engage in technical parsing of the criminal law, the take-away point for readers of this book is that a person may be convicted of felony cruelty to animals even in cases where there is no direct evidence that the person harbored hatred, ill will, or spite for the animal he or she has treated cruelly. Many times, the surrounding circumstances along with the manner and the fact of a person's intentional cruel treatment of an animal will demonstrate that the person acted with malice, even if there is no direct evidence of the person's hatred, ill will, or spite for the animal.

In sum, it is clear that a defendant's express bad motive, ill will, or spite will suffice to prove that he or she acted with malice. While the issue has been shrouded in some confusion, the North Carolina Court of Appeals explicitly has held that the concept of implied malice is applicable in animal cruelty cases. And, though it does not appear that North Carolina courts have applied the "inherently dangerous act" formulation of

---

48. Judge Ervin explained that the court should not rely on the common law definition of malice, as reflected in the pattern jury instructions and used in homicide and other cases. If there is a statutory definition, it should govern. *Id.* at 510–11 (Ervin, J., concurring). *See also* 2A Sutherland Statutory Construction § 46:06, at 181 (6th ed. 2000) ("It is an elementary rule of statutory construction that effect must be given, if possible, to every word, clause and sentence of a statute.").

49. *Sexton*, 357 N.C. at 238; *see also* State v. Yarborough, ___ N.C. App. ___, 803 S.E.2d 700 (2017) (unpublished) (stating this principle in context of felony animal cruelty case).

malice to an animal cruelty case, it is conceivable that a case could involve facts where applying the formulation would be appropriate.

Torture, Torment, and Cruelly

The animal cruelty law includes another definition that has generated some confusion and attracted the attention of the courts. The law defines three terms interchangeably: torture, torment, and cruelly.[50] These three terms are used in different ways in the statute:

- *torment* is an act that may constitute misdemeanor cruelty;
- *torture* is an act that may constitute felony cruelty; and
- *cruelly* qualifies the term "beat," which may be an act of felony cruelty.

All three terms are defined to "include or refer to any act, omission, or neglect causing or permitting unjustifiable pain, suffering, or death."[51] This is an extremely broad definition, especially with respect to the term "torture." In the context of homicide, for example, courts have defined the term "torture" to mean "the course of conduct by one or more persons which intentionally inflicts grievous pain and suffering upon another for the purpose of punishment, persuasion, or sadistic pleasure."[52] In animal cruelty cases, it will be important to refer to the definition of torture set out in the statutes rather than in the common law.

In 2010 the North Carolina Court of Appeals discussed the term "torment" in the context of a cruelty case related to unsanitary living conditions. The court described the living conditions in detail, including the strong odor, filth, and presence of feces and urine throughout the house and on the animals. It concluded that the evidence was "sufficient to support a conclusion by a reasonable jury that defendant 'tormented' [the cat], causing it unjustifiable pain or suffering . . . ."[53] This was an important case because many animal services officials have struggled over the years with the question of whether unsanitary living conditions constitute cruelty. This case creates strong precedent that will help guide local officials going forward, but it is important to remember that the facts in this case were particularly egregious.[54] Not all unsanitary living conditions will likely rise to the level of torment.

---

50. G.S. 14-360(c).

51. *Id.*

52. State v. Lee, 348 N.C. 474, 488 (1998) (internal quotation marks omitted) (citation omitted).

53. State v. Mauer, 202 N.C. App. 546, 550–51 (2010).

54. An excerpt from the opinion illustrates the gravity of the situation in the home:

> When the officers were able to enter the residence, there was so much fecal matter and debris on the floor that the front door was difficult to open. The officers observed that all the doors and windows were closed and feces and urine covered "everything"—including all the floors, furniture, and counter tops.

Exceptions

There are several important exceptions to the misdemeanor and felony cruelty laws. These laws do not apply to[55]

- the taking of animals under the jurisdiction of the Wildlife Resources Commission (WRC) (except see discussion of wild birds below);
- activities conducted for the purpose of biomedical research or training;
- activities conducted for the purpose of producing livestock, poultry, or aquatic species;
- activities conducted for the primary purpose of providing food for human or animal consumption;
- activities conducted for veterinary purposes;
- the destruction of any animal for the purposes of protecting the public, other animals, property, or the public health; and
- the physical alteration of livestock or poultry for the purpose of conforming with breed or show standards.

To be excepted from the criminal law, these activities must be carried out lawfully.[56] For example, a person who uses an animal for biomedical research in a way not authorized by law may be charged with cruelty. In 2015 the legislature enacted a statute that broadly excepted from the application of state or local laws any activity related to the capture, captivity, treatment, or release of possums between December 29 of each year and January 2 of each subsequent year.[57] This broad exception arguably would preclude a criminal prosecution for animal cruelty based on a person's treatment of a possum during this period of time.

Some of the feces were fresh while some were old and had mold on them. The officers, as well as the cats, were unable to walk in the house without stepping in the feces and urine. The officers also observed that cats, covered in their own feces and urine, were leaving streak marks from jumping on the walls, windows, and doors trying to get out of the house."

Id. at 550.

55. G.S. 14-360(c)(1)–(5).

56. There is relatively little North Carolina appellate case law regarding the exemptions to the criminal cruelty laws. For a discussion of the history of the North Carolina exemptions and how a court might construe them, see William A. Reppy, Jr., *Broad Exemptions in Animal-Cruelty Statutes Unconstitutionally Deny Equal Protection of the Law*, LAW & CONTEMP. PROBS., Winter 2007, at 255. For a general discussion of the societal justifications for exemptions to criminal cruelty laws, see Daniel M. Ibrahim, *The Anticruelty Statute: A Study in Animal Welfare*, 1 J. ANIMAL L. & ETHICS 175 (2006). For a general discussion of exemptions to animal cruelty laws for agricultural purposes, see David J. Wolfson, *Beyond the Law: Agribusiness and the Systemic Abuse of Animals Raised for Food or Food Production*, 2 ANIMAL L. 123 (1996).

57. G.S. 113-291.13.

Wild Birds

The exception for the lawful taking of wildlife has some additional language referring to "wild birds" that has an interesting history that has generated some confusion in recent years. Under current wildlife laws, wild (undomesticated) birds are subject to the WRC's jurisdiction.[58] The term "wild bird" is defined to include "[m]igratory game birds; upland game birds; and all undomesticated feathered vertebrates."[59] The WRC is authorized by statute to adopt a regulation excluding specific birds or classes of birds from that definition "based upon the need for protection or regulation in the interests of conservation of wildlife resources."[60] The WRC adopted such a regulation, excluding the following five birds from the definition of "wild bird":

- the English sparrow (Passer domesticus),
- Eurasian collared dove (Streptopelia decaocto),
- pigeon (Columba livia),
- mute swan (Cygnus olor), and
- starling (Sturnus vulgaris).[61]

Because these species of birds are excluded from the definition of "wild bird," they are no longer subject to the jurisdiction of the WRC. As a result, they *are* subject to the animal cruelty law. In other words, the exception to the cruelty law does not apply to the birds that have been excluded from the definition of wild bird.

There is, however, an exception to the exclusion from the exception. In 2015 a pigeon shoot was scheduled in Rockingham County, North Carolina. The sheriff sought a temporary restraining order to stop the event because pigeons were protected by the cruelty law. The organizers cancelled the event.[62] Shortly thereafter, the legislature amended G.S. 14-360 to provide that pigeons (Columba livia) are not excluded from the exception.[63] This means that pigeons are not subject to the animal cruelty law.[64]

---

58. G.S. 113-132(b) (conferring "jurisdiction over the conservation of wildlife resources" to the Wildlife Resources Commission (WRC)); 113-129(17) (defining the term "wildlife resources" to include all "wild birds"); 113-129(15a) (defining the term "wild birds").

59. G.S. 113-129(15a).

60. *Id.*

61. Title 15A, chapter 10B, § .0121 of the North Carolina Administrative Code (hereinafter N.C.A.C.).

62. Danielle Battaglia, *Man Drops Pigeon Shoot Amid Protest*, Greensboro News & Record (Jan. 23, 2015), http://www.greensboro.com/rockingham_now/man-drops-pigeon-shoot-amid-protest/article_7e90d5ea-a2b1-11e4-a2a9-8fccc94871c7.html.

63. S.L. 2015-286, § 4.32(a), *amending* G.S. 14-360(c)(1).

64. The wild bird exception, as applied to pigeons, is convoluted. This area of the law has been controversial for many years, in fact. The exception for pigeons was litigated in a case called *Malloy v. Cooper,* 162 N.C. App. 504 (2004), which involved a biannual pigeon shoot. John Malloy, the plaintiff, sponsored the sporting activity on his property and was concerned that he would be charged with criminal cruelty in connection with the shoot. At the time of

Instigating and Promoting Cruelty

G.S. 14-361 makes it a Class 1 misdemeanor to "willfully set on foot, or instigate, or move to, carry on, or promote, or engage in, or do any act towards the furtherance of any act of cruelty to any animal."[65] It is not readily apparent that this statute criminalizes any conduct that would not otherwise be criminal under the common law concept of aiding and abetting. Under that concept, a person is punishable as a principal to a crime committed by another person when he or she knowingly advises, instigates, encourages, procures, or helps the other person to commit the crime and his or her actions or statements caused or contributed to the commission of the crime by the other person.[66] In fact, in a situation where a person has acted in furtherance of another person's commission of felony cruelty to animals, a charge of instigating or promoting cruelty under G.S. 14-361 rather than a charge of felony cruelty to animals based upon the concept of aiding and abetting would be favorable to the defendant because violations of G.S. 14-361 are punished as misdemeanors. No North Carolina appellate cases directly address G.S. 14-361, and it is worth noting that G.S. 14-360 explicitly contemplates that a person who causes or procures the cruel treatment of animals is subject to punishment as a principal for cruelty to animals.

Reporting Animal Cruelty

Any person may report suspected animal cruelty to law enforcement or animal services officials but there is no legal mandate to do so. A veterinarian licensed in North Carolina who has reasonable cause to believe that an animal has been subject to cruelty will be protected from civil and criminal liability—as well as any professional disciplinary action—for reporting cruelty, participating in a cruelty investigation, or testifying in

---

the litigation, the WRC exempted only "domestic pigeons," rather than "pigeons," from its jurisdiction. Malloy asked the court to interpret the law prior to his scheduled pigeon shoot.

The court of appeals concluded that because domestic and feral pigeons are genetically identical, the cruelty statute was "unconstitutionally vague" as applied: people would not know whether they were shooting a domestic pigeon (protected by the cruelty statute) or a feral pigeon (arguably not protected by the cruelty statute). The court explained that the law failed "to give a person a reasonable opportunity to know whether shooting particular pigeons is prohibited, and fail[ed] to provide standards for those applying the law." *Id.* at 510. Because the law was found to be unconstitutional as applied to Malloy's situation, the court stated that it was unenforceable against him. Shortly after the court issued its decision, the WRC amended its regulation to exempt all pigeons from the definition of "wild bird." 18 N.C. Reg. 1598, 1599 (Mar. 15, 2004) (amending 15A N.C.A.C. 10B, § .0121). As a result of that change, all pigeons, domestic and feral, were protected by the cruelty statute up until the most recent change to G.S. 14-360 in 2015.

65. G.S. 14-361.

66. SMITH, *supra* note 10, at 31. It is also worth noting that a person may be prosecuted as a principal based on the common law concepts of acting indirectly or acting in concert. Each of these concepts is discussed in the book cited in this footnote.

cruelty-related judicial proceedings.[67] The immunity will not apply if the veterinarian acted in bad faith or with a malicious purpose. There is, however, a rebuttable presumption that the veterinarian acted in good faith. The state law also protects veterinarians from disciplinary actions by the North Carolina Veterinary Medical Board for *failing* to report suspected cruelty.[68]

Animal Fighting Exhibitions

In addition to the misdemeanor and felony cruelty laws discussed above, several statutes address specific acts that, broadly speaking, may be seen as cruel, including animal fighting. Three separate statutes, G.S. 14-362, 14-362.1, and 14-362.2, govern cockfighting, dogfighting and baiting, and exhibitions featuring fights between or among all other animals.

North Carolina law does not define the terms "fighting" and "baiting," but some other jurisdictions do. The District of Columbia, for example, defines "fighting" as "an organized event wherein there is a display of combat between [two] or more animals in which the fighting, killing, maiming, or injuring of an animal is a significant feature, or main purpose, of the event."[69] Under District of Columbia law, to "bait" means "to attack with violence, to provoke, or to harass an animal with one or more animals for the purpose of training an animal for, or to cause an animal to engage in, fights with or among other animals."[70]

Cockfighting—G.S. 14-362

A person is guilty of a Class I felony if he or she

    (1) (a) instigates,
        (b) promotes,
        (c) conducts,
        (d) is employed at,
        (e) allows property under his or her ownership or control to be used for,
        (f) participates as a spectator at, *or*
        (g) profits from
    (2) an exhibition featuring the fighting of a cock.[71]

---

67. G.S. 14-360.1 (this provision was added to the statute in 2007. S.L. 2007-232).
68. *Id.*
69. D.C. CODE § 22-1006.01 (2017).
70. *Id.*
71. G.S. 14-362.

The law further states that a lease of property that is either used for or intended to be used for a cockfighting exhibition is void and that a landlord who learns that the property is being used or will be used for cockfighting must evict the tenant immediately. Some states have also elected to criminalize the ownership of fighting cocks and fighting implements, but North Carolina has not done so.[72]

Dogfighting and Baiting—G.S. 14-362.2

The dogfighting and dog baiting[73] law is similar to the cockfighting law. A person is guilty of a Class H felony if he or she

    (1) (a) instigates,
          (b) promotes,
          (c) conducts,
          (d) is employed at,
          (e) provides a dog for,
          (f) allows property under his or her ownership or control to be used for,
          (g) gambles on,
          (h) profits from, *or*
          (i) participates as a spectator at
    (2) (a) an exhibition featuring the fighting of a dog with another dog or other animal *or*
          (b) an exhibition featuring the baiting of a dog.[74]

The law includes the same language as the cockfighting law in regard to leases of property used for fighting and the duty of a landlord to evict tenants immediately.

The dogfighting and dog baiting law also provides that a person is guilty of a Class H felony if he or she

    (1) (a) owns,
          (b) possesses, *or*
          (c) trains
    (2) a dog

---

72. *See, e.g.,* Colo. Rev. Stat. Ann. § 18-9-204 (2017); Md. Code Ann., Crim. Law § 10-608 (2017). The respective statutes criminalize both the ownership of cocks and implements in Colorado and Maryland. *See also* Humane Soc'y of the U.S., *Fact Sheet, Cockfighting: State Laws* (Apr. 2013), humanesociety.org (providing a survey of cockfighting laws in all fifty states), http://www.humanesociety.org/assets/pdfs/animal_fighting/cockfighting_chart_2013.pdf.

73. The terms "dogfighting" and "dog baiting" are used throughout this section as shorthand to refer to "exhibitions featuring the baiting of a dog or the fighting of a dog with another dog or with another animal."

74. G.S. 14-362.2(a); 14-362.2(c).

(3) (a) with the intent that the dog be used in an exhibition featuring the baiting of that dog *or*

(b) with the intent that the dog be used in an exhibition featuring the fighting of that dog with another dog or other animal.[75]

The dogfighting and baiting law does not prohibit the use of dogs

- for lawful hunting activities governed by the Wildlife Resources Commission;[76]
- as herding dogs engaged in the working of domesticated livestock for agricultural, entertainment, or sporting purposes;[77] or
- in certain earthdog trials.[78]

An *earthdog trial* is a sporting event in which certain breeds of dogs, specifically terriers and dachshunds, attempt to locate a "quarry" (such as a caged rat) that is in an underground den. According to the American Kennel Club, the trials are designed to test the dog's "natural aptitude and trained hunting and working behaviors when exposed to an underground hunting situation."[79] To be considered exempt from the fighting and baiting law, earthdog trials must be sanctioned or sponsored by an entity approved by the commissioner of agriculture, and the quarry must be kept separate from the dogs by a sturdy barrier and have access to food and water.

Fighting of Other Animals—G.S. 14-362.1

The third and final criminal animal fighting statute applies to all animals other than cocks and dogs.[80] This law is virtually identical to the dogfighting and baiting law, with two exceptions. First, it does not specifically prohibit gambling on fighting exhibitions involving these animals, even though gambling on such exhibitions is illegal under a different criminal statute.[81] Second, the criminal penalties are different. A person who

---

75. G.S. 14-362.2(b).

76. G.S. 14-362.2(d) (added by S.L. 2006-113).

77. G.S. 14-362.2(f) (added by S.L. 2007-181).

78. G.S. 14-362.2(e) (added by S.L. 2007-180).

79. *See* Am. Kennel Club, *Earthdog: Get Started*, https://www.akc.org/sports/earthdog/getting-started/ (last visited June 11, 2018).

80. G.S. 14-362.1.

81. G.S. 14-292 ("[A]ny person or organization that operates any game of chance or any person who plays at or bets on any game of chance at which any money, property or other thing of value is bet, whether the same be in stake or not, shall be guilty of a Class 2 misdemeanor."). Under the law, betting on animal fighting exhibitions likely would be considered a "game of chance" rather than a game of skill, even though there may be some skill involved on the part of the animals. *See, e.g.*, State v. Brown, 221 N.C. 301, 307 (1942) (concluding that betting on horse racing is a game of chance, regardless of the fact that racing involves skill on the part of the jockey and the horse).

violates G.S. 14-362.1 is guilty of a Class 2 misdemeanor. A subsequent violation for specified acts within three years is a Class I felony.[82]

Spectators at Fighting Exhibitions

All three of the state's animal fighting laws described above make it a crime to be a spectator at a fighting exhibition.[83]

In 2001 a person convicted of being a spectator at a dogfight challenged the constitutionality of this provision, arguing that in enacting it, the state had exceeded the scope of its authority. The North Carolina Court of Appeals upheld the law, explaining that it is a valid exercise of the state's police power because it is "substantially related" to the object of discouraging dogfighting exhibitions: "If no one attended the dogfights, either for amusement or profit, dogfighting as a group activity would be in jeopardy."[84] The court went on to uphold the prohibition on participating in a dogfight as a spectator against the defendant's contentions that it was unconstitutionally vague and overbroad.[85]

Table 2.2, below, shows the actions prohibited/not prohibited in the three state laws governing animal fighting exhibitions. The dogfighting law is the most comprehensive, while the cockfighting law (included under the column marked "Birds") is the least comprehensive.

---

82. It is a felony only if the second offense is for one of the following: instigating, promoting, conducting, being employed at, providing an animal for, or profiting from an animal fighting exhibition. The felony penalty does not apply to owning or possessing an animal, training an animal to fight, or participating as a spectator at an exhibition. G.S. 14-362.1(d).

83. Being a spectator at a dogfighting exhibition is a crime in every state except Montana. *See* Mich. State Univ., Animal Legal & Historical Ctr., *Chart of State Dogfighting Laws* (2014), https://www.animallaw.info/article/chart-state-dogfighting-laws.

84. State v. Arnold, 147 N.C. App. 670, 674 (2001), *aff'd per curiam*, 356 N.C. 291 (2002).

85. *Id.* at 674–75. One of the three judges dissented from the decision. He agreed with the majority's conclusion that the dogfighting law is constitutional but believed that the state should have offered more evidence establishing that the defendant in this case actually "participated" as a spectator. Specifically, the judge seemed troubled by the fact that the law enforcement official who arrested the spectators testified that "he did not observe whether defendant was actually watching the dogfight." *Id.* at 676–77 (Wynn, J., dissenting). A similar animal fighting spectator law was challenged in Colorado when a journalist videotaping and reporting on a dogfight was convicted. People v. Bergen, 883 P.2d 532 (Colo. App. 1994). The court rejected the reporter's argument that he should not have been arrested because his journalistic activities were protected by the First Amendment. The court explained that the law did not prevent the reporter from gathering information about dogfighting but did prohibit anyone from attending a dogfight.

Table 2.2. A Comparison of North Carolina's Criminal Laws Governing Animal Fighting Exhibitions

Prohibited Behavior	Type of Animal Covered by Statute		
	Birds	Dogs	Other
Instigating a fight	X	X	X
Promoting a fight	X	X	X
Conducting a fight	X	X	X
Being employed at a fight		X	X
Providing an animal for a fight		X	X
Allowing property owned or controlled to be used for a fight	X	X	X
Participating as a spectator at a fight	X	X	X
Gambling on a fight		X	
Profiting from a fight	X	X	X
Owning, possessing, or training an animal for use in fighting exhibitions		X	X

Animal Fighting under Federal Law

At the federal level, the Animal Welfare Act criminalizes various activities related to any "animal fighting venture"—defined as an "event . . . [which] involves a fight . . . between at least [two] animals [and is conducted] for purposes of sport, wagering, or entertainment."[86] The federal law generally supplements state laws governing fighting and only overrides a state or local animal fighting law if it is in "direct and irreconcilable conflict" with the federal statute.[87]

The following six activities are prohibited under the federal law:

- sponsoring or exhibiting an animal in an animal fighting venture;[88]
- attending an animal fighting venture;[89]
- causing a person under the age of 16 to attend an animal fighting venture;[90]

---

86. 7 U.S.C. § 2156(g)(1). Hunting-related activities are excluded from the definition.

87. 7 U.S.C. § 2156(i) ("The provisions of this chapter shall not supersede or otherwise invalidate any such State, local, or municipal legislation or ordinance relating to animal fighting ventures except in case of a direct and irreconcilable conflict between any requirements thereunder and this chapter or any rule, regulation, or standard hereunder.").

88. 7 U.S.C. § 2156(a)(1). There is a narrow exception to the law that applies to fighting ventures involving live birds (i.e., cockfights) in states where the venture is legal.

89. 7 U.S.C. § 2156(a)(2). This provision was added to the federal law in 2014. Pub. L. No. 113-79, tit. XII, § 12308, 128 Stat. 990 (2014).

90. *Id.*

- buying, selling, possessing, training, delivering, receiving, or transporting an animal for the purpose of having it participate in an animal fighting venture;[91]
- using the mail service or any instrumentality of interstate commerce to promote or in any other manner further an animal fighting venture;[92] and
- buying, selling, delivering, or transporting in interstate or foreign commerce a knife, gaff, or any other sharp instrument attached, or designed to be attached, to the leg of a bird for use in an animal fighting venture.[93]

All six of these federal crimes require that the person acted "knowingly."

Because of constitutional limitations on federal authority, these provisions all relate to the transport of the animals, equipment, or information through interstate or foreign commerce.[94] Thus, a fighting venture or sale of cockfighting implements that is wholly intrastate would likely not be subject to these federal laws. This federal law is enforced by the Animal and Plant Health Inspection Service and the Office of the Inspector General of the U.S. Department of Agriculture.[95] Penalties vary depending on the offense, ranging from up to one year of imprisonment for attending a fighting venture to up to five years for sponsoring a venture or buying an animal for a venture.[96] Fines may also be imposed.[97] Congress increased the penalties in 2007, with the expectation that increasing them to felonies would lead to more prosecutions.[98]

---

91. 7 U.S.C. § 2156(b).

92. 7 U.S.C. § 2156(c). This portion of the law does not apply when the conduct is performed "outside the limits of the States of the United States."

93. 7 U.S.C. § 2156(e). Congress added this language in April 2007.

94. *See e.g.,* United States v. Gibert, 677 F.3d 613 (4th Cir. 2012) (upholding the statute as a constitutional exercise of federal authority to regulate interstate commerce); Slavin v. United States, 403 F.3d 522 (8th Cir. 2005) (same).

95. The Department of Agriculture has been criticized in the past for failing to adequately enforce the Animal Welfare Act. *See, e.g.,* Shigehiko Ito, *Beyond Standing: A Search for a New Solution in Animal Welfare,* 46 Santa Clara L. Rev. 377, 378 (2006).

96. 18 U.S.C. § 49.

97. *Id.*

98. Animal Fighting Prohibition Enforcement Act of 2007, H.R. 137, 110th Cong. (2007). The House committee report endorsing the legislation explained that increasing the penalty to a felony would lead to more prosecutions. H.R. Rep. No. 110-27, pt. 1, at 2 (2007) ("Prohibitions against knowingly selling, buying, transporting, delivering, or receiving an animal in interstate or foreign commerce for the purposes of participation in an animal fighting venture were added to the Animal Welfare Act in 1976, with misdemeanor penalties of up to $5,000 in fines and up to 1 year in prison. Since then, Federal authorities have pursued fewer than a half dozen animal fighting cases, despite receiving numerous tips from informants and requests to assist with state and local prosecutions. The animal fighting industry continues to thrive within the United States, despite 50 State laws that ban dogfighting and 48 State laws that ban cockfighting. . . . By increasing penalties to the felony level, H.R. 137 will give prosecutors greater incentive to pursue cases against unlawful animal fighting ventures, and strengthen deterrence against them.").

Other Criminal Cruelty-Related Laws

Federal and state laws also criminalize other specific activities that involve cruelty or mistreatment of animals.

Depictions of Animal Cruelty

In 2010 the U.S. Supreme Court found unconstitutional a federal law that criminalized the creation and possession of depictions of animal cruelty.[99] The court concluded that the law was drafted so broadly that it violated the free speech protections afforded by the First Amendment. Later in 2010, Congress enacted a revised version of the law that is intended to remedy the constitutional problems.[100] Under the new law, it is a federal crime

(1) to knowingly create an obscene "animal crush video" if the video is to be distributed in, or is using a means of facility of, interstate or foreign commerce or

(2) to knowingly sell, market, advertise, exchange, or distribute such a video in, or by using a means or facility of, interstate or foreign commerce.

An "animal crush video" is defined broadly to include depictions of "actual conduct in which 1 or more living non-human mammals, birds, reptiles, or amphibians is intentionally crushed, burned, drowned, suffocated, impaled, or otherwise subjected to serious bodily injury."[101] The law is drafted to encompass only depictions that are "obscene," because courts have long held that obscene speech is not entitled to First Amendment protection.[102] While the law does not define the term "obscene," the congressional findings explain that many animal crush videos are obscene because they appeal to the prurient interest in sex; are patently offensive; and lack serious literary, artistic, political, or scientific value.[103] There are several exceptions to the law, including depictions of veterinary or agricultural practices, hunting, trapping, and fishing.

Poison Control

In North Carolina, three separate statutes address the poisoning of animals. Under G.S. 14-368, it is a Class 2 misdemeanor to throw or leave a poisonous shrub, plant, tree, or vegetable exposed in certain public areas.[104] Under G.S. 14-401, it is a Class 1

---

99. United States v. Stevens, 559 U.S. 460 (2010) (addressing constitutionality of 18 U.S.C. § 48).

100. 18 U.S.C. § 48 (as amended by Pub. L. No. 111-294 (2010)).

101. 18 U.S.C. § 48(a)(1).

102. *See* Miller v. California, 413 U.S. 15, 23 (1973) ("This much has been categorically settled by the Court, that obscene material is unprotected by the First Amendment.").

103. Pub. L. No. 111-294.

104. G.S. 14-368. The statute covers the following areas: "any public square, street, lane, alley or open lot in any city, town or village, or . . . any public road."

misdemeanor to place strychnine, other poisonous compounds, or ground glass on any food left in certain open areas. The same statute also makes it a Class 1 misdemeanor to leave open containers of antifreeze containing ethylene glycol in those same open areas.[105] The third poisoning statute, G.S. 14-163, makes it a Class I felony to poison another person's "horse, mule, hog, sheep or other livestock."[106]

Law Enforcement, Assistance, and Search and Rescue Animals

G.S. 14-163.1 specifically prohibits certain conduct involving law enforcement agency animals, assistance animals, or search and rescue animals. Under the statute, an animal is considered a "law enforcement agency animal" if it "is trained and may be used to assist a law enforcement officer in the performance of the officer's official duties."[107] An "assistance animal" is one that is trained and may be used to assist "any person who (i) has a physical or mental impairment which substantially limits one or more major life activities; (ii) has a record of such an impairment; or (iii) is regarded as having such an impairment."[108] An animal is a "search and rescue animal" if it is "trained and may be used to assist in a search and rescue operation."[109]

Killing a Law Enforcement, Assistance, or Search and Rescue Animal

A person is guilty of a Class H felony if he or she

    (1) willfully

    (2) kills

    (3) (a) a law enforcement agency animal,

        (b) an assistance animal, *or*

        (c) a search and rescue animal

    (4) (a) knowing that the animal is a type of animal described in element 3, above, *or*

        (b) having reason to know that the animal is a type of animal described in element 3.[110]

---

105. G.S. 14-401. These substances must not be placed in "any public square, street, lane, alley or on any lot in any village, town or city or on any public road, open field, woods, or yard in the country."

106. G.S. 14-163.

107. G.S. 14-163.1(a)(2).

108. G.S. 168A-3(7A) (defining "person with a disability"). Under G.S. 14-163.1(a)(1), an "assistance animal" is "an animal that is trained and may be used to assist a 'person with a disability' as defined in G.S. 168A-3."

109. G.S. 14-163.1(a)(3a). Search and rescue animals were added to the law in 2009. S.L. 2009-460.

110. G.S. 14-163.1(a1).

Causing Serious Harm to a Law Enforcement, Assistance, or Search and Rescue Animal

A person is guilty of a Class I felony if he or she

    (1) willfully

    (2) (a) causes *or*

        (b) attempts to cause

    (3) serious harm to

    (4) (a) a law enforcement agency animal,

        (b) an assistance animal, *or*

        (c) a search and rescue animal

    (5) (a) knowing that the animal is a type of animal described in element 4, above, *or*

        (b) having reason to know that the animal is a type of animal described in element 4.[111]

The term "serious harm" as used in element 3 of this crime is defined as harm that does any of the following:

- creates a substantial risk of death,
- causes maiming or substantial loss or impairment of bodily function,
- causes acute pain of a duration that results in substantial suffering,
- requires retraining of the animal, or
- requires retirement of the animal.[112]

Causing Harm to a Law Enforcement, Assistance, or Search and Rescue Animal

A person is guilty of a Class 1 misdemeanor if he or she

    (1) willfully

    (2) (a) causes *or*

        (b) attempts to cause

    (3) harm to

    (4) (a) a law enforcement agency animal,

        (b) an assistance animal, *or*

        (c) a search and rescue animal

    (5) (a) knowing that the animal is a type of animal described in element 4, above, *or*

        (b) having reason to know that the animal is a type of animal described in element 4.[113]

---

111. G.S. 14-163.1(b).
112. G.S. 14-163.1(a)(4).
113. G.S. 14-163.1(c).

The term "harm" as used in element 3 of this crime is defined as "[a]ny injury, illness, or other psychological impairment; or any behavioral impairment that impedes or interferes with duties performed by" the animal.[114]

Taunting, etc., a Law Enforcement, Assistance, or Search and Rescue Animal

A person is guilty of a Class 2 misdemeanor if he or she

(1) willfully
(2) (a) taunts,
    (b) teases,
    (c) harasses,
    (d) delays,
    (e) obstructs, *or*
    (f) attempts to delay or obstruct
(3) (a) a law enforcement agency animal,
    (b) an assistance animal, *or*
    (c) a search and rescue animal
(4) in the performance of the animal's duties
(5) (a) knowing that the animal is a type of animal described in element 3, above, *or*
    (b) having reason to know that the animal is a type of animal described in element 3.[115]

If a person is convicted of one of the above crimes, the court is directed to order restitution for costs such as veterinary care, medical care, and boarding expenses for the animal; replacement and retraining expenses; and the salary of the animal's handler (if a law enforcement agency or search and rescue animal) for time lost while the animal was unavailable.[116] In addition, a court may consider as an aggravating factor for sentencing purposes evidence indicating that the animal seriously harmed or killed was engaged in the performance of its official duties.[117]

Under federal law, it is a crime to willfully and maliciously harm a dog or horse used by a federal agency to enforce the law, detect criminal activity, or apprehend criminals.[118]

114. G.S. 14-163.1(a)(3).
115. G.S. 14-163.1(d).
116. G.S. 14-163.1(d1).
117. G.S. 15A-1340.16(d)(6a).
118. 18 U.S.C. § 1368.

Other Cruelty-Related Misdemeanors

Abandonment

It is a Class 2 misdemeanor in North Carolina for a person who owns, possesses, or has charge or custody of an animal to willfully abandon it without a justifiable excuse.[119]

Unlawful Restraint

A person will be guilty of a Class 1 misdemeanor if he or she maliciously restrains a dog using a chain or wire that is much larger or heavier than is needed to restrain the dog safely.[120] In the context of this law, the term "maliciously" means that the person used the restraint (1) intentionally and (2) with malice or bad motive.

Conveying Animals

It is a Class 1 misdemeanor to convey an animal in or upon a vehicle or other conveyance in a cruel or inhuman manner.[121] The law provides that when someone is taken into custody for a violation of this law, the officer has the authority to take charge of the conveyance and take steps to recover the costs of maintaining it while the person is in custody.[122]

Disposition of Certain Young Animals

It is a Class 3 misdemeanor in North Carolina to sell, offer for sale, barter, or give away as premiums (or prizes) certain young animals as pets or novelties. The law applies to chicks, ducklings, or other fowl, and to rabbits under eight weeks of age.[123]

Killing, Molesting, or Injuring Livestock

It is a Class 2 misdemeanor to kill, maim, or injure livestock lawfully running at large under certain circumstances.[124]

---

119. G.S. 14-361.1.

120. G.S. 14-362.3.

121. G.S. 14-363.

122. Specifically, the law allows the officer to incur expenses necessary to keep and sustain the vehicle and to impose a lien on the vehicle that the defendant must pay before reclaiming the vehicle.

123. G.S. 14-363.1.

124. G.S. 14-366 ("If any person shall unlawfully and on purpose drive any livestock, lawfully running at large in the range, from said range, or shall kill, maim or injure any livestock, lawfully running at large in the range or in the field or pasture of the owner, whether done with actual intent to injure the owner, or to drive the stock from the range, or with any other unlawful intent, every such person, his counselors, aiders, and abettors, shall be guilty of a Class 2 misdemeanor: provided, that nothing herein contained shall prohibit any person from driving out of the range any stock unlawfully brought from other states or places.").

Local Laws

Many jurisdictions have enacted ordinances that regulate conduct that has a degree of overlap with the cruelty laws discussed in this chapter. As discussed in Chapter 1, a local cruelty ordinance may regulate the same conduct as a state or federal law, but it must not duplicate or undermine the other law. Rather, it should impose higher standards or expectations within the jurisdiction. Given the broad scope of state and federal cruelty-related laws, local government officials drafting local ordinances need to be familiar with these laws to ensure that they do not run afoul of the restrictions described earlier in this book.[125]

In addition to the general limitations on a local government's ordinance-making authority discussed in Chapter 1, the legislature recently enacted a very specific limitation related to animals that has a direct impact on local animal cruelty or abuse ordinances.[126] The legislation enacted two nearly identical statutes—one for counties and another for municipalities.[127] The statutes prohibit local ordinances that regulate "standards of care" for "farm animals." The term "standards of care" is defined to include

- the construction, repair, or improvement of farm animal shelter or housing;
- restrictions on the types of feed or medicines that may be administered to farm animals; and
- exercise and social interaction requirements.

The exclusive list of farm animals subject to this limitation is as follows: cattle, oxen, bison, sheep, swine, goats, horses, ponies, mules, donkeys, hinnies, llamas, alpacas, lagomorphs, ratites, and poultry. The only difference between the statute governing counties and municipalities relates to poultry. For counties, the restriction applies to any ordinance governing poultry. For municipalities, the restriction applies only to poultry flocks of greater than twenty birds.

Because the new law relates to "standards of care," it overlaps with the concept of cruelty in many ways. State and local officials often rely on cruelty or abuse laws when animals have been deprived of adequate food, water, or shelter, or are kept in unsanitary conditions. If a local ordinance defines "animal" broadly enough to include the types of farm animals identified in this new law, it should either be revised or simply not enforced in the context of standards of care for those farm animals. Local laws are still valid and enforceable with respect to farm animals if the acts do not fall within the scope of "standards of care."

---

125. *See generally* chapter 1.

126. S.L. 2015-192. This legislation was introduced shortly after a controversy in Buncombe County related to an ordinance regulating shelter for horses and other animals. Joel Burgess, *Buncombe County Balks on Horse Rules*, Citizen-Times (Asheville) (Feb. 8, 2015), http://www.citizen-times.com/story/news/local/2015/02/08/asheville-buncombe-county-horse-controversy-shelters-animal-welfare-commissioners-ellen-frost-miranda-debruhl/23091281/.

127. G.S. 153A-145.4; 160A-203.1.

Animals Confined in Motor Vehicles

In 2013 the legislature added a new statute that is specifically focused on rescuing animals, other than livestock, that are confined in motor vehicles.[128] Under this law, if there is probable cause to believe that an animal is confined in a motor vehicle and may be at risk, several types of public officials may take action to release the animal.[129]

The types of officials who can take action are animal services officials, law enforcement officers, firefighters, rescue squad workers, and animal cruelty investigators appointed pursuant to G.S. 19A-45. An official may intervene if there is probable cause to believe that the animal is confined under conditions "that are likely to cause suffering, injury, or death to the animal due to heat, cold, lack of adequate ventilation, or . . . other endangering conditions."[130] Before attempting to rescue an animal, the official must first make a reasonable effort to locate the owner or other person responsible for the animal. After making such an effort, the official may "enter the motor vehicle by any reasonable means under the circumstances . . . ."[131]

Seizure and Confiscation of Animals

Law enforcement officers may decide to seize an animal as evidence in the course of investigating an animal cruelty case.[132] Because animal owners have a possessory interest in their animals,[133] any seizure of an animal must be done in a manner that is consistent with applicable law. Extensive discussion of search and seizure law is beyond the scope of this book, but other resources available from the School of Government

---

128. G.S. 14-363.3. When this bill was initially introduced, it proposed establishing a new Class 1 misdemeanor related to confinement in motor vehicles. *See* H. 612, Gen. Assemb., Reg. Sess. (N.C. 2013), http://ncleg.net/Sessions/2013/Bills/House/PDF/H612v1.pdf. That version of the bill did not pass, but the compromise language authorizing rescue measures was incorporated into another bill. S.L. 2013-377, § 6.

129. G.S. 14 363.3.

130. *Id.*

131. *Id.*

132. Article 4 of G.S. Chapter 19A authorizes boards of county commissioners to appoint "animal cruelty investigators" who may take custody of an animal in certain circumstances, and G.S. 67-30 authorizes counties to appoint "animal control officers" who also may take custody of an animal in certain circumstances. The term "law enforcement officers" as used in the text does not refer to either of these positions but, rather, refers to police officers, sheriff's deputies, wildlife law enforcement officers, and other like state and local law enforcement officers. The authority of animal cruelty investigators and animal services officials to seize an animal is discussed elsewhere in this book.

133. *See e.g.*, State v. Nance, 149 N.C. App. 734, 739–40 (2002) (seizure of defendant's horses implicated the Fourth Amendment because it deprived defendant of her possessory interest in the horses).

may be helpful.[134] If a person is convicted of a cruelty-related crime, the judge in the case has discretion to "order a final determination of the custody" of the animal.[135]

Recovering Sheltering Costs in Cruelty Cases

Often when a person is charged with a cruelty-related criminal offense, an animal shelter takes custody of the animal at issue. If a shelter is operated by or under contract with a county or municipality, the local government may incur significant expenses in the course of providing care and shelter for the animal. Local governments and animal shelters may petition the court to recover sheltering costs pursuant to G.S. 19A-70. This cost-recovery mechanism is discussed in Chapter 7, Animal Shelters.

Tracking Animal Cruelty

In 2016 the Federal Bureau of Investigation (FBI) made a significant change to the way that animal cruelty cases are tracked in a federal government database, the National Incident-Based Reporting System (NIBRS).[136] Previously, these types of prosecutions were tracked only in a catch-all category labeled "all other offenses" in the FBI's Uniform Crime Reporting (UCR) system. As such, it was difficult to focus any data analysis exclusively on animal-related crimes. With this shift in data tracking at the federal level, cruelty offenses now have their own category, similar to homicide, arson, and assault. For the purposes of reporting, the FBI defines cruelty as "intentionally, knowingly, or recklessly taking an action that mistreats or kills any animal without just cause, such as torturing, tormenting, mutilation, maiming, poisoning, or abandonment."[137] One of the goals driving this change is to elevate attention to these cases at the local level in order to expand protections for animals. Another goal is to provide data to help law enforcement officials identify people who may not only hurt animals but also people.[138]

---

134. *See* Robert L. Farb, Arrest, Search, and Investigation in North Carolina (UNC School of Government, 5th ed. 2016) (Chapter 4 of this book discusses the procedure for obtaining a search warrant and the consequences of an unlawful search or seizure).

135. G.S. 14-363.2.

136. FBI, *News*, "Tracking Animal Cruelty: FBI Collecting Data on Crimes Against Animals" (Feb. 1, 2016), https://www.fbi.gov/news/stories/-tracking-animal-cruelty; Colby Itkowitz, *A Big Win for Animals: The FBI Now Tracks Animal Abuse Like it Tracks Homicides*, Washington Post (Jan. 6, 2016), https://www.washingtonpost.com/news/inspired-life/wp/2016/01/06/a-big-win-for-animals-the-fbi-now-tracks-animal-abuse-like-it-tracks-homicides/?utm_term=.269351b7bf79.

137. Itkowitz, *supra* note 136.

138. For more information about the research connecting animal abuse and other types of violence, see Allie Phillips, Nat'l Dist. Attorneys' Ass'n, Understanding the

The first year of animal cruelty–related data was reported in the 2016 NIBRS, which showed that there were 1,126 animal cruelty offenses nationwide.[139] This data is not comprehensive, however, because state and local law enforcement agencies are not required to contribute data to this database.[140] North Carolina contributes data to the UCR system, but no North Carolina law enforcement agency is listed as participating in the NIBRS as of 2016, the most recent year for which published data is available.[141] North Carolina crime statistics are available from the State Bureau of Investigation (SBI).[142]

Conclusion

All three levels of government—federal, state, and local—address animal cruelty in different contexts and assign different penalties. The criminal laws discussed above provide several possible avenues for responding to alleged cruelty, while the civil remedies discussed in the next chapter offer individuals and government officials an entirely different remedy—a civil injunction. Both the civil and criminal remedies should be considered when evaluating the appropriate response to an act of animal cruelty.

LINK BETWEEN VIOLENCE TO ANIMALS AND PEOPLE: A GUIDEBOOK FOR CRIMINAL JUSTICE PROFESSIONALS (2014), http://www.ndaa.org/pdf/The%20Link%20Monograph-2014.pdf. *See also* the website of the National Link Coalition: http://nationallinkcoalition.org/ (last visited June 2, 2017) (collecting resources about the link between animal abuse and violence towards people).

139. *See* FBI, *2016 National Incident-Based Reporting System*, https://ucr.fbi.gov/nibrs/2016 (last visited Apr. 5, 2018).

140. FBI, *supra* note 139.

141. *See* FBI, *supra* note 139.

142. *See* North Carolina SBI, *Crime Reporting*, http://crimereporting.ncsbi.gov/ (last visited Apr. 5, 2018) (crime statistics are searchable by year).

Appendix. Relevant Sections of the North Carolina General Statutes (G.S.)

Article 23 [of G.S. Chapter 14].
Trespasses to Personal Property.
. . .

§ 14-163. Poisoning livestock.

If any person shall willfully and unlawfully poison any horse, mule, hog, sheep or other livestock, the property of another, such person shall be punished as a Class I felon.

§ 14-163.1. Assaulting a law enforcement agency animal, an assistance animal, or a search and rescue animal.

(a)   The following definitions apply in this section:

   (1)   Assistance animal. – An animal that is trained and may be used to assist a "person with a disability" as defined in G.S. 168A-3. The term "assistance animal" is not limited to a dog and includes any animal trained to assist a person with a disability as provided in Article 1 of Chapter 168 of the General Statutes.

   (2)   Law enforcement agency animal. – An animal that is trained and may be used to assist a law enforcement officer in the performance of the officer's official duties.

   (3)   Harm. – Any injury, illness, or other physiological impairment; or any behavioral impairment that impedes or interferes with duties performed by a law enforcement agency animal or an assistance animal.

   (3a)   Search and rescue animal. – An animal that is trained and may be used to assist in a search and rescue operation.

   (4)   Serious harm. – Harm that does any of the following:

      a.   Creates a substantial risk of death.

      b.   Causes maiming or causes substantial loss or impairment of bodily function.

      c.   Causes acute pain of a duration that results in substantial suffering.

      d.   Requires retraining of the law enforcement agency animal or assistance animal.

      e.   Requires retirement of the law enforcement agency animal or assistance animal from performing duties.

(a1)   Any person who knows or has reason to know that an animal is a law enforcement agency animal, an assistance animal, or a search and rescue animal and who willfully kills the animal is guilty of a Class H felony.

(b)   Any person who knows or has reason to know that an animal is a law enforcement agency animal, an assistance animal, or a search and rescue animal and who willfully causes or attempts to cause serious harm to the animal is guilty of a Class I felony.

(c)   Unless the conduct is covered under some other provision of law providing greater punishment, any person who knows or has reason to know that an animal is a law enforcement agency animal, an assistance animal, or a search and rescue animal and who willfully causes or attempts to cause harm to the animal is guilty of a Class 1 misdemeanor.

(d)   Unless the conduct is covered under some other provision of law providing greater punishment, any person who knows or has reason to know that an animal is a law enforcement agency animal, an assistance animal, or a search and rescue animal and who willfully taunts, teases, harasses, delays, obstructs, or attempts to delay or obstruct the animal in the performance of its duty as a law enforcement agency animal, an assistance animal, or a search and rescue animal is guilty of a Class 2 misdemeanor.

(d1) A defendant convicted of a violation of this section shall be ordered to make restitution to the person with a disability, or to a person, group, or law enforcement agency who owns or is responsible for the care of the law enforcement agency animal or search and rescue animal for any of the following as appropriate:

    (1) Veterinary, medical care, and boarding expenses for the law enforcement agency animal, the assistance animal, or the search and rescue animal.

    (2) Medical expenses for the person with the disability relating to the harm inflicted upon the assistance animal.

    (3) Replacement and training or retraining expenses for the law enforcement agency animal, the assistance animal, or the search and rescue animal.

    (4) Expenses incurred to provide temporary mobility services to the person with a disability.

    (5) Wages or income lost while the person with a disability is with the assistance animal receiving training or retraining.

    (6) The salary of the law enforcement agency animal handler as a result of the lost services to the agency during the time the handler is with the law enforcement agency animal receiving training or retraining.

    (6a) The salary of the search and rescue animal handler as a result of the search and rescue services lost during the time the handler is with the search and rescue animal receiving training or retraining.

    (7) Any other expense reasonably incurred as a result of the offense.

(e) This section shall not apply to a licensed veterinarian whose conduct is in accordance with Article 11 of Chapter 90 of the General Statutes.

(f) Self-defense is an affirmative defense to a violation of this section.

(g) Nothing in this section shall affect any civil remedies available for violation of this section.

Article 47 [of G.S. Chapter 14].
Cruelty to Animals.

§ 14-360. Cruelty to animals; construction of section.

(a) If any person shall intentionally overdrive, overload, wound, injure, torment, kill, or deprive of necessary sustenance, or cause or procure to be overdriven, overloaded, wounded, injured, tormented, killed, or deprived of necessary sustenance, any animal, every such offender shall for every such offense be guilty of a Class 1 misdemeanor.

(a1) If any person shall maliciously kill, or cause or procure to be killed, any animal by intentional deprivation of necessary sustenance, that person shall be guilty of a Class H felony.

(b) If any person shall maliciously torture, mutilate, maim, cruelly beat, disfigure, poison, or kill, or cause or procure to be tortured, mutilated, maimed, cruelly beaten, disfigured, poisoned, or killed, any animal, every such offender shall for every such offense be guilty of a Class H felony. However, nothing in this section shall be construed to increase the penalty for cockfighting provided for in G.S. 14-362.

(c) As used in this section, the words "torture", "torment", and "cruelly" include or refer to any act, omission, or neglect causing or permitting unjustifiable pain, suffering, or death. As used in this section, the word "intentionally" refers to an act committed knowingly and without justifiable excuse, while the word "maliciously" means an act committed intentionally and with malice or bad motive. As used in this section, the term "animal" includes every living vertebrate in the classes Amphibia, Reptilia, Aves, and Mammalia except human beings. However, this section shall not apply to the following activities:

(1) The lawful taking of animals under the jurisdiction and regulation of the Wildlife Resources Commission, except that this section shall apply to those birds other than pigeons exempted by the Wildlife Resources Commission from its definition of "wild birds" pursuant to G.S. 113-129(15a).

(2) Lawful activities conducted for purposes of biomedical research or training or for purposes of production of livestock, poultry, or aquatic species.

(2a) Lawful activities conducted for the primary purpose of providing food for human or animal consumption.

(3) Activities conducted for lawful veterinary purposes.

(4) The lawful destruction of any animal for the purposes of protecting the public, other animals, property, or the public health.

(5) The physical alteration of livestock or poultry for the purpose of conforming with breed or show standards.

§ 14-360.1. Immunity for veterinarian reporting animal cruelty.

Any veterinarian licensed in this State who has reasonable cause to believe that an animal has been the subject of animal cruelty in violation of G.S. 14-360 and who makes a report of animal cruelty, or who participates in any investigation or testifies in any judicial proceeding that arises from a report of animal cruelty, shall be immune from civil liability, criminal liability, and liability from professional disciplinary action and shall not be in breach of any veterinarianpatient confidentiality, unless the veterinarian acted in bad faith or with a malicious purpose. It shall be a rebuttable presumption that the veterinarian acted in good faith. A failure by a veterinarian to make a report of animal cruelty shall not constitute grounds for disciplinary action under G.S. 90-187.8.

§ 14-361. Instigating or promoting cruelty to animals.

If any person shall willfully set on foot, or instigate, or move to, carry on, or promote, or engage in, or do any act towards the furtherance of any act of cruelty to any animal, he shall be guilty of a Class 1 misdemeanor.

§ 14-361.1. Abandonment of animals.

Any person being the owner or possessor, or having charge or custody of an animal, who willfully and without justifiable excuse abandons the animal is guilty of a Class 2 misdemeanor.

§ 14-362. Cockfighting.

A person who instigates, promotes, conducts, is employed at, allows property under his ownership or control to be used for, participates as a spectator at, or profits from an exhibition featuring the fighting of a cock is guilty of a Class I felony. A lease of property that is used or is intended to be used for an exhibition featuring the fighting of a cock is void, and a lessor who knows this use is made or is intended to be made of his property is under a duty to evict the lessee immediately.

§ 14-362.1. Animal fights and baiting, other than cock fights, dog fights and dog baiting.

(a) A person who instigates, promotes, conducts, is employed at, provides an animal for, allows property under his ownership or control to be used for, or profits from an exhibition featuring the fighting or baiting of an animal, other than a cock or a dog, is guilty of a Class 2 misdemeanor. A lease of property that is used or is intended to be used for an exhibition featuring the fighting or baiting of an animal, other than a cock or a dog, is void, and a lessor who knows this use is made or is intended to be made of his property is under a duty to evict the lessee immediately.

(b)   A person who owns, possesses, or trains an animal, other than a cock or a dog, with the intent that the animal be used in an exhibition featuring the fighting or baiting of that animal or any other animal is guilty of a Class 2 misdemeanor.

(c)   A person who participates as a spectator at an exhibition featuring the fighting or baiting of an animal, other than a cock or a dog, is guilty of a Class 2 misdemeanor.

(d)   A person who commits an offense under subsection (a) within three years after being convicted of an offense under this section is guilty of a Class I felony.

(e)   This section does not prohibit the lawful taking or training of animals under the jurisdiction and regulation of the Wildlife Resources Commission.

§ 14-362.2. Dog fighting and baiting.

(a)   A person who instigates, promotes, conducts, is employed at, provides a dog for, allows property under the person's ownership or control to be used for, gambles on, or profits from an exhibition featuring the baiting of a dog or the fighting of a dog with another dog or with another animal is guilty of a Class H felony. A lease of property that is used or is intended to be used for an exhibition featuring the baiting of a dog or the fighting of a dog with another dog or with another animal is void, and a lessor who knows this use is made or is intended to be made of the lessor's property is under a duty to evict the lessee immediately.

(b)   A person who owns, possesses, or trains a dog with the intent that the dog be used in an exhibition featuring the baiting of that dog or the fighting of that dog with another dog or with another animal is guilty of a Class H felony.

(c)   A person who participates as a spectator at an exhibition featuring the baiting of a dog or the fighting of a dog with another dog or with another animal is guilty of a Class H felony.

(d)   This section does not prohibit the use of dogs in the lawful taking of animals under the jurisdiction and regulation of the Wildlife Resources Commission.

(e)   This section does not prohibit the use of dogs in earthdog trials that are sanctioned or sponsored by entities approved by the Commissioner of Agriculture that meet standards that protect the health and safety of the dogs. Quarry at an earthdog trial shall at all times be kept separate from the dogs by a sturdy barrier, such as a cage, and have access to food and water.

(f)   This section does not apply to the use of herding dogs engaged in the working of domesticated livestock for agricultural, entertainment, or sporting purposes.

§ 14-362.3. Restraining dogs in a cruel manner.

A person who maliciously restrains a dog using a chain or wire grossly in excess of the size necessary to restrain the dog safely is guilty of a Class 1 misdemeanor. For purposes of this section, "maliciously" means the person imposed the restraint intentionally and with malice or bad motive.

§ 14-363. Conveying animals in a cruel manner.

If any person shall carry or cause to be carried in or upon any vehicle or other conveyance, any animal in a cruel or inhuman manner, he shall be guilty of a Class 1 misdemeanor. Whenever an offender shall be taken into custody therefor by any officer, the officer may take charge of such vehicle or other conveyance and its contents, and deposit the same in some safe place of custody. The necessary expenses which may be incurred for taking charge of and keeping and sustaining the vehicle or other conveyance shall be a lien thereon, to be paid before the same can be lawfully reclaimed; or the said expenses, or any part thereof remaining unpaid, may be recovered by the person incurring the same of the owner of such animal in an action therefor.

§ 14-363.1. Living baby chicks or other fowl, or rabbits under eight weeks of age; disposing of as pets or novelties forbidden.

If any person, firm or corporation shall sell, or offer for sale, barter or give away as premiums living baby chicks, ducklings, or other fowl or rabbits under eight weeks of age as pets or novelties, such person, firm or corporation shall be guilty of a Class 3 misdemeanor. Provided, that nothing contained in this section shall be construed to prohibit the sale of nondomesticated species of chicks, ducklings, or other fowl, or of other fowl from proper brooder facilities by hatcheries or stores engaged in the business of selling them for purposes other than for pets or novelties.

§ 14-363.2. Confiscation of cruelly treated animals.

Conviction of any offense contained in this Article may result in confiscation of cruelly treated animals belonging to the accused and it shall be proper for the court in its discretion to order a final determination of the custody of the confiscated animals.

§ 14-363.3. Confinement of animals in motor vehicles.

(a)   In order to protect the health and safety of an animal, any animal control officer, animal cruelty investigator appointed under G.S. 19A-45, law enforcement officer, firefighter, or rescue squad worker, who has probable cause to believe that an animal is confined in a motor vehicle under conditions that are likely to cause suffering, injury, or death to the animal due to heat, cold, lack of adequate ventilation, or under other endangering conditions, may enter the motor vehicle by any reasonable means under the circumstances after making a reasonable effort to locate the owner or other person responsible for the animal.

(b)   Nothing in this section shall be construed to apply to the transportation of horses, cattle, sheep, swine, poultry, or other livestock.

Article 49 [of G.S. Chapter 14].
Protection of Livestock Running at Large.

§ 14-366. Molesting or injuring livestock.

If any person shall unlawfully and on purpose drive any livestock, lawfully running at large in the range, from said range, or shall kill, maim or injure any livestock, lawfully running at large in the range or in the field or pasture of the owner, whether done with actual intent to injure the owner, or to drive the stock from the range, or with any other unlawful intent, every such person, his counselors, aiders, and abettors, shall be guilty of a Class 2 misdemeanor: provided, that nothing herein contained shall prohibit any person from driving out of the range any stock unlawfully brought from other states or places. In any indictment under this section it shall not be necessary to name in the bill or prove on the trial the owner of the stock molested, maimed, killed or injured. Any person violating any provision of this section shall be guilty of a Class 2 misdemeanor.

§ 14-368. Placing poisonous shrubs and vegetables in public places.

If any person shall throw into or leave exposed in any public square, street, lane, alley or open lot in any city, town or village, or in any public road, any mock orange or other poisonous shrub, plant, tree or vegetable, he shall be liable in damages to any person injured thereby and shall also be guilty of a Class 2 misdemeanor.

Article 52 [of G.S. Chapter 14].
Miscellaneous Police Regulations.

. . .

§ 14-401. Putting poisonous foodstuffs, antifreeze, etc., in certain public places, prohibited.

It shall be unlawful for any person, firm or corporation to put or place (i) any strychnine, other poisonous compounds or ground glass on any beef or other foodstuffs of any kind, or (ii) any antifreeze that contains ethylene glycol and is not in a closed container, in any public square, street, lane, alley or on any lot in any village, town or city or on any public road, open field, woods or yard in the country. Any person, firm or corporation who violates the provisions of this section shall be liable in damages to the person injured thereby and also shall be guilty of a Class 1 misdemeanor. This section shall not apply to the poisoning of insects or worms for the purpose of protecting crops or gardens by spraying plants, crops, or trees, to poisons used in rat extermination, or to the accidental release of antifreeze containing ethylene glycol.

. . .

Article 6 [of G.S.Chapter 153A].
Miscellaneous Police Regulations.

. . .

§ 153A-127. Abuse of animals.

A county may by ordinance define and prohibit the abuse of animals.

. . .

§ 153A-145.4. Limitations on standards of care for farm animals.

Notwithstanding any other provision of law, no county ordinance may regulate standards of care for farm animals. For purposes of this section, "standards of care for farm animals" includes the following: the construction, repair, or improvement of farm animal shelter or housing; restrictions on the types of feed or medicines that may be administered to farm animals; and exercise and social interaction requirements. For purposes of this section, the term "farm animals" includes the following domesticated animals: cattle, oxen, bison, sheep, swine, goats, horses, ponies, mules, donkeys, hinnies, llamas, alpacas, lagomorphs, ratites, and poultry.

. . .

Article 8 [of G.S. Chapter 160A].
Miscellaneous Police Regulations.

. . .

§ 160A-182. Abuse of animals.

A city may by ordinance define and prohibit the abuse of animals.

. . .

§ 160A-203.1. Limitations on standards of care for farm animals.

Notwithstanding any other provision of law, no city ordinance may regulate standards of care for farm animals. For purposes of this section, "standards of care for farm animals" includes the following: the construction, repair, or improvement of farm animal shelter or housing; restrictions on the types of feed or medicines that may be administered to farm animals; and exercise and social interaction requirements. For purposes of this section, the term "farm animals" includes the following domesticated animals: cattle, oxen, bison, sheep, swine, goats, horses, ponies, mules, donkeys, hinnies, llamas, alpacas, lagomorphs, ratites, and poultry flocks of greater than 20 birds.

. . .

Chapter 3
Civil Cruelty

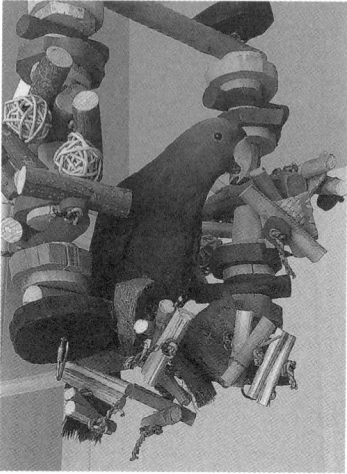

In addition to the criminal statutes governing animal cruelty and animal fighting exhibitions reviewed in Chapter 2, North Carolina law provides civil remedies for protecting animals from persons who abuse, neglect, or otherwise treat them cruelly. This chapter addresses those civil remedies. It first summarizes the process through which any person, regardless of his or her relationship to an animal, may ask a court to order another person to stop treating an animal cruelly. Next, it addresses the laws governing a unique class of public official—animal cruelty investigators. Then the chapter briefly reviews three mechanisms available for recovering some of the costs plaintiffs might incur for the shelter and care of animals taken from their owners while civil cruelty cases are pending. Finally, it provides a brief overview of federal law that requires humane care for animals by specific types of people and in certain settings.

Civil Cruelty Actions under State Law

Article 1 of Chapter 19A of the North Carolina General Statutes (hereinafter G.S.), entitled "Civil Remedy for the Protection of Animals," establishes a civil process that allows a court to impose restrictions it deems necessary to protect an animal that is being treated cruelly.[1] In general, this civil remedy is designed to stop someone from treating an animal cruelly. It is not designed to compensate owners financially for losses related to an animal's injury or death. For example, if Andy is upset with Bob because Bob injured or killed Andy's pet, Andy may want to pursue criminal cruelty charges to see that Bob is punished; or perhaps Andy may want to file a civil tort claim against Bob to recover money damages related to the loss of his pet. The civil remedy discussed in this chapter provides for neither of these actions. Rather, its primary purpose is to provide for *injunctions*—court orders "commanding or preventing an action."[2]

The civil remedy is available to protect any animal that is a "living vertebrate in the classes Amphibia, Reptilia, Aves, and Mammalia except human beings."[3] The terms "cruelty" and "cruel treatment" are defined to include "every act, omission, or neglect whereby unjustifiable physical pain, suffering, or death is caused or permitted."[4] These definitions mirror those used in the criminal cruelty laws.[5]

---

1. Chapter 19A, Article 1 of the North Carolina General Statutes (hereinafter G.S.).

2. *Injunction*, BLACK'S LAW DICTIONARY (10th ed. 2014).

3. G.S. 19A-1(1) (defining the term "animals"). The statutory definition does not include fish or insects, though one scholar has recommended expanding the definition. *See* William A. Reppy Jr., *Citizen Standing to Enforce Anti-Cruelty Laws by Obtaining Injunctions: The North Carolina Experience*, 11 ANIMAL L. 39, 45 (2005).

4. G.S. 19A-1(2).

5. *See* G.S. 14-360(c) (providing definitions of "cruelly" and "animal" in the context of the criminal cruelty laws).

North Carolina's civil remedy is an important complement to the criminal laws related to animal cruelty because, as discussed in more detail below, the civil remedy may be pursued by anyone and allows for animals to be protected from cruel treatment relatively quickly, regardless of the status of any criminal cruelty prosecution.[6] One author also explained that a civil remedy provides local officials with the option of forgoing criminal prosecution altogether in certain circumstances while still achieving the desired goals:

> This may be the case for some animal hoarders who are well-intentioned but ill-equipped—financially and/or mentally—to care for the animals they have taken in. Removal of the animals by injunction puts an immediate end to the suffering and is likely to be viewed as sufficient punishment by the hoarder to also serve a deterrent function. It also permits the public body to take the civil route where proving the case to the criminal standard of beyond a reasonable doubt is unlikely.[7]

The sections that follow discuss North Carolina's civil remedy in detail, describing the process for initiating the action, the types of relief available, the nature of hearings associated with the action, and other relevant information.

Standing

In general, an individual must have what is known as "standing" in order to bring a civil lawsuit.[8] In other states, the issue of a plaintiff's standing to bring suit is often the first point of argument in any cruelty litigation.[9] In North Carolina, though, standing is typically not an issue in civil animal cruelty cases. The state law explicitly confers standing to "*any* person" to bring a civil action for animal cruelty, "even though the

---

6. Penny Conly Ellison, *Time to Give Anticruelty Laws Some Teeth—Bridging the Enforcement Gap*, 3 J. ANIMAL L. & ETHICS 1, 2 (2009) (asserting that criminal prosecution of animal cruelty is infrequent and that a civil remedy, like North Carolina's law, is an important and useful alternative).

7. *Id.* at 3–4.

8. *See, e.g.*, Lujan v. Defenders of Wildlife, 504 U.S. 555 (1992) (discussing federal constitutional standing doctrine). *See also Standing*, BLACK'S LAW DICTIONARY (10th ed. 2014) (defining "standing" as "[a] party's right to make a legal claim or seek judicial enforcement of a duty or right.").

9. *See* Delcianna J. Winders, *Confronting Barriers to the Courtroom for Animal Advocates*, 13 ANIMAL L. 1, 6 (2006) (quoting Joyce Tischler, co-founder of the Animal Legal Defense Fund: "We didn't set out to make standing law. We didn't want to become standing experts. Dealing with the issue of standing . . . has been a practical necessity, because we are challenged in every case we file."). For cases addressing the issue of standing in cruelty cases, see *American Society for Prevention of Cruelty to Animals v. Ringling Bros. & Barnum & Bailey Circus*, 317 F.3d 334, 338 (D.C. Cir. 2003) (holding that a former circus animal handler had standing), and *Animal Legal Defense Fund, Inc. v. Glickman*, 154 F.3d 426, 445 (D.C. Cir. 1998) (recognizing that a visitor to a zoo had standing).

person does not have a possessory or ownership right in an animal."[10] The term "person" includes political and corporate bodies as well as individuals.[11] Thus, an animal protection society, local government, neighbor, or perfect stranger can bring a private lawsuit alleging animal cruelty.[12]

In 2007, a defendant in a civil cruelty case challenged the constitutionality of the expansive standing provision in the civil cruelty law.[13] The North Carolina Court of Appeals rejected the argument, explaining that the General Assembly intended that "the broadest category of persons or organizations be deemed '[a] real party in interest' when contesting cruelty to animals" and that the state constitution presented no barrier to such a law.[14]

Process

The two primary players in these civil actions are the plaintiff and the defendant. The plaintiff is the person who files the action alleging that another person is treating an animal cruelly. The defendant in a civil cruelty case may be any person who either owns or has possession of the animal.[15] As mentioned above, the primary mechanism by which the civil remedy operates is by authorizing a court to issue an injunction that protects the animal at issue from further cruel treatment. The law contemplates two

---

10. G.S. 19A-2 (emphasis added).

11. G.S. 19A-1(3). The statute cites the definition of "person" in G.S. 12-3, which refers to "bodies politic and corporate, as well as to individuals, unless the context clearly shows to the contrary." G.S. 12-3(6). *See also* Reppy, *supra* note 3, at 41–44 (discussing the broad standing provisions and explaining that the statute was amended in 2003 to clarify that local governments have standing).

12. Before the civil cruelty law was adopted, courts were unwilling to issue injunctions to prevent actions that may have constituted animal cruelty under the existing criminal law. In 1962, for example, the North Carolina Supreme Court rejected a plaintiff's request to enjoin a rabbit hunt allegedly conducted in a cruel manner. Yandell v. Am. Legion Post No. 113, 256 N.C. 691, 693 (1962). The court explained that "ordinarily the violation of a criminal statute is not sufficient to invoke the equitable jurisdiction of the court." *Id.*

13. Animal Legal Def. Fund v. Woodley, 181 N.C. App. 594 (2007).

14. *Id.* at 596 (quoting Justice for Animals, Inc. v. Robeson Cty., 164 N.C. App. 366, 371 (2004)); *see also* Justice for Animals, Inc. v. Lenoir Cty. SPCA, Inc., 168 N.C. App. 298, 304, *modified and aff'd*, 360 N.C. 48 (2005). In *Woodley*, the basis for the constitutional challenge was Article IV, Section 13 of the North Carolina Constitution, which states: "[t]here shall be in this State but one form of action for the enforcement or protection of private rights or the redress of private wrongs, which shall be denominated a civil action, and in which there shall be a right to have issues of fact tried before a jury." The appeals court explained that this provision does not relate to standing but was intended only to "abolish[] the distinction between actions at law and suits in equity." *Woodley*, 181 N.C. App. at 596 (citing Reynolds v. Reynolds, 208 N.C. 578, 624 (1935)).

15. G.S. 19A-2. The term "person" is defined broadly to include both individuals and political and corporate bodies. *Id.* § 12-3. A defendant could be, for example, a private individual, an animal shelter, a circus company, or a pet store.

types of injunctions that may be issued in a civil cruelty case—a *preliminary injunction* and a *permanent injunction*. A court is authorized to issue a preliminary injunction upon the filing of a verified complaint[16] and is authorized to issue a permanent injunction after the case has been heard on the merits.[17] Though the most salient feature of the civil cruelty remedy is the opportunity it presents for an injunction to be issued relatively quickly after the action is filed, the remedy is a bona fide civil action intended to culminate in a trial on the merits where one party will prevail. Consequently, the civil cruelty remedy largely is subject to the same legal landscape that influences any civil action, including the Rules of Civil Procedure. A full discussion of litigating a civil action and the Rules of Civil Procedure is beyond the scope of this book, but a person pursuing the civil remedy for cruelty to animals should be aware that the Rules govern the action and have substantial influence on how it proceeds. The process for initiating an action and the injunctions that may be issued are discussed in more detail below.

Initiating the Action

A civil cruelty action typically is initiated when a plaintiff files a complaint against a defendant in the district court in the county in which cruelty to an animal has allegedly occurred.[18] Unlike other types of civil actions, no court costs or fees must be paid prior to a final judicial determination on the merits of the case.[19] As mentioned, civil cruelty actions are subject to the North Carolina Rules of Civil Procedure, except to the extent that a differing procedure is prescribed by statute.[20] A complaint is a form of civil pleading, and, among other things, Rule 8 of the state Rules of Civil Procedure requires that a pleading contain a demand for "the relief to which the party deems himself entitled."[21] Thus, a plaintiff seeking an injunction should state that fact in the complaint.[22]

---

16. G.S. 19A-3(a).

17. G.S. 19A-4(a). The court also is broadly authorized to "enter orders as the court deems appropriate" after a hearing on the merits. *Id.*

18. *See* G.S. 19A-3 (describing judge's authority to issue preliminary injunction after verified complaint is filed in district court in county where cruelty allegedly occurred); 19A-4 (providing that a district court judge in the county in which the action was brought shall determine the merits of the action). *Cf. In re* King, 79 N.C. App. 139, 143 (1986) ("A civil action is initiated upon the filing of a complaint with the court or the issuance of a summons pursuant to Rule 3 of the North Carolina Rules of Civil Procedure."). As the preceding quotation suggests, a civil action may be initiated by issuance of a summons, but a plaintiff must be granted permission by the court to initiate an action in this manner. *See* G.S. 1A-1, Rule 3.

19. G.S. 19A-46(d).

20. *See* G.S. 1A-1, Rule 1.

21. G.S. 1A-1, Rule 8(A)(2).

22. *Cf.* Animal Legal Def. Fund v. Woodley, 181 N.C. App. 594, 595 (2007) (noting that plaintiff's complaint sought preliminary and permanent injunctions).

In cases where a plaintiff intends to seek a preliminary injunction, the complaint must be verified.[23] The requirement that the complaint be verified means that the person filing the complaint must file an affidavit "stat[ing] in substance that the contents of the [complaint] are true to the knowledge of the person making the verification, except as to those matters stated on information and belief, and as to those matters he believes them to be true."[24] Verified complaints "must be sworn to before a notary public or other officer of the court authorized to administer oaths."[25] The North Carolina Court of Appeals has held that a verified complaint is required in a civil cruelty action only when a plaintiff seeks a preliminary injunction as a form of relief—it is not necessary that a complaint be verified in order to confer subject matter jurisdiction over the action to the court.[26]

Preliminary Injunction

A preliminary injunction is "an interlocutory injunction issued after notice and hearing which restrains a party pending trial on the merits."[27] G.S. 19A-3 authorizes the judge in a civil cruelty case, as a matter of discretion, to issue a preliminary injunction upon the filing of a verified complaint and prior to a hearing on the merits.[28]

The statute further provides that issuance of a preliminary injunction should be in "accordance with G.S. 1A-1, Rule 65."[29] Rule 65 of the North Carolina Rules of Civil Procedure mandates that "[n]o preliminary injunction shall be issued without notice to the adverse party."[30] It appears that the notice to which the adverse party is entitled in the context of a preliminary injunction is notice of a preliminary injunction hearing, not merely notice of the initiation of the civil action[31] and the accompanying incidental fact that the plaintiff is seeking a preliminary injunction as relief.[32] The court should

---

23. G.S. 19A-3(a).

24. G.S. 1A-1, Rule 11(b).

25. Fansler v. Honeycutt, 221 N.C. App. 226, 229 (2012) (internal quotation marks omitted) (citation omitted). *See also* G.S. 1-148 ("Any officer competent to take the acknowledgment of deeds, and any judge or clerk of the General Court of Justice, notary public, in or out of the State, or magistrate, is competent to take affidavits for the verification of pleadings, in any court or county in the State, and for general purposes.").

26. *Woodley*, 181 N.C. App. at 595.

27. Setzer v. Annas, 286 N.C. 534, 537 (1975).

28. G.S. 19A-3(a).

29. *Id.*

30. G.S. 1A-1, Rule 65(a).

31. Notice to the adverse party of the initiation of the civil action is dictated by the Rules of Civil Procedure, which describe a comprehensive procedural framework for the litigation of civil actions that is beyond the scope of this book.

32. *See, e.g.,* Perry v. Baxley Dev., Inc., 188 N.C. App. 158, 162 (2008) (trial court abused its discretion by failing to set aside preliminary injunction where defendant did not receive proper notice of the hearing on the issuance of the preliminary injunction).

hold a hearing prior to issuing a preliminary injunction.[33] G.S. 1-485, the civil procedure statute dealing generally with preliminary injunctions, describes three circumstances where a preliminary injunction may be issued. Arguably, none of the circumstances described are good fits with a civil cruelty action because each speaks to situations where a party will be injured or a party's rights will be violated if the injunction is not issued. As already discussed, the civil cruelty action may be pursued by any person, and it will not always be the case that the person prosecuting the action will suffer an injury or have his or her rights violated absent the issuance of an injunction. Regardless, G.S. 19A-3 says that issuance of a preliminary injunction is a "matter of discretion" for the judge, and the spirit of G.S. 1-485 suggests that the injunction should be issued when it is necessary to restrain the commission or continuance of acts of cruelty towards the animal at issue.[34]

Plaintiffs usually have to post a bond sufficient to cover any costs a defendant might incur before a court will issue a preliminary injunction.[35] The bond will be used to reimburse the defendant if the court later determines that the injunction was improper. The court sets the amount of the bond or, in some situations, may conclude that no bond is required.[36] No bond will be required if the case is initiated by an officially appointed animal cruelty investigator[37] or by the state or a local government.[38] The court could, however, later assess damages against a state or local government plaintiff if it ultimately dissolves an injunction.[39]

---

33. *See* Setzer v. Annas, 286 N.C. 534, 537 (1975) (preliminary injunction is issued after a hearing). *See also* Justice for Animals, Inc. v. Robeson Cty., 164 N.C. App. 366, 368 (noting that trial court entered temporary restraining order effective "until such time as this matter can be brought on for hearing as to whether or not there should be a preliminary injunction entered ordering preliminary relief, in anticipation of trial"); Animal Legal Def. Fund v. Woodley, 181 N.C. App. 594, 595 (2007) (noting that trial court held hearing prior to issuance of preliminary injunction).

34. *See* G.S. 1-485(1). *See also* Calloway v. Onderdonk, 158 N.C. App. 743 (2003) (unpublished) (not paginated on Westlaw) ("The trial court enjoys broad discretion in proceedings under Chapter 19A.").

35. G.S. 1A-1, Rule 65(c) ("No . . . preliminary injunction shall issue except upon the giving of security by the applicant, in such sum as the judge deems proper, for the payment of such costs and damages as may be incurred or suffered by any party who is found to have been wrongfully enjoined or restrained.").

36. *See* Keith v. Day, 60 N.C. App. 559, 561–62 (1983).

37. For a discussion of the role of animal cruelty investigators, see page 66, *infra*.

38. G.S. 1A-1, Rule 65(c) ("No such security shall be required of the State of North Carolina or of any county or municipality thereof, or any officer or agency thereof acting in an official capacity, but damages may be awarded against such party in accord with this rule.").

39. *Id. See also* G.S. 1A-1, Rule 65(e) ("An order or judgment dissolving an injunction or restraining order may include an award of damages against the party procuring the injunction and the sureties on his undertaking without a showing of malice or want of probable cause in

The plaintiff may request permission to provide for the animal's care, and the preliminary injunction may give the plaintiff the right to do so.[40] The court has the discretion to issue a preliminary injunction authorizing the plaintiff to take possession of the animal as custodian if it concludes, based on the plaintiff's complaint, that the "condition giving rise to the cruel treatment . . . requires the animal to be removed" from the defendant's custody.[41] If temporary custody is awarded to the plaintiff, the plaintiff is allowed to place the animal with a foster care provider.[42]

While the animal is in the plaintiff's temporary custody, the plaintiff may decide that the animal needs veterinary care. The law provides the plaintiff with clear authority to obtain any such care (except euthanasia).[43] Before seeking veterinary care, however, the plaintiff is required to consult with or attempt to consult with the defendant about the care. Note that the law does not require the plaintiff to obtain the defendant's permission to seek veterinary care; it only requires that the plaintiff consult, or attempt to consult, with the defendant. Even if the defendant disagrees with the plaintiff's decision, the plaintiff may provide veterinary care for the animal.

The plaintiff may not have the animal euthanized without either the written consent of the defendant or a court order.[44] The court may issue such an order if it finds that the animal is suffering as a result of a terminal illness or terminal injury.

Permanent Injunction

In civil cruelty actions, G.S. 19A-4 provides that a district court judge in the county in which the action was brought must determine the merits of the action by a trial without a jury.[45] As is the case with any civil trial, the parties may present evidence and argue their case.[46] Though the statute does not identify a standard of proof for a trial on the merits, "[i]n ordinary civil actions, the verdict should be based on the preponderance of the evidence."[47] After determining the merits of the action, the judge is authorized to "enter orders as [he or she] deems appropriate, including a permanent injunction and dismissal of the action along with dissolution of any preliminary injunction that [has] been issued."[48] The statute contemplates that the court will enter a final judgment in

---

procuring the injunction. The damages may be determined by the judge, or he may direct that they be determined by a referee or jury.")

40. G.S. 19A-3(a) ("Every . . . preliminary injunction, if the plaintiff so requests, may give the plaintiff the right to provide suitable care for the animal.").

41. *Id.*

42. G.S. 19A-3(c).

43. G.S. 19A-3(b).

44. *Id.*

45. G.S. 19A-4(a).

46. *Id.*

47. Wyatt v. Queen City Coach Co., 229 N.C. 340, 342 (1948).

48. G.S. 19A-4(a).

the action, identifying the prevailing party and making any necessary findings of fact and conclusions of law.[49] If the court's final judgment entitles the defendant to regain possession of an animal that is in the custody of another person, "the custodian shall return the animal, including taking any necessary steps to retrieve the animal from a foster care provider."[50] The judge has the option, however, of extending the alternative custody and care arrangements until the time for appeal expires or until all appeals have been exhausted.[51]

G.S. 19A-4 appears to contemplate situations where a plaintiff prevails in the cruelty action but where the animal nevertheless can be safely returned to the defendant. The court's order should outline any restrictions placed on the defendant.[52] If the judge determines, based upon a preponderance of the evidence, that even if a permanent injunction were issued there still would be a "substantial risk that the animal would be subjected to further cruelty if returned to the possession of the defendant,"[53] the judge may terminate the defendant's ownership and right of possession. In such a case, the judge can transfer ownership and right of possession to another person or entity, such as the plaintiff or a foster care provider. For good cause shown, the judge may impose restrictions on the defendant's ability to acquire, own, or possess animals in the future.[54]

Exceptions

Under G.S. 19A-1.1, the following activities are excepted from the civil remedy statute:

1. the taking of animals that are under the jurisdiction of the Wildlife Resources Commission, with special provisions for wild birds;[55]

2. activities conducted for purposes of biomedical research or training;

3. activities conducted for purposes of production of livestock, poultry, or aquatic species;

---

49. *See* G.S. 19A-4(c) (referring to the contents of the "final judgment").

50. *Id.*

51. G.S. 19A-4(d).

52. The order must explain the reasons for the order and describe in detail the act or acts enjoined or restrained. G.S. 1A-1, Rule 65(d).

53. G.S. 19A-4(b). The "preponderance of the evidence" standard sometimes is also referred to as the "greater weight of the evidence." *See, e.g.,* Cincinnati Butchers Supply Co. v. Conoly, 204 N.C. 677, 679 (1933) (explaining that the two terms are synonymous).

54. G.S. 19A-4(b).

55. The law provides that a "wild bird" exempted from regulation by the Wildlife Resources Commission pursuant to G.S. 113-129(15a) may be the subject of a civil cruelty action. G.S. 19A-1.1(1). The same language is used in the criminal cruelty law and was the subject of extensive litigation. For a detailed discussion of the litigation related to the wild bird provision, see Chapter 2, page 29, *supra.*

4. activities conducted for the primary purpose of providing food for human or animal consumption;

5. activities conducted for veterinary purposes;

6. destruction of any animal for the purposes of protecting the public, other animals, or the public health;

7. activities for sport; and

8. the taking and holding in captivity of a wild animal by a licensed sportsman for use or display in an annual, seasonal, or cultural event, so long as the animal is captured from the wild and returned to the wild at or near the area where it was captured.

A court may not issue an injunction against a person for participating in any of these excepted activities, as long as the activities are carried out lawfully. But a person could seek an injunction against, for example, a researcher using an animal for biomedical experimentation in a way that is not authorized by law and that causes the animal unjustifiable pain, suffering, or death.

The first six exceptions in the civil statute mirror those in the criminal cruelty statute. The last two exceptions are included only in the civil remedy. The exception for "activities for sport" is vague and has not been litigated.

The last exception was incorporated into the law in response to controversy surrounding a civil cruelty case that sought to end a traditional practice in western North Carolina of lowering a live possum in a box on New Year's Eve, referred to as the "Possum Drop."[56] Following the initial round of litigation, the legislature added this exception to the cruelty law and at the same time amended the wildlife laws governing licenses to capture live animals.[57] Subsequently, another private lawsuit was filed challenging the validity of the captivity permit obtained by the person organizing the Possum Drop. In response, the legislature enacted a new law in 2015 that created an even broader exception applicable to possums:

> No State or local statutes, rules, regulations, or ordinances related to the capture, captivity, treatment, or release of wildlife shall apply to the Virginia

---

56. Jon Ostendorff, *Possum Drop Gets State Approval*, Citizen-Times (Asheville) (Dec. 20, 2013), http://www.citizen-times.com/story/news/2013/12/20/possum-drop-gets-state-approval/4148381/.

57. S.L. 2013-3. The legislation added language to the sections of the wildlife laws that authorize the Wildlife Resources Commission to issue captivity permits. Those sections now allow captivity permits to be issued "for scientific, educational, exhibition, or other purposes." G.S. 113-272.5(a); 113-274(c).

opossum (Didelphis virginiana) between the dates of December 29 of each year and January 2 of each subsequent year.[58]

In response to this change in the law, the state court of appeals dismissed the pending challenges to the validity of the captivity permits because they were moot.[59] With such a broad exemption in place related to the "treatment" of possums, it seems unlikely that a civil cruelty action based on the treatment of a possum during this limited time window (December 29 through January 2) would be successful. For other times of the year, possums are subject to the jurisdiction of the Wildlife Resources Commission and, therefore, any lawful taking of a possum would be exempt from the civil animal cruelty laws.

Cruelty Investigators

In North Carolina, counties have the option of enlisting private citizens to assist in cruelty investigations. Article 4 of G.S. Chapter 19A provides the framework for appointing volunteers as "animal cruelty investigators" and outlines their authority and responsibilities.

Appointment

Boards of county commissioners may appoint one or more persons to serve as animal cruelty investigators. These investigators must serve "without any compensation or other employee benefits," which implies that they may not be county employees.[60] It is important to remember, though, that a local government employee does not need to be an appointed animal cruelty investigator in order to investigate animal cruelty and pursue civil remedies. Both appointed animal cruelty investigators and local government employees working in animal services will be investigating and seeking to enforce the same body of animal cruelty law. The primary difference between the two groups is that animal cruelty investigators have the authority to seize animals pursuant to a magistrate's order (discussed further below). A local government official must rely on consent, a search warrant or other court order, or exigent circumstances to seize an animal.[61]

---

58. S.L. 2015-73 (adding new G.S. 113-291.13). *See also* Valerie Bauerlein, *Live Opossum Drop to Resume Its Place in Brasstown New Year's Celebration*, Wall Street Journal (Dec. 30, 2015), https://www.wsj.com/articles/live-opossum-drop-to-resume-its-place-in-brasstown-new-years-celebration-1451513677.

59. People for the Ethical Treatment of Animals v. Myers, 246 N.C. App. 571 (2016).

60. G.S. 19A-45(a).

61. *See generally* Robert L. Farb, Arrest, Search, and Investigation in North Carolina (5th ed. 2016) (chapter 4 of this book discusses the procedure for obtaining a search

When appointing investigators, the commissioners are allowed to consider candidates nominated by animal welfare organizations, but they may consider other candidates as well.[62] Cruelty investigators are required to take at least six hours a year of continuing education approved by the board of county commissioners. This training must be "designed to give the investigator expertise in the investigation of complaints relating to the care and treatment of animals."[63]

Before making an appointment, the commissioners may choose to enter into an agreement requiring the investigator or an animal welfare organization to assume responsibility for the costs of caring for any animals they seize. Note that this type of agreement is permitted, not required, by state law. The board of commissioners also may agree to reimburse the investigator for necessary and actual expenses related to investigations.[64]

Investigators are appointed for one-year terms and are not limited to any given number of terms. They must take the oath of office and wear badges that (1) are approved by the board of commissioners and (2) identify them as animal cruelty investigators.[65] The investigators must supply and pay for their badges "at no cost to the county."[66]

Seizure Authority

A cruelty investigator typically pursues a civil animal cruelty case in the same manner as described in the above section. Cruelty investigators have, however, one additional tool at their disposal: when an animal is being cruelly treated, they can request, obtain, and execute a seizure order *before* filing a civil cruelty action. To do so, the investigator must first file a sworn complaint with a magistrate requesting an order allowing the investigator to provide suitable care for and take immediate custody of the animal. If the magistrate finds "probable cause to believe that the animal is being cruelly treated

---

warrant and the consequences of an unlawful search or seizure). In *State v. Nance*, 149 N.C. App. 734 (2002), the court determined that the Fourth Amendment rights of a horse owner were violated when animal services officials seized horses from her property without a warrant or her consent and where no exigent circumstances existed.

62. The law specifically authorizes the board to consider "persons nominated by any society incorporated under North Carolina law for the prevention of cruelty to animals." G.S. 19A-45(a).

63. G.S. 19A-49.

64. G.S. 19A-45(d).

65. G.S. 19A-45(b). Chapter 11 of the North Carolina General Statutes governs the administration of oaths to members of the General Assembly and others appointed or elected to public office. It identifies who may administer the oath, defines when affirmation may be substituted for an oath, and prescribes its specific language. *See* Trey Allen, *One Oath or Two? What Is THE Oath of Office?*, COATES' CANONS: NC LOC. GOV'T L. blog (UNC School of Government, Jan. 27, 2017), https://canons.sog.unc.edu/one-oath-or-two-what-is-the-oath-of-office/.

66. G.S. 19A-45(b).

and that it is necessary for the investigator to immediately take custody of it," he or she must issue an order authorizing immediate seizure.[67] The order is only valid for twenty-four hours.

When seizing the animal, the investigator must leave with the owner a copy of the magistrate's order and a written statement describing

- the animal seized,
- the place where the animal will be taken,
- the reason for taking the animal, and
- the investigator's intent to file a civil cruelty case.[68]

If the investigator does not know who owns the animal, a copy of the above information should be affixed to the premises or vehicle where the animal was found.[69] If anyone is present when the investigator arrives, the investigator must give notice of his or her identity and purpose before entering the premises or vehicle.

When seizing an animal, an investigator may ask to be accompanied by an animal control or law enforcement officer. He or she may *forcibly* enter a building or a vehicle only

- when reasonably certain that the animal is on the premises or in the vehicle,
- when reasonably certain that no people are on the premises or in the vehicle,
- if forcible entry is necessary to seize the animal as authorized by the order,
- when accompanied by a law enforcement officer,
- during daylight hours, and
- when the order is issued by a district court judge (rather than a magistrate).[70]

After seizing the animal, the investigator must return the seizure order to the clerk of court along with a written inventory of the animal or animals seized.[71] The investigator must take the animal to a safe and secure place and provide suitable care for it. When an investigator has seized an animal, he or she is obligated to file a civil cruelty action "as soon as possible."[72]

A person who interferes with an animal cruelty investigator in the performance of his or her official duties may be charged with a misdemeanor.[73]

As discussed in greater detail in the previous chapter, animal cruelty investigators are among the officials who are permitted under G.S. 14-363.3 to rescue animals confined in motor vehicles when there is probable cause to believe the animal is at risk. That

---

67. G.S. 19A-46(a).
68. G.S. 19A-46(c).
69. *Id.*
70. G.S. 19A-46(b) and (e).
71. G.S. 19A-46(a).
72. G.S. 19A-46(c).
73. G.S. 19A-48 (Class 1 misdemeanor).

authority is distinct from the seizure authority discussed in this section and does not depend upon a magistrate's order.

Recovering the Custodian's Costs

If a plaintiff assumes custody of an animal during the course of a civil cruelty case, he or she will incur some costs related to its care: food, shelter, and veterinary care. A plaintiff also assumes responsibility for certain court costs and fees associated with bringing the action, although the law provides that such costs need not be paid until the court makes its final decision on the merits of the action.[74]

The law provides three mechanisms for recovering some or all of those costs. The first mechanism is fairly simple: if the plaintiff wins a civil animal cruelty case, state law provides that court costs are to be paid by the defendant.[75] Costs typically include the filing fees and other court-related expenses involved in bringing the action.[76] In cruelty cases, however, the judge, in his or her discretion, may also include the costs of any food, water, shelter, and care—including veterinary care—the plaintiff provided during the course of the proceeding.[77] If the judge decides to include those expenses as court costs, the defendant will be required to pay them.

The second cost-recovery mechanism is available only to animal cruelty investigators. If an investigator seizes and provides care for an animal during the course of a civil cruelty case, the animal's owner may be held liable for the "necessary expenses" incurred in caring for the animal, including veterinary care.[78] The cost of these expenses is a charge against the animal's owner and a lien on the animal,[79] meaning that if the owner fails to pay for the care provided to the animal after it was seized, the investigator may be able to sell the animal to recover some or all of the expenses. State law provides a detailed framework for enforcing liens through public or private sale, including deadlines and specific notice requirements.[80]

---

74. G.S. 19A-46(d) ("[A]ny person who commences a proceeding under this article [G.S. Chapter 19A, Article 4; animal cruelty investigators] or Article 1 [civil remedy for the protection of animals] shall not be required to pay any court costs or fees prior to a final judicial determination as provided in G.S. 19A-4 [permanent injunction], at which time those costs shall be paid pursuant to the provisions of G.S. 6-18.").

75. G.S. 6-18(5) ("Costs shall be allowed of course to the plaintiff, upon a recovery, in . . . an action brought under Article 1 of Chapter 19A.").

76. *See* G.S. 7A-305 (specifying the court costs that apply in civil actions).

77. G.S. 19A-4(b).

78. G.S. 19A-47.

79. *Id.*

80. *See generally* G.S. 44A-4.

The third cost-recovery mechanism is the option to petition the court to recover sheltering costs pursuant to G.S. 19A-70. This option is discussed in chapter 7, "Animal Shelters."

Federal Law

The federal Animal Welfare Act governs treatment of animals in certain types of facilities and by certain types of individuals and organizations.[81] When enacting this body of law, Congress focused on the role of the federal government in regulating animals and activities that "are either in interstate or foreign commerce or substantially affect such commerce or the free flow thereof . . . ."[82] It also specifically emphasized the need to regulate "the transportation, purchase, sale, housing, care, handling, and treatment of animals by carriers or by persons or organizations engaged in" research, animal exhibitions, or pet sales.[83] Therefore, the act applies to research facilities, dealers, exhibitors, handlers, and carriers.[84] As discussed in chapter 1, there is also a section of this law that addresses animal fighting ventures.[85]

In short, the federal law requires dealers and exhibitors to obtain licenses.[86] Other regulated entities, including research facilities and carriers, must register with the federal government.[87] The federal statutes and regulations specify requirements for the humane handling, care, treatment, and transportation of animals by all of these regulated entities.[88] If a regulated entity fails to comply, the U.S. Department of Agriculture (USDA) can take action on licenses, impose fines, seek injunctions, and even

---

81. 7 U.S.C. §§ 2131–2156. *See also* 9 C.F.R. ch. 1, subch. A.

82. 7 U.S.C. § 2131. Multiple cases have challenged the constitutionality of these laws, arguing that the federal government has overstepped its authority. In most cases, the constitutional challenge has failed. *See, e.g.,* United States v. Gibert, 677 F.3d 613, 626-27 (4th Cir. 2012) (upholding the provisions of the Animal Welfare Act related to animal fighting ventures as an appropriate exercise of federal authority pursuant to the Commerce Clause); 907 Whitehead St., Inc. v. Sec'y of U.S. Dep't of Agric., 701 F.3d 1345, 1350–51 (11th Cir. 2012) (upholding the constitutionality of the Animal Welfare Act with respect to licensure of animal exhibitors). *But see* United States v. Stevens, 559 U.S. 460 (2010) (invalidating provision of the Animal Welfare Act criminalizing depictions of animal cruelty, i.e., "animal crush videos," as overbroad and in violation of the First Amendment).

83. 7 U.S.C. § 2131.

84. These terms are defined in 7 U.S.C. § 2132.

85. 7 U.S.C. § 2156.

86. 7 U.S.C. §§ 2133–2134.

87. 7 U.S.C. § 2136.

88. 7 U.S.C. § 2143.

pursue criminal penalties.[89] For example, the USDA investigated an animal exhibitor in Catawba County and filed a 110-count complaint against the exhibitor in 2014, citing willful violations of the federal law.[90] In 2016, the exhibitor entered into a consent agreement with the federal government that addressed complaints and deficiencies documented over several years.[91] The consent agreement provided for a license suspension, a probationary period, and a prohibition on exhibition of nonhuman primates.

Because this body of law is administered and enforced exclusively by the federal government,[92] there is no direct role for local officials. They may, however, have an opportunity to coordinate with and support federal officials in their enforcement. Local officials may also pursue enforcement of state and local laws concurrently with federal enforcement. In 2015, the North Carolina Court of Appeals was asked to weigh in on the question of whether the federal Animal Welfare Act preempted—or overrode— the state's animal cruelty laws.[93] In this case, the plaintiffs filed a complaint against a private zoo in state district court. The plaintiffs were seeking an injunction under the state's cruelty laws in G.S. Chapter 19A. The state district court dismissed the case, asserting that because the zoo was a licensed exhibitor under federal law, the federal Animal Welfare Act governed treatment of the animals and state law did not apply. The plaintiffs appealed that decision to the court of appeals, which concluded that the lower court had made a mistake. It explained that the federal law does not preempt state law and that, in fact, the two bodies of law "both protect against the inhumane treatment of animals" and "apply equally and do not conflict so much as they operate cooperatively."[94]

---

89. 7 U.S.C. § 2146 (general enforcement provisions, including criminal penalties for interference with an investigation); § 2149 (violations by licensees, including suspension, revocation, and civil and criminal penalties); § 2159 (injunctions).

90. Joe Marusak, *Feds File 110-Count Complaint against Catawba Animal Park*, CHARLOTTE OBSERVER (Dec. 5, 2014), http://www.charlotteobserver.com/news/local/crime/article9241277.html#storylink=cpy.

91. *In re* Beal, AWA No. 15-0016, 2016 WL 369395 (U.S.D.A. Jan. 8, 2016).

92. Some concerns have been raised about the adequacy of federal oversight and enforcement. *See, e.g.*, Shigehiko Ito, *Beyond Standing: A Search for a New Solution in Animal Welfare*, 46 SANTA CLARA L. REV. 377, 378 (2006); People for the Ethical Treatment of Animals v. U.S. Dep't of Agric., 861 F.3d 502 (4th Cir. 2017) (holding that the agency's process for licensure renewals for exhibitors was entitled to deference).

93. Salzer v. King Kong Zoo, 242 N.C. App. 120 (2015).

94. *Id.* at 124.

Local Laws

As discussed in Chapter 2, local governments have long had the authority to adopt laws governing the treatment of animals.[95] These local ordinances may not contradict or duplicate state law, but they often supplement it. For example, several jurisdictions have adopted tethering ordinances in recent years. Some of the laws prohibit tethering completely,[96] some allow it for limited periods of time,[97] and others permit it if certain conditions are satisfied.[98] While one might be able to assert that tethering in some circumstances rises to the level of torment or cruelty under existing state laws, these local laws provide clear prohibitions that, because of their specificity, may be easier to enforce. A local law also has the benefit of offering some more flexible enforcement alternatives. In the context of civil enforcement, for example, an ordinance may authorize a local government to impose monetary fines on an owner or keeper. For a more detailed discussion of the role of ordinances in cruelty cases, see chapter 2.

Conclusion

This chapter, in conjunction with Chapter 2, summarizes and analyzes the many different legal tools available under state law for addressing animal cruelty. In some situations, an injunction may be the most appropriate remedy, while in others a criminal prosecution may prove more effective. Sometimes both are necessary. Local government officials, animal services officials, and animal cruelty investigators dealing with an instance of animal cruelty will need to understand and consider all the options the law makes available to them.

---

95. G.S. 153A-127 (counties); 160A-182 (cities).

96. *See, e.g.*, New Hanover County, N.C., Code of Ordinances § 5-30, City of Roanoke Rapids, N.C., Code of Ordinances § 91.22.

97. *See, e.g.*, Orange County, N.C., Code of Ordinances § 4-41(k) (authorizing tethering for up to three hours in a twenty-four-hour period); City of Laurinburg, N.C., Code of Ordinances § 4-19 (authorizing tethering for up to one hour in a twenty-four-hour period).

98. *See, e.g.*, Catawba County, N.C., Code of Ordinances § 6-41(6) (prohibiting "[c]haining or tethering an animal to a stationary object for a period of time or under conditions that an animal control officer deems harmful or potentially harmful to the animal" and including several examples of improper tethering); Surry County, N.C., Code of Ordinances art. VII, §§ 3–3a (prohibiting tethering to a moving cable trolley and allowing tethering if certain conditions are met).

Appendix. Relevant Sections of the North Carolina General Statutes (G.S.)

Article 1 [of G.S. Chapter 19A].
Civil Remedy for Protection of Animals.

§ 19A-1. Definitions.

The following definitions apply in this Article:
  (1)   The term "animals" includes every living vertebrate in the classes Amphibia, Reptilia, Aves, and Mammalia except human beings.
  (2)   The terms "cruelty" and "cruel treatment" include every act, omission, or neglect whereby unjustifiable physical pain, suffering, or death is caused or permitted.
  (3)   The term "person" has the same meaning as in G.S. 12-3.

§ 19A-1.1. Exemptions.

This Article shall not apply to the following:
  (1)   The lawful taking of animals under the jurisdiction and regulation of the Wildlife Resources Commission, except that this Article applies to those birds other than pigeons exempted by the Wildlife Resources Commission from its definition of "wild birds" pursuant to G.S. 113-129(15a).
  (2)   Lawful activities conducted for purposes of biomedical research or training or for purposes of production of livestock, poultry, or aquatic species.
  (3)   Lawful activities conducted for the primary purpose of providing food for human or animal consumption.
  (4)   Activities conducted for lawful veterinary purposes.
  (5)   The lawful destruction of any animal for the purposes of protecting the public, other animals, or the public health.
  (6)   Lawful activities for sport.
  (7)   The taking and holding in captivity of a wild animal by a licensed sportsman for use or display in an annual, seasonal, or cultural event, so long as the animal is captured from the wild and returned to the wild at or near the area where it was captured.

§ 19A-2. Purpose.

It shall be the purpose of this Article to provide a civil remedy for the protection and humane treatment of animals in addition to any criminal remedies that are available and it shall be proper in any action to combine causes of action against one or more defendants for the protection of one or more animals. A real party in interest as plaintiff shall be held to include any person even though the person does not have a possessory or ownership right in an animal; a real party in interest as defendant shall include any person who owns or has possession of an animal. Venue for any action filed under this Article shall only be in the county where any violation is alleged to have occurred.

§ 19A-3. Preliminary injunction; care of animal pending hearing on the merits.

  (a)   Upon the filing of a verified complaint in the district court in the county in which cruelty to an animal has allegedly occurred, the judge may, as a matter of discretion, issue a preliminary injunction in accordance with the procedures set forth in G.S. 1A-1, Rule 65. Every such preliminary injunction, if the plaintiff so requests, may give the plaintiff the right to provide suitable care for the animal. If it appears on the face of the complaint that the condition giving rise to the cruel treatment of an animal requires the animal to be removed from its owner or other person who possesses it, then it shall be proper for the court in the preliminary injunction to allow the plaintiff to take possession of the animal as custodian.

(b)   The plaintiff as custodian may employ a veterinarian to provide necessary medical care for the animal without any additional court order. Prior to taking such action, the plaintiff as custodian shall consult with, or attempt to consult with, the defendant in the action, but the plaintiff as custodian may authorize such care without the defendant's consent. Notwithstanding the provisions of this subsection, the plaintiff as custodian may not have an animal euthanized without written consent of the defendant or a court order that authorizes euthanasia upon the court's finding that the animal is suffering due to terminal illness or terminal injury.

(c)   The plaintiff as custodian may place an animal with a foster care provider. The foster care provider shall return the animal to the plaintiff as custodian on demand.

§ 19A-4. Permanent injunction.

(a)   In accordance with G.S. 1A-1, Rule 65, a district court judge in the county in which the original action was brought shall determine the merits of the action by trial without a jury, and upon hearing such evidence as may be presented, shall enter orders as the court deems appropriate, including a permanent injunction and dismissal of the action along with dissolution of any preliminary injunction that had been issued.

(b)   If the plaintiff prevails, the court in its discretion may include the costs of food, water, shelter, and care, including medical care, provided to the animal, less any amounts deposited by the defendant under G.S. 19A-70, as part of the costs allowed to the plaintiff under G.S. 6-18. In addition, if the court finds by a preponderance of the evidence that even if a permanent injunction were issued there would exist a substantial risk that the animal would be subjected to further cruelty if returned to the possession of the defendant, the court may terminate the defendant's ownership and right of possession of the animal and transfer ownership and right of possession to the plaintiff or other appropriate successor owner. For good cause shown, the court may also enjoin the defendant from acquiring new animals for a specified period of time or limit the number of animals the defendant may own or possess during a specified period of time.

(c)   If the final judgment entitles the defendant to regain possession of the animal, the custodian shall return the animal, including taking any necessary steps to retrieve the animal from a foster care provider.

(d)   The court shall consider and may provide for custody and care of the animal until the time to appeal expires or all appeals have been exhausted.

Article 4 [of G.S. Chapter 19].
Animal Cruelty Investigators.

§ 19A-45. Appointment of animal cruelty investigators; term of office; removal; badge; oath; bond.

(a)   The board of county commissioners is authorized to appoint one or more animal cruelty investigators to serve without any compensation or other employee benefits in his county. In making these appointments, the board may consider persons nominated by any society incorporated under North Carolina law for the prevention of cruelty to animals. Prior to making any such appointment, the board of county commissioners is authorized to enter into an agreement whereby any necessary expenses of caring for seized animals not collectable pursuant to G.S. 19A-47 may be paid by the animal cruelty investigator or by any society incorporated under North Carolina law for the prevention of cruelty to animals that is willing to bear such expense.

(b) Animal cruelty investigators shall serve a one-year term subject to removal for cause by the board of county commissioners. Animal cruelty investigators shall, while in the performance of their official duties, wear in plain view a badge of a design approved by the board identifying them as animal cruelty investigators, and provided at no cost to the county.

(c) Animal cruelty investigators shall take and subscribe the oath of office required of public officials. The oath shall be filed with the clerk of superior court. Animal cruelty investigators shall not be required to post any bond.

(d) Upon approval by the board of county commissioners, the animal cruelty investigator or investigators may be reimbursed for all necessary and actual expenses, to be paid by the county.

§ 19A-46. Powers; magistrate's order; execution of order; petition; notice to owner.

(a) Whenever any animal is being cruelly treated as defined in G.S. 19A-1(2), an animal cruelty investigator may file with a magistrate a sworn complaint requesting an order allowing the investigator to provide suitable care for and take immediate custody of the animal. The magistrate shall issue the order only when he finds probable cause to believe that the animal is being cruelly treated and that it is necessary for the investigator to immediately take custody of it. Any magistrate's order issued under this section shall be valid for only 24 hours after its issuance. After he executes the order, the animal cruelty investigator shall return it with a written inventory of the animals seized to the clerk of court in the county where the order was issued.

(b) The animal cruelty investigator may request a law-enforcement officer or animal control officer to accompany him to help him seize the animal. An investigator may forcibly enter any premises or vehicle when necessary to execute the order only if he reasonably believes that the premises or vehicle is unoccupied by any person and that the animal is on the premises or in the vehicle. Forcible entry shall be used only when the animal cruelty investigator is accompanied by a law-enforcement officer. In any case, he must give notice of his identity and purpose to anyone who may be present before entering said premises. Forcible entry shall only be used during the daylight hours.

(c) When he has taken custody of such an animal, the animal cruelty investigator shall file a complaint pursuant to Article 1 of this Chapter as soon as possible. When he seizes the animal, he shall leave with the owner, if known, or affixed to the premises or vehicle a copy of the magistrate's order and a written notice of a description of the animal, the place where the animal will be taken, the reason for taking the animal, and the investigator's intent to file a complaint in district court requesting custody of the animal pursuant to Article 1 of this Chapter.

(d) Notwithstanding the provisions of G.S. 7A-305(c), any person who commences a proceeding under this Article or Article 1 of this Chapter shall not be required to pay any court costs or fees prior to a final judicial determination as provided in G.S. 19A-4, at which time those costs shall be paid pursuant to the provisions of G.S. 6-18.

(e) Any judicial order authorizing forcible entry shall be issued by a district court judge.

§ 19A-47. Care of seized animals.

The investigator must take any animal he seizes directly to some safe and secure place and provide suitable care for it. The necessary expenses of caring for seized animals, including necessary veterinary care, shall be a charge against the animal's owner and a lien on the animal to be enforced as provided by G.S. 44A-4.

§ 19A-48. Interference unlawful.

It shall be a Class 1 misdemeanor, to interfere with an animal cruelty investigator in the performance of his official duties.

§ 19A-49. Educational requirements.

Each animal cruelty investigator at his own expense must attend annually a course of at least six hours instruction offered by the North Carolina Humane Federation or some other agency. The course shall be designed to give the investigator expertise in the investigation of complaints relating to the care and treatment of animals. Failure to attend a course approved by the board of county commissioners shall be cause for removal from office.

Article 6 [of G.S. Chapter 19A].
Care of Animal Subjected to Illegal Treatment.

§ 19A-70. Care of animal subjected to illegal treatment.

(a)   In every arrest under any provision of Article 47 of Chapter 14 of the General Statutes or under G.S. 67-4.3 or upon the commencement of an action under Article 1 of this Chapter by a county or municipality, by a county-approved animal cruelty investigator, by other county or municipal official, or by an organization operating a county or municipal shelter under contract, if an animal shelter takes custody of an animal, the operator of the shelter may file a petition with the court requesting that the defendant be ordered to deposit funds in an amount sufficient to secure payment of all the reasonable expenses expected to be incurred by the animal shelter in caring for and providing for the animal pending the disposition of the litigation. For purposes of this section, "reasonable expenses" includes the cost of providing food, water, shelter, and care, including medical care, for at least 30 days.

(b)   Upon receipt of a petition, the court shall set a hearing on the petition to determine the need to care for and provide for the animal pending the disposition of the litigation. The hearing shall be conducted no less than 10 and no more than 15 business days after the petition is filed. The operator of the animal shelter shall mail written notice of the hearing and a copy of the petition to the defendant at the address contained in the criminal charges or the complaint or summons by which a civil action was initiated. If the defendant is in a local detention facility at the time the petition is filed, the operator of the animal shelter shall also provide notice to the custodian of the detention facility.

(c)   The court shall set the amount of funds necessary for 30 days' care after taking into consideration all of the facts and circumstances of the case, including the need to care for and provide for the animal pending the disposition of the litigation, the recommendation of the operator of the animal shelter, the estimated cost of caring for and providing for the animal, and the defendant's ability to pay. If the court determines that the defendant is unable to deposit funds, the court may consider issuing an order under subsection (f) of this section.

    Any order for funds to be deposited pursuant to this section shall state that if the operator of the animal shelter files an affidavit with the clerk of superior court, at least two business days prior to the expiration of a 30-day period, stating that, to the best of the affiant's knowledge, the case against the defendant has not yet been resolved, the order shall be automatically renewed every 30 days until the case is resolved.

(d)   If the court orders that funds be deposited, the amount of funds necessary for 30 days shall be posted with the clerk of superior court. The defendant shall also deposit the same amount with the clerk of superior court every 30 days thereafter until the litigation is resolved, unless the defendant requests a hearing no less than five business days prior to the expiration of a 30-day period. If the defendant fails to deposit the funds within five business days of the initial hearing, or five business days of the expiration of a 30-day period, the animal is forfeited by operation of law. If funds have been deposited in accordance with this section, the operator of the animal shelter may draw from the funds the actual costs incurred in caring for the animal.

In the event of forfeiture, the animal shelter may determine whether the animal is suitable for adoption and whether adoption can be arranged for the animal. The animal may not be adopted by the defendant or by any person residing in the defendant's household. If the adopted animal is a dog used for fighting, the animal shelter shall notify any persons adopting the dog of the liability provisions for owners of dangerous dogs under Article 1A of Chapter 67 of the General Statutes. If no adoption can be arranged after the forfeiture, or the animal is unsuitable for adoption, the shelter shall humanely euthanize the animal.

(e) The deposit of funds shall not prevent the animal shelter from disposing of the animal prior to the expiration of the 30-day period covered by the deposit if the court makes a final determination of the charges or claims against the defendant. Upon determination, the defendant is entitled to a refund for any portion of the deposit not incurred as expenses by the animal shelter. A person who is acquitted of all criminal charges or not found to have committed animal cruelty in a civil action under Article 1 of this Chapter is entitled to a refund of the deposit remaining after any draws from the deposit in accordance with subsection (d) of this section.

(f) Pursuant to subsection (c) of this section, the court may order a defendant to provide necessary food, water, shelter, and care, including any necessary medical care, for any animal that is the basis of the charges or claims against the defendant without the removal of the animal from the existing location and until the charges or claims against the defendant are adjudicated. If the court issues such an order, the court shall provide for an animal control officer or other law enforcement officer to make regular visits to the location to ensure that the animal is receiving necessary food, water, shelter, and care, including any necessary medical care, and to impound the animal if it is not receiving those necessities.

Article 22 [of G.S. Chapter 113].
Regulation of Wildlife.

. . .

§ 113-291.13. Application of wildlife laws to opossums.

No State or local statutes, rules, regulations, or ordinances related to the capture, captivity, treatment, or release of wildlife shall apply to the Virginia opossum (Didelphis virginiana) between the dates of December 29 of each year and January 2 of each subsequent year.

. . .

Article 6 [of G.S. Chapter 153A].
Delegation and Exercise of the General Police Power.

. . .

§ 153A-127. Abuse of animals.

A county may by ordinance define and prohibit the abuse of animals.

. . .

Article 8 [of G.S. Chapter 160A].
Delegation and Exercise of the General Police Power.

. . .

§ 160A-182. Abuse of animals.

A city may by ordinance define and prohibit the abuse of animals.

. . .

Chapter 4
Dangerous Dogs

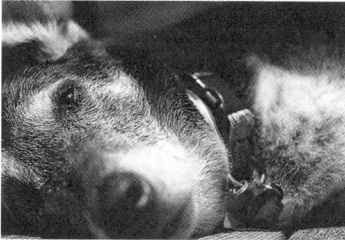

Every local government in North Carolina has probably faced the problem of a dog that is threatening or dangerous to people or to other animals. Article 1A of Chapter 67 of the North Carolina General Statutes (hereinafter G.S.) provides a framework for handling these situations;[1] it defines the term "dangerous dog" and imposes certain restrictions and obligations on the owners of such dogs. Many local governments have developed systems for addressing the issue of dangerous dogs, which can become a complex problem. This chapter reviews the state's framework for dealing with dangerous dogs and discusses some of the different approaches adopted in local ordinances across the state. It also briefly discusses the law governing civil claims for money damages based on harm or property damage caused by a dangerous dog as well as the authority of local governments to adopt breed-specific laws.

State Law

Definition

Before describing how North Carolina law addresses dangerous dogs, it is important to understand how certain terms are defined and used in the law. The statutory definition of the term "dangerous dog" can be confusing at first blush because there is some overlap between two of the four categories of dangerous dogs described by the definition. According to G.S. 67-4.1, a dangerous dog is one that

- is owned or harbored primarily or in part for the purpose of dogfighting;[2]
- is trained for dogfighting;[3]
- has, without provocation, killed or inflicted severe injury on a person;[4] or
- is determined to be potentially dangerous by a person or board authorized by a local government to make such judgments.[5]

The first two categories are relatively clear. If a dog is owned, harbored, or trained for dogfighting, it is automatically considered a dangerous dog under the law. The third category also is relatively clear—any dog that has killed or inflicted severe injury on a person is automatically considered a dangerous dog under the law. The term "severe injury" is defined by the statute as a physical injury that either (1) results in broken bones or disfiguring lacerations or (2) requires cosmetic surgery or hospitalization.[6] Note that this third category requires that the killing or injury be "without provocation." Inclusion

---

1. Article 1A of Chapter 67 of the North Carolina General Statutes (hereinafter G.S.).
2. G.S. 67-4.1(a)(1)b.
3. *Id.*
4. G.S. 67-4.1(a)(1)a.1.
5. G.S. 67-4.1(a)(1)a.2.
6. G.S. 67-4.1(a)(5).

of the term "without provocation" is largely redundant because, as discussed in more detail below, most types of provoked attacks already are subject to an exception that renders the law inapplicable.

The fourth category is perhaps the most confusing section of the state law. The first three categories provide that any dog that meets certain criteria is automatically considered a dangerous dog. The fourth category is different in that it requires a local government official or board to make a formal determination that the dog meets the definition of "potentially dangerous dog" (PDD) set out in subsection (a)(2) of the statute. If the dog meets the definition, it will be classified as a PDD, which is one type of dangerous dog. In other words, if the local government decides that a dog is potentially dangerous, the dog will be treated as a dangerous dog for the purposes of enforcing state law.

An animal may be designated as a PDD under G.S. 67-4.1(a)(2) if it exhibits one of three types of behavior:

- **Injuring a person.** A local government may conclude that a dog is a PDD if it inflicts a bite on a person that results in broken bones or disfiguring lacerations or requires cosmetic surgery or hospitalization. Note that this language is almost identical to the definition of the term "severe injury" provided by G.S. 67-4.1(a)(5). Therefore, it appears that a dog that inflicts such a physical injury is automatically considered a dangerous dog *and* may also be formally declared a potentially dangerous dog.
- **Injuring a domestic animal.** A local government may conclude that a dog is a PDD if it kills or inflicts severe injury on a "domestic animal" when not on the dog owner's real property. The definition of "severe injury" discussed above applies in this context as well (i.e., broken bones, disfiguring lacerations, cosmetic surgery, or hospitalization of the animal).
- **Approaching in terrorizing manner.** A local government may conclude that a dog is a PDD if it approaches a person in a vicious or terrorizing manner in an apparent attitude of attack when not on the dog owner's property.[7]

Because there is potential for some definitional overlap between the terms "dangerous dog" and "potentially dangerous dog," it can be difficult to understand precisely

---

7. In *Caswell County v. Hanks*, 120 N.C. App. 489 (1995), the state court of appeals upheld the constitutionality of this part of the definition of PDD. The court explained that the law is not unconstitutionally vague because it "provides sufficient notice for defendants and others to determine what conduct is proscribed." 120 N.C. App. at 493. The court also determined that the statute was not unconstitutionally overbroad because the state was not attempting to "regulate activities which sweep unnecessarily broadly and thereby invade the area of protected freedoms." *Id.* at 492 (internal quotation marks omitted) (citation omitted).

how the law should be applied. It may be helpful to refer to the following summary of the six situations in which a dog will be considered a dangerous dog under state law:

- when it is owned or harbored primarily or in part for the purpose of dogfighting,
- when it is trained for dogfighting,
- when it kills or inflicts severe injury on a person without provocation,
- when a local government representative or board decides that the dog has inflicted severe injury on a person,
- when a local government representative or board decides that the dog has killed or inflicted severe injury upon a domestic animal when not on the dog owner's property, or
- when a local government representative or board decides that the dog approached a person when not on the owner's property in a vicious or terrorizing manner in an apparent attitude of attack.

The law includes several exceptions.[8] First, a dog that has injured a person will not be considered dangerous if the victim

- was, at the time of the injury, committing a willful trespass or other tort;
- was, at the time of the injury, tormenting, abusing, or assaulting the dog;
- had tormented, abused, or assaulted the dog in the past;[9] or
- was, at the time of injury, committing or attempting to commit a crime.[10]

Second, the law will not recognize a dog as dangerous when it is used by a law enforcement officer to carry out official duties[11] or is used in a lawful hunt.[12] Finally, the state law will not apply to a dog that acted when the injury or damage was sustained by a domestic animal and the dog

- was on its owner's property or under its owner's control;
- was working as a hunting, herding, or predator control dog; and
- is of the species or type of domestic animal appropriate to the work of the dog (i.e., activities related to hunting, herding, and predator control).[13]

---

8. G.S. 67-4.1(b).

9. G.S. 67-4.1(b)(4). The drafting of this element of the exceptions subsection is awkward in that it is unclear whether the clause "at the time of the injury" modifies all of the provocative behaviors listed after that language or only the trespass-related behavior, which is listed first. For the purposes of this summary, it seems reasonable to conclude that the clause does *not* modify the language referring to a person who "had tormented, abused, or assaulted" the dog because the language is clearly in the past tense.

10. *Id.*

11. G.S. 67-4.1(b)(1).

12. G.S. 67-4.1(b)(2).

13. G.S. 67-4.1(b)(3).

It is not clear what type of proof would be required for a dog owner to take advantage of this particular exception. The owner may, for example, be required to provide evidence of specialized training. The term "predator control dog" is not defined in the law. Because the term "predator" is commonly understood to refer to animals that kill other animals in order to live,[14] one can infer that a predator control dog is one that is trained or expected to keep wild animals (such as foxes) from killing other animals on the owner's property (such as chickens).

Making PDD Determinations

Local governments must identify a person or a board that will be charged with determining whether a dog is potentially dangerous. The law neither prescribes a process for making such determinations nor identifies a particular type of person or board to be charged with this responsibility. In some jurisdictions, an individual animal services officer or supervisor may make the determination; in others, a board established for this purpose does so. If a dog is found to be potentially dangerous, the local government must notify the owner in writing of (1) the determination and (2) the reasons for the determination.[15] While not specifically required by the statute, the notice should also explain the process for appealing the determination.

Appealing PDD Determinations

Local governments are required under G.S. 67-4.1 to designate a board to hear appeals from determinations that a dog is potentially dangerous.[16] The law does not dictate the number of people that must serve on the appeals board or the type of person or professional that must be represented. The law does, however, exclude individuals who were involved in the initial determination.[17] All other decisions related to the size and composition of the appeals board are left to the local government. In response to this flexibility, jurisdictions have adopted a wide variety of approaches to constituting the board, such as

- using an existing appointed board, such as the board of health or animal services advisory committee;

14. *See predator*, Merriam Webster's Collegiate Dictionary (11th ed. 2003) ("one that preys, destroys, or devours").

15. G.S. 67-4.1(c).

16. *Id.*

17. The statute directs the local government to designate "a separate Board to hear any appeal." G.S. 67-4.1(c). It is clear from this language that the membership of an appeals board should be different from the membership of the board that made the initial determination. As a result, it is possible to infer that independence on the part of the appeals board is expected. Therefore, in jurisdictions that allow one individual (rather than a board) to make the initial determination that a dog is potentially dangerous, it seems appropriate to exclude that person from the appeals board.

- using an existing elected body, such as the town council;
- using a pre-established, regular subcommittee of an existing board or body;
- creating an ad hoc committee drawn from the members of an existing board or body;
- creating a board comprised of members with specific expertise or interests;[18] and
- establishing a pool of potential members with different types of expertise.[19]

To appeal a determination that a dog is potentially dangerous, the owner must file written objections with the appeals board "within three days."[20] Because this "three day" language is vague, it would be prudent for the local government to provide more specific guidance to the owner at the time of the determination. For example, the local government should decide whether

- the three-day period starts on the day the owner receives notice of the determination or several days thereafter (particularly if the determination is mailed to the owner),
- the three days are calendar days or working days, and
- the written objections must be postmarked or delivered to the appeals board by the third day.

This level of specificity in the written notice should help the owner better understand the appeals process.

Once the owner has filed an objection to a potentially dangerous dog determination, the appeals process begins and the board must schedule a hearing within ten days of the filing of the objection. This appeal should be treated as a quasi-judicial proceeding, which means that the proceeding will be more informal than a judicial proceeding but still must be conducted fairly and in accord with general principles of due process.[21] Though North Carolina appellate courts have not addressed the procedural requirements for an appeal of a PDD determination, the following principles outlined by the

---

18. *See, e.g.*, Lincoln County, N.C., Code of Ordinances § 92.07(E)(5) ("The Board of Animal Appeals will consist of five members . . . . The following will be considered when appointing the Board of Animal Appeals: (a) A person that is familiar with animals and works with them on a regular basis (e.g., a veterinarian or technician who works in a veterinary clinic); (b) A person who is active in animal welfare issues; (c) A law enforcement officer; and (d) Two citizens at large (preferably one that does not own a dog)").

19. Orange County, N.C., Code of Ordinances § 4-53.

20. G.S. 67-4.1(c).

21. *See generally* Aimee Wall, *Is the Dog Really "Potentially Dangerous?,"* Coates' Canons: NC Loc. Gov't L. blog (UNC School of Government, Dec. 20, 2013), http://canons.sog.unc.edu/is-the-dog-really-potentially-dangerous/ (drawing on research and legal principles discussed in blog posts by School of Government faculty member David Owens). *See also* David W. Owens & Adam Lovelady, Quasi-Judicial Handbook: A Guide for Boards Making Development Regulation Decisions (UNC School of Government, 2017).

North Carolina Supreme Court in the land use context may serve as helpful guidance for a board conducting a PDD appeal:

- **Follow procedures in the statute and any included in a relevant ordinance.** As mentioned, the statute describing PDD appeals says little about the procedure that a board should follow when an owner appeals a PDD determination. However, many local governments have supplemented the state law with more detailed directions. These procedures are sometimes found in ordinances, but they are also found in departmental or board policies. Boards conducting PDD appeal hearings should be aware of any procedures that have been formally adopted and should comply with them carefully.
- **Conduct hearings in accordance with fair-trial standards.** At a hearing on a PDD appeal, both the dog owner and the party who made the PDD determination should be given the opportunity to offer evidence, cross-examine witnesses, inspect documents or other tangible evidence, and offer evidence in explanation and rebuttal. Testifying witnesses also should be sworn.[22]
- **Base findings of fact only upon competent, material, and substantial evidence.** While PDD appeal hearings need not be conducted in accord with the rules of evidence applicable to formal judicial proceedings, a board nevertheless should base its findings of fact on solid evidence. Broadly speaking, a witness should testify only to those matters of which he or she has personal knowledge, and a board should be mindful of ensuring that the testimony it hears or the evidence it receives is relevant to the determination of the appeal.
- **Issue a written decision that states a factual basis.** Though not required by statute, many jurisdictions issue written decisions in PDD appeals, and doing so is a good practice. A written decision that announces the board's final determination of whether a dog is a PDD and includes the factual basis for that determination provides clarity for the parties and a record of the proceedings and decision.

If the appeals board upholds the initial determination, the owner has ten days to file a notice of appeal and petition for review in superior court. A superior court judge will not base his or her decision on the evidence and information collected by the appeals board but will conduct a de novo review, hearing "the case on its merits from beginning to end as if no hearing had been held by the Board and without any presumption in favor of the Board's decision."[23] Decisions made at the superior court level may be further appealed to the state court of appeals and state supreme court.

---

22. *Cf.* Humble Oil & Ref. Co. v. Board of Aldermen of Town of Chapel Hill, 284 N.C. 458 (1974) (identifying these features as among the "essential element[s]" of a fair trial in the context of quasi-judicial zoning hearings).

23. Caswell Cty. v. Hanks, 120 N.C. App. 489, 491 (1995).

Consequences for Owners of Dangerous Dogs

The primary consequences of the state dangerous dog law are that it imposes certain criminally enforceable restrictions and obligations upon owners of dangerous dogs and also provides that owners are strictly liable in civil damages for injuries or property damage inflicted by such dogs.

Owners vs. Keepers

The state dangerous dog law, G.S. 67-4.1, speaks only to restrictions, obligations, and strict civil liability for *owners* of dangerous dogs. The statute defines the term "owner" as "any person or legal entity that has a possessory property right in a dog."[24] In *Lee v. Rice*, the North Carolina Court of Appeals concluded that a person who simply owned real property where a dangerous dog was housed by a tenant could not be held civilly liable as an "owner," as that term is defined in G.S. 67-4.1, without more evidence that the property owner had a possessory property right in the dog.[25] Consistent with the statutory definition, the court may apply the same analysis to the term as used throughout the dangerous dog law—requiring evidence of a possessory property right before recognizing a person as an owner. *Lee* involved a civil tort claim where the defendant could have been held liable based on being either the owner or the keeper of the dog, and the court noted a longstanding distinction between those terms.[26] In contrast to an owner who has a possessory interest in a dog, a keeper is "one who, either with or without the owner's permission, undertakes to manage, control, or care for the animal as owners in general are accustomed to do."[27]

The distinction between the terms can be important because, as mentioned, the state dangerous dog law imposes obligations upon and provides criminal penalties for owners of dangerous dogs;[28] no provision of the statute imposes obligations upon or provides criminal penalties for non-owner keepers of dangerous dogs. This is not to say, however, that a non-owner keeper of a dangerous dog is not regulated under state law. For example, the civil tort claim at issue in *Lee* imposes liability on an owner or a keeper, though the defendant in that case did not satisfy either definition. As another example, G.S. 14-362.2 criminalizes numerous activities related to dogfighting that do not require that a person be the owner of the dog.[29]

---

24. G.S. 67-4.1(a)(3).

25. 154 N.C. App. 471, 475–76 (2002).

26. *Id.* at 474. *See also* Swain v. Tillett, 269 N.C. 46, 51 (1967) ("It is apparent that a keeper may or may not be [an animal's] owner.").

27. *Lee*, 154 N.C. App. at 474.

28. These consequences are discussed in more detail below.

29. *See, e.g.,* G.S. 14-362.2(b) (person who trains a dog with the intent that the dog be used in a dogfighting exhibition is guilty of a Class H felony). It is also conceivable that a non-owner keeper could be charged with a homicide or assault crime in certain circumstances.

Criminal Consequences

Under state law, an owner of a dangerous dog faces several important criminally enforceable restrictions on the owner's manner of care for the dog as well as criminal liability for certain attacks by the dog. The restrictions upon owners are set out in G.S. 67-4.2, and violating the statute is a Class 3 misdemeanor. First, the dog must not be left unattended on the owner's property "unless the dog is confined indoors, in a securely enclosed and locked pen, or in another structure designed to restrain the dog."[30] Second, the dog must not be allowed off the owner's property unless it is leashed (or otherwise restrained) and muzzled.[31] Third, if the owner sells or gives the dog to someone else, the owner must notify the other person of the dog's dangerous behavior.[32] If a local government has made a formal determination that the dog is a potentially dangerous dog, the owner must notify the other person of that fact and must notify the local government authority that made the formal determination of the transfer of the dog, along with the name and address of the person to whom the dog is being transferred.[33] As mentioned above, it is a Class 3 misdemeanor to fail to comply with the restrictions and notification requirements set out in G.S. 67-4.2.[34]

Under G.S. 67-4.3, if a dangerous dog attacks someone and causes physical injuries that require medical care costing more than $100, its owner may be charged with a Class 1 misdemeanor.[35]

It is important to recognize the difference between the two statutes providing criminal penalties and to keep the elements of the crimes they describe clear in any prosecution. In 2011, the North Carolina Court of Appeals considered a case involving a mismatch between the charging document and the sentence imposed.[36] In that case, dogs that had already been declared potentially dangerous attacked a person while off the owner's property, causing injuries that required medical care costing thousands of dollars. When the dogs' owner was charged criminally, the charging document charged a violation of G.S. 67-4.2, the Class 3 misdemeanor statute that relates to failing to confine dangerous dogs. The charging document also included language referring to the attack and to the physical injuries suffered by the victim, but it did not cite G.S. 67-4.3, the Class 1 misdemeanor statute that relates to attacks by dangerous dogs, nor did it state that the medical expenses incurred by the victim exceeded $100, an essential

---

30. G.S. 67-4.2(a)(1).
31. G.S. 67-4.2(a)(2).
32. G.S. 67-4.2(b)(2).
33. G.S. 67-4.2(b)(1), (2).
34. G.S. 67-4.2(c).
35. G.S. 67-4.3. As discussed above, it also is possible in such a situation that the owner could face additional criminal liability under G.S. Chapter 14.
36. State v. Burge, 212 N.C. App. 220 (2011).

element of that crime.[37] At trial, the jury found the dogs' owner guilty. The trial court's judgment specified that the owner had been found guilty of a violation of G.S. 67-4.2 but erroneously classified this offense as a Class 1 misdemeanor. On appeal, the court of appeals concluded that because the cost of the necessary medical care was an essential element of a violation of G.S. 67-4.3, the charging document was insufficient to charge that offense and, thus, the dogs' owner could not have been convicted of the Class 1 misdemeanor.[38] The case was remanded for sentencing as a Class 3 misdemeanor.

Civil Consequences

In addition to the potential criminal liability described above, an owner of a dangerous dog may be sued in civil court for money damages for harm to persons or property caused by the dog. Historically, North Carolina has recognized two distinct theories of liability in cases involving harm caused by dangerous dogs. One cause of action is a traditional negligence claim, which North Carolina courts have permitted plaintiffs to prosecute against both owners and non-owners of the dog that caused the harm.[39] The essence of such a claim is a plaintiff's allegation that he or she suffered an injury or loss because of a person's failure to exercise the appropriate degree of care for the safety of others. This theory of liability is not discussed in detail here because it is, simply, a traditional negligence claim[40] and because whether a dog is dangerous, in fact or as a statutory matter, is not necessarily a central issue under this theory of liability.[41]

---

37. The court was not concerned about the failure to include the correct citation in the charging documents. *See Burge*, 212 N.C. App. at 223 ("The statutory cite in the charging document is not controlling if the wording of the charge sets out the elements of another statutory offense and adequately informs the defendant of the charge against him.").

38. The court's conclusion rested on the principle of criminal procedure that a court does not have jurisdiction to convict a criminal defendant of a crime for which he or she has not been properly charged. The question of whether the dogs' owner could have been convicted of the Class 1 misdemeanor as a factual matter, assuming that crime had been properly charged, was not before the court.

39. *See, e.g.*, Holcomb v. Colonial Assocs., L.L.C., 358 N.C. 501, 506–07 (2004) (allowing a negligence claim against a landlord for injuries caused by a tenant's dog even though the landlord was not an owner or keeper of the dog); Williams v. Tysinger, 328 N.C. 55, 60 (1991) (allowing a negligence claim against owners of a horse).

40. For more information about the negligence theory of civil liability, see JOHN I. LAZAR, ANIMAL CONTROL LAW 1988 SUPPLEMENT: CIVIL LIABILITY FOR THE MISDEEDS OF ANIMALS 9 (1989), and ANN McCOLL, 1990 UPDATE TO ANIMAL CONTROL LAW FOR NORTH CAROLINA LOCAL GOVERNMENTS AND ANIMAL CONTROL LAW 1988 SUPPLEMENT: CIVIL LIABILITY FOR THE MISDEEDS OF ANIMALS 14 (1991). *See also Tysinger*, 328 N.C. at 60 (overruling a court of appeals case cited in the McColl publication for the proposition that pursuing a claim for the wrongful keeping of a vicious animal is the exclusive remedy for injuries caused by an animal; *Tysinger* makes it clear that both theories of liability discussed in the main text remain viable causes of action in North Carolina).

41. For example, if a person were to leave an infant unattended in the company of a Great Dane and the dog were to injure the child, it would not be necessary to show that the dog

The other historically recognized civil cause of action is for the wrongful keeping of a vicious animal, a claim that may be prosecuted only against an owner or a keeper[42] of a dog and which does not require proof of negligence.[43] Because no proof of negligence is required, the claim is based on strict liability.[44] Prior to the adoption of G.S. Chapter 67, there was some confusion among commentators regarding whether North Carolina actually recognized the two theories of liability just outlined or whether the appearance of two theories was an illusion of dicta in court opinions, though the prevailing thought was that there were in fact two theories of liability.[45] The adoption of Chapter 67 cleared the matter up, to an extent.[46] G.S. 67-4.4 states that "[t]he owner of a dangerous dog shall be strictly liable in civil damages for any injuries or property damage the dog inflicts upon a person, his property, or another animal." Thus, it is clear from the statute that there is a strict liability cause of action against an owner of a dangerous dog, and North Carolina case law suggests that a keeper also may be subject to strict liability despite the fact that G.S. 67-4.4 makes no explicit mention of keepers.[47]

The showing a plaintiff must make in order to prevail on the strict liability cause of action is typically framed in the case law as follows: the plaintiff must show that

> "(1) the animal was dangerous, vicious, mischievous, or ferocious, or one termed in law as possessing a vicious propensity; and (2) that the owner or keeper knew or should have known of the animal's vicious propensity, character, and habits."[48]

This statement of the required showing is a shorthand description of a plaintiff's burden. In order for a plaintiff to actually recover damages from a person, the plaintiff would

---

was dangerous or vicious in order to make out a prima facie negligence cause of action. *See Tysinger*, 328 N.C. at 60 (stating that the cause of action does implicate the general propensities of the animal in question but does not depend on the animal being vicious or dangerous).

42. Though claims against keepers are discussed here, be mindful that G.S. Chapter 67 speaks only of special rules of liability with regard to *owners* of dangerous dogs.

43. See *Holcomb*, 358 N.C. at 506–07 (describing this claim as one of "strict liability"). *See also Liability: strict liability*, BLACK'S LAW DICTIONARY (10th ed. 2014) (defining "strict liability" as "[l]iability that does not depend on proof of negligence or intent to do harm but that is based instead on a duty to compensate the harms proximately caused by the activity or behavior subject to the liability rule").

44. *Holcomb*, 358 N.C. at 506–07.

45. See LAZAR, *supra* note 40, at 7–8 (stating that there appeared to be two theories of liability but that the issue had not been conclusively decided).

46. The *Tysinger* case, cited above, also makes it clear that there are two distinct causes of action in North Carolina. The case was decided after the adoption of Chapter 67.

47. *See Holcomb*, 358 N.C. at 506 (so suggesting in dicta); Lee v. Rice, 154 N.C. App. 471 (2002) (seemingly accepting that a keeper may be held strictly liable, though the issue was not directly addressed by the court).

48. Sellers v. Morris, 233 N.C. 560, 561 (1951); *Lee*, 154 N.C. App. at 474.

additionally have to prove that the person was in fact the owner or keeper of the dog at issue, that the dog proximately caused the plaintiff's injury, and that damages ensued.[49]

In a case where a dog has been determined to be a potentially dangerous dog (PDD) prior to the incident giving rise to the civil lawsuit, a plaintiff proceeding against an owner who owned the dog at the time of the PDD determination could rely on the determination to prove that the animal was "one termed in law as possessing a vicious propensity." Additionally, assuming compliance with the notice requirements of G.S. 67-4.1(c), the PDD determination would suffice to prove that such an owner had notice of the dog's vicious propensity. Thus, all that would remain for a plaintiff to prove would be the issue of ownership at the time of the incident giving rise to the claim, the issue of proximate cause, and the measure of damages.

In a case where a plaintiff is proceeding against a defendant who is a keeper of a PDD or an owner who acquired a PDD after the determination of the dog's status had been made, the plaintiff would additionally need to prove that the defendant knew or should have known of the animal's vicious propensity. G.S. Chapter 67 does not provide for any direct notice of an animal's PDD status from a local government to a person who is not the owner of a PDD at the time the PDD determination is made. G.S. 67-4.2 obligates the owner of a PDD to provide notice of the dog's PDD status to a person to whom the owner transfers the dog, but it is possible that an owner could fail to do so and that a person could thereby take a PDD without actual notice of the dog's status. There is no statutory mechanism for providing actual notice of a dog's PDD status to keepers.

In a case involving a dog that satisfies the statutory definition of a dangerous dog but that has not been formally determined to be a PDD, a plaintiff obviously does not have the benefit of proving any element of the strict liability claim using a preexisting determination that the dog is one termed in law as possessing a vicious propensity. Of course, a plaintiff could rely on the statutory definitions of the terms "dangerous dog" and "potentially dangerous dog," along with evidence of the dog's behavior or treatment, in order to prove that the dog would be one termed in law as possessing a vicious propensity.

Euthanizing Dangerous Dogs

While state law governing dangerous dogs does not provide explicit authority for a local government to euthanize a dog that has been declared dangerous, there are several reasons these dogs may ultimately be euthanized:

- The owner may decide to surrender the dog to the shelter or have it euthanized privately because he or she is not willing or able to comply with the restrictions imposed.

---

49. *See* LAZAR, *supra* note 40, at 1 (identifying these additional necessary allegations).

- A jurisdiction may have adopted an ordinance that provides for euthanasia in some circumstances. For example, Cumberland County authorizes immobilizing or killing dogs if people or other animals are at risk.[50]
- An animal services or law enforcement official may need to euthanize an animal in an emergency.

In addition to the consequences specified in state law regarding dangerous dogs, many local ordinances include additional requirements or restrictions, such as requiring owners of such dogs to register or obtain permits for the dogs, to post signage about the presence of dangerous dogs, or even to give up animals in some circumstances.[51] Local ordinances are discussed in more detail below.

Recovering Sheltering Costs in Dangerous Dog Cases

Dogs that are or that may be dangerous are typically impounded for a period of time at an animal shelter. If a shelter is operated by or under contract with a county or municipality, the local government may incur significant expenses in the course of providing care and shelter for the animal. Local governments and animal shelters may petition the court to recover sheltering costs pursuant to G.S. 19A-70. This cost-recovery mechanism is discussed in chapter 7, "Animal Shelters."

Vicious Animals

In addition to the dangerous dog authority outlined in G.S. Chapter 67, local public health directors have separate authority to declare any animal—not just dogs—as "vicious and a menace to the public health."[52] This authority is available when an animal has made an unprovoked attack on a person and caused bodily harm.[53] Once an animal has been declared vicious, it must be confined to its owner's property except when (1) accompanied by a responsible adult and (2) restrained on a leash. Though local health directors have this authority, they rarely use it to address problems with dogs because the dangerous dog laws are much more specific. If, however, a local health director does declare a dog vicious and the owner fails to comply with the restrictions, the owner

---

50. CUMBERLAND COUNTY, N.C., CODE OF ORDINANCES § 3-39.

51. For example, in Cumberland County, a person may not own a dog that has killed a person, except in limited circumstances. CUMBERLAND COUNTY, N.C., CODE OF ORDINANCES § 3-36(4).

52. G.S. 130A-200.

53. *Id.* The statute does not use the term "unprovoked" but, rather, provides that the animal must not have been "teased, molested, provoked, beaten, tortured, or otherwise harmed."

may be charged with a Class 1 misdemeanor.[54] Additionally, the health director may seek an injunction in superior court.[55]

Dogs Killing Livestock and Other Animals

Several older state laws in G.S. Chapter 67 specifically address the issue of dogs that kill livestock, wildlife, and even people:

- If a district court judge concludes that a dog killed a sheep, another domestic animal, or a person and the owner or keeper of the dog refuses to kill the dog, the owner or keeper may be charged with a Class 3 misdemeanor.[56] In addition, any person is then authorized to kill the dog if it is found at large.[57]
- Any person is allowed to kill a dog that is killing sheep, cattle, hogs, goats, or poultry.[58]
- Certain wildlife officials and their agents are authorized to humanely destroy a dog if it trails, runs, injures, or kills any deer or bear in protected wildlife areas during the closed season.[59]

These laws should be interpreted and applied in the context of other relevant laws, such as the animal cruelty laws.[60] A person should not, for example, kill a dog pursuant to one of the older state laws in Chapter 67 in any way that could be considered inhumane or cruel. The cruelty laws recognize that a person may intentionally kill an animal if the killing is justifiable.[61] When a dog has killed a sheep or cow, for example, one could argue that the older state laws in Chapter 67 discussed above provide sufficient justification and authority to destroy the dog, so long as the destruction of the dog is accomplished in compliance with the laws. An animal should not, however, be subjected to unnecessary suffering in the process. Additionally, a person who intends to kill a dog based upon the statutes discussed above would be well advised to be certain that the killing falls within the authorization of the statute, as the animal cruelty laws

---

54. G.S. 130A-25. This statute does not classify the misdemeanor but another statute, G.S. 14-3(a), provides that unclassified misdemeanors are punishable as Class 1 misdemeanors.

55. G.S. 130A-18.

56. G.S. 67-3.

57. *Id.*

58. G.S. 67-14.

59. G.S. 67-14.1.

60. G.S. Chapter 14, Article 47.

61. *See, e.g.,* G.S. 14-360(c)(4) (providing that G.S. 14-360, the criminal statute prohibiting cruelty to animals, does not apply to "[t]he lawful destruction of any animal for the purposes of protecting the public, other animals, property, or the public health").

criminalize wrongful intentional killing of any animal regardless of whether the killing is accomplished in a humane manner.[62]

Though there is little North Carolina law on the issue, it is worth noting that laws that authorize the killing of a dog or other animal are sometimes attacked based on the theory that they are unconstitutional because they allow deprivation of property without due process of law.[63] It is possible to find North Carolina cases upholding such laws in the face of constitutional attack,[64] and it has been said that this position coincides with the majority position nationally.[65] It is also worth noting that a person who wrongfully kills a dog or other animal may be subject to civil liability.[66]

Local Ordinances

As discussed in chapter 1, cities and counties have broad power to regulate animals by ordinance, and many local governments have used this power to adopt dangerous dog ordinances over the years.[67] A number of local governments have ordinances that were already in place when the state's statutory framework for dangerous dogs was enacted in 1989, and some ordinances have been adopted or amended since that time. State law does not override the local ordinances in this field but, rather, provides that the state statutes must not be "construed to prevent a city or county from adopting or enforcing its own program for control of dangerous dogs."[68]

Some jurisdictions have not adopted ordinances, and thus they rely entirely on the existing body of state law. A few jurisdictions have adopted ordinances that simply reiterate the state's dangerous dog law. This approach is not recommended because, as discussed earlier in this book, the "elements of an offense defined by a city ordinance [may not be] identical to the elements of an offense defined by State or federal law."[69]

---

62. G.S. 14-360(a) (person who intentionally kills any animal without justification guilty of Class 1 misdemeanor); 14-360(b) (person who maliciously kills any animal guilty of Class H felony).

63. Patrice Solberg, North Carolina Dog Law Manual 7 (1978).

64. *See, e.g.,* Mowery v. Salisbury, 82 N.C. 175 (1880) (suggesting without detailed analysis that such laws are constitutional).

65. Solberg, *supra* note 63.

66. *See* Scott v. Cates, 175 N.C. 336, 336 (1918) (stating that it is settled state law "[t]hat an action may be maintained to recover damages for the unlawful killing or injuring of the dog of another").

67. Recall that in addition to their general police powers, local governments have specific authority to "regulate, restrict, or prohibit the possession or harboring . . . of animals which are dangerous to persons or property." G.S. 153A-131 (counties); 160A-187 (cities).

68. G.S. 67-4.5.

69. *See* G.S. 160A-174(b) (identifying the preemption principles applicable to city ordinances); State v. Tenore, 280 N.C. 238, 247 (1972) (extending those same preemption principles to county ordinances).

Some have adopted ordinances that cross-reference the state law and supplement it with procedural details, such as the composition of appeals boards, or include more specificity related to restrictions imposed by state law, such as detailed information about the type or construction of the enclosures required for dangerous dogs. Other jurisdictions have adopted more robust and comprehensive schemes for addressing dangerous dogs. A few examples of more robust ordinance provisions are highlighted at the end of this chapter. Note that these are provided as examples for consideration only; they are not offered as recommendations or models.

Several local governments across the state have considered, but rejected, the idea of adopting ordinances restricting or prohibiting private citizens from owning specific breeds of dogs, such as pit bulls. The discussion typically begins after someone in the city or county is attacked by a particular breed of dog. A local government considering such ordinances must decide (1) whether breed-specific legislation is the best policy tool available for addressing the jurisdiction's concerns and (2) whether it has the authority to adopt an ordinance restricting that type of animal. With respect to the first issue, advocates of breed-specific legislation often cite dog-bite statistics related to particular breeds, while those opposed argue that more comprehensive legislation addressing dangerous dogs, animal bites, and owner and victim behavior will have a greater impact.[70]

With respect to the second issue—the scope of the government's authority—North Carolina local governments probably do have the authority to enact breed-specific ordinances.[71] As discussed above, cities and counties have broad authority to regulate dogs within their jurisdictions through both their general police powers and their authority

---

70. *See, e.g.,* Gary J. Patronek et al., *Co-occurrence of Potentially Preventable Factors in 256 Dog Bite-Related Fatalities in the United States (2000-2009),* 243 J. Am. Veterinary Med. Ass'n 1726 (2013) (concluding that breed was not a coincident, preventable factor in dog bite-related fatalities); Carrie M. Shuler et al., *Canine and Human Factors Related to Dog Bite Injuries,* 232 J. Am. Veterinary Med. Ass'n 542 (2008) (identifying breed as one factor related to dog bite injuries, but emphasizing others as more significant); Johannes Schalamon et al., *Analysis of Dog Bites in Children Who are Younger than 17 Years,* 117 Pediatrics e374 (2006) (identifying breed-related behavior of dogs as one of a range of factors influencing dog bites); Jeffrey J. Sacks et al., *Breeds of Dogs Involved in Fatal Human Attacks in the United States between 1979 and 1998,* 217 J Am. Veterinary Med. Ass'n 836, 836 (2000) (evaluating breeds of dogs involved in fatal attacks and concluding that breed "should not be the primary factory driving public policy concerning dangerous dogs"); Devin Burstein, *Breed Specific Legislation: Unfair Prejudice and Ineffective Policy,* 10 Animal L. 313, 313 (2004) (arguing that breed-specific laws are not effective and create a "false sense of security for the public"); Humane Soc'y of the U.S., *All Dogs Are Equal, Fact Sheet,* humanesociety.org, http://www.humanesociety.org/issues/breed-specific-legislation/fact_sheets/breed-specific-legislation-all-dogs-are-equal.html?credit=web_id625934014 (last visited June 2, 2016).

71. Jeanette Cox, *Ordinances Targeting Pit Bull Dogs Must Be Drafted Carefully,* Loc. Gov't L. Bull. No. 106 (Nov. 2004), https://www.sog.unc.edu/sites/www.sog.unc.edu/files/reports/lglb106_0.pdf. The author discusses constitutional challenges to breed-specific legislation in other jurisdictions, with a specific focus on challenges based on vagueness, equal

to regulate dangerous animals. This authority would probably extend to regulation of particular breeds if the jurisdiction has a rational reason for believing that the breed is dangerous and that regulation is needed to protect the public.[72] Courts in other states have found that breed-specific ordinances are valid exercises of local government police power in certain circumstances.[73] Before moving forward with such an ordinance, though, a local government should review breed-specific laws in other states and carefully craft the ordinance to avoid potential constitutional defects.[74]

The primary constitutional challenges that are raised against breed-specific laws include the following: (1) that the law is unconstitutionally vague, (2) that the jurisdiction does not have a rational basis for implementing the law or that the means of implementing the law is not rational, (3) that the law violates procedural due process, and (4) that the law violates equal protection.[75] The party challenging the constitutionality of a breed-specific law bears the burden of showing that the law is invalid.[76]

An argument that a breed-specific law is unconstitutionally vague generally involves an allegation that the law defines categories of regulated breeds with insufficient defi-

---

protection, and due process. She recommends that North Carolina jurisdictions interested in adopting a breed-specific ordinance

- identify a rational basis for regulating the breed;
- list specific breeds regulated;
- provide a uniform standard for determining when the ordinance applies to a mixed-breed dog;
- create a procedure for dog owners to ask whether their dogs fall within the ordinance;
- provide for civil, rather than criminal, sanctions; and
- provide a hearing to a dog's owner if and when the government intends to destroy his or her dog.

The author also discusses alternatives to breed-specific legislation, such as rigorous enforcement of state and local dangerous dog laws.

72. *See* State v. Maynard, 195 N.C. App. 757, 758–59 (2009) (internal quotation marks omitted) (citations omitted) (providing that, as a general proposition, a local government's police power "may be exercised in order to protect or promote the health, morals, order, safety and general welfare of society").

73. *See, e.g.,* Bess v. Bracken Cty. Fiscal Ct., 210 S.W.3d 177, 182 (Ky. Ct. App. 2006) (breed-specific ordinance banning ownership of certain breed was valid exercise of local government police power in case where local government's determination that breed was inherently vicious and dangerous was supported by evidence); Toledo v. Tellings, 871 N.E.2d 1152 (Ohio 2007) (local government ordinance including certain breed within definition of "vicious dog" was valid exercise of police power).

74. Cox, *supra* note 71.

75. *Id.*

76. *Maynard*, 195 N.C. App. at 759.

niteness, such that ordinary people cannot understand what dogs are regulated, and that this vagueness encourages arbitrary and discriminatory enforcement.[77]

An argument that a jurisdiction does not have a rational basis[78] for implementing a breed-specific law usually involves an allegation that the law regulates the targeted breed in an arbitrary fashion and, thus, impermissibly burdens a dog owner's rights. Generally, this line of argument involves an allegation that the targeted breed is not especially dangerous compared to other breeds and that there is not a rational reason to single the breed out for regulation.[79] Assuming that there is a rational basis for implementing a breed-specific law, the means by which the law regulates the targeted breed also must be rational.[80]

An argument that a breed-specific law violates an owner's right to procedural due process generally involves an allegation that the law does not provide an owner with sufficient notice and opportunity to be heard regarding the regulation of his or her dog.[81] What degree of process is sufficient depends upon the nature of the particular law.

An argument that a breed-specific law violates principles of equal protection generally involves an allegation that the law impermissibly classifies owners of the targeted breed and treats them differently from owners of non-targeted breeds.[82] In order to satisfy constitutional equal protection requirements, the classification and differential treatment must be rationally related to the public safety interest that serves as the typical justification for breed-specific laws.[83]

---

77. *See, e.g.*, Dias v. City & Cty. of Denver, 567 F.3d 1169, 1179 (10th Cir. 2009) (upholding a breed-specific law against a facial vagueness challenge).

78. Courts generally find that there is not a fundamental right to own a dog, regardless of the breed, and consequently evaluate these challenges using rational basis scrutiny rather than the strict scrutiny applied to laws that impinge upon a fundamental right. *See, e.g., id.* This discussion assumes that a court will apply rational basis scrutiny.

79. *Toledo,* 871 N.E.2d at 1154 (noting this argument).

80. *See, e.g., Dias,* 567 F.3d at 1183 (plaintiffs alleged that absolute prohibition on owning particular breed was irrational means by which to pursue city's legitimate interest in animal control).

81. *See, e.g.*, Garcia v. Village of Tijeras, 767 P.2d 355, 361 (N.M. 1988) (addressing this argument with respect to an ordinance that authorized destruction of the targeted breed).

82. *See, e.g., id.*

83. Courts generally find that classifying owners based upon the breed of dog is not a suspect classification and consequently evaluate these challenges using rational basis scrutiny rather than the strict scrutiny applied to laws that involve suspect classifications. *See id.* This discussion assumes that a court will apply rational basis scrutiny.

Appendix A. Relevant Sections of the North Carolina General Statutes (G.S.)

Article 1A [of G.S. Chapter 67].
Dangerous Dogs.

§ 67-4.1. Definitions and procedures.

(a)   As used in this Article, unless the context clearly requires otherwise and except as modified in subsection (b) of this section, the term:

   (1)   "Dangerous dog" means

      a.   A dog that:

         1.   Without provocation has killed or inflicted severe injury on a person; or

         2.   Is determined by the person or Board designated by the county or municipal authority responsible for animal control to be potentially dangerous because the dog has engaged in one or more of the behaviors listed in subdivision (2) of this subsection.

      b.   Any dog owned or harbored primarily or in part for the purpose of dog fighting, or any dog trained for dog fighting.

   (2)   "Potentially dangerous dog" means a dog that the person or Board designated by the county or municipal authority responsible for animal control determines to have:

      a.   Inflicted a bite on a person that resulted in broken bones or disfiguring lacerations or required cosmetic surgery or hospitalization; or

      b.   Killed or inflicted severe injury upon a domestic animal when not on the owner's real property; or

      c.   Approached a person when not on the owner's property in a vicious or terrorizing manner in an apparent attitude of attack.

   (3)   "Owner" means any person or legal entity that has a possessory property right in a dog.

   (4)   "Owner's real property" means any real property owned or leased by the owner of the dog, but does not include any public right-of-way or a common area of a condominium, apartment complex, or townhouse development.

   (5)   "Severe injury" means any physical injury that results in broken bones or disfiguring lacerations or required cosmetic surgery or hospitalization.

(b)   The provisions of this Article do not apply to:

   (1)   A dog being used by a law enforcement officer to carry out the law enforcement officer's official duties;

   (2)   A dog being used in a lawful hunt;

   (3)   A dog where the injury or damage inflicted by the dog was sustained by a domestic animal while the dog was working as a hunting dog, herding dog, or predator control dog on the property of, or under the control of, its owner or keeper, and the damage or injury was to a species or type of domestic animal appropriate to the work of the dog; or

   (4)   A dog where the injury inflicted by the dog was sustained by a person who, at the time of the injury, was committing a willful trespass or other tort, was tormenting, abusing, or assaulting the dog, had tormented, abused, or assaulted the dog, or was committing or attempting to commit a crime.

(c)   The county or municipal authority responsible for animal control shall designate a person or a Board to be responsible for determining when a dog is a "potentially dangerous dog" and shall designate a separate Board to hear any appeal. The person or Board making the determination that a dog is a "potentially dangerous dog" must notify the owner in writing, giving the reasons for the determination, before the dog may be considered potentially dangerous under this Article. The owner may appeal the determination by filing written objections with the appellate Board within three days. The appellate Board shall schedule a hearing within 10 days of the filing of the objections. Any appeal from the final decision of such appellate Board shall be taken to the superior court by filing notice of appeal and a petition for review within 10 days of the final decision of the appellate Board. Appeals from rulings of the appellate Board shall be heard in the superior court division. The appeal shall be heard de novo before a superior court judge sitting in the county in which the appellate Board whose ruling is being appealed is located.

§ 67-4.2. Precautions against attacks by dangerous dogs.

(a)   It is unlawful for an owner to:
    (1)   Leave a dangerous dog unattended on the owner's real property unless the dog is confined indoors, in a securely enclosed and locked pen, or in another structure designed to restrain the dog;
    (2)   Permit a dangerous dog to go beyond the owner's real property unless the dog is leashed and muzzled or is otherwise securely restrained and muzzled.

(b)   If the owner of a dangerous dog transfers ownership or possession of the dog to another person (as defined in G.S. 12-3(6)), the owner shall provide written notice to:
    (1)   The authority that made the determination under this Article, stating the name and address of the new owner or possessor of the dog; and
    (2)   The person taking ownership or possession of the dog, specifying the dog's dangerous behavior and the authority's determination.

(c)   Violation of this section is a Class 3 misdemeanor.

§ 67-4.3. Penalty for attacks by dangerous dogs.

The owner of a dangerous dog that attacks a person and causes physical injuries requiring medical treatment in excess of one hundred dollars ($100.00) shall be guilty of a Class 1 misdemeanor.

§ 67-4.4. Strict liability.

The owner of a dangerous dog shall be strictly liable in civil damages for any injuries or property damage the dog inflicts upon a person, his property, or another animal.

§ 67-4.5. Local ordinances.

Nothing in this Article shall be construed to prevent a city or county from adopting or enforcing its own program for control of dangerous dogs.

Article 6 [of G.S. Chapter 130A].
Communicable Diseases.

• • •

§ 130A-200. Confinement or leashing of vicious animals.

A local health director may declare an animal to be vicious and a menace to the public health when the animal has attacked a person causing bodily harm without being teased, molested, provoked, beaten, tortured or otherwise harmed. When an animal has been declared to be vicious and a menace to the public health, the local health director shall order the animal to be confined to its owner's property. However, the animal may be permitted to leave its owner's property when accompanied by a responsible adult and restrained on a leash.

Appendix B. Relevant North Carolina Local Government Ordinances, by Topic

Redefining "Dangerous Dog" and "Potentially Dangerous Dog"

The Catawba County Code of Ordinances expands on the definitions provided in state law and creates tiers based on the gravity of the offense.[a]

Sec. 6-131. - Determination of dangerous and potentially dangerous dogs.

. . .

(1) *Dangerous dog.* A dangerous dog will be classified as either a level 1 or level 2 dangerous dog.
   a. *Level 1*:
      1. The dog will be classified as level 1 if the dog:
         i. Killed a person;
         ii. When not on the owner's real property, inflicted severe injury to a person;
         iii. Was previously declared a level 2 dangerous dog and while out of the secure enclosure bit a person;
         iv. Was previously declared a level 2 dangerous dog and while out of the secure enclosure and not on the owner's real property bit another domestic animal;
         v. Was previously declared a potentially dangerous dog and inflicted severe injury to a person; or
         vi. Was previously declared a potentially dangerous dog and when not on the owner's real property killed or inflicted severe injury to a domestic animal.
      2. The assistant director of emergency services shall order the level 1 dangerous dog to be humanely destroyed.
   b. *Level 2*:
      1. The dog will be classified as level 2 if the dog:
         i. When on the owner's real property inflicted severe injury to a person;
         ii. Was owned or harbored primarily or in part for the purpose of dog fighting, or trained for dog fighting, in violation of G.S. 14-362.2;
         iii. Was previously declared a potentially dangerous dog and when not on the owner's real property bit another domestic animal but did not cause a severe injury; or
         iv. Was previously declared a potentially dangerous dog and bit a person but did not cause a severe injury.
      2. The owner must confine the level 2 dangerous dog as outlined in sections 6-133(a) and (b).
(2) *Potentially dangerous dog.* If a potentially dangerous dog is redeemed by the owner, the owner must keep the dog under restraint and comply with section 6-133(c) below. A dog will be classified as a potentially dangerous if the dog:
   (a) When not on the owner's real property killed or inflicted severe injury upon a domestic animal; or
   (b) When not on the owner's real property approached a person in a vicious or terrorizing manner in an apparent attitude of attack; or
   (c) Inflicted an unprovoked bite to a human.

---

a. CATAWBA COUNTY, N.C., CODE OF ORDINANCES § 6-131

Appeals Process

Cumberland County's Code of Ordinances outlines the process for conducting a dangerous dog appeal.[b]

Sec. 3-33. - Determination that a dog is potentially dangerous; appeals.

(a) *Generally.* Upon receipt of a report submitted in accordance with section 3-32, or upon the receipt of any other complaint, or when he has reasonable suspicion that a dog is potentially dangerous, the director or his designee shall make a determination whether or not such dog is a potentially dangerous dog. Any determination that a dog is potentially dangerous shall be made in a writing stating the facts relied upon by the director to make his determination. The written declaration shall be personally delivered to the owner of the subject dog or shall be mailed by certified mail, return receipt requested, to the owner. If the determination is made that the subject dog is potentially dangerous, the written determination shall order compliance with the appropriate provisions of this article and the director may impose reasonable conditions to maintain the public health and safety. The director may pursue such other civil or criminal penalties and remedies as authorized by this chapter or state law.

(b) [*Determination by director.*] If, at any time after the receipt of any report or complaint made pursuant to section 3-32, the director determines that the conditions under which the subject dog is being kept or confined do not adequately protect the public health or safety, the director shall require that the subject dog be impounded at the department's shelter until completion of the investigation and any appeal of the decision of the director.

(c) *Appeals from determinations.*
  (1) The owner of any dog determined by the director to be potentially dangerous may appeal the decision of the director to the appeal board within three business days of receiving notice of the determination. Appeal to the appeal board may be taken by filing written objections to the director's determination with the clerk for the appeal board.
  (2) The appeal board shall schedule and hear such appeal within ten days of the filing of the written objections or at such later time as the appellant consents.
  (3) The vote of the appeal board shall be taken, and the announcement of its decision shall be made, in an open public meeting. A written statement of the decision of the appeal board shall be delivered to the director and the appellant. The notice shall be sent by certified mail, return receipt requested, and filed concurrently with the director and the Cumberland County Attorney.

(d) [*Conduct of appeal.*] An appeal hearing before the appeal board shall be conducted as follows:
  (1) The hearing shall be subject to the open meetings law, and the required notice shall be posted and given as applicable;
  (2) The chairperson of the appeal board shall preside at the hearing;
  (3) The director shall be represented by the county attorney;
  (4) The county attorney shall present the director's case;
  (5) The appellant may be represented by an attorney;
  (6) The director and the appellant may make any statements, present any evidence, or offer any witnesses on their behalf, on any relevant issue;
  (7) The chairperson of the appeal board shall rule on the admissibility of any evidence and on any procedural issues that might arise;
  (8) The director and the appellant shall be entitled to cross-examine any witnesses;

b. CUMBERLAND COUNTY, N.C., CODE OF ORDINANCES § 3-33.

(9)   The hearing shall be quasi-judicial in nature and all testimony shall be under oath;

(10) The appellant shall be entitled to obtain a transcript of the proceeding at his own cost;

(11) The appeal board shall announce its decision at an open meeting and render it in writing as expeditiously as possible at or following the hearing. Its decision shall contain findings of fact and conclusions in support of its decision.

(e)   [*Purpose of appeal.*] The purpose of the hearing before the appeal board shall be to determine whether or not the determination of the director is in the best interests of the public health, safety and welfare.

(f)   [*Function of appeal board.*] The function of the appeal board shall be to affirm, reverse, or modify the determination of the director which has been appealed. Any conditions imposed by the appeal board shall be reasonable, relevant to the issues in the matter, and have the effect of promoting the public health, safety and welfare.

(g)   [*Hearing.*] The hearing shall be administrative in nature and the decision of the appeal board shall be final.

Enclosure Specifications

Guilford County's Code of Ordinances requires dog owners to construct enclosures that meet detailed specifications.[c]

Sec. 5-12. - Dangerous or vicious animals restricted.

. . .

(e)   *Enclosures for dangerous or vicious animals.* If an animal has been determined to be dangerous or vicious, as specified in this section, and at the appeals board's discretion, the owner may retain the animal upon satisfying the following conditions. The owner must erect, within 30 days of declaration of dangerous or vicious status by an animal control officer or law enforcement officer, or in the event of an appeal, within 15 days from the decision of the appeals board a proper structure and display warning signs. This structure must be inspected and approved by a code enforcement official; designated animal control officer; or installed by a qualified professional as meeting the following requirements and standards (Note: With appropriate findings, the appeals panel may require alternative method(s) of enforcement of equal to or more restrictive than the requirements such forth below.)

(1)   The structure must be a minimum size of 15 feet by six feet by six feet with a floor consisting of a concrete pad at least four inches thick. If more than one animal is to be kept in the enclosure, the floor area must provide at least 45 square feet for each animal. The walls and roof of the structure must be constructed of welded chain link of a minimum thickness of 12 gauge, supported by galvanized steel poles at least two and one-half inches in diameter. The vertical support poles must be sunk in concrete-filled holes at least 18 inches deep and at least eight inches in diameter. The chainlink fencing must be anchored to the concrete pad with galvanized steel anchors placed at intervals of no more than 12 inches along the perimeter of the pad. The entire structure must be freestanding and not be attached or anchored to any existing fence, building, or structure. The structure must be secured by a child-resistant lock.

(2)   A warning sign of at least 120 square inches must be visible from each exposure of the structure which is visible to any adjoining property. Each sign must have a graphic representation of an appropriate animal such that the dangerousness or viciousness of the animal is communicated to those who cannot read, including young children.

---

c. GUILFORD COUNTY, N.C., CODE OF ORDINANCES § 5-12.

(3) The owner of the animal will be responsible for ensuring that the enclosure is maintained in such a condition as to meet the requirements of this chapter. Failure to maintain or repair the enclosure shall subject the owner to penalty under this chapter.

(4) Prior to inspection of the enclosure by the appropriate personnel as described in (e) above the owner shall pay the current fee for the inspection of an accessory building. The animal shall not be returned to the owner's property until such time as this enclosure and warning signs have been approved. While this structure is being erected, the animal must be boarded at the county animal shelter at the owner's expense. A deposit may be required by the owner equal to the estimated costs, including veterinary care for ten days boarding. Failure to pay said deposit when required shall be deemed a waiver of all rights regarding the animal.

· · ·

Mandatory Notifications

The Town of Garner, in its Code of Ordinances, requires owners of dangerous dogs to provide notice to the town if certain incidents occur.[d]

Sec. 3-20. - Required notification to the animal control program by owners of dangerous animals or dangerous dogs.

The owner of an animal declared dangerous under this article shall inform the animal control officer or a Garner Police Officer, as soon as practicable, but not later than twenty-four (24) hours, after the occurrence of any of the following:

(1) An attack or biting upon any human being committed by the dangerous animal in the owner's care or control.

(2) An attack or biting upon any domesticated animal or pet while the dangerous animal is off the owner's property.

(3) The destruction of or damage to property of another by the dangerous animal.

(4) The roaming or escape of any dangerous animal required to be restrained or confined to a secure enclosure.

Tracking

Several local governments require owners to facilitate the tracking of dangerous dogs using tools such as microchips, registration, and permitting. The Code of Ordinances of Boiling Springs Lake, for example, requires both registration and permits.[e]

---

d. TOWN OF GARNER, N.C., CODE OF ORDINANCES § 3-20.
e. CITY OF BOILING SPRINGS LAKE, N.C., CODE OF ORDINANCES §§ 3-102 to 3-103.

Chapter 3 – ANIMALS

. . .

ARTICLE V. - POTENTIALLY DANGEROUS OR VICIOUS DOGS

. . .

Sec. 3-102. - Registration required.

(a) *Generally.* Any person owning, keeping, or harboring a dog determined as set forth above to be dangerous, potentially dangerous, or vicious shall register such dog with the ACO[f] within five (5) days of such determination. In lieu of a determination hearing, an owner, keeper or harborer of a dog suspected of being dangerous, potentially dangerous, or vicious may register such dog voluntarily; such registration shall be an admission and determination that the dog is dangerous, potentially dangerous, or vicious.

(b) *Relief from civil penalty.* Voluntary registration of a dangerous, potentially dangerous, or vicious dog by the owner, keeper or harborer thereof within thirty (30) days of the effective date of this article or prior to the determination that a suspect dog is dangerous, potentially dangerous, or vicious or within five (5) days of an event establishing reasonable cause to believe that a dog is dangerous or vicious or of the acquisition of a dangerous or vicious dog, whichever later occurs, shall relieve such person from the assessment of a civil penalty under the provisions of this article for any violation of this article occurring between such date, event or acquisition and the date of registration.

(c) *Permanent identification mark required.* Each dog registered as set forth above shall be assigned by the ACO a registration number, which shall be affixed to the dog by permanent tattoo or some other permanent means by or at the expense of the owner, keeper or harborer of the dog. No person shall remove such identification mark once it is assigned and affixed.

Sec. 3-103. - Permit required.

(a) *Generally.* After registration of a dangerous dog or a determination that the dog is dangerous, no person shall own, keep or harbor such dog thereafter within the territorial jurisdiction of the City of Bolling Spring Lakes without applying for and obtaining a permit from the ACO.

(b) *Issuance of permit.* A permit shall be issued by the ACO only upon submission of a complete, verified application, payment of the permit fee, and a finding by the ACO, or the designee thereof, that arrangements for housing of the dog and other public health and safety provisions required by this article are in place, and that each dangerous dog for which a permit is issued does not pose an unreasonable threat to the public health, safety and general welfare, if the permittee complies with the provisions of this article and the conditions of the permit. Each permit shall be conditioned on continued compliance with the provisions of this article and other provisions of the City Code, on continued compliance with and maintenance of the arrangements for housing and safety set forth in the permit application, and any special conditions that the ACO deems reasonably necessary to protect the public health, safety and general welfare in view of the particular circumstances and history of the dog concerned.

(c) *Temporary permits.* Following the registration of a dangerous or vicious dog or the apprehension and confinement of a suspect dog pursuant to the provisions of this article, the ACO may issue, upon application and for good cause shown, a temporary permit allowing the owner, keeper or harborer of a registered dangerous dog or dog suspected

---

f. "ACO" is the acronym for Animal Control Office.

of being dangerous to retain possession of such dog or to confine such dog at a veterinary facility or kennel approved by such officer. A temporary permit also may be issued to allow the transport of a vicious dog from the territorial jurisdiction of the City of Boiling Spring Lakes. A temporary permit shall be issued subject to the same conditions to which a regular permit is subject and to any other conditions the ACO deems to be necessary to protect the public health, safety and welfare in a manner consistent with the provisions of this article. A temporary permit shall be valid only until the earlier of its revocation or the issuance or denial of a permit under the provisions of subsection (b) of this section.

(d)   *Term of permits and renewal thereof.* No permit shall be issued under subsection (b) of this section for a period in excess of three (3) years and may, in the discretion of the ACO, be issued for a lesser period. Permits may be renewed, subject to the same terms and conditions required for initial permits.

(e)   *Revocation of permits.* The ACO may, upon notice and hearing and for good cause shown, revoke any permit or modify any terms, conditions or provisions thereof. In the event that the ACO deems it necessary to protect the public health or safety from any imminent threat or danger thereto, the ACO may, without hearing, suspend any permit or any portion thereof for a period not to exceed thirty (30) days. Good cause for revocation or modification of a permit shall include, without limitation, the violation of or failure to comply with any provision of this article or with any term, condition or provision of a permit.

(f)   *Inspections.* The ACO shall cause inspections to be made of the premises of a permittee to determine compliance with the provisions of this article.

(g)   *Insurance.* Every person owning, keeping or harboring a dog that has been declared dangerous, potentially dangerous, or vicious shall purchase and maintain a policy of liability insurance covering any injury or property damage caused by the dog. Minimum policy limits shall be: One hundred thousand dollars ($100,000.00) personal injury or property damage, per occurrence. The owner, keeper or harborer of a dog that has been declared dangerous, potentially dangerous, or vicious shall cause a certificate of insurance to be furnished to the ACO annually by their insurance carrier. Every calendar day that the required insurance is not in full force and effect shall constitute a Class III violation of this article pursuant to subsection 3-106(a).

Chapter 5
Rabies Control

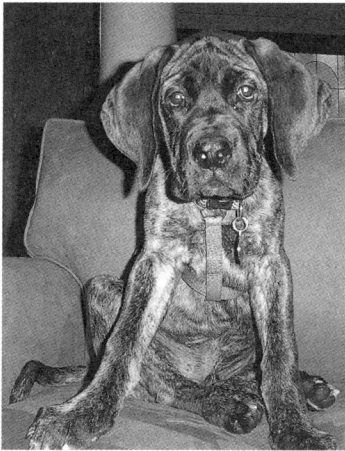

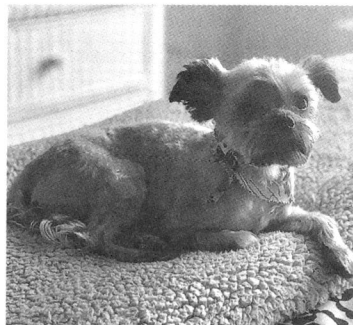

Rabies is a viral infection that may be transmitted to humans through the bite of infected animals such as raccoons, bats, and dogs.[1] If left untreated, the disease is almost always fatal for humans.[2] In North Carolina, public health, animal services, and wildlife management officials work together to enforce state and local laws designed to minimize the spread of rabies and the risk of human exposure.

Like many other states, North Carolina has adopted a set of statutes and regulations governing the control of rabies. These statewide laws not only require the vaccination of cats, dogs, and ferrets but also provide a detailed framework for responding to animal bites and other potential exposures to the rabies virus. The relevant statutes can be found in Article 6, Part 6 of Chapter 130A of the North Carolina General Statutes (hereinafter G.S.)—the public health chapter.[3]

This chapter provides a brief summary of the history of those rabies control laws and offers an overview of their major components, including recent changes related to post-exposure management.

---

1. According to the Centers for Disease Control and Prevention (hereinafter CDC), the virus can also be contracted when an infected animal's saliva or nervous system tissue comes in direct contact with a person's eyes, nose, mouth, or an open wound. CDC, *Rabies: How Is Rabies Transmitted?*, CDC.GOV (Apr. 22, 2011), http://www.cdc.gov/rabies/transmission/index.html.

2. If a person is bitten by an animal that has or may have rabies, a health care provider will most likely treat the wound and administer a series of vaccines intended to prevent rabies in humans (postexposure antirabies prophylaxis). *See* Susan E. Manning et al., CDC, *Human Rabies Prevention—United States, 2008: Recommendations of the Advisory Committee on Immunization Practices*, 57 MORBIDITY & MORTALITY WKLY. REP. 1 (May 23, 2008), https://www.cdc.gov/mmwr/PDF/rr/rr5703.pdf. Until recently, most people believed that in the absence of prophylaxis treatment the disease would be fatal to humans. At least six people are known to have survived an active rabies infection, with the most recent being in 2004 in Wisconsin. Rodney E. Willoughby Jr. et al., *Survival after Treatment of Rabies with Induction of Coma*, 352 NEW. ENG. J. MED. 2508 (2005); CDC, *Recovery of a Patient from Clinical Rabies—Wisconsin, 2004*, 53 MORBIDITY & MORTALITY WKLY. REP. 1171–73 (Dec. 24, 2004), www.cdc.gov/mmwr/preview/mmwrhtml/mm5350a1.htm.

3. The state Commission for Public Health has also adopted a few regulations governing rabies control. *See, e.g.,* Title 10A, Chapter 41G, §§ .0101–.0103 of the North Carolina Administrative Code (hereinafter N.C.A.C.) (addressing rabies vaccinations).

"Mad" Dogs

The earliest rabies control laws in North Carolina governed the killing of "mad" dogs.[4] Any dog that exhibited symptoms of rabies infection—agitation, loss of appetite, and unusually aggressive behavior—could be considered a "mad" dog.[5]

North Carolina has two "mad dog" laws. The first provides that an owner who knows, or has "good reason to believe," that his or her dog has been bitten by a mad dog must immediately kill his or her dog. Failure to do so may result in both civil and criminal penalties.[6] The second law authorizes any person to kill any mad dog.[7] These two laws predate the modern statutory scheme designed to control rabies and, therefore, may have been superseded.

---

4. The laws date back to the early nineteenth century and have changed very little over time. In 1817, the law read as follows:

> Whereas that most dreadful of all maladies, Hydrophobia, has become much more common than formerly by reason of the negligence of the owners of dogs: For remedy whereof.
>
> 1. Be it enacted. That whenever the owner of any dog shall know, or have good reason to believe, that his or her dog, or any dog belonging to his or her slave, or any other person in his or her employment, has been bitten by a mad dog, and shall neglect or refuse immediately to kill the same, he or she so refusing or neglecting shall pay the sum of twenty-five pounds . . .
>
> 2. And be it further enacted. That he or she so refusing or neglecting as aforesaid, shall be further liable to pay all damages which may be sustained by any person or persons whatsoever, by the bite of any dog belonging as aforesaid.

Laws of the State of N.C. (Potter's Revisal, 1821), vol. II, ch. 945, p. 1405 (1817).

The fine became fifty dollars in 1837, and the criminal penalty appears to have been added in 1883. N.C. Rev. Stat. 1837, ch. 70 (fine); N.C. Code 1883, § 2499 (misdemeanor).

5. *See, e.g.*, Buck v. Brady, 73 A. 277, 278–79 (Md. 1909) (describing the symptoms of a rabid dog).

6. Chapter 67, Section 4 of the North Carolina General Statutes (hereinafter G.S.). The law provides that if the dog that was bitten by a mad dog ("victim 1") subsequently bites a person or animal ("victim 2") and the owner of victim 1 is sued civilly, the owner of victim 1 must pay victim 2 (or if victim 2 is an animal, its owner) fifty dollars as well as any damages. Victim 1's owner will also be guilty of a Class 3 misdemeanor. *Id.*

7. G.S. 67-14. The statute also allows the killing of any dog that is killing sheep, cattle, hogs, goats, or poultry. This statute can be traced as far back as 1919. N.C. Code, ch. 31, art. 3, § 1682 (1920).

Vaccination Requirements

Vaccination of pets is the cornerstone requirement of modern rabies control. Under state law, every owner of a dog, cat, or ferret over four months of age is required to have the animal vaccinated against rabies.[8] State regulations authorize the use of any vaccine licensed by the federal government[9] and outline the requirements for the timing of vaccinations, with some being required on an annual basis and others required every three years.[10]

While many pet owners take their animals to private veterinarians for rabies vaccinations, local health departments are required to organize (or assist other county departments in organizing) at least one countywide public vaccination clinic per year.[11] Most counties offer multiple clinics each year. Boards of county commissioners set the clinic vaccination fee, which is limited by statute to the actual cost of the vaccine, the certificate, and the collar tag, plus an administrative fee of up to ten dollars per vaccination. Often the county coordinates these public clinics with the assistance and support of private veterinarians in the community. For example, the county may organize and advertise the clinic, while veterinarians participate at public locations or in their own offices.

Vaccinations may be administered by licensed veterinarians, registered veterinary technicians (under the supervision of a licensed veterinarian), or certified rabies vaccinators (CRVs). Individuals wishing to become CRVs must (1) be appointed as such by the local health director, (2) receive at least four hours of training from the state public health veterinarian (located in the N.C. Department of Health and Human Services), and (3) receive written certification from the state public health veterinarian indicating that they are able to administer vaccines.[12] Local health directors are required to appoint CRVs if a licensed veterinarian is not available to participate in the county vaccination clinic. If a veterinarian is available, the health director has the option of appointing one or more CRVs for the county. Appointed CRVs must make themselves available to participate in the county vaccination clinics.

---

8. G.S. 130A-185. While state law does not currently require other types of animals to be vaccinated, a local government could adopt such a requirement. For example, Buncombe County authorizes the local board of health or health director to order the vaccination of other domestic animals in the event of a rabies outbreak or epidemic. BUNCOMBE COUNTY, N.C., CODE OF ORDINANCES § 6-56(a)(1).

9. 10A N.C.A.C. 41G, § .0103 (Approved Rabies Vaccines).

10. 10A N.C.A.C. 41G, § .0101 (Time of Rabies Vaccination).

11. G.S. 130A-187.

12. G.S. 130A-185; 130A-186. If an animal is vaccinated by a CRV, it must be revaccinated the following year even if the vaccine is one that is approved for three years. 10A N.C.A.C. 41G, § .0101(a).

The North Carolina Department of Health and Human Services, Division of Public Health (DPH) recommends that the local health director have policies and procedures in place to ensure that the director retains overall supervisory responsibility for rabies vaccinations performed by CRVs.[13] Specifically, DPH suggests that the director maintain records regarding each appointment, including details regarding the location(s) where the CRV may administer vaccines and the name of the CRV's direct supervisor. If the director has concerns about a CRV's performance, DPH recommends that the director consider requiring remedial training, re-certification, or termination of the appointment.[14]

The person who administers a vaccination must give the animal's owner a copy of a vaccination certificate and a rabies tag.[15] At a minimum, the tags must include the year issued, a vaccination number, the words "rabies vaccine," and either "North Carolina" or the initials "N.C."[16] DPH sells tags, links, and rivets, as do private companies. The fee for rabies vaccination tags obtained from DPH is not specified in statute, but there are some limitations on how it may be calculated. It may include the actual cost of the tag, links, and rivets; transportation costs (presumably related to distributing the tags); and an additional $.15 per tag to be used to fund rabies education and prevention programs.[17] DPH maintains a public list of entities that have purchased tags from the State, which can aid in the process of reuniting lost animals with their owners.[18]

Dogs are required to wear their tags at all times, but local governments may exempt cats and ferrets from the requirement.[19] Cabarrus County, for example, exempts cats from the tag requirement but requires that cat owners maintain the certificates as evidence of vaccination.[20] Guilford County does not exempt cats but allows them to wear an "ear tag" in lieu of the traditional collar tag.[21]

Some local governments have adopted ordinances or board of health rules that supplement the tag requirements in various ways. For example, the local law may prohibit

---

13. *See* N.C. Div. of Pub. Health, North Carolina Rabies Control Manual (Feb. 2013) (hereinafter N.C. Rabies Control Manual), http://epi.publichealth.nc.gov/cd/lhds/manuals/rabies/toc.html. The section of the manual offering CRV guidance for local health directors is available at http://epi.publichealth.nc.gov/cd/lhds/manuals/rabies/docs/crv_for_lhds.pdf.

14. The local health director may terminate a vaccinator's appointment at any time. G.S. 130A-186.

15. G.S. 130A-189; 130A-190.

16. G.S. 130A-190.

17. G.S. 130A-190(b).

18. *See* N.C. Dep't of Health & Human Servs., *Rabies: Rabies Tag Lists* (updated Jan. 26, 2018), http://epi.publichealth.nc.gov/cd/rabies/figures.html#tags.

19. G.S. 130A-190.

20. Cabarrus County, N.C., Code of Ordinances § 10-99.

21. Guilford County, N.C., Code of Ordinances § 5-32(c).

the use of a rabies tag for any animal other than the one that received the vaccination.[22] Local ordinances or rules should not, however, establish requirements that conflict with or are less stringent than those set out in the state law.[23]

People who bring a dog, cat, or ferret to North Carolina from another state or country also have a duty to protect against the spread of rabies. The state statute governing import and export of these animals provides that they may enter the state if they either (1) have a certificate from a licensed veterinarian or (2) comply with additional vaccination and confinement requirements.[24]

Veterinarian's Certificate

In order to comply with state law, the veterinarian's certificate must demonstrate that the animal is apparently free from rabies, has not been exposed to rabies, and is currently vaccinated against rabies. Interestingly, DPH's website states that the agency is "officially eliminating the requirement for incoming dogs/cats/ferrets to be accompanied by an ICVI (health certificate)."[25] In lieu of a certificate, the agency explains, the "only requirement for these animals is that they be currently vaccinated against rabies when entering the state" or that they comply with the vaccination/confinement option set out below. The guidance from the state agency appears to conflict with state statutes. As a result, an owner traveling into North Carolina will need to decide whether to rely on the more relaxed DPH interpretation of state law or to comply with the more stringent state provisions.

Vaccination/Confinement

In the absence of a certificate or possibly current vaccination status, the animal must be securely confined upon entry into the state, vaccinated within one week, and then confined for a further two weeks after vaccination.[26] This law does not apply to animals

---

22. *See, e.g.*, CUMBERLAND COUNTY, N.C., CODE OF ORDINANCES § 3-40(k).

23. For example, Hyde County's animal control ordinance requires that dogs and cats "running at large" wear a rabies tag, which could erroneously lead members of the public to believe that the tags are not required for dogs kept at home or not otherwise "at large." HYDE COUNTY, N.C., CODE OF ORDINANCES § 4-5. *See also* CLEVELAND COUNTY, N.C., CODE OF ORDINANCES § 3-31(4) (exempts dogs from the tag requirement when they are participating in an organized hunting activity as long as their owners are in possession of the tags during the activity).

24. G.S. 130A-193.

25. *See* N.C. Dep't of Health & Human Servs., Div. of Public Health, *Diseases & Topics: Import/Export Requirements for Domestic Dogs, Cats & Ferrets* (updated Nov. 13, 2017), http://epi.publichealth.nc.gov/cd/diseases/importexport.html. "ICVI" is the acronym for interstate certificate of veterinary inspection.

26. G.S. 130A-193(a).

brought into the state for exhibition purposes, as long as they are confined and not permitted to run at large.[27]

Before transporting animals from North Carolina to another state or country, it is important to research the applicable law of the destination state. The U.S. Department of Agriculture maintains a searchable database of laws that govern traveling with pets from state to state or out of the country.[28]

Enforcement of Vaccination Requirements

Local governments are expected to enforce state vaccination requirements by finding animals without tags, issuing warnings to owners, and possibly pursuing criminal or civil remedies.

- **Canvassing.** "Animal control officers" are required to canvass their jurisdictions to find animals not wearing rabies tags.[29] The term "canvass" suggests that officials have a duty to proactively tour the jurisdiction seeking out animals in violation of the law.[30] Presumably, this requirement does not extend to cats or ferrets in jurisdictions that have adopted ordinances exempting them from the tag requirement.
- **Warning.** If an officer finds a dog, cat, or ferret without a rabies tag but the animal is wearing a tag that identifies its owner, or if the officer knows who owns the animal, the officer must provide written notice to the owner that (1) explains the vaccination requirements and (2) directs the owner to provide a copy of the animal's current vaccination certificate "within three days of the notification."[31]
- **Impounding.** If an officer finds a dog, cat, or ferret without a rabies tag and does not know who owns the animal, he or she has the authority to impound

---

27. G.S. 130A-193(b).

28. *See* U.S. Dep't of Agric., Animal & Plant Health Inspection Service (APHIS), *APHIS Pet Travel*, https://www.aphis.usda.gov/aphis/pet-travel (last visited Apr. 10, 2018).

29. G.S. 130A-192. The term "animal control officer" is defined broadly in the law to mean "[a] city or county employee whose responsibility includes animal control." G.S. 130A-184(1). The titles for these officials will vary from jurisdiction to jurisdiction based on how animal services are delivered in that particular community. They may be law enforcement officials, public health officials, animal services officials, or animal control officials.

30. The definitional variants of the term "canvass" found in the dictionary include going through a region to solicit votes, orders, or opinions and also conducting a thorough investigation. *See canvass*, Merriam Webster's Collegiate Dictionary (11th ed. 2003).

31. G.S. 130A-192.

it.[32] Note that the officer is not *required* to impound the animal; state law grants local governments the authority to seize the animal but does not require them to impound all dogs, cats, and ferrets found without rabies tags. An officer who does seize an animal is required to make a reasonable effort to locate its owner, which may include scanning the animal to determine if it has a microchip. For more information about impoundment, see Chapter 7.

- **Pursuing civil or criminal enforcement.** If an owner fails to comply with the vaccination requirements or to produce proof of vaccination when required, the owner may be charged with a Class 1 misdemeanor.[33] In lieu of criminal prosecution, a local government could also consider seeking an injunction.[34]

Some local governments have imposed fines or other penalties for ordinance violations related to vaccination status. Because the vaccination requirements are in state law, local ordinance enforcement tools are not appropriate and should not be used.[35]

Exposure and Potential Exposure

To minimize health risks to humans, North Carolina law creates a framework for handling situations in which a person is exposed or potentially exposed to rabies. The components of the framework include mandatory reporting, confinement of animals, and, in some cases, destruction of animals. The responsibilities of public health and animal services officials vary depending on the situation and the level of health risk, as outlined below.

Animals Biting Humans

When an animal potentially exposes a human to rabies, several reporting laws come into play.

---

32. *Id.* If an animal is wearing an identification tag, animal services officials may still have authority to impound the animal pursuant to a local ordinance. For example, Orange County has declared that animals found not wearing currently valid rabies tags are public nuisances and may be impounded pursuant to a process described by ordinance. *See* ORANGE COUNTY, N.C., CODE OF ORDINANCES § 4-43.

33. G.S. 130A-25; 14-3.

34. G.S. 130A-18.

35. G.S. 160A-174(b)(6) prohibits ordinances if the "elements of an offense defined by a city ordinance are identical to the elements of an offense defined by State or federal law." While this limitation is named only in the law governing municipalities, the courts have consistently applied it to counties as well. *See* State v. Tenore, 280 N.C. 238, 248 (1972). Some local ordinances repeat the rabies vaccination requirements and then establish enforcement tools, such as fines, that differ from those tools available in state law. Because the ordinance is not authorized or valid, the enforcement tools would also not be authorized. See Chapter 1 for further discussion of the interaction between state law and local ordinances.

- **Physician reporting.** When a physician treats a person for an animal bite, the physician has a duty under G.S. 130A-196(a) to notify the local health director within twenty-four hours. The report must include the bite victim's name, age, and sex.[36] The statute provides that the physician's duty to report is triggered if the bite is by "an animal known to be a potential carrier of rabies," which could arguably include any mammal.[37]
- **Person responsible for an animal.** When a dog, cat, or ferret bites a person, the animal's owner (or the person possessing or in control of the animal) must notify the local health director immediately.[38] The report must include the names and addresses of the victim and the animal's owner.[39] Note that this law applies to all dogs, cats, and ferrets that bite someone, regardless of the animal's vaccination status.
- **Bite victim.** Immediately after a person has been bitten by a dog, cat, or ferret, the victim, or the victim's parent, guardian, or person standing in loco parentis of the person, is also required to notify the health director.[40] The report must include the name and address of the victim and the animal's owner, if known.[41]

After a dog, cat, or ferret bites a person, the offending animal must be immediately confined for ten days.[42] If the animal is a stray or is feral, animal services officials must make a reasonable attempt to locate the owner. If they are unable to do so within seventy-two hours of the event (or ninety-six hours if the bite occurred on a weekend or state holiday), the local health director may allow the animal to be euthanized. The animal's head would then be removed so that it could be sent to a lab to determine whether the rabies virus was present at the time of the bite.[43] Animals that are not strays or not feral are subject to the ten-day confinement period regardless of vaccination status.

The ten-day confinement period is important because it allows health officials to determine whether the animal was capable of transmitting rabies to the bite victim. An animal that is infected with the rabies virus will appear healthy during an incubation period that can range from a few weeks up to six months.[44] After the incubation period, the disease will have traveled into the animal's brain and the animal will begin to shed

---

36. G.S. 130A-196(a).

37. *Id. See also* CDC, *supra* note 1 ("All species of mammals are susceptible to rabies virus infection, but only a few species are important as reservoirs for the disease.").

38. G.S. 130A-196(a).

39. *Id.*

40. *Id.*

41. *Id.*

42. G.S. 130A-196(b).

43. G.S. 130A-196(a).

44. *See* CDC, *Rabies: The Path of the Rabies Virus*, CDC.GOV (updated Oct. 27, 2017), http://www.cdc.gov/rabies/transmission/body.html ("The reason there is so much variation in the time between exposure and the onset of the disease is that many factors come into play

the virus in its saliva. Once this begins to happen, the animal will quickly become ill and die within ten days. It is during this short window of time that an infected animal will be able to pass the virus on to another animal or to a human through a bite.[45] Therefore, the law is designed to allow monitoring of biting animals to determine whether they are in this critical ten-day window. If, during the confinement, the animal exhibits symptoms compatible with rabies, local health officials will take immediate action to evaluate the animal, euthanize it if appropriate, and have it tested. Depending on the circumstances, health officials may or may not recommend that the bite victim receive treatment (postexposure prophylaxis) before the results of the testing are complete.

The local health director is responsible for designating the place of confinement, which could be a veterinarian's office, a public or private animal shelter, or even the owner's property. Some health directors are comfortable allowing an owner to confine the animal on his or her own property under some circumstances, but many are not. State law leaves this decision entirely up to the health director.[46] Regardless of where the animal is confined, the owner is responsible for any costs related to the confinement.[47]

An owner who fails to confine the animal as required by the health director may be charged with a Class 2 misdemeanor, and, if an owner refuses to confine the animal in accordance with the instructions of the health director, the director may order the seizure and confinement of the animal.[48] For example, in 2011, a Chatham County dog owner was charged with a misdemeanor and the county health director began the process of issuing a seizure order when the owner removed his dog from the veterinary office where it had been confined.[49]

Potential Animal Exposures

If a dog, cat, or ferret is exposed to rabies, there are several factors the health director will consider when deciding how best to manage the situation. Before exploring the management of potential exposures, it is important to understand what constitutes an exposure.

---

including the site of the exposure, the type of rabies virus, and any immunity in the animal or person exposed.").

45. *Id. See also* Nat'l Ass'n of State Pub. Health Veterinarians (NASPHV), Compendium of Animal Rabies Prevention & Control Comm., *Compendium of Animal Rabies Prevention and Control, 2016*, 248 J. A. Veterinary Med. Assoc'n 505, 511 (2016), http://www.nasphv.org/Documents/NASPHVRabiesCompendium.pdf.

46. The health director also has the authority to allow "a dog trained and used by a law enforcement agency to be released from confinement to perform official duties upon submission of proof that the dog has been vaccinated for rabies." G.S. 130A-196(b).

47. *Id.*

48. *Id.*

49. *See* Dan E. Way, *Suspect Frees His Dog from Quarantine, Faces Charges*, Herald-Sun (Durham) (Feb. 2, 2011).

Under state law, a dog, cat, or ferret is considered to have been exposed to rabies if the health director "reasonably suspects" that the animal has been exposed to the saliva or nerve tissue (e.g., cerebrospinal fluid, brain or spinal cord tissue) of either

(1) a proven rabid animal or
(2) an animal reasonably suspected of having rabies that is not available for laboratory diagnosis.[50]

An "unavailable" wild mammal may be "reasonably suspected of having rabies" if, for example, it is an animal that is considered to have a high risk for rabies transmission, including raccoons, skunks, foxes, bats, bobcats, coyotes, and groundhogs (i.e., woodchucks).[51] Other types of wild mammals, such as squirrels, may also be "reasonably suspected of having rabies" based on the "animal's behavior, health, or circumstances (unprovoked attack, or history that pet rodent or rabbit was housed outside in a rabies endemic area)."[52] For encounters with unavailable domestic animals, the health director will likely proceed under the assumption that the animal is "reasonably suspected of having rabies" and that an exposure may have occurred.

Note that because the statutory language speaks to a situation where the local health director "reasonably suspects" that an animal has been exposed to the saliva or nervous tissue of a rabid or potentially rabid animal, the law provides the local health director with significant discretion in deciding whether a dog, cat, or ferret has been exposed to rabies. It may be of some help in exercising this discretion to note that the National Association of State Public Health Veterinarians (NASPHV) states that rabies exposure occurs when "the virus is introduced into bite wounds, into open cuts in skin, or onto mucous membranes from saliva or other potentially infectious material such as neural tissue."[53] Table 5.1, below, includes descriptions of the types of exposures identified by the North Carolina Department of Health and Human Services, Division of Public Health (DPH).

---

50. G.S. 130A-197.

51. *See* N.C. Rabies Control Manual, *supra* note 13. The relevant section of the manual is available at http://epi.publichealth.nc.gov/cd/lhds/manuals/rabies/docs/testing_criteria.pdf); *see also* Manning et al., *supra* note 2, at 1 ("Most reported cases of rabies occur among carnivores, primarily raccoons, skunks, and foxes and various species of bats."; also describing types of exposure and criteria for determining when an exposure may have occurred); NASPHV, *supra* note 45, at 509 ("Wild mammalian carnivores, skunks, and bats that are not available or suitable for testing should be regarded as rabid.").

52. *See* N.C. Rabies Control Manual, *supra* note 13, at 2. The relevant section of the manual is available at http://epi.publichealth.nc.gov/cd/lhds/manuals/rabies/docs/testing_criteria.pdf.

53. NASPHV, *supra* note 45, at 506.

Table 5.1. DPH Rabies Exposure Types, Descriptions

Bite	Any penetration of the skin by the teeth of a rabid or potentially rabid animal.
Open wound exposure	Introduction of saliva or nerve tissue (e.g., cerebrospinal fluid, brain or spinal cord tissue) from a rabid or potentially rabid animal into an open wound or open break in the skin. This includes scratches where introduction of saliva or nerve tissue cannot be ruled out.
Mucous membrane exposure	Introduction of saliva or nerve tissue from a rabid or potentially rabid animal onto any mucous membrane (e.g., eyes, nose, mouth).
Bats and other exposures	Any interaction with a rabid or potentially rabid animal where a bite, open wound, or mucous membrane exposure cannot be definitively ruled out and where there is a reasonable suspicion or probability of exposure, including • direct physical contact with a bat when a bite or scratch cannot be ruled out, • a bat found in a room with a sleeping person, • a bat found in a room with an unattended child, • a bat found in a room with an intoxicated or mentally compromised person, or • a bat found in close proximity to an unattended child outdoors.

If the health director reasonably suspects that an animal has been exposed to rabies, state law requires that the director follow the recommendations for postexposure management issued by the NASPHV.[54] Those recommendations, issued in March 2016, provide as follows:

- **Never been vaccinated.** Dogs, cats, and ferrets that have never been vaccinated should be euthanized immediately or placed in strict quarantine for four months (dogs and cats) or six months (ferrets). The quarantine should be in an enclosure that precludes direct contact with people or other animals. If quarantined, the animal should be vaccinated within ninety-six hours of exposure. If the vaccination is delayed, the local health director may consider extending the quarantine period.[55]

---

54. G.S. 130A-197. *See also* NASPHV, *supra* note 45. The state Division of Public Health updated the *North Carolina Rabies Control Manual* to incorporate the new NASPHV recommendations. *See* N.C. Rabies Control Manual, *supra* note 13. The relevant section of the manual is available at http://epi.publichealth.nc.gov/cd/lhds/manuals/rabies/animal_mgmt.html.

55. When deciding whether to extend the period, some of the factors the local health director should consider include the severity of the exposure, the length of delay in vaccination, the animal's current health status, and the vaccination history. *See* N.C. Rabies Control Manual,

- **Vaccinated with appropriate documentation.** A dog or cat that has appropriate documentation[56] showing that it is either current on its vaccinations or was vaccinated at least once previously should receive a booster vaccination within ninety-six hours of exposure. In addition, the owner should keep the animal under his or her control and observe it for forty-five days for signs of illness.[57] If the booster is delayed, the local health director may consider increasing the observation period.

- **Vaccination without documentation.** If an owner reports that the dog or cat has had a rabies vaccination in the past but does not have the appropriate documentation to prove it, the guidance offers two options:
  - Follow the quarantine approach described above for animals that have never been vaccinated or
  - Consider allowing blood testing to evaluate whether there is evidence of a robust immune response upon booster vaccination.[58]

- **Ferrets.** A ferret with appropriate documentation that is current on its vaccinations is treated the same as a dog or cat that is current on its vaccinations. A ferret with or without appropriate documentation that has a lapsed vaccination should be "evaluated on a case-by-case basis" to determine the appropriate management.

---

supra note 13. The relevant section of the manual is available at http://epi.publichealth.nc.gov/ cd/lhds/manuals/rabies/docs/NASPHVRabiesCompAlgDogCat2016.pdf.

56. Pursuant to guidance issued by DPH, "appropriate documentation" would be "a rabies certificate or official veterinary record validating that the animal has received a USDA-licensed rabies vaccine at least once previously, and if a single vaccination, [that] the animal was vaccinated at least 28 days prior to the exposure." *See* N.C. Rabies Control Manual, *supra* note 13. The relevant section of the manual is available at http://epi.publichealth.nc.gov/ cd/lhds/manuals/rabies/docs/NASPHVRabiesCompAlgDogCat2016.pdf. The NASPHV has a form available (NASPHV Form 51) that would meet this requirement. Form 51 is available at http://nasphv.org/Documents/RabiesVacCert.pdf.

57. DPH describes "owner observation" as "under the owner's strict supervision and control (leash walk, fenced yard, no travel or boarding unless approved by the [local health director], no outings at doggie park or other parks, etc.)." *See* N.C. Rabies Control Manual, *supra* note 13. The relevant section of the manual is available at http://epi.publichealth.nc.gov/cd/ lhds/manuals/rabies/docs/NASPHVRabiesCompAlgDogCat2016.pdf. The NASPHV guidance goes on further to suggest that the animal should have "no contact with animals or people other than the caretaker(s) until the local health director has released the animal from the 45 day observation period." *Id.*

58. Protocols for blood testing, called Prospective Serologic Monitoring, are available from both the NASPHV (http://www.nasphv.org/Documents/NASPHVSerologicMonitoring2016.pdf) and DPH (http://epi.publichealth.nc.gov/cd/lhds/manuals/rabies/docs/ProspectiveSerological Monitoring_Nov2016.pdf).

Figure 5.1. Recommendations for Postexposure Management (Cats and Dogs)

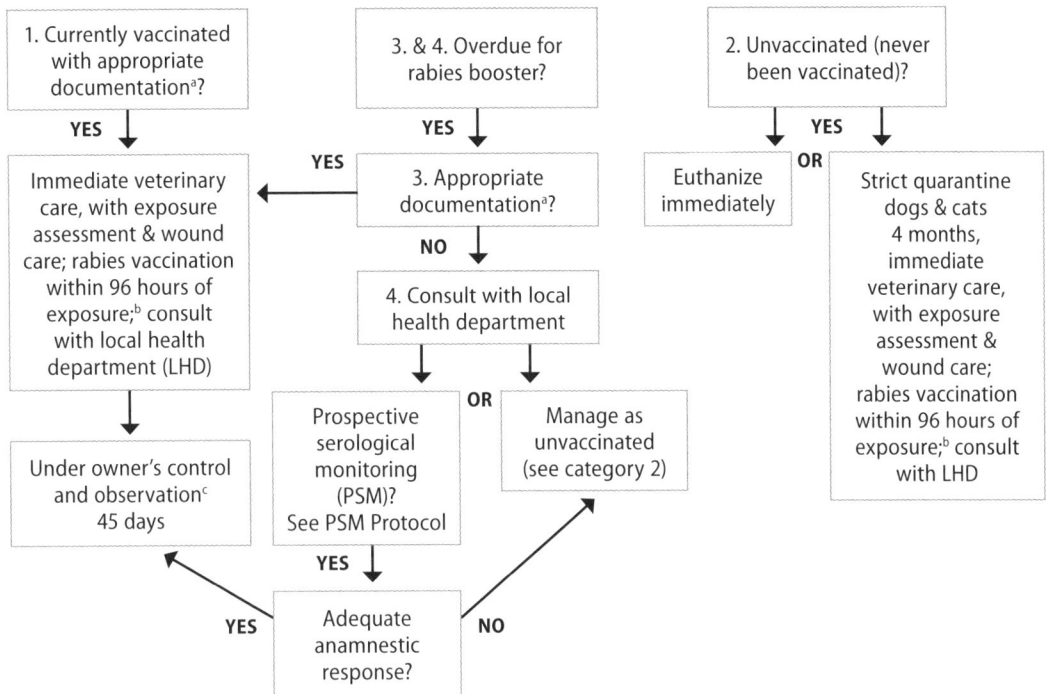

a. Appropriate documentation: A rabies certificate or official veterinary record validating that the animal has received a USDA-licensed rabies vaccine at least once previously, and if a single vaccination, the animal was vaccinated at least 28 days prior to the exposure date (G.S. 130A-185 and 130A-197).

b. If rabies booster or vaccination is delayed, LHD may consider increasing observation period (case-by-case) or quarantine period (from 4 to 6 month), considering severity of exposure, length of delay in vaccination, current health status, and number of prior rabies vaccines and lapses.

c. Owner Observation: Under the owner's strict supervision and control (leash walk, fenced yard, no travel or boarding unless approved by the LHD, no outings at doggie park or other parks, etc.). There should be no contact with animals or people other than the caretaker(s) until the local health director has released the animal from the 45-day observation period.

Source: N.C. DIV. OF PUB. HEALTH, NORTH CAROLINA RABIES CONTROL MANUAL (Feb. 2013), http://epi.publichealth.nc.gov/cd/lhds/manuals/rabies/toc.html; NASPHV (Oct. 14, 2016), http://epi.publichealth.nc.gov/cd/lhds/rabies/docs/NASPHVRabiesCompAlgDogCat2016.pdf.

This approach to postexposure management is new for North Carolina.[59] Prior to October 2017, if a dog, cat, or ferret was exposed to rabies but did not have current vaccinations or appropriate documentation, the animal would have either been quarantined for up to six months or euthanized. With the changes in the law, local health directors—who still have exclusive authority to make decisions regarding postexposure

59. In 2017, the General Assembly enacted legislation that effectively adopted the NASPHV recommendations by reference. S.L. 2017-106. The change went into effect October 1, 2017.

management—will be developing new practices and procedures for their communities that align with the NASPHV recommendations.

Animal Suspected of Having or Diagnosed with Rabies

If any animal is suspected of having rabies, the owner or person in possession of the animal must immediately notify his or her local health director or an animal services official.[60] For example, a person might suspect that his or her dog has rabies because it is behaving erratically or exhibiting other symptoms. Once notified, the health director must designate a place for the animal to be securely confined for a period of ten days. If the animal dies during that period, its head must be sent to the state's public health laboratory for testing.[61] In lieu of confinement, the state public health veterinarian may require destruction of any animal suspected of having rabies.[62]

If an animal is diagnosed by a veterinarian as having rabies, it must be destroyed and its head must be sent to the state's public health laboratory for testing.[63]

Rabies in the Community

The basic legal framework for rabies control at the individual animal level lies in the enforcement of preventive vaccination requirements and effective responses to potential rabies exposures. Local governments also have two additional tools they can use to meet the threat of a rabies outbreak in their communities: geographic quarantine and declaration of a rabies emergency.

---

60. G.S. 130A-198. While the law specifies that the notification be made to the *county* animal services official, notifying a municipal animal control official should also suffice.

61. DPH has issued guidelines regarding submission of specimens. The guidelines vary based on the type and size of animal and the relative risk involved. *See* N.C. Rabies Control Manual, *supra* note 13. The relevant section of the manual is available at http://epi.publichealth.nc.gov/cd/lhds/manuals/rabies/docs/testing_specimens.pdf.

62. Previously, the confinement requirements in G.S. 130A-198 distinguished between "dogs and cats" and "other animals." The ten-day confinement was required for dogs and cats, while the state public health veterinarian had the authority to order destruction of "other animals" (such as raccoons). When the statute was amended in 2009, the words "dog and cat" were deleted from the text and the more general term "animal" was inserted. S.L. 2009-327, § 13. As a result, this section of the law is somewhat ambiguous because it both *requires* ten-day confinement of animals and *allows* the state public health veterinarian to order destruction of "other animals."

63. G.S. 130A-199.

Geographic Quarantine

A local health director has the authority to order a rabies quarantine for a geographic area if the director determines that the disease is prevalent enough to endanger the lives of the human population.[64] When an area is under quarantine, dogs, cats, and ferrets must be confined to their owners' premises or to a veterinary hospital, kept on a leash, or be under the control and in the sight of a responsible adult. If a peace officer or animal services official sees a dog, cat, or ferret running uncontrolled in a quarantined area but is not able to catch it, the official is allowed to destroy the animal.

Use of the term "quarantine" in the context of rabies control could be somewhat confusing because the term is used in different ways in other sections of the state's public health laws. Specifically, the term "quarantine authority" defined in G.S. Chapter 130A includes orders that

- limit the freedom of movement or action of persons or animals that have been exposed to a communicable disease;
- limit access by any person or animal to an area or facility that may be contaminated with an infectious agent; and
- under certain circumstances, limit the freedom of movement or action of people who have not received immunizations.[65]

The term "quarantine authority" is often used in connection with "isolation authority."[66] Public health officials have a long history of using these two legal authorities to control the spread of communicable diseases and conditions. The definition above is consistent with the quarantine that a health director might order if a dog, cat, or ferret has been exposed to rabies or is suspected of having rabies.

However, the definition of quarantine authority above is inconsistent with the geographic quarantine concept in the section of the rabies law that provides for restricting the movement or action of animals within a certain geographic region. That definition refers specifically to (1) animals that either have been exposed to a communicable disease or have not been immunized and (2) areas and facilities that may be contaminated with an infectious agent. It does *not* address the ability of local health directors to order restrictions for an entire geographic region regardless of exposure to disease or immunization status.

Until this discrepancy in the law is resolved, it would be reasonable for local health directors to assume that they have two separate and distinct quarantine authorities in

---

64. G.S. 130A-194; 130A-195.

65. G.S. 130A-2(7a).

66. "Isolation authority" is available when a person or animal is infected or is reasonably suspected of being infected with rabies. G.S. 130A-2(3a). "Quarantine authority" is available when a person or animal has been exposed to or is reasonably suspected of having been exposed to rabies. *Id.* § 130A-2(7a).

the limited context of rabies control. The first is the authority to order *all* dogs, cats, and ferrets within a geographic region to be confined or restrained when rabies is prevalent.[67] The second is the more general isolation and quarantine authority available for all communicable diseases, including when a dog, cat, or ferret is exposed to or suspected of having rabies.[68]

Rabies Emergency

During the early 1990s, a new rabies epidemic began sweeping through North Carolina's wild animal population.[69] In response, the General Assembly enacted a law authorizing local health directors to ask the state health director to declare a rabies emergency in any jurisdiction where rabies is found in a wild animal (other than a bat).[70]

The primary benefit of declaring a rabies emergency in a jurisdiction is that it allows the state health director to ask the Wildlife Resources Commission (WRC) to develop a plan to minimize the threat to humans and domestic animals of rabies exposure from foxes, raccoons, skunks, or bobcats.[71] The plan developed by the WRC could, for example, suspend or liberalize hunting restrictions for those animals until the emergency has passed.

---

67. G.S. 130A-194; 130A-195.

68. G.S. 130A-197. For more information about this type of quarantine authority, see the discussion above regarding potential animal exposures to rabies. For a detailed discussion of the more expansive isolation and quarantine authorities, see Jill Moore, *The North Carolina Public Health System's Isolation and Quarantine Authority*, HEALTH L. BULL. No. 84 (July 2006), https://www.sog.unc.edu/sites/www.sog.unc.edu/files/reports/hlb84.pdf.

69. According to one report, North Carolina's confirmed cases of rabies almost doubled every year early in the decade. The state had 10 confirmed cases in 1990, 24 cases in 1991, 50 cases in 1992, and 106 cases in 1993. The number peaked in 1997 at 879 confirmed cases. In 2016, there were 251 confirmed cases. N.C. Dep't of Health & Human Servs., *Rabies: Facts & Figures* (updated Jan. 26, 2018), http://epi.publichealth.nc.gov/cd/rabies/figures.html. *See also* Martha Quillin, *Pets Are Vital Link in Battling Rabies*, NEWS & OBSERVER (Raleigh) (Mar. 17, 1996), at B1 (describing some of the history of the rabies outbreak in the early nineties).

70. G.S. 130A-201. Before declaring an emergency, the state health director must consult with the public health veterinarian (located in the N.C. Department of Health and Human Services) and the state agriculture veterinarian (located in the N.C. Department of Agriculture and Consumer Services).

71. The Wildlife Resources Commission has the authority to develop such plans pursuant to G.S. 113-291.2(a1).

Local Rabies Laws

Some local governments have chosen to adopt local ordinances and board of health rules addressing rabies.[72] Local governments do not have specific authority to regulate in this area, though elected bodies may rely on their general ordinance-making powers and boards of health upon their general rule-making authority.[73] As discussed in chapter 1, local laws should not (1) duplicate or contradict existing state laws related to rabies or (2) impose local penalties for violations of state law requirements. It may be appropriate to rely on local laws to supplement state law in some circumstances.[74] A local law could, for example, exempt cats or ferrets from the rabies tag requirement.

---

72. G.S. 130A-39 (boards of health); 153A-121 (county authority); 160A-174 (city authority).

73. A detailed discussion of ordinance and rule-making authority and limitations can be found in Chapter 1.

74. Cumberland County's ordinance, for example, explains that its rabies control provisions are designed "to supplement the state laws by providing a procedure for the enforcement of state laws relating to rabies control, in addition to the criminal penalties provided by the state." CUMBERLAND COUNTY, N.C., CODE OF ORDINANCES § 3-40(d). It is possible that a court could conclude that the state has "occupied the field" with respect to rabies, thus preempting any local regulation in this field. *See* Craig v. Cty. of Chatham, 356 N.C. 40 (2002) (holding that state law impliedly preempted local regulation of swine farm siting).

Appendix A. Relevant Sections of the North Carolina General Statutes (G.S.)

Article 1 [of G.S. Chapter 67].
Owner's Liability.

. . .

§ 67-4. Failing to kill mad dog.

If the owner of any dog shall know, or have good reason to believe, that his dog, or any dog belonging to any person under his control, has been bitten by a mad dog, and shall neglect or refuse immediately to kill the same, he shall forfeit and pay the sum of fifty dollars ($50.00) to him who will sue therefor; and the offender shall be liable to pay all damages which may be sustained by anyone, in his property or person, by the bite of any such dog, and shall be guilty of a Class 3 misdemeanor.

Article 2 [of G.S. Chapter 67].
License Taxes on Dogs.

. . .

§ 67-14. Mad dogs, dogs killing sheep, etc., may be killed.

Any person may kill any mad dog, and also any dog if he is killing sheep, cattle, hogs, goats, or poultry.

. . .

Article 6 [of G.S. Chapter 130A].
Communicable Diseases.

. . .

Part 6. Rabies.

§ 130A-184. Definitions.

The following definitions apply in this Part:

(1)   Animal Control Officer. – A city or county employee whose responsibility includes animal control. The term "Animal Control Officer" also includes agents of a private organization that is operating an animal shelter under contract with a city or county whenever those agents are performing animal control functions at the shelter.

(2)   Cat. – A domestic feline of the genus and species Felis catus.

(3)   Certified rabies vaccinator. – A person appointed and certified to administer rabies vaccine to animals in accordance with this Part.

(4)   Dog. – A domestic canine of the genus, species, and subspecies Canis lupus familiaris.

(4a)   Feral. – An animal that is not socialized.

(4b)   Ferret. – A domestic mammal of the genus, species, and subspecies Mustela putorius furo.

(5)   Rabies vaccine. – An animal rabies vaccine licensed by the United States Department of Agriculture and approved for use in this State by the Commission.

(6)   State Public Heath Veterinarian. – A person appointed by the Secretary to direct the State public health veterinary program.

(6a)   Stray. – An animal that meets both of the following conditions:
   a.   Is beyond the limits of confinement or lost.
   b.   Is not wearing any tags, microchips, tattoos, or other methods of identification.
(7)   Vaccination. – The administration of rabies vaccine by a person authorized to administer it under G.S. 130A-185.

§ 130A-185. Vaccination required.

(a)   Vaccination required. – The owner of an animal listed in this subsection over four months of age shall have the animal vaccinated against rabies:
   (1)   Cat.
   (2)   Dog.
   (3)   Ferret.
(b)   Vaccination. – Only animal rabies vaccine licensed by the United States Department of Agriculture and approved by the Commission shall be used on animals in this State. A rabies vaccine may only be administered by one or more of the following:
   (1)   A licensed veterinarian.
   (2)   A registered veterinary technician under the direct supervision of a licensed veterinarian.
   (3)   A certified rabies vaccinator.

§ 130A-186. Appointment and certification of certified rabies vaccinator.

In those counties where licensed veterinarians are not available to participate in all scheduled county rabies control clinics, the local health director shall appoint one or more persons for the purpose of administering rabies vaccine to animals in that county. Whether or not licensed veterinarians are available, the local health director may appoint one or more persons for the purpose of administering rabies vaccine to animals in their county and these persons will make themselves available to participate in the county rabies control program. The State Public Health Veterinarian shall provide at least four hours of training to those persons appointed by the local health director to administer rabies vaccine. Upon satisfactory completion of the training, the State Public Health Veterinarian shall certify in writing that the appointee has demonstrated a knowledge and procedure acceptable for the administration of rabies vaccine to animals. A certified rabies vaccinator shall be authorized to administer rabies vaccine to animals in the county until the appointment by the local health director has been terminated.

§ 130A-187. County rabies vaccination clinics.

(a)   Local Clinics. – The local health director shall organize or assist other county departments to organize at least one countywide rabies vaccination clinic per year for the purpose of vaccinating animals required to be vaccinated under this Part. Public notice of the time and place of rabies vaccination clinics shall be published in a newspaper having general circulation within the area.
(b)   Fee. – The county board of commissioners may establish a fee to be charged for a rabies vaccination given at a county rabies vaccination clinic. The fee amount may consist of the following:
   (1)   A charge for administering and storing the vaccine, not to exceed ten dollars ($10.00).
   (2)   The actual cost of the rabies vaccine, the vaccination certificate, and the rabies vaccination tag.

§ 130A-188

[Repealed by S.L. 2009-327, § 4, effective October 1, 2009.]

A person who administers a rabies vaccine shall complete a rabies vaccination certificate. The Commission shall adopt rules specifying the information that must be included on the certificate. An original rabies vaccination certificate shall be given to the owner of the animal that receives the rabies vaccine. A copy of the rabies vaccination certificate shall be retained by the licensed veterinarian or the certified rabies vaccinator. A copy shall also be given to the county agency responsible for animal control, provided the information given to the county agency shall not be used for commercial purposes.

§ 130A-190. Rabies vaccination tags.

(a)   Issuance. – A person who administers a rabies vaccine shall issue a rabies vaccination tag to the owner of the animal. The rabies vaccination tag shall show the year issued, a vaccination number, the words "North Carolina" or the initials "N.C." and the words "rabies vaccine." Dogs shall wear rabies vaccination tags at all times. Cats and ferrets must wear rabies vaccination tags unless they are exempt from wearing the tags by local ordinance.

(b)   Fee. – Rabies vaccination tags, links, and rivets may be obtained from the Department of Health and Human Services. The Secretary is authorized to collect a fee for the rabies tags, links, and rivets in accordance with this subsection. The fee for each tag is the sum of the following:

(1)   The actual cost of the rabies tag, links, and rivets.

(2)   Transportation costs.

(3)   Fifteen cents (15¢). This portion of the fee shall be used to fund rabies education and prevention programs.

(4)   [Repealed by S.L. 2010-31, § 11.4(h), effective October 1, 2010.]

(c)   [Repealed by S.L. 2007-487, § 1, effective January 1, 2008.]

§ 130A-191. Possession and distribution of rabies vaccine.

It shall be unlawful for persons other than licensed veterinarians, certified rabies vaccinators and persons engaged in the distribution of rabies vaccine to possess rabies vaccine. Persons engaged in the distribution of vaccines may distribute, sell and offer to sell rabies vaccine only to licensed veterinarians and certified rabies vaccinators.

§ 130A-192. Animals not wearing required rabies vaccination tags.

(a)   The Animal Control Officer shall canvass the county to determine if there are any animals not wearing the required rabies vaccination tag. If an animal required to wear a tag is found not wearing one, the Animal Control Officer shall check to see if the owner's identification can be found on the animal. If the animal is wearing an owner identification tag with information enabling the owner of the animal to be contacted, or if the Animal Control Officer otherwise knows who the owner is, the Animal Control Officer shall notify the owner in writing to have the animal vaccinated against rabies and to produce the required rabies vaccination certificate to the Animal Control Officer within three days of the notification. If the animal is not wearing an owner identification tag and the Animal Control Officer does not otherwise know who the owner is, the Animal Control Officer may impound the animal. The duration of the impoundment of these animals shall be established by the county board of commissioners, but the duration shall not be less than 72 hours. During the impoundment period, the Animal Control Officer shall make a reasonable effort to locate the owner of the animal. If the Animal Control Officer has access at no cost or at a reasonable cost to a microchip scanning device, the Animal Control Officer shall scan the animal and utilize any information that may be available through a microchip to locate the owner of the animal, if possible. If the animal is not reclaimed by its owner during the impoundment period, the animal shall be disposed of in one of the following manners: returned to the owner; adopted as a pet by a new owner; or put to death by a procedure approved by rules adopted by the Department of Agriculture and Consumer Services or, in the absence of such rules, by a procedure approved by the American Veterinary Medical Association, the Humane Society of the United States or of the American Humane Association.

(a1) Before an animal may be put to death, it shall be made available for adoption as provided in G.S. 19A32.1.

(a2) [Repealed by S.L. 2013-377, § 3, effective July 29, 2013.]

(a3) The Animal Control Officer shall maintain a record of all animals impounded under this section which shall include the date of impoundment, the length of impoundment, the method of disposal of the animal and the name of the person or institution to whom any animal has been released.

(b) through (e) [Repealed by S.L. 2013-377, § 3, effective July 29, 2013.]

§ 130A-93. Vaccination and confinement of animals brought into this State.

(a) Vaccination Required. – An animal brought into this State that is required to be vaccinated under this Part shall immediately be securely confined and shall be vaccinated against rabies within one week after entry. The animal shall remain confined for two weeks after vaccination.

(b) Exceptions. – The provisions of subsection (a) shall not apply to:

(1) An animal brought into this State for exhibition purposes if the animal is confined and not permitted to run at large.

(2) An animal brought into this State accompanied by a certificate issued by a licensed veterinarian showing that the animal is apparently free from and has not been exposed to rabies and that the animal is currently vaccinated against rabies.

§ 130A-194. Quarantine of districts infected with rabies.

An area may be declared under quarantine against rabies by the local health director when the disease exists to the extent that the lives of persons are endangered. When quarantine is declared, each animal in the area that is required to be vaccinated under this Part shall be confined on the premises of the owner or in a veterinary hospital unless the animal is on a leash or under the control and in the sight of a responsible adult.

§ 130A-195. Destroying stray or feral animals in quarantine districts.

When quarantine has been declared and stray or feral animals continue to run uncontrolled in the area, any peace officer or Animal Control Officer shall have the right, after reasonable effort has been made to apprehend the animals, to destroy the stray or feral animals and properly dispose of their bodies.

§ 130A-196. Notice and confinement of biting animals.

(a) Notice. – When a person has been bitten by an animal required to be vaccinated under this Part, the person or parent, guardian or person standing in loco parentis of the person, and the person owning the animal or in control or possession of the animal shall notify the local health director immediately and give the name and address of the person bitten and the owner of the animal. If the animal that bites a person is a stray or feral animal, the local agency responsible for animal control shall make a reasonable attempt to locate the owner of the animal. If the owner cannot be identified within 72 hours of the event, the local health director may authorize the animal be euthanized, and the head of the animal shall be immediately sent to the State Laboratory of Public Health for rabies diagnosis. If the event occurs on a weekend or State holiday the time period for owner identification shall be extended 24 hours.

A physician who attends a person bitten by an animal known to be a potential carrier of rabies shall report the incident within 24 hours to the local health director. The report must include the name, age, and sex of the person.

(b) Confinement. – When an animal required to be vaccinated under this Part bites a person, the animal shall be immediately confined for 10 days in a place designated by the local health director. The local health director may authorize a dog trained and used by a law enforcement agency to be released from confinement to perform official duties upon submission of proof that the dog has been vaccinated for rabies in compliance with this Part. After reviewing the circumstances of the particular case, the local health director may allow the owner to confine the animal on the owner's property. An owner who fails to confine an animal in accordance with the instructions of the local health director shall be guilty of a Class 2 misdemeanor. If the owner or the person who controls or possesses the animal that has bitten a person refuses to confine the animal as required by this subsection, the local health director may order seizure of the animal and its confinement for 10 days at the expense of the owner.

§ 130A-197. Management of dogs, cats, and ferrets exposed to rabies.

When the local health director reasonably suspects that an animal required to be vaccinated under this Part has been exposed to the saliva or nervous tissue of a proven rabid animal or animal reasonably suspected of having rabies that is not available for laboratory diagnosis, the animal shall be considered to have been exposed to rabies. The recommendations and guidelines for rabies post-exposure management specified by the National Association of State Public Health Veterinarians in the most current edition of the Compendium of Animal Rabies Prevention and Control shall be the required control measures.

§ 130A-198. Confinement.

A person who owns or has possession of an animal which is suspected of having rabies shall immediately notify the local health director or county Animal Control Officer and shall securely confine the animal in a place designated by the local health director. The animal shall be confined for a period of 10 days. Other animals may be destroyed at the discretion of the State Public Health Veterinarian.

§ 130A-199. Rabid animals to be destroyed; heads to be sent to State Laboratory of Public Health.

An animal diagnosed as having rabies by a licensed veterinarian shall be destroyed and its head sent to the State Laboratory of Public Health. The heads of all animals that die during a confinement period required by this Part shall be immediately sent to the State Laboratory of Public Health for rabies diagnosis.

§ 130A-200. Confinement or leashing of vicious animals.

A local health director may declare an animal to be vicious and a menace to the public health when the animal has attacked a person causing bodily harm without being teased, molested, provoked, beaten, tortured or otherwise harmed. When an animal has been declared to be vicious and a menace to the public health, the local health director shall order the animal to be confined to its owner's property. However, the animal may be permitted to leave its owner's property when accompanied by a responsible adult and restrained on a leash.

§ 130A-201. Rabies emergency.

A local health director in whose county or district rabies is found in the wild animal population as evidenced by a positive diagnosis of rabies in the past year in any wild animal, except a bat, may petition the State Health Director to declare a rabies emergency in the county or district. In determining whether a rabies emergency exists, the State Health Director shall consult with the Public Health Veterinarian and the State Agriculture Veterinarian and may consult with any other source of veterinary expertise the State Health Director deems advisable. Upon finding that a rabies emergency exists in a county or district, the State Health Director shall petition the Executive Director of the Wildlife Resources Commission to develop a plan pursuant to G.S. 113291.2(a1) to reduce the threat of rabies exposure to humans and domestic animals by foxes, raccoons, skunks, or bobcats in the county or district. Upon determination by the State Health Director that the rabies emergency no longer exists for a county or district, the State Health Director shall immediately notify the Executive Director of the Wildlife Resources Commission.

Article 3 [of G.S. Chapter 19A].
Animal Welfare Act.

. . .

§ 19A-32.1. Minimum holding period for animals in animal shelters; public viewing of animals in animal shelters; disposition of animals.

(a) Except as otherwise provided in this section, all animals received by an animal shelter or by an agent of an animal shelter shall be held for a minimum holding period of 72 hours, or for any longer minimum period established by a board of county commissioners, prior to being euthanized or otherwise disposed of.

(b) Before an animal may be euthanized or otherwise disposed of, it shall be made available for adoption under procedures that enable members of the public to inspect the animal, except in the following cases:

    (1) The animal has been found by the operator of the shelter to be unadoptable due to injury or defects of health or temperament.

    (2) The animal is seriously ill or injured, in which case the animal may be euthanized before the expiration of the minimum holding period if the manager of the animal shelter determines, in writing, that it is appropriate to do so. The writing shall include the reason for the determination.

    (3) The animal is being held as evidence in a pending criminal case.

(c) Except as otherwise provided in this subsection, a person who comes to an animal shelter attempting to locate a lost pet is entitled to view every animal held at the shelter, subject to rules providing for such viewing during at least four hours a day, three days a week. If the shelter is housing animals that must be kept apart from the general public for health reasons, public safety concerns, or in order to preserve evidence for criminal proceedings, the shelter shall make reasonable arrangements that allow pet owners to determine whether their lost pets are among those animals.

(d) During the minimum holding period, an animal shelter may place an animal it is holding into foster care by transferring possession of the animal to an approved foster care provider, an approved rescue organization, or the person who found the animal. If an animal shelter transfers possession of an animal under this subsection, at least one photograph depicting the head and face of the animal shall be displayed at the shelter in a conspicuous location that is available to the general public during hours of operation, and that photograph shall remain posted until the animal is disposed of as provided in subsection (f) of this section.

(e)   If a shelter places an animal in foster care, the shelter may, in writing, appoint the person or organization possessing the animal to be an agent of the shelter. After the expiration of the minimum holding period, the shelter may (i) direct the agent possessing the animal to return it to the shelter, (ii) allow the agent to adopt the animal consistent with the shelter's adoption policies, or (iii) extend the period of time that the agent holds the animal on behalf of the shelter. A shelter may terminate an agency created under this subsection at any time by directing the agent to deliver the animal to the shelter. The local government or organization operating the shelter, as principal in the agency relationship, shall not be liable to reimburse the agent for the costs of care of the animal and shall not be liable to the owner of the animal for harm to the animal caused by the agent, absent a written contract providing otherwise.

(f)   An animal that is surrendered to an animal shelter by the animal's owner and not reclaimed by that owner during the minimum holding period may be disposed of in one of the following manners:

  (1)   Returned to the owner.

  (2)   Adopted as a pet by a new owner.

  (3)   Euthanized by a procedure approved by rules adopted by the Department of Agriculture and Consumer Services or, in the absence of such rules, by a procedure approved by the American Veterinary Medical Association, the Humane Society of the United States, or the American Humane Association.

(g)   An animal that is surrendered to an animal shelter by the animal's owner may be disposed of before the expiration of the minimum holding period in a manner authorized under subsection (f) of this section if the owner provides to the shelter (i) some proof of ownership of the animal and (ii) a signed written consent to the disposition of the animal before the expiration of the minimum holding period.

(h)   If the owner of a dog surrenders the dog to an animal shelter, the owner shall state in writing whether the dog has bitten any individual within the 10 days preceding the date of surrender.

(i)   An animal shelter shall require every person to whom an animal is released to present one of the following valid forms of governmentissued photographic identification: (i) a drivers license, (ii) a special identification card issued under G.S. 20-37.7, (iii) a military identification card, or (iv) a passport. Upon presentation of the required photographic identification, the shelter shall document the name of the person, the type of photographic identification presented by the person, and the photographic identification number.

(j)   Animal shelters shall maintain a record of all animals impounded at the shelter, shall retain those records for a period of at least three years from the date of impoundment, and shall make those records available for inspection during regular inspections pursuant to this Article or upon the request of a representative of the Animal Welfare Section. These records shall contain, at a minimum:

  (1)   The date of impoundment.

  (2)   The length of impoundment.

  (3)   The disposition of each animal, including the name and address of any person to whom the animal is released, any institution that person represents, and the identifying information required under subsection (i) of this section.

  (4)   Other information required by rules adopted by the Board of Agriculture.

                              . . .

Appendix B. Relevant Regulations—North Carolina Administrative Code (hereinafter NCAC)

Title 10A, Chapter 41, Subchapter G
Veterinary Public Health
Section .0100 - Veterinary Public Health Program

10A NCAC 41G .0101   TIME OF RABIES VACCINATION

(a)   When rabies vaccine is administered by a certified rabies vaccinator to a dog or cat, the dog or cat shall be revaccinated annually.

(b)   When rabies vaccine is administered by a licensed veterinarian to a dog or cat, the dog or cat shall be revaccinated one year later and every three years thereafter, if a rabies vaccine licensed by the U.S. Department of Agriculture as a threeyear vaccine is used. Annual revaccination shall be required for all rabies vaccine used other than the U.S. Department of Agriculture threeyear vaccine. However, when a local board of health adopts a resolution stating that in order to control rabies and protect the public health annual vaccination is necessary within the area over which they have jurisdiction, then the dog or cat must be vaccinated annually regardless of the type vaccine used, until the resolution is repealed.

10A NCAC 41G .0102   FEES FOR RABIES TAGS, LINKS, AND RIVETS

[Repealed 2014.]

10A NCAC 41G .0103   APPROVED RABIES VACCINES

Any animal rabies vaccine licensed by the United States Department of Agriculture is approved for use on animals in North Carolina.

Chapter 6
Nuisance and At-Large Animals

Local animal control officials spend much of their time dealing with citizen complaints about nuisance animals and animals found wandering at large. Although a handful of narrowly tailored state laws address at-large animals, local animal officers' primary enforcement activities involve local nuisance ordinances. These ordinances vary tremendously in scope and in their level of detail; a few focus primarily on at-large animals and sanitation, while others define "nuisance" broadly to encompass a wide range of animal issues.

State Law

North Carolina has no statewide leash law or nuisance statute. The rabies law does provide a partial mechanism for addressing the issue of stray animals; as discussed in chapter 5, animal services officials may impound unidentified cats and dogs that are not wearing rabies tags.[1] If, however, the cat or dog at large is wearing its rabies tag, animal services officials have limited options under state law. One statute makes it a Class 3 misdemeanor to intentionally, knowingly, and willfully allow a dog over six months of age to run at large in the nighttime.[2] Several other narrowly worded state laws relate to specific nuisances and at-large animals.

- A person who owns or has possession of a female dog and knowingly permits the dog to run at large during estrus (i.e., "in heat" or "in season") may be charged with a Class 3 misdemeanor.[3]
- A person may be charged with a Class 3 misdemeanor if he or she (1) owns or keeps a dog that kills a domestic animal or person, (2) refuses to put the dog to death after being notified that satisfactory evidence of the dog's behavior has been presented to a district court judge, and (3) permits the dog to "go at liberty." In addition to defining the criminal charge, the law authorizes anyone finding the dog at large to kill it.[4]
- An owner or keeper whose dog, while off its home premises, kills or injures any livestock or fowl is liable for damages to the owner of the livestock or fowl.[5]
- If a dog is found unmuzzled and running at large in a wildlife refuge, sanctuary, or management area, wildlife officials may seize and impound the dog.[6] They are also authorized to destroy humanely any dog found tracking, running,

---

1. Chapter 130A, Section 192 of the North Carolina General Statutes (hereinafter G.S.).
2. G.S. 67-12.
3. G.S. 67-2.
4. G.S. 67-3.
5. G.S. 67-1.
6. G.S. 67-14.1(b).

injuring, or killing a deer or bear during a season in which hunting with dogs is prohibited.[7]

Though there is no statewide nuisance statute, North Carolina does recognize the common law tort of nuisance. Additionally, the common law tort of trespass by an animal or the common law tort of negligence may be applicable to some situations involving at-large animals.[8] Because the primary focus of this book is animal services law relevant to local governments, the private causes of action in tort for private nuisance, public nuisance, trespass, and negligence are not discussed in great detail here. The brief discussion that follows is meant simply to make local government actors aware of the private causes of action applicable to nuisance and at-large animals, regardless of a particular jurisdiction's local ordinance.

The common law tort of nuisance encompasses distinct causes of action based upon two classifications of nuisances: private nuisances and public nuisances.[9] Depending on the circumstances, animals may behave in such a manner as to constitute either type of nuisance.[10] "A private nuisance is defined as any substantial invasion of a person's interest in the private use and enjoyment of his land by any type of liability-forming conduct, not including trespass."[11] Though there is little North Carolina case law on the issue, courts in other states have found that at-large animals may constitute an actionable private nuisance.[12] Courts in other states also have found that animals may constitute an actionable private nuisance by other behavior, even when the behavior takes place on the animal owner's property; persistent barking of dogs is a common example.[13] Without regard to the existence of a local ordinance or a state nuisance statute, a person may initiate a common law private nuisance action against an animal owner as a civil lawsuit.

---

7. G.S. 67-14.1(a).

8. For more information on private causes of action, see JOHN I. LAZAR, ANIMAL CONTROL LAW 1988 SUPPLEMENT: CIVIL LIABILITY FOR THE MISDEEDS OF ANIMALS 9 (1989); ANN McCOLL, 1990 UPDATE TO ANIMAL CONTROL LAW FOR NORTH CAROLINA LOCAL GOVERNMENTS AND ANIMAL CONTROL LAW 1988 SUPPLEMENT: CIVIL LIABILITY FOR THE MISDEEDS OF ANIMALS 14 (1991); CHARLES E. DAYE & MARK W. MORRIS, NORTH CAROLINA LAW OF TORTS (3d ed. 2012).

9. See DAYE & MORRIS, supra note 8, at ch. 25.

10. See Mowery v. Salisbury, 82 N.C. 175, 177 (1880) (recognizing that dogs "may become nuisances in cities and populous towns if permitted without restraint to roam the streets").

11. DAYE & MORRIS, supra note 8, at § 25.20 (footnote omitted).

12. See, e.g., Wallace v. Grasso, 119 S.W.3d 567, 580 (Mo. Ct. App. 2003) (finding that defendant's failure to contain his dogs constituted a private nuisance because it interfered with the private use and enjoyment of neighbor plaintiff's property).

13. See, e.g., Tichenor v. Vore, 953 S.W.2d 171, 177–78 (Mo. Ct. App. 1997) (defendant's maintenance of dog kennel on his property to house his show dogs was private nuisance because of consistent barking that disturbed neighbors).

The law has long contemplated that animals may behave in such a manner as to constitute a public nuisance.[14] Indeed, this fact serves as one basis for local governments' authority to regulate animals through ordinance, a topic discussed in more detail below. "A public nuisance is any act or condition that disrupts public order, obstructs public rights, or undermines public morals or decency."[15] As with private nuisances, regardless of whether an applicable ordinance or state statute exists, in appropriate circumstances a person may initiate a common law public nuisance action against an animal owner as a civil lawsuit.

North Carolina cases recognize that a traditional negligence action may be prosecuted against an animal owner in situations where an animal has caused physical injury or property damage, and many of these situations involve at-large animals.[16] As a general proposition, "[i]t is the legal duty of a person having charge of animals to exercise ordinary care and the foresight of a prudent person in keeping them in restraint."[17] Additionally, "[t]he owner of a domestic animal is chargeable with knowledge of the general propensities of certain animals and he must exercise due care to prevent injury from reasonably anticipated conduct."[18] Of course, different animals have different propensities[19] and, consequently, the degree to which an owner must restrain an animal in order to exercise due care to prevent injury to others varies depending on the circumstances.[20] Many North Carolina cases based on a traditional negligence claim involve situations where an at-large animal has caused a motor vehicle wreck; such cases have been brought against dog owners as well as owners of larger domestic animals.[21]

---

14. *See, e.g.*, Perry v. Phipps, 32 N.C. 259 (1849) (recognizing that dogs may be a public nuisance in certain circumstances).

15. Daye & Morris, *supra* note 8, at § 25.20 (footnote omitted).

16. *See* Gardner v. Black, 217 N.C. 573 (1940) (stating that ordinary principles of negligence apply to situations where an at-large animal causes damages).

17. *Id*. at 576; 2 Am. Jur. 2d *Animals*, § 62 (1962).

18. Griner v. Smith, 43 N.C. App. 400, 407 (1979).

19. *Cf.* Williams v. Tysinger, 328 N.C. 55, 60 (1991) (stating that the general propensities of horses are such that they are capable of inflicting serious injury upon persons by ordinary behavior).

20. As an illustration of this notion, consider the case of *Hunnicutt v. Lundberg*, 94 N.C. App. 210, 212 (1989). *Hunnicutt* involved a situation where the defendant's small dogs caused an injury to her neighbor, and the neighbor sued for personal injury alleging that the defendant breached her duty to control the dogs. The court of appeals acknowledged that the defendant had a legal duty to control her dogs but concluded that she was properly performing that duty at the time of the incident because she had the dogs on leashes and had successfully used the leashes along with verbal commands to control the dogs in the past.

21. *See, e.g.*, Sink v. Moore, 67 N.C. 344 (1966) (wreck involving car, bicyclist, and dog); Herndon v. Allen, 253 N.C. 271 (1960) (wreck involving mule and tractor-trailer).

The common law tort of trespass by an animal is recognized in North Carolina and may be applicable to some situations involving at-large animals.[22] It appears that dogs and cats are afforded more leeway than other animals to trespass of their own volition onto the property of a person who is not their owner. Notably, the North Carolina Supreme Court has stated as follows with respect to dogs:

> [B]y natural instinct and habit an ordinary dog of most breeds is inclined to roam around and stray at times from its immediate habitat without causing injury or doing damage to persons or property. And in deference to this natural instinct of dogs the processes of the early common law eschewed the idea of requiring that they be kept shut up, and instead . . . allowed a reputable dog a modicum of liberty to follow his roaming instincts without imposing liability on its master.[23]

Other animals apparently are afforded less leeway to trespass of their own volition onto property that does not belong to their owner.[24] Despite the leeway afforded to dogs and cats, if a person intentionally or knowingly causes a dog or cat to trespass on the lands of another, the person may be liable for damages caused by the animal.[25] In addition, local ordinances may impose a greater duty upon dog or cat owners to prevent their animals from trespassing.

Local Ordinances

Many jurisdictions have adopted ordinances governing nuisance animals and animals found running at large. As discussed in more detail in chapter 1, cities and counties may rely on three sources of statutory authority for these laws. First, both levels of local government have broad police powers that give them the authority to adopt ordinances to "define, prohibit, regulate, or abate acts, omissions, or conditions detrimental to the health, safety or welfare of [their] citizens and the peace and dignity" of the city or county and to "define and abate nuisances."[26] Second, both have the authority to "regulate, restrict, or prohibit the possession or harboring . . . of animals which are dangerous to persons or property."[27] Finally, cities have specific authority to "regulate, restrict, or prohibit the keeping, running, or going at-large of any domestic animals, including dogs and cats."[28] By relying on this combination of statutes, local governments

---

22. *See generally* DAYE & MORRIS, *supra* note 8, at § 20.30.

23. Pegg v. Gray, 240 N.C. 548, 551 (1954).

24. *See* DAYE & MORRIS, *supra* note 8, at § 20.30.

25. *Id. See also Pegg*, 240 N.C. 548.

26. G.S. 153A-121(a) (counties); 160A-174(a) (cities).

27. G.S. 153A-131 (counties); 160A-187 (cities).

28. G.S. 160A-186.

have been able to regulate many animal-related nuisances within their jurisdictions using ordinances that directly address the topic at hand.[29]

Some types of nuisances may be creatively addressed through other types of ordinances. For example, some jurisdictions rely on zoning ordinances to restrict the number of animals allowed in residential areas,[30] and some jurisdictions rely on ordinances regarding municipal recreation facilities to regulate the behavior of animals at parks or other such facilities.[31]

As discussed above, the term "public nuisance" is commonly understood to mean a behavior or condition that unreasonably interferes with rights common to the general public. Rather than rely on this general legal concept, most ordinances include a definition or application of the given nuisance that is more specifically focused on animals. Many ordinances address such commonly encountered animal behaviors as

- running at large;
- barking, howling, or making other noises;
- chasing or snapping at people or vehicles;
- turning over garbage receptacles; and
- damaging real or personal property.[32]

Some nuisance ordinances also concern the care and keeping of animals,[33] addressing conduct such as

- keeping animals too close to a right-of-way;
- housing animals in unsanitary conditions;
- failing to confine a female animal in estrus;
- failing to remove animal feces from public or private property; and
- keeping certain types of animals, such as poultry and livestock, within city limits.

With some exceptions, local animal nuisance ordinances across the state promote similar policy goals and use comparable language. Some variation occurs, though, with

---

29. *See* State v. Harrell, 203 N.C. 210 (1932) (recognizing that municipalities have the authority to regulate dogs pursuant to their general police powers).

30. *See, e.g.,* CUMBERLAND COUNTY, N.C., ZONING ORDINANCE § 912 (restricting kennel operations in residential districts); *id.* § 203 (defining "kennel" as a premises where four or more adult dogs are kept commercially or as pets, subject to limited exceptions).

31. *See, e.g.,* CITY OF STATESVILLE, N.C., CODE OF ORDINANCES § 15-27 (prohibiting owners from allowing dogs to run at large within city recreation facilities).

32. *See, e.g.,* NEW HANOVER COUNTY, N.C., CODE OF ORDINANCES § 5-4 (specifically defining "public nuisance" to include such behaviors by way of example); *id.* § 5-32 (prohibiting such behaviors because they constitute "reasonable public nuisance complaints").

33. *See, e.g.,* GUILFORD COUNTY, N.C., CODE OF ORDINANCES § 5-10 (making it unlawful to "own, keep, possess or maintain an animal in such a manner as to constitute a public nuisance" and listing examples of manners of care and keeping that constitute a public nuisance).

respect to noise and sanitation issues. A number of animal noise ordinances include general prohibitions on "excessive," "continuous," or "untimely" barking, while others are more specific.

- Sanford's ordinance prohibits "[h]owling, barking, . . . or making other loud sounds or noises continuously for a period of ten minutes or more, or intermittently for one-half hour or more, at any time with the noise or sound disturbing the quiet comfort, repose, or health of a reasonable individual of normal sensitivities."[34]
- Cary's ordinance prohibits allowing an animal to make an "annoying sound" that interferes with the reasonable use and enjoyment of neighboring premises and deems any sound made by a cat or dog "which is made for more than 15 minutes during any thirty minute period" to be an "annoying sound."[35]
- Winston-Salem's ordinance governs dogs "which habitually and regularly bark, howl or whine for at least 15 minutes so as to result in serious annoyance to neighboring residents and [so] as to interfere with the reasonable use and enjoyment of the premises occupied by such residents."[36]

With respect to sanitation, or "pooper scooper," ordinances, jurisdictions typically take one of two approaches. They either establish a general prohibition on "soiling" or "defiling" private or public property[37] or specifically require the animal's custodian to remove feces deposited on public or private property unless the property owner has given permission for it to remain.[38] One jurisdiction, Apex, struggled with the enforcement of such an ordinance and adopted a slightly different approach. It requires the removal of feces but also requires that

> [a]ny person, while harboring, walking, in possession of or in charge of a dog on public property, public park property, public right-of-way or any private property without the permission of the private property owner, shall have in his or her possession a bag or other container that closes, which is suitable for removing feces deposited by the dog.[39]

By requiring the custodian of the animal to have a bag or other container, the ordinance eliminates the need to either "catch the dog in the act" or find witnesses who did.

---

34. City of Sanford, N.C., Code of Ordinances § 4-40(a)(4).

35. City of Cary, N.C., Code of Ordinances § 6-71(8).

36. City of Winston-Salem, N.C., Code of Ordinances § 6-9.

37. *See, e.g.,* Forsyth County, N.C., Code of Ordinances § 6-1; City of Brevard, N.C., Code of Ordinances § 14-1; Town of Surf City, N.C., Code of Ordinances § 3-1.

38. *See, e.g.,* Town of Garner, N.C., Code of Ordinances § 3-15(b)(6); City of Rocky Mount, N.C., Code of Ordinances §§ 4-22(a)(4), (5).

39. Town of Apex, N.C., Code of Ordinances § 4-1(b).

Just as with other types of ordinances, ordinances addressing animal-related nuisances and animals going at large sometimes are challenged by citizens who are opposed to or feel aggrieved by the ordinances. The general discussion of challenges to ordinances in Chapter 1 includes several examples of cases involving ordinances targeting nuisances and animals going at large. For purposes of the current discussion, it is worth noting that the court of appeals has upheld an ordinance prohibiting the keeping of a dog that conducts itself so as to be a public nuisance,[40] an ordinance that prohibited the keeping of an animal that makes excessive annoying noise,[41] and an ordinance that prohibited allowing dogs to run at large.[42] Refer to Chapter 1 for a fuller discussion of this issue.

Livestock Found At Large

It is a crime to allow livestock to run at large in North Carolina, with the exception of certain horses on the Outer Banks.[43] State law allows *any person*, including local governments, to impound livestock found at large,[44] though no state law requires that a person or local government do so. If the animal is impounded, the impounder must take steps to either locate the owner to return the animal or sell it at auction. There are several requirements that apply and procedures that must be followed in these situations.

The statutory definition of the term "livestock" includes, but is not limited to, equine animals, bovine animals, sheep, goats, llamas, and swine.[45] While the definition does not provide an exhaustive list of the types of animals that are considered livestock, the term most likely does not include poultry because a different statute specifically addresses poultry running at large.[46]

If a local government or person decides to impound livestock found running at large, the impounder must provide the animal with "a reasonably adequate quantity of good and wholesome feed and water."[47] Failure to do so constitutes a Class 3 misdemeanor.[48] The impounder is allowed to recover from the owner the reasonable costs of impounding and maintaining the animal, as well as damages to the impounder caused by the animal.[49] If an impounded animal is *not* receiving adequate food and water for

---

40. Gray v. Clark, 9 N.C. App. 319, 321 (1970).
41. State v. Taylor, 128 N.C. App. 616, 618 (1998).
42. State v. Pharo, 28 N.C. App. 171, 174 (1975).
43. G.S. 68-16; 68-42.
44. G.S. 68-17.
45. G.S. 68-15.
46. G.S. 68-25 (addressing poultry at large).
47. G.S. 68-22.
48. *Id.*
49. G.S. 68-17.

more than twenty-four hours, any person is authorized by law to enter the property to provide the animal with feed and water.[50] That person is allowed to recover from the owner any costs incurred and may not be charged with trespass.[51] Any person who willfully releases an impounded animal without the impounder's permission, or who receives an animal knowing that it was unlawfully released, may be charged with a Class 3 misdemeanor.[52]

If the impounder knows who owns the animal, the impounder has a legal duty to notify the owner immediately. The notice must include details regarding the expenses incurred for the impoundment and compensation required for damage caused by the animal, if any.[53] If the owner and the impounder cannot agree on the amount of money owed, there is an interesting and somewhat old-fashioned process set out in the General Statutes that allows "three disinterested landowners" to determine the amount owed.[54] If a majority of those three are not able to agree, the clerk of superior court is required to appoint a referee to decide the matter.[55]

If the owner does not redeem the animal within three days of either (1) receiving notice or (2) the final determination of how much is owed (as decided by the three landowners or by a referee), the impounder may begin the process of auctioning off the animal.[56] The first step in the process is to notify the sheriff's office in the county where the animal was found so that it can post a notice of sale on its website. The notice must describe the animal and specify the place, date, and hour of sale. Ten days after the notice is posted, the impounder may sell the animal at public auction.[57] The proceeds from the auction may be used to cover the "reasonable costs" incurred in caring for the animal and also to compensate the impounder for any damages it may have caused. Any balance must be paid to the owner.

If, at the time of impoundment, the impounder does not know who owns the animal, the impounder must provide notice of impoundment to the sheriff.[58] The notice must provide a full description of the animal, including all marks or brands, and specify when and where the animal was found.[59] The law does not require the sheriff to post this notice on its website or in any other place, but it seems that it would be reasonable and appropriate to do so.

---

50. G.S. 68-23.
51. *Id.*
52. G.S. 68-21.
53. G.S. 68-18.
54. G.S. 68-19.
55. *Id.*
56. G.S. 68-20.
57. *Id.*
58. G.S. 68-18.1.
59. *Id.*

If the owner does not come forward to claim the animal three days after the sheriff's office is notified of the impoundment, the impounder then asks the sheriff's office to post a notice of sale on its website. Ten days after the notice is posted, the impounder is allowed to sell the animal at public auction. After the impounder is reimbursed for reasonable costs incurred and compensated for any damage caused, the law requires that any balance be directed to the "school fund" for the county in which the animal was found.[60]

The law is silent about how the impounder should proceed if the auction is unsuccessful. Some local governments enlist foster homes to assist in caring for the animal or adopt it out to rescue organizations, who then care for the animal and may be able to find it a new home. The cost of maintaining the animal for an extended period can be significant, so local governments have a strong incentive to transfer the animal as quickly as possible.

Conclusion

While state statutory law governing animal-related nuisances is sparse, local governments have expansive authority to address such concerns via ordinance. Courts are likely to uphold such ordinances as long as the government is able to point to specific statutory authority, such as the authority granted to cities to regulate domestic animals, and articulate a rational reason why the law is an appropriate exercise of the government's police power.

---

60. The term "school fund" is antiquated and the allocation of funds to schools is a complicated subject that is beyond the scope of this book. In a situation where a balance remains after the proceeds of an auction have been distributed to the impounder and the owner, the county finance officer should be contacted for guidance about how to dispose of the balance in accordance with the spirit of the law. *Cf.* Kara Millonzi, *Locally-Collected Fines & Penalties: Calculating and Distributing Clear Proceeds*, COATES' CANONS: NC LOC. GOV'T L. blog (UNC School of Government, Dec. 8, 2011), https://canons.sog.unc.edu/locally-collected-fines-penalties-calculating-and-distributing-clear-proceeds/ (discussing the distribution of the proceeds of certain fines and penalties to public school systems).

Appendix. Relevant Sections of the North Carolina General Statutes (G.S.)

Article 1 [of G.S. Chapter 67].
Owner's Liability.

§ 67-1. Liability for injury to livestock or fowls.

If any dog, not being at the time on the premises of the owner or person having charge thereof, shall kill or injure any livestock or fowls, the owner or person having such dog in charge shall be liable for damages sustained by the injury, killing, or maiming of any livestock, and costs of suit.

§ 67-2. Permitting bitch at large.

If any person owning or having any bitch shall knowingly permit her to run at large during the erotic stage of copulation he shall be guilty of a Class 3 misdemeanor.

§ 67-3. Sheep-killing dogs to be killed.

If any person owning or having any dog that kills sheep or other domestic animals, or that kills a human being, upon satisfactory evidence of the same being made before any judge of the district court in the county, and the owner duly notified thereof, shall refuse to kill it, and shall permit such dog to go at liberty, he shall be guilty of a Class 3 misdemeanor, and the dog may be killed by anyone if found going at large.

. . .

Article 2 [of G.S. Chapter 67].
License Taxes on Dogs.

. . .

§ 67-12. Permitting dogs to run at large at night; penalty; liability for damage.

No person shall allow his dog over six months old to run at large in the nighttime unaccompanied by the owner or by some member of the owner's family, or some other person by the owner's permission. Any person intentionally, knowingly, and willfully violating this section shall be guilty of a Class 3 misdemeanor, and shall also be liable in damages to any person injured or suffering loss to his property or chattels.

. . .

§ 67-14.1. Dogs injuring deer or bear on wildlife management area may be killed; impounding unmuzzled dogs running at large.

(a) Any dog which trails, runs, injures or kills any deer or bear on any wildlife refuge, sanctuary or management area, now or hereafter so designated and managed by the Wildlife Resources Commission, during the closed season for hunting with dogs on such refuge or management area, is hereby declared to be a public nuisance, and any wildlife protector or other duly authorized agent or employee of the Wildlife Resources Commission may destroy, by humane method, any dog discovered trailing, running, injuring or killing any deer or bear in any such area during the closed season therein for hunting such game with dogs, without incurring liability by reason of his act in conformity with this section.

(b)   Any unmuzzled dog running at large upon any wildlife refuge, sanctuary, or management area, when unaccompanied by any person having such dog in charge, shall be seized and impounded by any wildlife protector, or other duly authorized agent or employee of the Wildlife Resources Commission.

(c)   The person impounding such dog shall cause a notice to be published at least once a week for two successive weeks in some newspaper published in the county wherein the dog was taken, or if none is published therein, in some newspaper having general circulation in the county. Such notice shall set forth a description of the dog, the place where it is impounded, and that the dog will be destroyed if not claimed and payment made for the advertisement, a catch fee of one dollar ($1.00) and the boarding, computed at the rate of fifty cents (50¢) per day, while impounded, by a certain date which date shall be not less than 15 days after the publication of the first notice. A similar notice shall be posted at the courthouse door.

(d)   The owner of the dog, or his agent, may recover such dog upon payment of the cost of the publication of the notices hereinbefore described together with a catch fee of one dollar ($1.00) and the expense, computed at the rate of fifty cents (50¢) per day, incurred while impounding and boarding the dog.

(e)   If any impounded dog is not recovered by the owner within 15 days after the publication of the first notice of the impounding, the dog may be destroyed in a humane manner by any wildlife protector or other duly authorized agent or employee of the North Carolina Wildlife Resources Commission, and no liability shall attach to any person acting in accordance with this section.

. . .

Article 6 [of G.S. Chapter 130A].
Communicable Diseases.

. . .

§ 130A-192. Animals not wearing required rabies vaccination tags.

(a)   The Animal Control Officer shall canvass the county to determine if there are any animals not wearing the required rabies vaccination tag. If an animal required to wear a tag is found not wearing one, the Animal Control Officer shall check to see if the owner's identification can be found on the animal. If the animal is wearing an owner identification tag with information enabling the owner of the animal to be contacted, or if the Animal Control Officer otherwise knows who the owner is, the Animal Control Officer shall notify the owner in writing to have the animal vaccinated against rabies and to produce the required rabies vaccination certificate to the Animal Control Officer within three days of the notification. If the animal is not wearing an owner identification tag and the Animal Control Officer does not otherwise know who the owner is, the Animal Control Officer may impound the animal. The duration of the impoundment of these animals shall be established by the county board of commissioners, but the duration shall not be less than 72 hours. During the impoundment period, the Animal Control Officer shall make a reasonable effort to locate the owner of the animal. If the Animal Control Officer has access at no cost or at a reasonable cost to a microchip scanning device, the Animal Control Officer shall scan the animal and utilize any information that may be available through a microchip to locate the owner of the animal, if possible. If the animal is not reclaimed by its owner during the impoundment period, the animal shall be disposed of in one of the following manners: returned to the owner; adopted as a pet by a new owner; or put to death by a procedure approved by rules adopted by the Department of Agriculture and Consumer Services or, in the absence of such rules, by a procedure approved by the American Veterinary Medical Association, the Humane Society of the United States or of the American Humane Association.

(a1)   Before an animal may be put to death, it shall be made available for adoption as provided in G.S. 19A-32.1.

(a2)   Repealed by Session Laws 2013-377, s. 3, effective July 29, 2013.

(a3)   The Animal Control Officer shall maintain a record of all animals impounded under this section which shall include the date of impoundment, the length of impoundment, the method of disposal of the animal and the name of the person or institution to whom any animal has been released.

(b) through (e) [Repealed by S.L. 2013-377, § 3, effective July 29, 2013.]

. . .

Article 6 [of G.S. Chapter 153A].
Delegation and Exercise of the General Police Power.

. . .

§ 153A-121. General ordinance-making power.

(a)   A county may by ordinance define, regulate, prohibit, or abate acts, omissions, or conditions detrimental to the health, safety, or welfare of its citizens and the peace and dignity of the county; and may define and abate nuisances.

(b)   This section does not authorize a county to regulate or control vehicular or pedestrian traffic on a street or highway under the control of the Board of Transportation, nor to regulate or control any right-of-way or right-of-passage belonging to a public utility, electric or telephone membership corporation, or public agency of the State. In addition, no county ordinance may regulate or control a highway right-of-way in a manner inconsistent with State law or an ordinance of the Board of Transportation.

(c)   This section does not impair the authority of local boards of health to adopt rules and regulations to protect and promote public health.

. . .

§ 153A-131. Possession or harboring of dangerous animals.

A county may by ordinance regulate, restrict, or prohibit the possession or harboring of animals which are dangerous to persons or property. No such ordinance shall have the effect of permitting any activity or condition with respect to a wild animal which is prohibited or more severely restricted by regulations of the Wildlife Resources Commission.

. . .

Article 8 [of G.S. Chapter 160A].
Delegation and Exercise of the General Police Power.

. . .

§ 160A-174. General ordinance-making power.

(a)   A city may by ordinance define, prohibit, regulate, or abate acts, omissions, or conditions, detrimental to the health, safety, or welfare of its citizens and the peace and dignity of the city, and may define and abate nuisances.

(b)   A city ordinance shall be consistent with the Constitution and laws of North Carolina and of the United States. An ordinance is not consistent with State or federal law when:

    (1)   The ordinance infringes a liberty guaranteed to the people by the State or federal Constitution;

    (2)   The ordinance makes unlawful an act, omission or condition which is expressly made lawful by State or federal law;

    (3)   The ordinance makes lawful an act, omission, or condition which is expressly made unlawful by State or federal law;

    (4)   The ordinance purports to regulate a subject that cities are expressly forbidden to regulate by State or federal law;

    (5)   The ordinance purports to regulate a field for which a State or federal statute clearly shows a legislative intent to provide a complete and integrated regulatory scheme to the exclusion of local regulation;

    (6)   The elements of an offense defined by a city ordinance are identical to the elements of an offense defined by State or federal law.

The fact that a State or federal law, standing alone, makes a given act, omission, or condition unlawful shall not preclude city ordinances requiring a higher standard of conduct or condition.

. . .

§ 160A-186. Regulation of domestic animals.

A city may by ordinance regulate, restrict, or prohibit the keeping, running, or going at large of any domestic animals, including dogs and cats. The ordinance may provide that animals allowed to run at large in violation of the ordinance may be seized and sold or destroyed after reasonable efforts to notify their owner.

. . .

§ 160A-187. Possession or harboring of dangerous animals.

A city may by ordinance regulate, restrict, or prohibit the possession or harboring within the city of animals which are dangerous to persons or property. No such ordinance shall have the effect of permitting any activity or condition with respect to a wild animal which is prohibited or more severely restricted by regulations of the Wildlife Resources Commission.

. . .

Article 3 [of G.S. Chapter 68].
Livestock Law.

§ 68-15. Term "livestock" defined.

The word "livestock" in this Chapter shall include, but shall not be limited to, equine animals, bovine animals, sheep, goats, llamas, and swine.

§ 68-16. Allowing livestock to run at large forbidden.

If any person shall allow his livestock to run at large, he shall be guilty of a Class 3 misdemeanor.

§ 68-17. Impounding livestock at large; right to recover costs and damages; abandoned livestock.

(a) Any person may take up any livestock running at large or straying and impound the same; and such impounder may recover from the owner the reasonable costs of impounding and maintaining the livestock as well as damages to the impounder caused by such livestock, and may retain the livestock, with the right to use with proper care until such recovery is had. Reasonable costs of impounding shall include any fees paid pursuant to G.S. 68-18.1 in order to locate the owner.

(b) Livestock is deemed to be abandoned when (i) it is placed in the custody of any other person for treatment, boarding, or care; (ii) the owner of the livestock does not retake custody of the animal within two months after the last day the owner paid a fee to the custodian for the treatment, boarding, or care of the livestock; and (iii) the custodian has made reasonable attempts to collect any past-due fees during the two-month period. If, after the end of the Senate Bill 615 Session Law 2017-108 Page 3 two-month period, the custodian of the abandoned livestock has been unsuccessful in collecting the past-due fees and the owner of the livestock has not retaken custody of the livestock, the custodian may sell or transfer the livestock by executing an affidavit that identifies the buyer or transferee of the livestock and certifies compliance with the criteria and requirements of this subsection. If the custodian is unable to sell or transfer the livestock, the custodian may, but shall not be required to, otherwise humanely dispose of the abandoned livestock. A custodian shall provide written notice of the provisions of this subsection in conspicuous type to the owner of livestock at the time the livestock is delivered for treatment, boarding, or care as follows: "Pursuant to N.C. General Statutes § 68-17(b), the owner of this facility is entitled to sell, transfer, or otherwise humanely dispose of any livestock abandoned at this facility."

§ 68-18. Notice and demand when owner known.

If the owner of impounded livestock is or becomes known to the impounder, actual notice of the whereabouts of the impounded livestock must be immediately given to the owner and the impounder must then make demand upon the owner of the livestock for the costs of impoundment and the damages to the impounder, if any, caused by such livestock.

§ 68-18.1. Notice when owner not known.

If the owner of the impounded livestock is not known or cannot be found, the impounder shall inform the sheriff of the county in which the livestock was found of the impoundment, giving a full description of the livestock impounded, including all marks or brands on the livestock, and shall state when and where the animal was taken up.

§ 68-19. Determination of damages by selected landowners or by referee.

If the owner and impounder cannot agree as to the cost of impounding and maintaining such livestock, as well as damages to the impounder caused by such livestock running at large, then such costs and damages shall be determined by three disinterested landowners, one to be selected by the owner of the livestock, one to be selected by the impounder and a third to be selected by the first two. If within 10 days a majority of the landowners so selected cannot agree, or if the owner of the livestock or the impounder fails to make his selection, or if the two selected fail to select a third, then the clerk of superior court of the county where the livestock is impounded shall select a referee. The determination of such costs and damages by the landowners or by the referee shall be final.

§ 68-20. Notice of sale and sale where owner fails to redeem or is unknown; application of proceeds.

If the owner fails to redeem his livestock within three days after the notice and demand as provided in G.S. 68-18 is received or within three days after the determination of the costs and damages as provided in G.S. 68-19, the impounder shall notify the local Sheriff's office and the Sheriff shall post a notice fully describing the livestock and stating the place, date, and hour of sale on the Web site of the Sheriff's department. After 10 days from such posting, the impounder shall sell the livestock at public auction. If the owner of the livestock remains unknown to the impounder, then, three days after publication of the notice required by G.S. 68-18.1, the impounder shall notify the local Sheriff's office and the Sheriff shall post a notice fully describing the livestock and stating the place, date, and hour of sale on the Web site of the Sheriff's department. After 10 days from such posting, the impounder shall sell the livestock at public auction. The proceeds of any such public sale shall be applied to pay the reasonable costs of impounding and maintaining the livestock and the damages to the impounder caused by the livestock. Reasonable costs of impounding shall include any fees paid pursuant to G.S. 68-18.1 in an attempt to locate the owner of the livestock. The balance, if any, shall be paid to the owner of the livestock, if known, or, if the owner is not known, then to the school fund of the county where the livestock was impounded.

§ 68-21. Illegally releasing or receiving impounded livestock misdemeanor.

If any person willfully releases any lawfully impounded livestock without the permission of the impounder or receives such livestock knowing that it was unlawfully released, he shall be guilty of a Class 3 misdemeanor.

§ 68-22. Impounded livestock to be fed and watered.

If any person shall impound or cause to be impounded any livestock and shall fail to supply to the livestock during the confinement a reasonably adequate quantity of good and wholesome feed and water, he shall be guilty of a Class 3 misdemeanor.

§ 68-23. Right to feed impounded livestock; owner liable.

When any livestock is impounded under the provisions of this Chapter and remains without reasonably adequate feed and water for more than 24 hours, any person may lawfully enter the area of impoundment to supply the livestock with feed and water. Such person shall not be liable in trespass for such entry and may recover of the owner or, if the owner is unknown, of the impounder of the livestock, the reasonable costs of the feed and water.

§ 68-24. Penalties for violation of this Article.

A violation of G.S. 68-16, 68-21 or 68-22 is a Class 3 misdemeanor.

§ 68-25. Domestic fowls running at large after notice.

(a)   If any person shall permit any turkeys, geese, chickens, ducks or other domestic fowls to run at large on the lands of any other person while such lands are under cultivation in any kind of grain or feedstuff or while being used for gardens or ornamental purposes, after having received actual or constructive notice of such running at large, the person is guilty of a Class 3 misdemeanor.

(b)   If any person permits any domestic fowls to run at large on the lands of a commercial poultry operation of any other person after having received actual or constructive notice of such running at large, the person is guilty of a Class 3 misdemeanor. For purposes of this subsection, a commercial poultry operation means any premises or operation where domestic poultry are fed, caged, housed, or otherwise kept for meat or egg production until sold or marketed.

(b1) [Repealed by S.L. 2011-412, § 3.1, effective October 15, 2011.]

(c) If it shall appear to any magistrate that after three days' notice any person persists in allowing his fowls to run at large in violation of this section and fails or refuses to keep them upon his own premises, then the said magistrate may, in his discretion, order any sheriff or other officer to kill the fowls when they are running at large as herein provided.

§ 68-42. Stock running at large prohibited; certain ponies excepted

From and after July 1, 1958, it shall be unlawful for any person, firm or corporation to allow his or its horses, cattle, goats, sheep, or hogs to run free or at large along the outer banks of this State. This Article shall not apply to horses known as marsh ponies or banks ponies on Ocracoke Island, Hyde County. This Article shall not apply to horses known as marsh ponies or banks ponies on Shackleford Banks between Beaufort Inlet and Barden's Inlet in Carteret County. Saving and excepting those animals known as "banker ponies" on the island of Ocracoke owned by the Boy Scouts and not exceeding 35 in number.

Chapter 7
Animal Shelters

State law does not require local governments to impound animals. Most local governments do, however, want to make arrangements to impound and house animals in some circumstances: a dog without a collar, a stray cat creating a nuisance in a neighborhood, a dog that has bitten someone and is being confined for observation pursuant to the rabies law, or a dog that is in the process of being declared potentially dangerous. It would be difficult for a local government to carry out its responsibilities in these situations without having the ability to impound animals.

Local governments are allowed to either (1) "establish, equip, operate, and maintain" an animal shelter or (2) fund a shelter operated by another entity, such as another local government or an animal welfare organization.[1] An "animal shelter" is a facility "used to house or contain seized, stray, homeless, quarantined, abandoned or unwanted animals" and which is owned by or under contract with a local government or an animal welfare organization.[2] Local governments take different approaches to sheltering. Some build and operate shelters, such as Onslow County[3] and Burlington.[4] Others, such as Polk County, contract with nonprofit organizations for all sheltering services.[5] Some municipalities, such as Kitty Hawk, contract with their counties for sheltering services.[6] Buncombe County has implemented a hybrid approach: it owns the shelter facility but contracts with the Asheville Humane Society to operate the shelter.[7]

---

1. Chapter 153A, Section 442 of the North Carolina General Statutes (hereinafter G.S.) (counties); G.S. 160A-493 (cities). Note that state law specifically authorizes local governments to enter into contracts with private entities "to carry out any public purpose that the [city/county] is authorized by law to engage in." *Id.* § 153A-449 (counties); 160A-20.1 (cities).

2. G.S. 19A-23(5).

3. *See* Onslow Cty. Animal Servs., *Animal Services*, http://www.onslowcountync.gov/AnimalServices/ (last visited May 11, 2018).

4. *See* City of Burlington, *Animal Services*, http://www.ci.burlington.nc.us/963/Animal-Services (last visited May 11, 2018). Note that this shelter serves Burlington and Alamance County, as well as several other municipalities within the county.

5. *See* Polk Cty. Sheriff's Off., *Animal Control Division*, http://www.polknc.org/animal_control.php#.W2RjiVVKjX4, which contracts with Foothills Humane Society, https://www.foothillshumanesociety.org.

6. *See* TOWN OF KITTY HAWK, N.C., CODE OF ORDINANCES § 4-22(b) ("Any dog or cat apprehended and impounded under this section by the town shall either be turned over and delivered to the county animal control office or the county animal control shelter to be processed in accordance with the provisions of the county animal control ordinance . . . .").

7. The Asheville Humane Society's website explains that the organization partnered with Buncombe County to open an "Animal Care Campus." The campus includes (1) the county animal shelter, which is owned by the county and operated by the nonprofit, and (2) an adoption and education center that is owned and operated exclusively by the nonprofit. Asheville Humane Society, *Buncombe County Animal Shelter FAQ*, http://www.ashevillehumane.org/buncombe-county-animal-shelter/faq (last visited May 11, 2018).

This chapter provides an overview of the legal landscape that governs regulation of public animal shelters, reviews a legal mechanism that is available to help local government shelters recover costs related to sheltering animals in cruelty and dangerous dog cases, and describes a relatively new law establishing an animal shelter support fund for local governments.

Regulation of Public Animal Shelters

State oversight of animal shelters owned and operated by local governments has been gradually growing and changing over the last fifteen years. For many years, only private animal shelters were subject to oversight by the North Carolina Department of Agriculture and Consumer Services (Department) pursuant to the state's Animal Welfare Act (AWA).[8] In 2005, the Act was amended to include shelters owned and operated by local governments.[9] As a result, public and private shelters are now required to register with the state and comply with the AWA. The AWA is enforced by the Animal Welfare Section, which is housed in the Department's Veterinary Division.[10] The Department has adopted various regulations regarding the operation of shelters in North Carolina.[11]

In 2009, the state became more directly involved in oversight of euthanasia practices in animal shelters. The Department adopted regulations that specify acceptable methods of euthanasia in shelters and establish certification requirements for individuals responsible for carrying out euthanasia.[12] Euthanasia is discussed in more detail later in this chapter.

Also in 2009, the General Assembly made quite a few changes to the state's rabies control law that had a direct impact on animal shelters. Many of the changes required shelters to do certain things, such as allow for public inspection of impounded animals and provide adoption opportunities. At the time those changes were made, the law did not provide a mechanism for the state to enforce these new requirements. In 2013, the law was further amended to move some of those new requirements from the rabies law

---

8. The North Carolina Animal Welfare Act is codified in Article 3 of G.S. Chapter 19A.

9. S.L. 2005-276, § 11.5(a) (modifying the definition of the term "animal shelter" in G.S. 19A-23 to include facilities owned, operated, or maintained by local governments).

10. G.S. 19A-25 (requiring the Department to investigate all reports of violations and granting Department staff a right of entry into shelters, which may be enforced by an order from superior court); *see also* N.C. Dep't of Agric. & Consumer Serv., Veterinary Div.: Animal Welfare Sec., *Frequently Asked Questions*, http://www.ncagr.gov/vet/aws/index.htm (last visited May 11, 2018) (explaining that the purpose of the 2005 changes in the law was to create a uniform system for the regulation of private and public animal shelters).

11. *See* Title 2, Chapter 52, Subchapter J of the North Carolina Administrative Code (hereinafter N.C.A.C.).

12. 2 N.C.A.C. 52J, § .0400 (Euthanasia Standards).

and integrate them into a new section in the AWA.[13] Now that the requirements are part of the AWA, the Animal Welfare Section has enforcement authority.

Registration

Animal shelters must apply for and receive a certificate of registration from the Animal Welfare Section before commencing operations.[14] Certificates are valid for one year unless they are suspended or revoked.[15] The state may deny an application or suspend or revoke a certificate for various reasons, such as making material misstatements in the application, willfully disregarding state law, or failing to provide adequate housing facilities or enclosures.[16] For example, the Department briefly suspended the registration of the Washington County Animal Shelter in October 2017 after multiple inspections indicated that the facility was out of compliance with statutory and regulatory requirements.[17] The shelter's registration was reinstated less than three weeks later because most of the problems were resolved and a corrective action plan was put in place regarding the remaining issues.[18]

Appeals of such decisions are handled as contested cases through the Office of Administrative Hearings.[19] For example, in 2015, the Department imposed a $5,000 fine on the Columbus County Animal Shelter for euthanizing animals before the expiration of the minimum holding period.[20] The county appealed the fine, arguing that the early euthanasia complied with the shelter's written policies. Ultimately, the Department and the county reached a settlement that involved a waiver of the fine.[21] In another recent

---

13. G.S. 19A-32.1.

14. G.S. 19A-26.

15. *Id.*

16. G.S. 19A-30 (outlining various grounds for denial, suspension, and revocation and detailing the process for taking such actions); 19A-35 (allowing revocation of license or registration for failure to adequately house, feed, and water animals; conduct is classified as a Class 3 misdemeanor).

17. Patricia Norris, DVM, MS, Director, Animal Welfare Sec., N.C. Dep't of Agric. & Consumer Servs., Veterinary Div., Notice of Suspension of Animal Shelter Registration and Notice of Violations (Oct. 2, 2017), http://www.ncagr.gov/vet/aws/documents/AWS-SU-2017-2.pdf.

18. Patricia Norris, DVM, MS, Director, Animal Welfare Sec., N.C. Dep't of Agric. & Consumer Servs., Veterinary Div., Re-Instatement of Animal Shelter Registration (Oct. 19, 2017), http://www.ncagr.gov/vet/aws/documents/REINSTATEMEMTLETTERWASHINGTON COUNTY.pdf.

19. G.S. 19A-30; 19A-32.

20. Patricia Norris, DVM, MS, Director, Animal Welfare Sec., N.C. Dep't of Agric. & Consumer Servs., Veterinary Div., Notice of Civil Penalty (June 18, 2015), http://www.ncagr.gov/ vet/aws/Inspections/Columbus_County/documents/ColumbusCoCivilPenalty6-18-15.pdf.

21. Agreement between the North Carolina Department of Agriculture and Consumer Services, Veterinary Division, Animal Welfare Section, and Columbus County Animal Control (Jan. 21, 2016), http://www.ncagr.gov/vet/aws/documents/FullySignedSettlement Agreement.pdf.

case, the Department imposed a $5,200 fine on the Forsyth County Department of Animal Control Animal Shelter for various violations, including recordkeeping and premature euthanasia.[22] The county appealed and the parties reached a settlement that required the county to provide updated information and participate in a "program review." The fine was reduced to $2,100.[23]

To obtain a license or certificate of registration, facilities must meet the detailed requirements for the housing and care of animals set forth in the Department's regulations.[24] Facilities must, for example, use a specified formula to calculate the minimum square footage of floor space for their primary enclosures for cats and dogs,[25] and they must ensure that enclosures and exercise areas are cleaned at least twice a day.[26] Regulations also govern the transporting of animals.[27]

Holding and Adoption

If a local government decides to own or operate an animal shelter or to contract with an entity for those services, the shelter will be subject to several requirements related to the holding and adoption of animals. When any cat or dog initially arrives at the shelter, the staff is required to record certain information, such as the origin of the animal, the date the shelter received it, and a description of the animal.[28] The shelter is further required to document veterinary care provided and the ultimate disposition of each animal, including specific details related to any death.[29]

As a general rule, shelters are required to hold animals for a minimum of seventy-two hours, unless the local government has established a longer minimum holding period.[30] Note that federal law requires a five-day holding period in certain limited circumstances (see discussion below). An animal may be euthanized before the expiration of the holding period if the shelter determines that the animal is seriously ill or injured and euthanasia is appropriate.[31] The shelter must document this determination

---

22. Patricia Norris, DVM, MS, Director, Animal Welfare Sec., N.C. Dep't of Agric. & Consumer Servs., Veterinary Div., Notice of Civil Penalty (Apr. 18, 2016), http://www.ncagr.gov/vet/aws/Inspections/Forsyth_County/documents/AWS-CP-2016-4.pdf.

23. Agreement between the North Carolina Department of Agriculture and Consumer Services, Veterinary Division, Animal Welfare Section, and the Forsyth County Animal Services Shelter (Aug. 30, 2016), http://www.ncagr.gov/vet/aws/documents/FORSYTH AGREEMENT.pdf.

24. *See* 2 N.C.A.C. 52J.

25. 2 N.C.A.C. 52J, § .0204(d).

26. 2 N.C.A.C. 52J, § .0207(a).

27. 2 N.C.A.C. 52J, §§ .0301–.0304.

28. G.S. 19A-32.1(j); 2 N.C.A.C. 52J, § .0101.

29. 2 N.C.A.C. 52J, § .0101.

30. G.S. 19A-32.1(a).

31. G.S. 19A-32.1(b)(2).

in writing.[32] After the expiration of the applicable minimum holding period, the shelter must make the animal available for adoption unless

- the shelter has determined that the animal is "unadoptable due to injury or defects of health or temperament,"
- the shelter has determined that the animal is seriously ill or injured,
- the animal is being held as evidence in a pending criminal case.

State law does not specify how long an animal must be made available for adoption after the expiration of the holding period.

Animals arrive at shelters in various ways. An owner may surrender his or her animal or a concerned citizen may deliver a stray animal to the shelter. A local official (animal services, law enforcement) may find a stray animal or pick up a nuisance animal. A law enforcement officer, possibly in collaboration with animal services, may seize an animal in the course of a criminal cruelty or dogfighting investigation. The shelter's obligations related to holding and adoption vary depending on the circumstances surrounding how the animal came to be impounded and how much information the shelter may have about the animal.

- **Surrendered animal.** An owner may surrender an animal for any reason. At the time of surrender, the owner may sign a consent form authorizing the shelter to euthanize the animal immediately.[33] When doing so, the owner must present proof of ownership. State law does not specify what constitutes proof of ownership but local government policies often do.[34] They may require, for example, veterinary bills, animal licenses, or vaccination records. If the animal is a dog, the owner must also indicate in writing whether the dog has bitten anyone within the previous ten days.[35] Presumably, this requirement is in place to ensure that the shelter complies with the rabies law, which requires confinement of a biting animal for ten days after the bite.[36] If the animal is surrendered, is not a dog that has bitten someone recently, and the owner does not consent to immediate euthanasia, the animal will be treated like other potentially adoptable animals.

---

32. *Id.*

33. G.S. 19A-32.1(g).

34. In Wake County, for example, owners are required to present photo identification and veterinary records and must complete a detailed questionnaire about the animal's temperament and history. *See* WakeGOV, Animal Center, *Surrendering a Pet*, http://www.wakegov.com/pets/shelter/Pages/surrender.aspx (last visited May 11, 2018).

35. G.S. 19A-32.1(h).

36. G.S. 130A-196. Interestingly, this same requirement does not extend to cats or ferrets, which are also subject to the same rabies law. *See* chapter 5.

- **Known owner.** If an animal arrives at the shelter and has a tag or a microchip identifying its owner,[37] the shelter will attempt to notify the owner that the animal has been impounded.[38] An owner will typically be required to pay a fee to redeem the animal. If the owner does not redeem the animal after the applicable minimum holding period, the shelter must make it available for adoption unless one of the exceptions described above applies.
- **Unknown owner.** If an animal's owner is unknown, the shelter must hold it for the applicable minimum holding period before taking any action. The shelter must have a policy in place that allows members of the public to view all animals being held at the shelter so that they have an opportunity to find lost pets.[39] The policy must allow for viewing to take place at least three days a week for at least four hours each day. For animals that are being kept apart from the general public for health or safety reasons or to preserve evidence in a criminal case, the shelter must make "reasonable arrangements" so as to allow owners a chance to determine if one of those animals is their lost pet.[40] If the animal is transferred to a foster care provider or rescue organization during the minimum holding period, the shelter must display a photograph of the animal (head and face). Many shelters also post photos of the animals on their websites or contract with another organization that hosts pictures of lost pets.[41] After the holding period has passed, the shelter must make an animal available for adoption unless one of the exceptions described above applies.

---

37. If a shelter has access to a microchip scanner, it will typically scan each animal brought into the facility. There is a provision in state law that mandates scanning if (1) an animal is impounded based on a violation of the rabies law and (2) the shelter has access to a microchip-scanning device. G.S. 130A-192(a).

38. State law requires that animal control officials "make a reasonable attempt to locate the owner" of an animal impounded for a rabies violation. G.S. 130A-192. This mandate does not necessarily extend to other impounded animals but it is presumably standard practice for sheltering professionals.

39. G.S. 19A-32.1(c).

40. The law does not provide any more guidance about how the shelter should manage these types of situations. It may be reasonable to post pictures of animals that are not available for public viewing. A separate section of the law allows photographs to be used when animals are placed in foster care or with a rescue organization during the minimum holding period. One could argue that if a photograph is sufficient in those situations, it also would be sufficient when an animal must be kept apart from the general public.

41. *See, e.g.*, Moore Cty. Animal Servs., *Lost & Found*, https://www.moorecountync.gov/sheriff/animal-services/lost-found (last visited May 11, 2018) (displaying photographs of stray animals that have arrived at the shelter); Orange Cty. Animal Servs., *Lost and Found Pets*, http://www.orangecountync.gov/departments/animalservices/lost_pets.php (last visited May 11, 2018) (same).

- **Seized in a criminal case.** If an animal is seized in a criminal case, the shelter will typically coordinate with law enforcement officials and prosecutors to make plans regarding disposition of the animal. The animal owner may be allowed to redeem the animal and may be required to pay a redemption fee. Occasionally, an owner will voluntarily surrender the animal to the shelter. Finally, in some cases, seized animals will be held for a significant amount of time and the shelter operator may seek to have the owner pay for costs associated with the animal's care.[42]

Before a shelter releases an animal, the person receiving the animal must present one of four types of government-issued identification.[43] The shelter must document the type of identification presented.[44]

Euthanasia

Over the last fifteen years, North Carolina law governing euthanasia in animal shelters has changed significantly in three primary areas: (1) approved methods of euthanasia, (2) certification of staff performing euthanasia, and (3) access to controlled substances.

Methods

Until fairly recently, state oversight of euthanasia methods was limited. A state rabies statute provided that shelters could euthanize animals using methods approved by one of three national organizations: the American Veterinary Medical Association (AVMA), the Humane Society of the United States (HSUS), or the American Humane Association (AHA). The law did not, however, include any mechanism for the state to enforce this requirement. In 2005, the legislature imported that mandate into the state Animal Welfare Act (AWA), directed the Board of Agriculture to adopt regulations governing methods, and provided the Department with enforcement authority.[45]

The most controversial issue facing both the legislature and the Board was whether to allow shelters to use carbon monoxide (CO) gas for euthanasia. At that point in time, both the HSUS and the AHA did not authorize the use of CO gas, but the AVMA authorized its use in limited circumstances. The Board ultimately adopted regulations that (1) incorporated the guidance from the three organizations by reference and

---

42. G.S. 19A-70. See discussion in Chapter 2.

43. G.S. 19A-32.1(i). The four types of authorized identification are a driver's license, a special identification card issued pursuant to G.S. 20-37.7, a military identification card, and a passport.

44. G.S. 19A-32.1(j)(3).

45. G.S. 19A-24(a)(5) (authorizing euthanasia methods approved by the AVMA, HSUS, and AHA); 02 N.C.A.C. 52J, § .0401 (incorporating the recommendations of the national organizations by reference).

(2) established conditions designed to address safety and efficacy of the use of CO gas as a method.[46]

In 2013, the AVMA revised its guidance on euthanasia, imposing much more significant limitations on the use of CO gas by shelters.[47] The guidance states that the preferred method of euthanasia in shelters is injection of a barbiturate (e.g., pentobarbital) or a barbituric acid derivative.[48] The other two organizations, the HSUS and the AHA, both agree with this recommendation.[49] The AVMA recognizes that other methods may be appropriate in limited circumstances. With respect to CO gas specifically, the AVMA guidelines now state as follows:

> [CO] is not recommended for routine euthanasia of cats and dogs. It may be considered in unusual or rare circumstances, such as natural disasters and large-scale disease outbreaks. Alternate methods with fewer conditions and disadvantages are recommended for companion animals where feasible.[50]

Because most of the euthanasia performed by animal shelters is "routine euthanasia of cats and dogs," local government shelters should now use this method only very rarely, if at all. The AVMA does not prohibit the use of CO gas or classify it as an "unacceptable method." Rather, the method is classified as "acceptable with conditions," which means that it may be used if the conditions specified in the guidelines are followed. The conditions relate to staff training, chamber construction, ventilation, lighting, quality of gas used, and ability to regulate gas flow.[51] State law also imposes similar conditions on the use of CO gas and prohibits its use on certain types of animals, including those that are very young, pregnant, or near death.[52]

---

46. G.S. 19A-24(a)(5) (authorizing the Board to allow for the use of carbon monoxide gas); 02 N.C.A.C. 52J, § .0600 (Euthanasia by Carbon Monoxide).

47. Am. Veterinary Med. Ass'n, AVMA Guidelines for the Euthanasia of Animals: 2013 Edition (2013), https://www.avma.org/KB/Policies/Pages/Euthanasia-Guidelines.aspx.

48. *Id.* at 47.

49. *See* Am. Humane, *Position Statement: Gassing of Shelter Animals* (Aug. 25, 2016), https://www.americanhumane.org/position-statement/gassing-of-shelter-animals/ (last visited May 11, 2018) ("American Humane considers euthanasia by injection (EBI) to be the only acceptable and humane means of euthanasia for all shelter animals."); Humane Soc'y of the U.S., *Statement on Euthanasia*, humanesociety.org, http://www.humanesociety.org/about/policy_statements/statement_euthanasia.html?credit=web_globalfooter_id93480558 (last visited May 11, 2018) ("[EBI] is the most humane method available because it causes rapid loss of consciousness and an immediate inability to feel pain. Other methods—such as carbon monoxide gas chambers—that cause distress, fear, or pain in the animal, are not acceptable.").

50. Am. Veterinary Med. Ass'n, *supra* note 47, at 45.

51. *Id.* at 22–23.

52. G.S. 19A-24(a)(5); 2 N.C.A.C. 52J, §§ .0601–.0609.

In "extraordinary circumstances," the regulations allow shelter staff to euthanize an animal by shooting it or using another "extreme" method approved by one of the three national organizations.[53] The rules explain that an "extraordinary circumstance or situation includes a situation which is offsite from the shelter, in which an animal poses an immediate risk to animal, human or public health and in which no alternative, less extreme measure of euthanasia is feasible. It also includes circumstances or situations in which it would be inhumane to transport an animal to another location to perform euthanasia."[54]

Staff Certification

After the authority for oversight of shelters was shifted to the North Carolina Department of Agriculture and Consumer Services (Department), the Board of Agriculture adopted a regulatory scheme that governs the training and certification of animal shelter staff who are authorized to perform euthanasia.[55] The law now provides that only the following three categories of professionals are allowed to euthanize an animal in a shelter: veterinarians, certified euthanasia technicians (CETs), or probationary CETs.[56] This restriction does not, however, apply to extraordinary circumstances as described above.[57]

State law sets forth detailed requirements related to the application, training, authority, and recertification of CETs.[58] The Department has broad authority to discipline CETs. For example, it can refuse to issue or renew a certification, revoke or suspend a certification, or place a CET on probation.[59] Disciplinary actions may be appealed to the Office of Administrative Hearings.

---

53. 2 N.C.A.C. 52J, § .0700.

54. 2 N.C.A.C. 52J, §§ .0701–.0702.

55. The Board of Agriculture initially developed the regulatory scheme shortly after oversight responsibility was shifted to the Department. The draft rules were not adopted as law at that time because it was determined that the rule-making body lacked the appropriate statutory authority. The General Assembly quickly remedied this problem in 2008 by enacting relatively comprehensive statutory authority. S.L. 2008-198, § 2.(a) (amending G.S. 19A-24 to add paragraph (b)).

56. G.S. 19A-24(b) (directing the Board of Agriculture to adopt rules governing certification); 02 N.C.A.C. 52J, § .0402 (limiting the type of individual who can perform euthanasia).

57. 2 N.C.A.C. 52J, § .0704.

58. *See generally* 2 N.C.A.C. 52J, § .0400 (Euthanasia Standards).

59. 2 N.C.A.C. 52J, § .0409. Examples of disciplinary actions can be found online at the Department of Agriculture and Consumer Services' website: http://www.ncagr.gov/vet/aws/CETsPenalty.htm (last visited May 11, 2018).

Access to Controlled Substances

For many years, animal shelters did not have direct access to the controlled substances, such as sodium pentobarbital, needed to perform euthanasia by injection. Most local governments entered into contracts with local veterinarians who agreed to provide the shelters access to the drugs and to supervise their use of the drugs. This approach presented both administrative and, in some instances, financial challenges. In 2010, the General Assembly changed the controlled substances law to allow animal shelters to directly access sodium pentobarbital and other drugs used for euthanasia.[60] A shelter's manager and chief operating officer are the only individuals authorized to acquire the drugs, but CETs are allowed to possess and administer them on the shelter's premises. This same legislation also established a requirement that CETs submit to criminal background checks.[61]

Penalties

State law provides both civil and criminal penalties for violations related to animal shelter conditions. The director of the Animal Welfare Section has the authority to impose civil monetary penalties against any person who violates either the AWA or its implementing regulations.[62] The maximum penalty for a violation is $5,000, but the director is required to consider the degree and extent of the harm caused by the violation when determining the amount. The proceeds of penalties collected under this law are placed in a fund dedicated to the public schools.[63] Examples of recent violations and penalties assessed are in Table 7.1, below.

Criminal penalties for violations related to shelter conditions are more narrowly tailored. As mentioned above, it is a Class 3 misdemeanor for a person who is registered pursuant to state law to fail to adequately house, feed, and water animals in his or her care.[64] When a person is charged with this crime, the state has the authority to seize and impound the animals. If the person is subsequently convicted, the state may sell or euthanize the animals.[65] It is also conceivable that, in extreme circumstances, an animal shelter operator could be found guilty of animal cruelty (see Chapter 2).

---

60. S.L. 2010-127 (amending G.S. 90-101).

61. *Id.* (amending G.S. 19A-24 and adding new G.S. 114-19.29).

62. G.S. 19A-40.

63. *See* Article 31A of G.S. Chapter 115C. When a civil fine is collected by a state agency, the agency is allowed to retain a small portion of the proceeds to cover the costs incurred in collecting the fine. That amount may not exceed 20 percent of the total amount collected. G.S. 115C-457.2.

64. G.S. 19A-35.

65. *Id.*

Table 7.1. Civil Penalties for Violations of Laws and Regulations on Shelter Conditions

Violation	Number of Violations	Total Penalty Assesed
Euthanasia prior to expiration of the 72-hour holding period	15 animals	$1,500 [a]
	81 animals	$8,100 [b]
Euthanasia performed by uncertified personnel	205 animals	$2,050 [c]
Inadequate veterinary care	4 animals	$4,000 [d]
	2 animals	$2,300 [e]
Inadequate shelter facilities	12 shelters	$2,400 [f]
Failure to vaccinate	1 animal	$100 [g]
	6 animals	$1,200 [h]
Inadequate feeding	2 animals	$1,000 [i]
Inadequate recordkeeping	3 records	$300 [j]
	Numerous records	$500 [k]
Failure to comply with requirements for animals staying for extended periods (long-term care)	1 animal	$500 [l]

a. Patricia Norris, DVM, MS, Director, Animal Welfare Sec., N.C. Dep't of Agric. & Consumer Servs., Veterinary Div. (hereinafter Norris, Veterinary Div.), Notice of Civil Penalty and Notice of Warning to Edwin Causey, Sampson County Manager (Mar. 12, 2018), http://www.ncagr.gov/vet/aws/Inspections/Sampson_County/documents/AWS-CP-2018-1SampsonCountyAnimal Shelter3-12-18.pdf.

b. Patricia Norris, Veterinary Div., Notice of Civil Penalty to Jaime Laughter, Transylvania County Manager (Sept. 22, 2015), http://www.ncagr.gov/vet/aws/Inspections/Transylvania_County/documents/TransylvaniaCoCP9-22-15.pdf.

c. Id.

d. Norris, Veterinary Div., Notice of Civil Penalty to J. Dudley Watts, Jr., Forsyth County Manager (Apr. 18, 2016), http://www.ncagr.gov/vet/aws/Inspections/Forsyth_County/documents/AWS-CP-2016-4.pdf.

e. Norris, Veterinary Div., Notice of Civil Penalty and Notice of Warning to Edwin Causey, Sampson County Manager (Mar. 12, 2018), http://www.ncagr.gov/vet/aws/Inspections/Sampson_County/documents/AWS-CP-2018-1SampsonCounty AnimalShelter3-12-18.pdf.

f. Norris, Veterinary Div., Notice of Civil Penalty to Clarence Grier, Guilford Deputy County Manager (July 26, 2017), http://www.ncagr.gov/vet/aws/Inspections/Guilford_County/documents/AWS-2017-11GuilfordCoAnimalShelter7-26-17.pdf.

g. Id.; Norris, Veterinary Div., Notice of Civil Penalty to Eric Evans, Edgecombe County Manager (July 10, 2017), http://www.ncagr.gov/vet/aws/documents/AWSCP2017-8EdgecombeCounty.pdf.

h. Norris, Veterinary Div., Notice of Civil Penalty and Notice of Warning to Clarence Grier, Guilford Deputy County Manager (Oct. 4, 2017), http://www.ncagr.gov/vet/aws/documents/AWS-CP-2017-13GuilfordCounty.pdf.

i. Norris, Veterinary Div., Notice of Civil Penalty and Notice of Warning to Edwin Causey, Sampson County Manager (Mar. 12, 2018), http://www.ncagr.gov/vet/aws/Inspections/Sampson_County/documents/AWS-CP-2018-1SampsonCounty AnimalShelter3-12-18.pdf.

j. Norris, Veterinary Div., Notice of Civil Penalty to Eric Evans, Edgecombe County Manager (July 10, 2017), http://www.ncagr.gov/vet/aws/documents/AWSCP2017-8EdgecombeCounty.pdf.

k. Norris, Veterinary Div., Notice of Civil Penalty to J. Dudley Watts, Jr., Forsyth County Manager (Apr. 18, 2016), http://www.ncagr.gov/vet/aws/Inspections/Forsyth_County/documents/AWS-CP-2016-4.pdf.

l. Norris, Veterinary Div., Notice of Civil Penalty to Eric Evans, Edgecombe County Manager (July 10, 2017), http://www.ncagr.gov/vet/aws/documents/AWSCP2017-8EdgecombeCounty.pdf.

Federal Law

While most of the law governing public animal shelters is found in state statutes, there is a body of law at the federal level that is worth noting. The federal Animal Welfare Act (AWA), which is administered by the Animal and Plant Health Inspection Service (APHIS)[66] of the U.S. Department of Agriculture (USDA), regulates several different categories of animal operations. It focuses on operations that use animals for research, sell animals to the public, transport animals, and use animals in exhibits.[67] One provision of the federal law applies directly to local government animal shelters. It requires shelters to hold all dogs and cats for a minimum of five days before selling them to a dealer.[68] A dealer is, in short, (1) a person who buys, sells, or transports any animal (alive or dead) for compensation or profit for use as a pet or for research, teaching, or exhibition or (2) a person who buys, sells, or transports any dog for hunting, security, or breeding purposes.[69] This five-day holding requirement also applies to private entities (such as humane societies) that are under contract with a state, county or city, or research facility licensed by the USDA. The law authorizes the USDA to conduct investigations and inspections, impose civil money penalties, and apply for injunctions.[70]

Recovering Sheltering Costs

Shelters are often asked to shelter animals seized as part of cruelty or dangerous dog cases.[71] If a shelter is operated by or under contract with a county or municipality, the local government may incur significant expenses in the course of providing care and shelter for these animals. Under G.S. 19A-70, animal shelters may ask the court to order defendants to pay for some of the cost of caring for the animals.[72] The law also provides for forfeiture of the animal in some circumstances.

---

66. *See* U.S. Dep't of Agric., Animal & Plant Health Inspection Serv., *Animal Welfare*, www.aphis.usda.gov/animal_welfare/index.shtml (last visited May 11, 2018) (explaining this administrative responsibility).

67. *See generally* 7 U.S.C. §§ 2131–2159.

68. 7 U.S.C. § 2158(a).

69. 7 U.S.C. § 2132(f). The definition does not include a retail pet store except such store which sells any animals to a research facility, an exhibitor, or a dealer." *Id.*

70. 7 U.S.C. §§ 2146–2147; § 2149; § 2159.

71. The circumstances under which a shelter takes custody of an animal vary. Sometimes, an animal is seized as evidence of a crime pursuant to a body of criminal law regarding seizures of property that is beyond the scope of this book. *See, e.g.*, ROBERT L. FARB, ARREST, SEARCH, AND INVESTIGATION IN NORTH CAROLINA 447 (UNC School of Government, 5th ed. 2016) (describing process of seizing animal pursuant to a search warrant). Other times, an animal is seized by an animal cruelty investigator pursuant to a magistrate's order. Seizures by animal cruelty investigators are discussed in more detail in chapter 3.

72. G.S. 19A-70(a).

This cost-recovery mechanism is available only in the following cases:

- A person has been arrested for any violation of the criminal animal cruelty laws in G.S. Chapter 14.
- A person has been arrested pursuant to G.S. 67-4.3 after a dangerous dog has attacked another person and caused physical injuries requiring medical treatment costing more than $100.
- A civil animal cruelty action has been initiated pursuant to G.S. Chapter 19A, Article 1. This provision only applies if the action is initiated by a local government, an animal cruelty investigator, or by an organization operating a county or municipal shelter under contract.

Note that G.S. 19A-70 is tied to violations of state law. It does not apply if a local government is pursuing an ordinance violation.

The process for pursuing this option is as follows:

- **File a petition.** The shelter operator may petition the court to order the defendant to deposit with the court enough money to cover the "reasonable expenses" of caring for the animal while the litigation is pending. Reasonable expenses include the cost of providing food, water, shelter, and care, including medical care. The initial petition should itemize the costs expected to be incurred for thirty days.
- **Hearing.** Once such a petition is filed, the court is required to conduct a hearing no earlier than ten business days and no later than fifteen business days after the filing date. The shelter operator must mail notice of the hearing and a copy of the petition to the defendant.[73] At the hearing, the judge should determine how much money is needed to care for the animal for thirty calendar days (not business days). In making this determination, the judge should consider not only the needs of the animal but also the defendant's ability to pay.
- **Order.** The judge may either (1) order the defendant to deposit funds sufficient to care for the animal for thirty days or (2), if the judge concludes that the defendant is financially unable to deposit the necessary funds, he or she may order the defendant to provide suitable care for the animal at the animal's current location while the litigation is pending.[74]

---

73. If the defendant is in jail, the shelter operator must also provide notice to the custodian of the jail. G.S. 19A-70(b).

74. In conjunction with such an order, an animal control or law enforcement officer must make regular visits to the animal to ensure that it is receiving proper care. If the officer concludes that the animal is not being cared for appropriately, it may be impounded. G.S. 19A-70(f).

- **Deposit funds.** When the judge orders the defendant to deposit funds, the money must be deposited with the clerk of superior court within five days of the initial hearing. Once the funds are posted, the shelter operator is allowed to draw from the funds an amount reflecting the actual costs incurred in caring for the animal. While the litigation is pending, the defendant is required to continue depositing funds within five business days of the end of every thirty-day period, unless the defendant requests a hearing at least five business days before expiration of the period.

- **Extension.** If the case is not resolved within the initial thirty days, the shelter operator may request an extension of the order for additional thirty-day periods until the litigation is resolved. To do so, the operator must file an affidavit with the clerk of superior court stating that to the best of his or her knowledge, the case has not been resolved. This affidavit must be filed at least two business days prior to the expiration of each thirty-day period. Upon receipt of the affidavit, the initial order is automatically renewed for an additional thirty days.[75]

- **Forfeiture.** If the defendant fails to either request a review hearing or deposit funds as directed by the court, the animal is automatically forfeited.

Since the cost-recovery statute was enacted in 2005, a few key questions and concerns have come up with regard to implementation. Two issues have generated confusion related to the initiation of a proceeding. The first concerns the language in the statute that requires an "arrest" in a criminal cruelty or dangerous dog case. In many of these cases, particularly the misdemeanors, law enforcement officers may prefer to seek a criminal summons rather than arrest the individual involved. Because the statute requires an arrest, some officials have elected to alter their practices to arrest defendants in order to preserve the right to petition for cost recovery.

The second issue relates to the filing of the petition. G.S. 19A-70 states that the shelter operator must file the petition with "the court." It does not specify which court is appropriate. As a result, practice varies across the state. In some districts, the attorney representing the shelter operator works closely with the district attorney's office and files the petition in the court with jurisdiction over the criminal proceeding. In other districts, the district attorney's office or judges have decided that such a petition is not appropriate in the criminal proceeding. In those districts, shelter operators have elected to file the petition as a special proceeding in superior court. Anecdotal reports suggest that the unique nature of the cost-recovery petition, combined with the lack

---

75. Interestingly, it appears that the defendant's duty to deposit funds every thirty days is independent of the shelter's duty to submit an affidavit requesting extension of the order. This may simply be a drafting error. It seems reasonable to infer that if the shelter does not request an extension, the original order automatically expires.

of procedural detail in the statute, has caused uncertainty among shelter operators, district attorneys, and judges about how and where petitions should be filed. As of this writing, there has not been any clarification on this issue from North Carolina appellate courts or the General Assembly.

The next issue that has arisen in connection with the cost-recovery law involves the constitutionality of its forfeiture provision. Specifically, some have questioned whether it is constitutional to permanently deprive a defendant of his or her property in a criminal proceeding prior to conviction. North Carolina courts have not addressed this question in the context of the animal forfeiture provision of this statute. As a general matter, the government may deprive a person of his or her property (including animals) prior to the person being convicted of a crime if the deprivation is a remedial measure, rather than punishment, and if the government's deprivation procedure comports with the constitutional requirements of due process.[76] As the central concern of the cost-recovery statute is the collection of funds necessary for the care of a seized animal, a strong argument can be made that the statute is remedial rather than punitive in nature. Assuming that a court would find the statute to be remedial, the question becomes whether the statute provides a person due process prior to forfeiture of an animal. Generally speaking, "due process requires notice and a hearing before the government may deprive an individual of liberty or property."[77] As discussed above, the cost-recovery statute provides for both notice and a hearing prior to forfeiture. As noted, however, the constitutionality of the statute has not been litigated in North Carolina.

Perhaps in response to the concerns about the forfeiture provision's constitutionality or the procedural challenges involved in cost-recovery pursuant to G.S. 19A-70, some animal services and law enforcement officials encourage defendants to sign a form effecting the surrender of their animals. It is certainly reasonable to provide the animal's

---

76. *See, e.g.,* Henry v. Edmisten, 315 N.C. 474, 494–95 (1986) (state and federal constitutional principles of due process prohibit the state from punishing a person except after conviction at trial; the state is not prohibited from depriving a person of his or her property as a remedial, rather than a punitive, measure prior to conviction so long as the state provides constitutionally sufficient due process).

77. State v. Poole, 228 N.C. App. 248, 260 (2013). In an unpublished case, a federal district court held that an animal forfeiture law in Kentucky was unconstitutional on due process grounds. Louisville Kennel Club, Inc. v. Louisville/Jefferson Cty. Metro Gov't, No. CIV.A. 3:07-CV-230-S, 2009 WL 3210690, at *9 (W.D. Ky. Oct. 2, 2009) (unpublished). The law at issue in the case afforded an animal owner a post-confiscation hearing where the only issue before the judge was whether there was probable cause for the confiscation. If the judge found probable cause, the owner was required to post a pre-conviction bond in a fixed amount every thirty days; the law provided that the animal would be forfeited if the defendant failed to post the bond. The court concluded that "the risk of erroneous deprivation" of the property was high, particularly if the defendant was acquitted, and that the government had not articulated a reason that would justify failing to provide additional procedural protections prior to forfeiture, such as another hearing before forfeiture or a late payment process. *Id.* at *10.

owner with an option to surrender in these cases, but it is important that the surrender be an informed and completely voluntary one. If a surrender is voluntary, a person's right to due process prior to being deprived of his or her property is not implicated—the person has freely relinquished his or her interest in the animal. On the other hand, if a surrender is not truly voluntary, a person's due process rights are implicated because the government has interfered with a person's protected property interest. There may be some confusion when a person is asked to surrender an animal at the same time a petition is pending that could result in forfeiture. In a case from North Dakota, animal services officials seized dogs and presented the owner with two forms—a surrender form and a notice of confiscation form. They asked her to sign both forms, which she did, but she later appealed the confiscation. The state argued that there had been no confiscation, asserting that the owner had, by signing the forms, relinquished her interest in the dogs, thereby waiving her property rights associated with them. The court held that the surrender form was invalid and explained that "waiver under duress is not voluntary."[78] Animal services officials in North Carolina should proceed carefully to ensure that animal owners fully understand their rights at the time any animal is seized.

Animal Shelter Support Fund

In 2015, the General Assembly established a new fund to reimburse local governments for certain animal shelter–related expenses that are incurred if either (1) a shelter's registration is denied, suspended, or revoked or (2) there is an unforeseen catastrophic disaster at a shelter.[79] Local governments may seek reimbursement for "direct operational costs," which include veterinary costs, sanitation costs, animal sustenance and supplies, and temporary housing and sheltering.[80] Local governments receiving support from the fund must share in the costs. The mandated contribution varies based on the given county's development tier.[81] As of May 2018, no county has requested reimbursement from the fund.[82]

---

78. *In re* Peterson's Dogs, 758 N.W.2d 749 (N.D. 2008).

79. G.S. Chapter 19A, Article 5A.

80. G.S. 19A-68; 2 N.C.A.C. 52J, § .0901 (regulation detailing the types of expenditures eligible for reimbursement under each of these four categories).

81. G.S. 19A-68. Tier 1 counties have a 1:3 funds match, while Tier 3 counties have a 1:1 match. *See* G.S. 143B-437.08 for details regarding the criteria for development tiers.

82. Email from Patricia Norris, DVM, MS, Director, Animal Welfare Sec., N.C. Dep't of Agric. & Consumer Servs., Veterinary Div., to Aimee Wall, UNC School of Government (June 5, 2018) (on file with author).

Appendix A. Relevant Sections of the North Carolina General Statutes (G.S.)

Article 3 [of G.S. Chapter 19A].
Animal Welfare Act.

§ 19A-20. Title of Article.
This Article may be cited as the Animal Welfare Act.

§ 19A-21. Purposes.
The purposes of this Article are (i) to protect the owners of dogs and cats from the theft of such pets; (ii) to prevent the sale or use of stolen pets; (iii) to insure that animals, as items of commerce, are provided humane care and treatment by regulating the transportation, sale, purchase, housing, care, handling and treatment of such animals by persons or organizations engaged in transporting, buying, or selling them for such use; (iv) to insure that animals confined in pet shops, kennels, animal shelters and auction markets are provided humane care and treatment; (v) to prohibit the sale, trade or adoption of those animals which show physical signs of infection, communicable disease, or congenital abnormalities, unless veterinary care is assured subsequent to sale, trade or adoption.

§ 19A-22. Animal Welfare Section in Animal Health Division of Department of Agriculture and Consumer Services created; Director.
There is hereby created within the Animal Health Division of the North Carolina Department of Agriculture and Consumer Services, a new section thereof, to be known as the Animal Welfare Section of said division.

  The Commissioner of Agriculture is hereby authorized to appoint a Director of said section whose duties and authority shall be determined by the Commissioner subject to the approval of the Board of Agriculture and subject to the provisions of this Article.

§ 19A-23. Definitions.
For the purposes of this Article, the following terms, when used in the Article or the rules or orders made pursuant thereto, shall be construed respectively to mean:
  (1) "Adequate feed" means the provision at suitable intervals, not to exceed 24 hours, of a quantity of wholesome foodstuff suitable for the species and age, sufficient to maintain a reasonable level of nutrition in each animal. Such foodstuff shall be served in a sanitized receptacle, dish, or container.
  (2) "Adequate water" means a constant access to a supply of clean, fresh, potable water provided in a sanitary manner or provided at suitable intervals for the species and not to exceed 24 hours at any interval.
  (3) "Ambient temperature" means the temperature surrounding the animal.
  (4) "Animal" means any domestic dog (Canis familiaris), or domestic cat (Felis domestica).
  (5) "Animal shelter" means a facility which is used to house or contain seized, stray, homeless, quarantined, abandoned or unwanted animals and which is under contract with, owned, operated, or maintained by a county, city, town, or other municipality, or by a duly incorporated humane society, animal welfare society, society for the prevention of cruelty to animals, or other nonprofit organization devoted to the welfare, protection, rehabilitation, or humane treatment of animals.

(5a) "Approved foster care provider" means an individual, nonprofit corporation, or association that cares for stray animals that has been favorably assessed by the operator of the animal shelter through the application of written standards.

(5b) "Approved rescue organization" means a nonprofit corporation or association that cares for stray animals that has been favorably assessed by the operator of the animal shelter through the application of written standards.

(5c) "Boarding kennel" means a facility or establishment which regularly offers to the public the service of boarding dogs or cats or both for a fee. Such a facility or establishment may, in addition to providing shelter, food and water, offer grooming or other services for dogs and/or cats.

(6) "Commissioner" means the Commissioner of Agriculture of the State of North Carolina.

(7) "Dealer" means any person who sells, exchanges, or donates, or offers to sell, exchange, or donate animals to another dealer, pet shop, or research facility; provided, however, that an individual who breeds and raises on his own premises no more than the offspring of five canine or feline females per year, unless bred and raised specifically for research purposes shall not be considered to be a dealer for the purposes of this Article.

(8) "Director" means the Director of the Animal Welfare Section of the Animal Health Division of the Department of Agriculture and Consumer Services.

(9) "Euthanasia" means the humane destruction of an animal accomplished by a method that involves rapid unconsciousness and immediate death or by a method that involves anesthesia, produced by an agent which causes painless loss of consciousness, and death during such loss of consciousness.

(10) "Housing facility" means any room, building, or area used to contain a primary enclosure or enclosures.

(11) "Person" means any individual, partnership, firm, jointstock company, corporation, association, trust, estate, or other legal entity.

(12) "Pet shop" means a person or establishment that acquires for the purposes of resale animals bred by others whether as owner, agent, or on consignment, and that sells, trades or offers to sell or trade such animals to the general public at retail or wholesale.

(13) "Primary enclosure" means any structure used to immediately restrict an animal or animals to a limited amount of space, such as a room, pen, cage compartment or hutch.

(14) "Public auction" means any place or location where dogs or cats are sold at auction to the highest bidder regardless of whether such dogs or cats are offered as individuals, as a group, or by weight.

(15) "Research facility" means any place, laboratory, or institution at which scientific tests, experiments, or investigations involving the use of living animals are carried out, conducted, or attempted.

(16) "Sanitize" means to make physically clean and to remove and destroy to a practical minimum, agents injurious to health.

§ 19A-24. Powers of Board of Agriculture.

(a) The Board of Agriculture shall:

(1) Establish standards for the care of animals at animal shelters, boarding kennels, pet shops, and public auctions. A boarding kennel that offers dog day care services and has a ratio of dogs to employees or supervisors, or both employees and supervisors, of not more than 10 to one, shall not as to such services be subject to any regulations that restrict the number of dogs that are permitted within any primary enclosure.

(2) Prescribe the manner in which animals may be transported to and from registered or licensed premises.

(3) Require licensees and holders of certificates to keep records of the purchase and sale of animals and to identify animals at their establishments.

(4) Adopt rules to implement this Article, including federal regulations promulgated under Title 7, Chapter 54, of the United States Code.

(5) Adopt rules on the euthanasia of animals in the possession or custody of any person required to obtain a certificate of registration under this Article. An animal shall only be put to death by a method and delivery of method approved by the American Veterinary Medical Association, the Humane Society of the United States, or the American Humane Association. The Department shall establish rules for the euthanasia process using any one or combination of methods and standards prescribed by the three aforementioned organizations. The rules shall address the equipment, the process, and the separation of animals, in addition to the animals' age and condition. If the gas method of euthanasia is approved, rules shall require (i) that only commercially compressed carbon monoxide gas is approved for use, and (ii) that the gas must be delivered in a commercially manufactured chamber that allows for the individual separation of animals. Rules shall also mandate training for any person who participates in the euthanasia process.

(b) In addition to rules on the euthanasia of animals adopted pursuant to subdivision (5) of subsection (a) of this section, the Board of Agriculture shall adopt rules for the certification of euthanasia technicians. The rules may provide for:

(1) Written and practical examinations for persons who perform euthanasia.

(2) Issuance of certification to persons who have successfully completed both training and examinations to become a euthanasia technician.

(3) Recertification of euthanasia technicians on a periodic basis.

(4) Standards and procedures for the approval of persons who conduct training of euthanasia technicians.

(5) Approval of materials for use in euthanasia technician training.

(6) Minimum certification criteria for persons seeking to become euthanasia technicians including, but not limited to: age; previous related experience; criminal record; and other qualifications that are related to an applicant's fitness to perform euthanasia.

(7) Denial, suspension, or revocation of certification of euthanasia technicians who:

    a. Violate any provision of this Article or rules adopted pursuant to this Article;

    b. Have been convicted of or entered a plea of guilty or nolo contendere to:

        1. Any felony;

        2. Any misdemeanor or infraction involving animal abuse or neglect; or

        3. Any other offense related to animal euthanasia, the duties or responsibilities of a euthanasia technician, or a euthanasia technician's fitness for certification;

    c. Make any false statement, give false information, or omit material information in connection with an application for certification or for renewal or reinstatement of certification as a euthanasia technician; or

    d. Otherwise are or become ineligible for certification.

(8) Provision of the names of persons who perform euthanasia at animal shelters and for the animal shelter to notify the Department when those persons are no longer affiliated, employed, or serving as a volunteer with the shelter.

(9) Certified euthanasia technicians to notify the Department when they are no longer employed by or are serving as a volunteer at an animal shelter.

(10) The duties, responsibilities, and standards of conduct for certified euthanasia technicians.

(c)   Regardless of the extent to which the Board exercises its authority under subsection (b) of this section, the Department may deny, revoke, or suspend the certification of a euthanasia technician who has been convicted of or entered a plea of guilty or nolo contendere to a felony involving the illegal use, possession, sale, manufacture, distribution, or transportation of a controlled substance, drug, or narcotic.

(d)   Persons seeking certification as euthanasia technicians, or a renewal of such certification, shall provide the Department a fingerprint card in a format acceptable to the Department, a form signed by the person consenting to a criminal record check and the use of the person's fingerprints, and such other identifying information as may be required by the State or national data banks. The Department may deny certification to persons who refuse to provide the fingerprint card or consent to the criminal background check. Fees required by the Department of Public Safety for conducting the criminal background check shall be collected by the Department and remitted to the Department of Public Safety along with the fingerprint card and consent form.

§ 19A-25. Employees; investigations; right of entry.

For the enforcement of the provisions of this Article, the Director is authorized, subject to the approval of the Commissioner to appoint employees as are necessary in order to carry out and enforce the provisions of this Article, and to assign them interchangeably with other employees of the Animal Health Division. The Director shall cause the investigation of all reports of violations of the provisions of this Article, and the rules adopted pursuant to the provisions hereof; provided further, that if any person shall deny the Director or his representative admittance to his property, either person shall be entitled to secure from any superior court judge a court order granting such admittance.

§ 19A-26. Certificate of registration required for animal shelter.

No person shall operate an animal shelter unless a certificate of registration for such animal shelter shall have been granted by the Director. Application for such certificate shall be made in the manner provided by the Director. No fee shall be required for such application or certificate. Certificates of registration shall be valid for a period of one year or until suspended or revoked and may be renewed for like periods upon application in the manner provided.

. . .

§ 19A-30. Refusal, suspension or revocation of certificate or license.

The Director may refuse to issue or renew or may suspend or revoke a certificate of registration for any animal shelter or a license for any public auction, kennel, pet shop, or dealer, if after an impartial investigation as provided in this Article he determines that any one or more of the following grounds apply:

(1)   Material misstatement in the application for the original certificate of registration or license or in the application for any renewal under this Article;

(2)   Willful disregard or violation of this Article or any rules issued pursuant thereto;

(3)   Failure to provide adequate housing facilities and/or primary enclosures for the purposes of this Article, or if the feeding, watering, sanitizing and housing practices at the animal shelter, public auction, pet shop, or kennel are not consistent with the intent of this Article or the rules adopted under this Article;

(4)   Allowing one's license under this Article to be used by an unlicensed person;

(5)   Conviction of any crime an essential element of which is misstatement, fraud, or dishonesty, or conviction of any felony;

(6) Making substantial misrepresentations or false promises of a character likely to influence, persuade, or induce in connection with the business of a public auction, commercial kennel, pet shop, or dealer;

(7) Pursuing a continued course of misrepresentation of or making false promises through advertising, salesmen, agents, or otherwise in connection with the business to be licensed;

(8) Failure to possess the necessary qualifications or to meet the requirements of this Article for the issuance or holding of a certificate of registration or license.

The Director shall, before refusing to issue or renew and before suspension or revocation of a certificate of registration or a license, give to the applicant or holder thereof a written notice containing a statement indicating in what respects the applicant or holder has failed to satisfy the requirements for the holding of a certificate of registration or a license. If a certificate of registration or a license is suspended or revoked under the provisions hereof, the holder shall have five days from such suspension or revocation to surrender all certificates of registration or licenses issued thereunder to the Director or his authorized representative.

A person to whom a certificate of registration or a license is denied, suspended, or revoked by the Director may contest the action by filing a petition under G.S. 150B-23 within five days after the denial, suspension, or revocation.

Any licensee whose license is revoked under the provisions of this Article shall not be eligible to apply for a new license hereunder until one year has elapsed from the date of the order revoking said license or if an appeal is taken from said order of revocation, one year from the date of the order or final judgment sustaining said revocation. Any person who has been an officer, agent, or employee of a licensee whose license has been revoked or suspended and who is responsible for or participated in the violation upon which the order of suspension or revocation was based, shall not be licensed within the period during which the order of suspension or revocation is in effect.

. . .

§ 19A-32. Procedure for review of Director's decisions.

A denial, suspension, or revocation of a certificate or license under this Article shall be made in accordance with Chapter 150B of the General Statutes.

§ 19A-32.1. Minimum holding period for animals in animal shelters; public viewing of animals in animal shelters; disposition of animals.

(a) Except as otherwise provided in this section, all animals received by an animal shelter or by an agent of an animal shelter shall be held for a minimum holding period of 72 hours, or for any longer minimum period established by a board of county commissioners, prior to being euthanized or otherwise disposed of.

(b) Before an animal may be euthanized or otherwise disposed of, it shall be made available for adoption under procedures that enable members of the public to inspect the animal, except in the following cases:

(1) The animal has been found by the operator of the shelter to be unadoptable due to injury or defects of health or temperament.

(2) The animal is seriously ill or injured, in which case the animal may be euthanized before the expiration of the minimum holding period if the manager of the animal shelter determines, in writing, that it is appropriate to do so. The writing shall include the reason for the determination.

(3) The animal is being held as evidence in a pending criminal case.

(c) Except as otherwise provided in this subsection, a person who comes to an animal shelter attempting to locate a lost pet is entitled to view every animal held at the shelter, subject to rules providing for such viewing during at least four hours a day, three days a week. If the shelter is housing animals that must be kept apart from the general public for health reasons, public safety concerns, or in order to preserve evidence for criminal proceedings, the shelter shall make reasonable arrangements that allow pet owners to determine whether their lost pets are among those animals.

(d)   During the minimum holding period, an animal shelter may place an animal it is holding into foster care by transferring possession of the animal to an approved foster care provider, an approved rescue organization, or the person who found the animal. If an animal shelter transfers possession of an animal under this subsection, at least one photograph depicting the head and face of the animal shall be displayed at the shelter in a conspicuous location that is available to the general public during hours of operation, and that photograph shall remain posted until the animal is disposed of as provided in subsection (f) of this section.

(e)   If a shelter places an animal in foster care, the shelter may, in writing, appoint the person or organization possessing the animal to be an agent of the shelter. After the expiration of the minimum holding period, the shelter may (i) direct the agent possessing the animal to return it to the shelter, (ii) allow the agent to adopt the animal consistent with the shelter's adoption policies, or (iii) extend the period of time that the agent holds the animal on behalf of the shelter. A shelter may terminate an agency created under this subsection at any time by directing the agent to deliver the animal to the shelter. The local government or organization operating the shelter, as principal in the agency relationship, shall not be liable to reimburse the agent for the costs of care of the animal and shall not be liable to the owner of the animal for harm to the animal caused by the agent, absent a written contract providing otherwise.

(f)   An animal that is surrendered to an animal shelter by the animal's owner and not reclaimed by that owner during the minimum holding period may be disposed of in one of the following manners:
   (1)   Returned to the owner.
   (2)   Adopted as a pet by a new owner.
   (3)   Euthanized by a procedure approved by rules adopted by the Department of Agriculture and Consumer Services or, in the absence of such rules, by a procedure approved by the American Veterinary Medical Association, the Humane Society of the United States, or the American Humane Association.

(g)   An animal that is surrendered to an animal shelter by the animal's owner may be disposed of before the expiration of the minimum holding period in a manner authorized under subsection (f) of this section if the owner provides to the shelter (i) some proof of ownership of the animal and (ii) a signed written consent to the disposition of the animal before the expiration of the minimum holding period.

(h)   If the owner of a dog surrenders the dog to an animal shelter, the owner shall state in writing whether the dog has bitten any individual within the 10 days preceding the date of surrender.

(i)   An animal shelter shall require every person to whom an animal is released to present one of the following valid forms of governmentissued photographic identification: (i) a drivers license, (ii) a special identification card issued under G.S. 20-37.7, (iii) a military identification card, or (iv) a passport. Upon presentation of the required photographic identification, the shelter shall document the name of the person, the type of photographic identification presented by the person, and the photographic identification number.

(j)   Animal shelters shall maintain a record of all animals impounded at the shelter, shall retain those records for a period of at least three years from the date of impoundment, and shall make those records available for inspection during regular inspections pursuant to this Article or upon the request of a representative of the Animal Welfare Section. These records shall contain, at a minimum:
   (1)   The date of impoundment.

(2) The length of impoundment.
(3) The disposition of each animal, including the name and address of any person to whom the animal is released, any institution that person represents, and the identifying information required under subsection (i) of this section.
(4) Other information required by rules adopted by the Board of Agriculture.

. . .

§ 19A-35. Penalty for failure to adequately care for animals; disposition of animals.

Failure of any person licensed or registered under this Article to adequately house, feed, and water animals in his possession or custody shall constitute a Class 3 misdemeanor, and such person shall be subject to a fine of not less than five dollars ($5.00) per animal or more than a total of one thousand dollars ($1,000). Such animals shall be subject to seizure and impoundment and upon conviction may be sold or euthanized at the discretion of the Director and such failure shall also constitute grounds for revocation of license after public hearing.

§ 19A-36. Penalty for violation of Article by dog warden.

Violation of any provision of this Article which relates to the seizing, impoundment, and custody of an animal by a dog warden shall constitute a Class 3 misdemeanor and the person convicted thereof shall be subject to a fine of not less than fifty dollars ($50.00) and not more than one hundred dollars ($100.00), and each animal handled in violation shall constitute a separate offense.

§ 19A-37. Application of Article.

This Article shall not apply to a place or establishment which is operated under the immediate supervision of a duly licensed veterinarian as a hospital where animals are harbored, boarded, and cared for incidental to the treatment, prevention, or alleviation of disease processes during the routine practice of the profession of veterinary medicine. This Article shall not apply to any dealer, pet shop, public auction, commercial kennel or research facility during the period such dealer or research facility is in the possession of a valid license or registration granted by the Secretary of Agriculture pursuant to Title 7, Chapter 54, of the United States Code. This Article shall not apply to any individual who occasionally boards an animal on a noncommercial basis, although such individual may receive nominal sums to cover the cost of such boarding.

. . .

§ 19A-40. Civil Penalties.

The Director may assess a civil penalty of not more than five thousand dollars ($5,000) against any person who violates a provision of this Article or any rule promulgated thereunder. In determining the amount of the penalty, the Director shall consider the degree and extent of harm caused by the violation. The clear proceeds of civil penalties assessed pursuant to this section shall be remitted to the Civil Penalty and Forfeiture Fund in accordance with G.S. 115C-457.2.

§ 19A-41. Legal representation by the Attorney General.

It shall be the duty of the Attorney General to represent the Commissioner of Agriculture and the Department of Agriculture and Consumer Services, or to designate some member of his staff to represent the Commissioner and the Department, in all actions or proceedings in connection with this Article.

Article 5A [of G.S. Chapter 19A].
Animal Shelter Support Fund.

§ 19A-67. Animal Shelter Support Fund.

    (a)   Creation. – The Animal Shelter Support Fund is established as a special fund in the Department of Agriculture and Consumer Services. The Fund consists of appropriations by the General Assembly or contributions and grants from public or private sources.

    (b)   Use. – The Fund shall be used by the Animal Welfare Section of the Department of Agriculture and Consumer Services to reimburse local governments for expenses related to their operation of a registered animal shelter due to any of the following:

        (1)   The denial, suspension, or revocation of the shelter's registration.

        (2)   An unforeseen catastrophic disaster at an animal shelter.

    (c)   Rules. – The Board of Agriculture shall issue rules detailing eligible expenses and application guidelines that comply with the requirements of this Article.

    (d)   Reversion. – Any appropriated and unencumbered funds remaining at the end of each fiscal year in excess of two hundred fifty thousand dollars ($250,000) shall revert to the General Fund.

§ 19A-68. Distributions to counties and cities from Animal Shelter Support Fund.

    (a)   Reimbursable Costs. – Local governments eligible for distributions from the Animal Shelter Support Fund may receive reimbursement only for the direct operational costs of the animal shelter following an event described in G.S. 19A-67(b). For purposes of this subsection, direct operational costs shall include veterinary services, sanitation services and needs, animal sustenance and supplies, and temporary housing and sheltering. Counties and cities shall not be reimbursed for administrative costs or capital expenditures for facilities and equipment.

    (b)   CostShare. – A local government requesting distributions from the Animal Shelter Support Fund must provide a local match based on their most recent development tier designation as defined in G.S. 143B-437.08. Local governments located in development tier one counties must provide a match equivalent to one dollar ($1.00) for every three dollars ($3.00) distributed from the Fund. Local governments located in development tier two counties must provide a match equivalent to one dollar ($1.00) for every two dollars ($2.00) distributed from the Fund. Local governments located in development tier three counties must provide a match equivalent to one dollar ($1.00) for every one dollar ($1.00) distributed from the Fund.

    (c)   Application. – A county or city eligible for reimbursement from the Animal Shelter Support Fund shall apply to the Department of Agriculture and Consumer Services within 60 days of when the reimbursable cost has been incurred. The application shall be submitted in the form required by the Department and shall include an itemized listing of the costs for which reimbursement is sought.

    (d)   Distribution. – The Department shall make payments from the Animal Shelter Support Fund to eligible counties and cities that have made timely application for reimbursement within 30 days of receipt of requests.

§ 19A-69. Report.

The Department shall report annually to the Joint Legislative Commission on Governmental Operations and the Fiscal Research Division no later than March 1. The report shall contain information regarding all revenues and expenditures of the Animal Shelter Support Fund.

Article 6 [of G.S. Chapter 19A].
Care of Animal Subjected to Illegal Treatment.

§ 19A-70. Care of animal subjected to illegal treatment.

(a) In every arrest under any provision of Article 47 of Chapter 14 of the General Statutes or under G.S. 67-4.3 or upon the commencement of an action under Article 1 of this Chapter by a county or municipality, by a countyapproved animal cruelty investigator, by other county or municipal official, or by an organization operating a county or municipal shelter under contract, if an animal shelter takes custody of an animal, the operator of the shelter may file a petition with the court requesting that the defendant be ordered to deposit funds in an amount sufficient to secure payment of all the reasonable expenses expected to be incurred by the animal shelter in caring for and providing for the animal pending the disposition of the litigation. For purposes of this section, "reasonable expenses" includes the cost of providing food, water, shelter, and care, including medical care, for at least 30 days.

(b) Upon receipt of a petition, the court shall set a hearing on the petition to determine the need to care for and provide for the animal pending the disposition of the litigation. The hearing shall be conducted no less than 10 and no more than 15 business days after the petition is filed. The operator of the animal shelter shall mail written notice of the hearing and a copy of the petition to the defendant at the address contained in the criminal charges or the complaint or summons by which a civil action was initiated. If the defendant is in a local detention facility at the time the petition is filed, the operator of the animal shelter shall also provide notice to the custodian of the detention facility.

(c) The court shall set the amount of funds necessary for 30 days' care after taking into consideration all of the facts and circumstances of the case, including the need to care for and provide for the animal pending the disposition of the litigation, the recommendation of the operator of the animal shelter, the estimated cost of caring for and providing for the animal, and the defendant's ability to pay. If the court determines that the defendant is unable to deposit funds, the court may consider issuing an order under subsection (f) of this section.

 Any order for funds to be deposited pursuant to this section shall state that if the operator of the animal shelter files an affidavit with the clerk of superior court, at least two business days prior to the expiration of a 30day period, stating that, to the best of the affiant's knowledge, the case against the defendant has not yet been resolved, the order shall be automatically renewed every 30 days until the case is resolved.

(d) If the court orders that funds be deposited, the amount of funds necessary for 30 days shall be posted with the clerk of superior court. The defendant shall also deposit the same amount with the clerk of superior court every 30 days thereafter until the litigation is resolved, unless the defendant requests a hearing no less than five business days prior to the expiration of a 30day period. If the defendant fails to deposit the funds within five business days of the initial hearing, or five business days of the expiration of a 30day period, the animal is forfeited by operation of law. If funds have been deposited in accordance with this section, the operator of the animal shelter may draw from the funds the actual costs incurred in caring for the animal.

 In the event of forfeiture, the animal shelter may determine whether the animal is suitable for adoption and whether adoption can be arranged for the animal. The animal may not be adopted by the defendant or by any person residing In the defendant's household. If the adopted animal is a dog used for fighting, the animal shelter shall notify any persons adopting the dog of the liability provisions for owners of dangerous dogs under Article 1A of Chapter 67 of the General Statutes. If no adoption can be arranged after the forfeiture, or the animal is unsuitable for adoption, the shelter shall humanely euthanize the animal.

(e)   The deposit of funds shall not prevent the animal shelter from disposing of the animal prior to the expiration of the 30day period covered by the deposit if the court makes a final determination of the charges or claims against the defendant. Upon determination, the defendant is entitled to a refund for any portion of the deposit not incurred as expenses by the animal shelter. A person who is acquitted of all criminal charges or not found to have committed animal cruelty in a civil action under Article 1 of this Chapter is entitled to a refund of the deposit remaining after any draws from the deposit in accordance with subsection (d) of this section.

(f)   Pursuant to subsection (c) of this section, the court may order a defendant to provide necessary food, water, shelter, and care, including any necessary medical care, for any animal that is the basis of the charges or claims against the defendant without the removal of the animal from the existing location and until the charges or claims against the defendant are adjudicated. If the court issues such an order, the court shall provide for an animal control officer or other law enforcement officer to make regular visits to the location to ensure that the animal is receiving necessary food, water, shelter, and care, including any necessary medical care, and to impound the animal if it is not receiving those necessities.

Article 23 [of G.S. Chapter 153A].
Miscellaneous Provisions.

. . .

§ 153A-442. Animal shelters.

A county may establish, equip, operate, and maintain an animal shelter or may contribute to the support of an animal shelter, and for these purposes may appropriate funds not otherwise limited as to use by law. The animal shelters shall meet the same standards as animal shelters regulated by the Department of Agriculture pursuant to its authority under Chapter 19A of the General Statutes.

. . .

§ 153A-449. Contracts with private entities; contractors must use E-Verify.

(a)   Authority. – A county may contract with and appropriate money to any person, association, or corporation, in order to carry out any public purpose that the county is authorized by law to engage in. A county may not require a private contractor under this section to abide by any restriction that the county could not impose on all employers in the county, such as paying minimum wage or providing paid sick leave to its employees, as a condition of bidding on a contract.

(b)   [Repealed by S.L. 2015-294, § 1(c), effective October 1, 2015, and applicable to contracts entered into on or after that date.]

Article 3 [of G.S. Chapter 160A].
Contracts.

. . .

§ 160A-20.1. Contracts with private entities; contractors must use E-Verify.

(a)   Authority. – A city may contract with and appropriate money to any person, association, or corporation, in order to carry out any public purpose that the city is authorized by law to engage in. A city may not require a private contractor under this section to abide by any restriction that the city could not impose on all employers in the city, such as paying minimum wage or providing paid sick leave to its employees, as a condition of bidding on a contract.

(b) Repealed by Session Laws 2015-294, § 1(b), effective October 1, 2015, and applicable to contracts entered into on or after that date.

Article 21 [of G.S. Chapter 160A].
Miscellaneous.

. . .

§ 160A-493. Animal shelters.

A city may establish, equip, operate, and maintain an animal shelter or may contribute to the support of an animal shelter, and for these purposes may appropriate funds not otherwise limited as to use by law. The animal shelters shall meet the same standards as animal shelters regulated by the Department of Agriculture pursuant to its authority under Chapter 19A of the General Statutes.

Appendix B. Relevant Regulations—North Carolina Administrative Code (hereinafter NCAC)

Title 2, Chapter 52, Subchapter J
Animal Welfare Section

Section .0100 – Record Keeping and Licensing

02 NCAC 52J .0101   RECORDS; ANIMAL SHELTERS, ETC.

Operators of all animal shelters, pet shops, public auctions, and dealers shall maintain records on all dogs and cats showing the following:
(1) origin of animals (including names and addresses of consignors) and date animals were received;
(2) description of animals including species, age, sex, breed, and color markings;
(3) location of animal if not kept at the licensed or registered facility;
(4) disposition of animals including name and address of person to whom animal is sold, traded or adopted and the date of such transaction; in the event of death, the record shall show the date, signs of illness, or cause of death if identified; if euthanized, the record shall show date and type of euthanasia; and
(5) record of veterinary care including treatments, immunization and date, time, description of medication (including name and dosage), and initials of person administering any product or procedure.

02 NCAC 52J .0102   RECORDS; BOARDING KENNELS

Operators of boarding kennels shall maintain records of all dogs and cats showing the following:
(1) name and address of owner or person responsible for animal, the date of entry and signature and address of individual to whom animal is released and the date of release;
(2) description of animal including breed, sex, age and color marking; and
(3) veterinary care provided while boarded, which shall include date, times, description of medication (including name and dosage) and initials of person administering product or procedure.

02 NCAC 52J .0103   INSPECTION OF RECORDS

All operators of animal shelters, pet shops, boarding kennels, public auctions, and persons operating as dealers shall make all required records available to the director or his authorized representative on request, during the business and cleaning hours listed on the license application. The operator must be able to match each animal to its record upon request. Records shall be maintained for a period of one year after the animal is released.

02 NCAC 52J .0104   DEFINITIONS

As used in this Subchapter:
(1) "Accessories" means any objects used in cleaning and sanitizing primary enclosures, exercise areas, or objects to which an animal may have access, including, but not limited to toys, blankets, food and water utensils, and bedding.

(2) "Adequate" means a condition which, when met, does not jeopardize an animal's comfort, safety or health.

(3) "Cage" means a primary enclosure which is enclosed on all sides and also on the top and bottom.

(4) "Husbandry" means the practice of daily care administered to animals.

(5) "Isolation" means the setting apart of an animal from all other animals, food, and equipment in the facility for the sole purpose of preventing the spread of disease.

(6) "License period" means July 1 through June 30.

(7) "Long term care" means the housing of an animal for a period of more than 30 consecutive days.

(8) "Properly cleaned" means the removal of carcasses, debris, food waste, excrement, or other organic material with adequate frequency.

(9) "Social interaction" means friendly physical contact or play between animals of the same species or with a person.

(10) "Suitable method of drainage" means drainage that allows for the elimination of water and waste products, prevents contamination of animals, allows animals to remain dry, and complies with applicable building codes and local ordinances.

(11) "Supervision of animals" means one person (at least 16 years of age) present, at all times, able to directly view each enclosure or common area.

Section .0200 – Facilities and Operating Standards

02 NCAC 52J .0201   GENERAL

(a) Housing facilities for dogs and cats shall be structurally sound and maintained in good repair to protect the animals from injury, contain the animals and restrict the entrance of other animals and people.

(b) All light fixtures and electrical outlets in animal areas shall be in compliance with the State Building Code.

(c) Facilities shall have reliable and safe electric power as necessary to comply with the Animal Welfare Act.

(d) Supplies of food and bedding shall be stored in facilities which adequately protect such supplies against infestation or contamination by vermin and insects. All open bags of food shall be stored in airtight containers with lids. Refrigeration shall be provided for supplies of perishable food.

(e) Provisions shall be made for the daily removal and disposal of animal and food waste, bedding and debris from the housing facility in accordance with local ordinances, to assure facility will be maintained in a clean and sanitary manner.

(f) Hot and cold running, potable water must be available. Facilities such as washroom, basin or sink shall be provided to maintain cleanliness among animal caretakers, animals, and animal food and water receptacles.

(g) Each facility shall have the ability to confirm ambient temperature.

(h) A separate five-foot perimeter fence is required if any animals have access to an outdoor enclosure, including unsupervised exercise areas.

(i) An adequate drainage system must be provided for the housing facility.

(j) All areas of a facility are subject to review or inspection by North Carolina Department of Agriculture and Consumer Services employees during normal business hours (8:00 a.m. through 5:30 p.m. Monday through Friday).

(k) All animals in a facility are subject to the requirements of the Animal Welfare Act, regardless of ownership.

(l) A licensee or registrant shall comply with all federal, state and local laws, rules and ordinances relating to or affecting the welfare of dogs and cats in its facility.

(m) No dog or cat shall be in a window display except during business hours and then only in compliance with standards set forth in this Section.

02 NCAC 52J .0202   INDOOR FACILITIES

(a) Indoor housing facilities for dogs and cats shall be adequately heated and cooled when necessary to protect the dogs and cats from cold and excessive heat and provide for their health and comfort. The ambient temperature shall not be allowed to fall below 50 degrees F. or exceed 85 degrees F.

(b) Indoor housing facilities for dogs and cats shall be adequately ventilated to provide for the health and comfort of the animals at all times. The facilities shall be provided with fresh air either by means of windows, doors, vents or air conditioning and shall be ventilated so as to minimize drafts. Air flow shall be adequate to minimize odors and moisture condensation.

(c) Indoor housing facilities for dogs and cats shall have adequate illumination to permit routine inspections, maintenance, cleaning and housekeeping of the facility and observation of the animals. Illumination shall provide regular diurnal lighting cycles of either natural or artificial light, uniformly diffused throughout the animal facilities.

(d) Interior building surfaces of indoor facilities with which animals come in contact shall be constructed and maintained so that they are impervious to moisture, and can be readily sanitized.

(e) A suitable method of drainage shall be provided to rapidly eliminate excess water from an indoor housing facility. If closed drain systems are used, they shall be equipped with traps and installed to prevent odors and backup of sewage. The drainage system shall be constructed to prevent cross-contamination among animals.

02 NCAC 52J .0203   OUTDOOR FACILITIES

(a) In outdoor facilities that are subject to the Animal Welfare Act, primary enclosures and walkways with which an animal comes in contact shall be constructed of sealed concrete or other surfaces impervious to moisture. Gravel may be used if maintained at a minimum depth of six inches and kept in a sanitary manner.

(b) Dogs and cats kept outdoors shall be provided housing to allow them to remain dry and comfortable during inclement weather. Housing shall be constructed of material which is impervious to moisture and which can be disinfected. One house shall be available for each animal within each enclosure except for a mother and its unweaned offspring.

(c) In addition to housing, the enclosure shall provide protection from excessive sun and inclement weather.

(d) Animal owners shall be advised at the time of reservation and admission if the animal will be kept in outside facilities.

(e) A suitable method of drainage shall be provided.

02 NCAC 52J .0204   PRIMARY ENCLOSURES

(a) Primary enclosures shall be constructed so as to prevent contamination from waste and wastewater from animals in other enclosures. All surfaces with which an animal comes in contact shall be impervious to moisture. For primary enclosures placed into service on or after January 1, 2005, no wood shall be within the animal's reach. For primary enclosures in use in a licensed or registered facility prior to January 1, 2005, any damaged wood must be replaced in a manner that does not permit contact with wood by the animal.

(b) Primary enclosures for dogs and cats shall be structurally sound and maintained in good repair and in a manner to prevent injury to animals and keep other animals out. Primary enclosures shall be constructed so as to provide space to allow each dog or cat to walk, urn about freely, and to easily stand, sit, or lie in a natural position. The height of a primary enclosure other than a cage shall be no less than five feet. All enclosures shall be constructed to prevent the escape of animals.

(c) Each primary enclosure shall be provided with a solid resting surface or surfaces adequate to comfortably hold all occupants of the primary enclosure at the same time. All resting surfaces must be of a non-porous or easily sanitized material, such as a towel, or a disposable material such as newspaper. The resting surface or surfaces shall be elevated in primary enclosures housing two or more cats.

(d) In addition to Paragraph (b) of this Rule, each dog shall be provided a minimum square footage of floor space equal to the mathematical square of the sum of the length of the dog in inches, as measured from the tip of its nose to the base of its tail, plus six inches, then divide the product by 144. The calculation is: (length of dog in inches + 6) x (length of dog in inches + 6) = required floor space in square inches. Required floor space in square inches ÷ 144 = required floor space in square feet. The calculation shall be expressed in square feet. Not more than four adult dogs shall be housed in the same primary enclosure without supervision.

(e) If more than four dogs are housed in a common area or enclosure, then there must be at least one person supervising each 10 dogs housed within each enclosure or common area.

(f) In addition to Paragraph (b) of this Rule, each feline older than six months housed in any primary enclosure shall be provided a minimum of four square feet of floor space which may include elevated resting surfaces. Each feline younger than six months shall be provided 1.5 square feet. Not more than 12 cats shall be housed in the same primary enclosure.

(g) In all cat enclosures, a receptacle containing clean litter shall be provided for waste. A minimum of one receptacle per three cats is required.

02 NCAC 52J .0205 FEEDING

(a) Dogs and cats shall be fed at least once each 24-hour period except as otherwise might be required to provide adequate veterinary care. Food shall be commercially prepared food which complies with laws applicable to animal feed or the food shall be provided by the owner. The food shall be free from contamination, wholesome, palatable, and of adequate quality and quantity appropriate for the given size, age, and condition of an animal to meet the daily requirements for nutritional value. Puppies and kittens less than six months of age shall be fed at least twice in each 24-hour period. An eight-hour interval between feedings is required if only two feedings are offered in a 24-hour period.

(b) Food receptacles shall be accessible to all dogs or cats and shall be located so as to minimize contamination by waste. For every adult animal, there must be at least one food receptacle offered. Food receptacles shall be durable and shall be kept clean and sanitized. Damaged receptacles shall be replaced. Disposable food receptacles may be used but must be discarded after each feeding.

(c) Food and water receptacles in outdoor facilities shall be protected from the elements.

02 NCAC 52J .0206 WATERING

Animals shall have continuous access to fresh water, except as might otherwise be required to provide adequate veterinary care. Watering receptacles shall be durable and kept clean and sanitized. Damaged receptacles shall be replaced.

02 NCAC 52J .0207 SANITATION

(a) Waste shall be removed from primary enclosures and exercise areas to prevent contamination of the dogs or cats contained therein and to reduce disease hazards and odors. Enclosures and exercise areas for dogs and cats must be properly cleaned a minimum of two times per day. The animal must be able to walk or lie down without coming in contact with any waste or debris. When a hosing or flushing method is used for cleaning an enclosure, dogs or cats contained therein shall be removed during the cleaning process, and adequate measures shall be taken to protect the animals in other such enclosures from being contaminated with water and other wastes.

(b) Sanitation shall be as follows:

   (1)   Prior to the introduction of dogs or cats into empty primary enclosures previously occupied, enclosures and accessories shall be sanitized in the manner provided in Subparagraph (b)(3) of this Rule.

   (2)   In addition to primary enclosures being properly cleaned a minimum of two times per day, enclosures and accessories shall be sanitized a minimum of once every seven days in the manner provided in Subparagraph (b)(3) of this Rule if the same animal is housed in the same enclosure more than seven days.

   (3)   Cages, rooms and hardsurfaced pens or runs shall be sanitized by:

      (A)   washing them with hot water (180 degrees F.) and soap or detergent as in a mechanical cage washer; or

      (B)   washing all soiled surfaces with a detergent solution to remove all organic matter followed by application of a safe and effective disinfectant; or

      (C)   cleaning all soiled surfaces with live steam.

   (4)   Food and water receptacles shall be sanitized daily with hot water, detergent, and disinfectant.

   (5)   Soiled linens and cloth products shall be mechanically washed with detergent and sanitized.

   (6)   Any area accessible to multiple animals shall be kept clean and sanitary.

(c) Premises (buildings and grounds) shall be kept clean and in good repair in order to protect the animals from injury and to facilitate the prescribed husbandry practices set forth in this Rule. Premises shall remain free of accumulations of trash, junk, waste products, and discarded matter. Weeds, grasses, and bushes must be controlled so as to facilitate cleaning of the premises and to improve pest control, and to protect the health and well-being of the animals.

(d) An effective program for the control of insects, ectoparasites, and avian and mammalian pests shall be established and maintained.

02 NCAC 52J .0208   EMPLOYEES

A sufficient number of employees shall be utilized to maintain the prescribed level of husbandry practices set forth in this Rule. Such practices shall be under the supervision of an animal caretaker who has a background in animal husbandry or care.

02 NCAC 52J .0209   CLASSIFICATION AND SEPARATION

Animals housed in the same primary enclosure shall be maintained in compatible groups, with the following additional restrictions:

   (1)   Females in season (estrus) shall not be housed in the same primary enclosure with males, except for planned breeding purposes. Breeding shall not be allowed in animal shelters.

   (2)   In boarding kennels, animals of different owners shall not have contact with other animals, unless written permission is obtained from the animal's owner. Any dog or cat exhibiting an aggressive disposition shall be housed individually in a primary enclosure.

   (3)   Puppies or kittens less than four months of age shall not be housed in the same primary enclosure with adult dogs or cats other than their dams, except when permanently maintained in breeding colonies, or if requested in writing, by the animals' owner, as in a boarding kennel. Puppies or kittens between 4 and 16 weeks of age shall have daily access to human social interaction, excluding animals which pose a danger to humans or other animals.

(4)   Dogs shall not be housed in the same primary enclosure with cats, nor shall dogs or cats be housed in the same primary enclosure with any other species of animals. Exceptions are allowed at boarding kennels, if requested in writing by the animals' owner.

(5)   All facilities shall designate an isolation area for animals being treated or observed for communicable diseases. Dogs or cats in isolation that are being treated for a communicable disease shall be separated from other dogs or cats and other susceptible species of animals in such a manner as to minimize dissemination of such disease. A sign shall be posted at the cage or isolation area when in use, giving notice of a communicable disease.

(6)   Animals in long term care which are intended for adoption or sale must be provided the following:
    (a)   Daily access to both human and same species social interaction.
    (b)   Daily access to space other than the primary enclosure.
    (c)   A species and size-appropriate toy, unless it poses a health threat.

(7)   All animals shall be confined in primary enclosures or exercise areas.

02 NCAC 52J .0210   VETERINARY CARE

(a) A written program of veterinary care to include disease control and prevention, vaccination, euthanasia, and adequate veterinary care shall be established with the assistance of a licensed veterinarian by any person who is required to be licensed or registered under the Animal Welfare Act, Article 3 of Chapter 19A of the General Statutes.

(b) If there is a disease problem that persists for more than 30 days at the facility, the facility operator shall obtain and follow a veterinarian's written recommendations for correcting the problem.

(c) Each dog and cat shall be observed daily by the animal caretaker in charge, or by someone under his direct supervision. Sick or diseased, injured, lame, or blind dogs or cats shall be provided with veterinary care or be euthanized, provided that this shall not affect compliance with any state or local law requiring the holding, for a specified period, of animals suspected of being diseased. If euthanasia is performed at a certified facility, a list of personnel approved to perform euthanasia shall be maintained in a Policy and Procedure Manual as described in 02 NCAC 52J .0800. Diseased or deformed animals shall be sold or adopted only under the policy set forth in the "Program of Veterinary Care." Full written disclosure of the medical condition of the animal shall be provided to the new owner.

(d) All animals in a licensed or registered facility shall be in compliance with the North Carolina rabies law, G.S. 130A, Article 6, Part 6. However, no shelter shall be disapproved following inspection or otherwise cited for failure to inoculate any dog or cat known to be less than 12 weeks old or until such animals have been in the shelter at least 15 days.

Section .0300 – Transportation Standards

02 NCAC 52J .0301   VEHICLES

(a) Vehicles used in transporting dogs and cats shall be mechanically sound and equipped to provide fresh air to all animals transported without harmful drafts.

(b) The animal cargo space shall be constructed and maintained so as to prevent engine exhaust fumes from getting to the animals.

(c) The interior of the animal cargo space shall be kept clean. It shall be sanitized as deemed necessary.

02 NCAC 52J .0302   PRIMARY ENCLOSURES USED IN TRANSPORTING DOGS AND CATS

(a) Primary enclosures such as compartments or transport cages, cartons, or crates used by persons subject to the Animal Welfare Act to transport cats and dogs shall be constructed, ventilated and designed to protect the health and insure the safety of the animals. Such enclosures shall be constructed or positioned in the vehicle in such a manner that:

(1)   Each animal in the vehicle has sufficient fresh air for normal breathing.

(2)   The openings of such enclosures are easily accessible for emergency removals at all times.

(3)   The animals are adequately protected from the elements.

The ambient temperature shall be maintained between 50 degrees F and 85 degrees F. A shelter shall be deemed as being in compliance if its vehicles' animal containment units are equipped with operable air-conditioning, forced-air cooling and heating or other temperature control mechanisms.

(b) Animals transported in the same primary enclosure shall be of the same species. Puppies or kittens less than four months of age shall not be transported in the same primary enclosure with adult dogs and cats other than their dams.

(c) Primary enclosures used to transport dogs and cats shall be large enough for each animal to turn about freely, and to easily stand, sit, or lie down in a natural position. Primary enclosures used to transport dogs and cats shall be secured to the vehicle to prevent sliding or tipping of the enclosure during transit.

(d) Animals shall not be placed in primary enclosures over other animals in transit unless such enclosure is constructed so as to prevent animal excreta from entering lower enclosures.

(e) All primary enclosures used to transport dogs and cats shall be sanitized between use for shipments.

02 NCAC 52J .0303   FOOD AND WATER REQUIREMENTS

If dogs and cats are transported for a period of more than 12 hours:

(1)   The vehicle shall stop at least once every 12 hours for a period of one hour. During the one hour stop, potable water shall be continuously provided for dogs and cats.

(2)   Adult dogs and cats shall be fed at least once during each 24 hour period. Puppies and kittens less than six months of age shall be fed every six hours.

(3)   Dogs shall be removed from the vehicle, given fresh water and given the opportunity for exercise if they have been confined in the vehicle for 36 hours.

02 NCAC 52J .0304   CARE IN TRANSIT

It shall be the responsibility of the attendant or driver to inspect animals frequently enough to assure health and comfort and to determine if they need emergency care and to obtain it if needed.

Section .0400 – Euthanasia Standards

02 NCAC 52J .0401   ADOPTION BY REFERENCE

A person required to obtain a certificate of registration pursuant to G.S. 19A, Article 3 may use any method of euthanasia approved by the American Veterinary Medical Association (AVMA), the Humane Society of the United States (HSUS), or the American Humane Association (AHA) which are hereby incorporated by reference, including subsequent amendments and editions. Copies of these documents may be obtained as follows:

(1)   AVMA Guidelines on Euthanasia may be accessed at no cost on their website at www.avma. org.

(2)   The HSUS Euthanasia Training Manual can be purchased through their website at www.hsus. org at a cost of nineteen dollars and ninety-five cents ($19.95).

(3)   The AHA publication, Euthanasia by Injection, can be purchased through their website at www.americanhumane.org at a cost of ten dollars ($10.00).

02 NCAC 52J .0402   AUTHORIZED PERSONS

Only a Certified Euthanasia Technician, Probationary Euthanasia Technician, or a veterinarian licensed to practice veterinary medicine in North Carolina may euthanize an animal in a certified animal shelter. A Certified Euthanasia Technician shall not euthanize animals using a method for which he or she is not currently certified except as specified in 02 NCAC 52J .0700.

02 NCAC 52J .0403   DEFINITIONS

As used in this Subchapter:
(1)   "Certified Euthanasia Technician" means a person employed by a certified facility who has been instructed in the proper methods of humane euthanasia, security and record keeping.
(2)   "Certified facility" means a certified animal shelter, kennel or pet shop that employs at least one Certified Euthanasia Technician or licensed veterinarian to perform euthanasia on animals at that certified facility.
(3)   "Approved Certified Euthanasia Technician trainer" means a person or organization that received permission from the Animal Welfare Section to provide training to applicants or individuals seeking to be Certified Euthanasia Technicians.
(4)   "Chemical Agent" means any chemical approved by the American Veterinary Medical Association, the Humane Society of the United States or the American Humane Association which is used to induce death.
(5)   "Applicant" means a person seeking certification as a Euthanasia Technician.
(6)   "Commercially manufactured chamber" means a chamber built with the intention for sale with the purpose of euthanizing animals, and which meets the requirements of 02 NCAC 52J .0600.
(7)   "Conviction of a criminal offense" means being found guilty, convicted, placed on probation or entering a guilty plea that is accepted by the court, forfeiture of bail, bond or collateral deposited to secure one's own appearance in a criminal proceeding or having received a withheld judgment, prayer for judgment continued or suspended sentence by a court of competent jurisdiction in this state, in a federal court or another state of any felony, as described by federal or state law, or any criminal act that in any way is related to practicing as a Certified Euthanasia Technician.

02 NCAC 52J .0404   CERTIFICATION REQUIREMENTS FOR EUTHANASIA TECHNICIANS

(a) Individuals who perform euthanasia must be trained and qualified as a Certified Euthanasia Technician as set forth in this Section.

(b) Individuals seeking certification as a Euthanasia Technician shall submit a written application documenting their qualifications to the Animal Welfare Section, North Carolina Department of Agriculture and Consumer Services, 1030 Mail Service Center, Raleigh, NC 27699-1030, on the form provided by the Animal Welfare Section.

(c) The Animal Welfare Section shall receive and review all applications for Euthanasia Technician certification and determine whether or not to issue the individual applicant proof of certification in the form of a printed certificate.

02 NCAC 52J .0405 CERTIFICATION STANDARDS

Applicants for certification as a Certified Euthanasia Technician shall be at least 18 years of age at the date they receive certification. Applicants are not eligible for certification if they have been convicted of a felony offense or a crime or infraction involving animal abuse or neglect and shall demonstrate compliance with this Section.

02 NCAC 52J .0406 APPLICATION REQUIREMENTS

An applicant for certification shall:
  (1) submit a completed and signed application form;
  (2) provide a document from an approved Certified Euthanasia Technician trainer establishing that the applicant has completed an approved course, passed the course written examination and passed a practical examination in the specific euthanasia techniques for which the applicant is seeking certification, or provide separate documentation of having taken an approved course and passed the written examination and having passed a practical examination given by a different approved Certified Euthanasia Technician trainer; and
  (3) specify in the application form the specific euthanasia techniques the applicant is requesting certification.

02 NCAC 52J .0407 TRAINING AND EXAMINATIONS

  (a) Training and examinations for euthanasia certification shall consist of:
  (1) Classroom lecture covering the entire list of subjects in Paragraph (b) of this Rule;
  (2) Earning a score of 80 percent correct on a written test provided by the Animal Welfare Section, demonstrating knowledge of the subjects listed in Paragraph (b) of this Rule; and
  (3) Passing a practical examination in each of the euthanasia methods for which the applicant is seeking certification.
  (b) The Animal Welfare Section shall develop Certified Euthanasia Technician training programs and materials or accredit training programs and materials to be offered by other individuals, schools, agencies or veterinary practices. The programs and materials shall conform to the processes set forth by the American Veterinary Medical Association, the Humane Society of the United States or the American Humane Association and shall include the following topics:
  (1) The theory and history of euthanasia methods and practice;
  (2) Animal anatomy;
  (3) Proper animal restraint, handling and methods for controlling animal stress;
  (4) Proper chemical agent dosages, record keeping and usage documentation, chemical agent, instrument and equipment storage, handling and disposal in accordance with rules and the Code of Federal Regulations;
  (5) Proper injection techniques;
  (6) Proper euthanasia techniques not utilizing injected chemical agents;
  (7) Proper and accurate verification of animal death;
  (8) Proper record keeping;
  (9) Proper disposal of euthanized animals;
  (10) Stress management for euthanasia personnel;
  (11) Proper methods and techniques of euthanasia under extraordinary circumstances;
  (12) Proper methods, techniques and chemicals inducing anesthesia and sedation in animals prior to euthanasia; and
  (13) Proper methods, techniques and chemicals used in the practical examination section for Certified Euthanasia Technician.

(c) The Animal Welfare Section shall prepare written examinations to be given to applicants. Following the classroom training detailed in Paragraph (b) of this Rule, the applicant shall take a written examination provided by the Animal Welfare Section that will be used by the approved trainer. Those passing the written examination are eligible for the practical examination of the methods of euthanasia for which the applicant seeks certification.

(d) The applicant must pass a practical examination on each method of euthanasia for which he or she seeks certification.

(e) Applicants for certification in Euthanasia by Injection shall demonstrate the following knowledge and competencies:

   (1)   Correctly calculate chemical agent dosage based upon the species, age, weight and condition of the animal;

   (2)   Correctly complete all required documentation;

   (3)   Correctly draw the properly calculated chemical dosage into a syringe and needle of a type and size appropriate for the animal;

   (4)   Correctly administer the chemical agent to the animal;

   (5)   Properly perform intravenous and intraperitoneal injections on dogs and intravenous or intraperitoneal injections on cats;

   (6)   Knowledge of the medical procedures and drugs necessary for an animal to be euthanized by cardiac injection;

   (7)   Demonstrate ability to verify death by:
      (A)   lack of respiration;
      (B)   lack of ocular reflexes;
      (C)   lack of a heartbeat;

   (8)   Knowledge about the human health risks associated with the use of chemical agents used for euthanasia including signs and symptoms associated with accidental exposure of the Certified Euthanasia Technician;

   (9)   Proper first aid for a person accidentally exposed to chemical agents used for euthanasia.

(f) Applicants for certification in Euthanasia by Gas Inhalation shall meet the standards set forth in this Paragraph:

   (1)   Demonstrate knowledge of the dangers and human health effects of exposure to carbon monoxide gas;

   (2)   Demonstrate knowledge about which animals Euthanasia by Gas Inhalation is approved and which species, age, medical or physical conditions make it improper to use Euthanasia by Gas Inhalation;

   (3)   Demonstrate proper techniques in placing animals into the chamber;

   (4)   Demonstrate knowledge about the maintenance, operation and cleaning of the chamber, fittings, gas cylinder, valves, and other parts of the equipment;

   (5)   Demonstrate proper operation of the chamber;

   (6)   Demonstrate ability to verify death by:
      (A)   lack of respiration;
      (B)   lack of ocular reflexes;
      (C)   lack of a heartbeat;

   (7)   Demonstrate knowledge about the human health risks associated with the use of carbon monoxide when used for euthanasia. Such knowledge shall also include signs and symptoms associated with accidental exposure of the Certified Euthanasia Technician;

   (8)   Demonstrate knowledge of proper first aid for a person accidentally exposed to carbon monoxide used for euthanasia.

02 NCAC 52J .0408   TRAINERS

(a) Certified Euthanasia Technician training shall be provided by the Animal Welfare Section or by companies or individuals meeting the following criteria:

(1)   Possess working knowledge of euthanasia conducted according to this Section;

(2)   Have actual experience in euthanasia of animals;

(3)   Have experience training staff in euthanasia; and

(4)   Provide references from individuals or organizations previously trained.

(b) Information taught shall conform to this Section and the guidelines set forth by the American Veterinary Medical Association, the Humane Society of the United States or the American Humane Association.

(c) Trainers shall disclose to their students and the Animal Welfare Section any affiliations with suppliers of equipment or supplies used in euthanasia.

(d) The Animal Welfare Section may make unannounced audit of instruction and testing by trainers.

(e) Prior to providing euthanasia training leading to certification as a Euthanasia Technician, the person or company shall obtain approval before each class for its training program from the Animal Welfare Section.

02 NCAC 52J .0409   PROBATIONARY EUTHANASIA TECHNICIANS

An individual who has passed the written exam, but has not taken and passed the practical examination may serve as a Probationary Euthanasia Technician under the direct supervision of:

(1)   a licensed veterinarian; or

(2)   a Certified Euthanasia Technician

for up to three consecutive months or until such time as the next practical euthanasia exam is conducted, whichever is longer. Certified animal shelters employing probationary euthanasia technicians must notify the Animal Welfare Section no later than five days prior to the probationary euthanasia technician's first day serving in that capacity.

02 NCAC 52J .0410   EXAM REQUIRED

An individual who has not passed the written exam may not serve as a Certified Euthanasia Technician or Probationary Euthanasia Technician.

02 NCAC 52J .0411   NEW APPLICATION

If the individual or applicant fails to pass the practical exam a second time and wishes to apply for certification again, the individual shall submit a new application to the Animal Welfare Section, attend a training program, pass the written exam and take and pass a practical examination on euthanasia. The Animal Welfare Section shall cancel the application of any applicant who fails the written examination twice.

02 NCAC 52J .0412   ISSUANCE OF CERTIFICATION

Upon the receipt of materials specified in this Section the Animal Welfare Section shall issue a Certificate.

02 NCAC 52J .0413   LENGTH OF CERTIFICATION

A Certificate issued by the Animal Welfare Section is valid for five years from the date of issuance unless it is revoked pursuant to this Section or upon termination of employment or volunteer status as described in this Section.

02 NCAC 52J .0414 TERMINATION OF EMPLOYMENT

Upon termination of employment or volunteer status from a certified facility, a Certified Euthanasia Technician shall not perform animal euthanasia in a certified facility until recertified by the Animal Welfare Section. The Certified Euthanasia Technician's certification shall be canceled effectively upon termination of employment or volunteer status. No later than 10 days from the date of the termination of a Certified Euthanasia Technician's employment or volunteer status at that certified facility the Certified Euthanasia Technician shall complete a form notifying the Animal Welfare Section of the termination of employment or volunteer status and shall return the form and the Certificate to the Animal Welfare Section.

02 NCAC 52J .0415 NOTICE OF TERMINATION

A certified facility shall notify the Animal Welfare Section in writing, no later than 10 days from the date of the termination of a Certified Euthanasia Technician's employment or volunteer status at that certified facility.

02 NCAC 52J .0416 RECERTIFICATION

(a) If a former Certified Euthanasia Technician is employed or is accepted as a volunteer at a certified facility before the expiration of his certification, the former Certified Euthanasia Technician or employer may request reinstatement of his/her certification from the Animal Welfare Section. The reinstated Certification shall be good for five years from the date of its initial issue.

(b) If a former Certified Euthanasia Technician is employed or is accepted as a volunteer at a certified facility after the expiration of his certification, the former Certified Euthanasia Technician may only euthanize animals under the direct supervision of a licensed veterinarian or currently certified euthanasia technician for three months or until he/she passes practical examination whichever is less. The former Certified Euthanasia Technician and the manager of the certified facility shall each notify the Animal Welfare Section within 10 days of the date the former Certified Euthanasia Technician is employed or accepted as a volunteer.

02 NCAC 52J .0417 CERTIFICATION RENEWAL

(a) Certifications may be renewed every five years provided that:
  (1) within the 12 months immediately preceding the application for certification renewal the Certified Euthanasia Technician has taken and passed a practical examination for each method of euthanasia for which they are seeking certification renewal;
  (2) the applicant receives up-to-date information about the method of euthanasia for which the applicant is seeking certification; and
  (3) the applicant receives training in stress management.
(b) The applicant shall submit an application for certification renewal to the Animal Welfare Section. The application shall be on a form created by the Animal Welfare Section and shall include a document from an approved Certified Euthanasia Technician trainer establishing that the applicant has passed a practical examination in the specific euthanasia techniques for which he or she is seeking certification.

02 NCAC 52J .0418 DUTIES

A Certified Euthanasia Technician may:
  (1) Prepare animals for euthanasia;
  (2) Record the identification number of the animal, its species, sex, breed description and date, dosages for drugs that are administered and amounts for drugs wasted;
  (3) Order euthanasia supplies;

(4) Maintain the security of all controlled substances and other drugs in accordance with applicable state and federal laws and regulations;

(5) Directly supervise probationary Euthanasia Technicians;

(6) Report to the appropriate government agencies violations or suspicions of a violation of the rules in this Subchapter or any abuse of drugs;

(7) Euthanize animals;

(8) Dispose of euthanized animals and expired or unwanted chemical agent(s) or the containers, instruments and equipment used in the administration of drugs in accordance with all applicable federal, state and local laws and regulations; and

(9) Notify the Animal Welfare Section as required in this Section upon leaving employment or volunteer status at a covered facility.

02 NCAC 52J .0419   GROUNDS FOR DISCIPLINE - CERTIFIED EUTHANASIA TECHNICIANS

The Department may refuse to issue, renew, or reinstate the certification of a Euthanasia Technician, or may deny, revoke, suspend, sanction, or place on probation, impose other forms of discipline, and enter into consent agreements and negotiated settlements with Certified Euthanasia Technician pursuant to the procedures set forth in G.S. 150B, Article 3, for any of the following reasons:

(1) Failure to Carry Out Duties. Failure to carry out the duties of a Certified Euthanasia Technician;

(2) Abuse of Chemical Substances. Abuse of any drug or chemical substance by:
  (a) Selling, diverting or giving away drugs or chemical substances;
  (b) Stealing drugs or chemical substances;
  (c) Misusing chemical substances; or
  (d) Abetting anyone in the foregoing activities;

(3) Euthanizing animals without supervision as required by this subchapter;

(4) Allowing uncertified individuals to euthanize animals;

(5) Allowing probationary Euthanasia Technicians to euthanize animals outside of the Certified Euthanasia Technician's personal presence;

(6) Fraud, misrepresentation, or deception in obtaining certification;

(7) Unethical or Unprofessional Conduct. Unethical or unprofessional conduct means to knowingly engage in conduct of a character likely to deceive or defraud the public. Such conduct includes working in conjunction with any agency or person illegally practicing as a Certified Euthanasia Technician; failing to provide sanitary facilities or apply sanitary procedures for the euthanizing of any animal; euthanizing animals in a manner that endangers the health or welfare of the public; gross ignorance, incompetence or inefficiency in the euthanizing of animals as determined by the practices generally and currently followed and accepted as approved by the American Veterinary Medical Association, the Humane Society of the United States or the American Humane Association; intentionally performing a duty, task or procedure involved in the euthanizing of animals for which the individual is not qualified; and swearing falsely in any testimony or affidavits relating to practicing as a Certified Euthanasia Technician;

(8) Conviction of any criminal offense as described in this Section;

(9) Improper Record Keeping. Failure to follow proper record keeping procedures as outlined in the rules in this Subchapter;

(10) Improper Security and Storage for Chemical Agents. Failure to provide and maintain proper security and storage for euthanasia and restraint drugs as established under applicable United States Drug Enforcement Administration and North Carolina Department of Health and Human Services statutes and rules;

(11) Improper Disposal of Chemical Agents and Equipment. Failure to dispose of drugs and the containers, instruments and equipment in a manner permitted by this Subchapter;

(12) Improper Labeling of Approved Chemical Agents. Failure to properly label approved euthanasia and restraint chemical agents;

(13) Revocation, Suspension or Limitation. The revocation, suspension, limitation, of a license, certificate or registration or any other disciplinary action by another state or United States jurisdiction or voluntary surrender of a license, certificate or registration by virtue of which one is licensed, certified or registered to practice as a Certified Euthanasia Technician in that state or jurisdiction on grounds other than nonpayment of the renewal fee;

(14) Failure of any applicant or certificate holder to cooperate with the North Carolina Department of Agriculture and Consumer Services during any investigation or inspection.

Section .0500 – Euthanasia by Injection

02 NCAC 52J .0501   INTRACARDIAC INJECTION

Intracardiac injection shall only be used on animals that have been anesthetized or heavily sedated.

Section .0600 – Euthanasia by Carbon Monoxide

02 NCAC 52J .0601   CARBON MONOXIDE EQUIPMENT

If carbon monoxide is used for euthanasia in a certified facility, the following requirements shall be met:
(1) Only commercially compressed, bottled gas shall be used;
(2) The gas shall be delivered in a commercially manufactured chamber that allows for the individual separation of animals;
(3) Animals placed inside of the chamber shall be of the same species;
(4) The chamber shall achieve a minimum six percent uniform concentration of carbon monoxide within two minutes of beginning the administration of the gas;
(5) Death shall occur within five minutes of beginning the administration of the gas; and
(6) Animals shall remain in the chamber with carbon monoxide for a minimum of 20 minutes.

02 NCAC 52J .0602   PROHIBITED USES

Carbon monoxide may not be used to euthanize animals in certified facilities in any manner inconsistent with guidelines for the use of carbon monoxide approved by the entities referenced in 02 NCAC 52J .0401. Additionally, carbon monoxide shall not be used to euthanize the following animals in certified facilities:
(1) Animals that appear to be less than 16 weeks of age;
(2) Animals that are pregnant;
(3) Animals that are near death.

02 NCAC 52J .0603   DEAD ANIMALS

Live animals shall not be placed into a euthanasia chamber with dead animals in certified facilities.

02 NCAC 52J .0604   INDIVIDUAL SEPARATION

Animals shall be individually separated within a euthanasia chamber in a certified facility.

02 NCAC 52J .0605   CHAMBER REQUIREMENTS

(a) A euthanasia chamber in a certified facility shall be located in a well-ventilated place, preferably outdoors.

(b) The chamber shall be in good working order.

(c) The chamber shall have strong airtight seals around the doors and viewports.

(d) The chamber shall have at least one port for viewing of the animals during euthanasia.

(e) The chamber shall be lit sufficiently to allow observation of an animal in any part of the chamber.

(f) Any chamber electrical wiring or components exposed to carbon monoxide must be warranted by the manufacturer to be explosion proof.

(g) Any light inside of the chamber shall be shatterproof.

(h) The chamber shall use exhaust ventilation to evacuate the gas from the chamber before the doors are opened upon completion of the process.

(i) If the chamber is located outdoors:

 (1)   The exhaust shall be vented at least eight feet above ground level.

 (2)   The minimum stack velocity shall be at least 3,000 feet per minute;

 (3)   If there is a roof above the chamber, the exhaust shall be vented at least three feet above the highest point of the roof; and

 (4)   The exhaust shall not be located within eight feet of any building air intakes.

(j) If the chamber is located indoors:

 (1)   The exhaust shall be vented to the outdoors at least three feet above the highest point of the roof;

 (2)   The exhaust shall not be located within eight feet of any building air intakes;

 (3)   The minimum stack velocity shall be at least 3,000 feet per minute; and

 (4)   At least two carbon monoxide detectors shall be placed in the room.

02 NCAC 52J .0606   INSPECTIONS AND RECORDS

(a) Chamber seals, exhaust flow, carbon monoxide monitors and other equipment used in the euthanasia process in certified facilities shall be inspected at least monthly and repaired or replaced as necessary.

(b) The chamber must be inspected at least annually by the manufacturer, its authorized representative or an industrial hygienist knowledgeable about the manufacture and operation of the chamber.

(c) A record shall be made of each inspection recording the results, the date of the inspection, and the name of the person performing the inspection. The record shall be maintained in the policy and procedure manual for at least two years.

02 NCAC 52J .0607   CLEANING CHAMBER

A euthanasia chamber at a certified facility shall be cleaned between uses.

02 NCAC 52J .0608   OPERATIONAL GUIDES AND INSTRUCTION MANUALS

Current operational guides and maintenance instruction manuals shall be kept in the room with the euthanasia chamber at all times in a certified facility.

02 NCAC 52J .0609   PERSONS REQUIRED TO BE PRESENT

A euthanasia chamber in a certified facility shall not be operated unless a Certified Euthanasia Technician or a veterinarian licensed in North Carolina and one other adult are present at the time of its use.

Section .0700 – Extraordinary Circumstances

02 NCAC 52J .0701 METHODS OF EUTHANASIA PERMITTED UNDER EXTRAORDINARY CIRCUMSTANCES AND SITUATIONS

For purposes of this Section, extraordinary circumstance or situation includes a situation which is offsite from the shelter, in which an animal poses an immediate risk to animal, human or public health and in which no alternative, less extreme measure of euthanasia is feasible. It also includes circumstances or situations in which it would be inhumane to transport an animal to another location to perform euthanasia.

02 NCAC 52J .0702 GUNSHOT OR OTHER METHODS

Under extraordinary circumstances and situations which occur offsite from the shelter, a shelter employee may use gunshot or other extreme method of euthanasia as set forth in the American Veterinary Medical Association, Humane Society of the United States or American Humane Association Guidelines incorporated by reference in 02 NCAC 52J .0401.

02 NCAC 52J .0703 METHODS AND STANDARDS

Methods of euthanasia used by a certified facility under an extraordinary circumstance or situation must be approved by the American Veterinary Medical Association, the Humane Society of the United States or the American Humane Association for use on that species of animal and must conform to standards set forth by that organization.

02 NCAC 52J .0704 TECHNICIAN NOT REQUIRED

If an extraordinary circumstance or situation occurs and euthanasia is necessary, the person performing the euthanasia is not required to be a Certified Euthanasia Technician at a certified facility.

02 NCAC 52J .0705 REPORTS

A licensee or registrant shall prepare a report of any euthanasia performed under extraordinary circumstances or situations, and keep the report on file for at least two years. The report shall include the date, time, identification of the animal, the name of the person performing the final euthanasia, the method of euthanasia and the reason for euthanasia of the animal as permitted by this Section.

Section .0800 – Policy and Procedure Manual

02 NCAC 52J .0801 MANUAL REQUIRED

Any animal shelter performing euthanasia shall have a current policy and procedure manual about euthanasia.

02 NCAC 52J .0802 CONTENTS

The policy and procedure manual shall set forth the shelter's equipment, process, and the procedures for individual separation of animals.

02 NCAC 52J .0803 ADDITIONAL CONTENTS

A certified facility's policy and procedure manual shall be kept consistent with the publications listed below and reflect the current information for each. The manual shall include:
    (1)   A copy of the current North Carolina Animal Welfare Act and the rules in this Subchapter;

(2) A copy of the 2000 Report of the American Veterinary Medical Association Panel on Euthanasia and any future revisions, replacements, supplements or changes thereto issued by that organization;

(3) A current copy of the Euthanasia Training Manual of the Humane Society of the United States;

(4) A copy of the publication on euthanasia by the American Humane Association;

(5) A list of methods of euthanasia allowed at the shelter and the policy and procedures for each method;

(6) A list of Certified Euthanasia Technicians, the methods of euthanasia in which they have received training, and the date of training;

(7) The name, address and contact information for the veterinarian responsible for the Annual Program of Veterinary Care;

(8) The name, address and contact information for veterinarians responsible for the veterinary medical care of the animals. The contact information shall include telephone numbers for working hours, weekends, nights and holidays;

(9) Euthanasia procedure to use in emergencies, after hours, holidays and weekends;

(10) Procedures to follow if no Certified Euthanasia Technician is present and euthanasia of an animal is necessary;

(11) Methods of verifying death of an animal after a euthanasia process is performed;

(12) The name and contact information of the supplier of materials. It shall include:
    (a) Bottled gas (if applicable);
    (b) Manufacturer of the chamber used to euthanize animals by inhalant gas (if applicable);
    (c) Injectable euthanasia solution;
    (d) Tranquilizer or anesthetic solution;

(13) Original of U.S. Drug Enforcement Administration certification permitting the use of controlled substances;

(14) A material safety data sheet for any chemical or gas used for euthanasia in that shelter;

(15) A material safety data sheet for any anesthetic or tranquilizer used in that facility;

(16) Notice of the signs and symptoms associated with human exposure to the agents used for euthanasia at the facility;

(17) First aid for people accidentally exposed to the agents used for euthanasia at the facility; and

(18) Contact information of the physician or medical facility providing medical treatment to employees of the facility. The information shall include the name of the medical facility, the telephone number for both working and after-hours contact and directions to the medical facility from the certified facility including a map. If the medical facility does not provide service after-hours, on weekends or on holidays, there must be contact information as described in this item for the nearest medical facility, urgent care clinic or emergency room that does provide care during that time.

Section .0900 – Animal Shelter Support Fund

02 NCAC 52J .0901   ELIGIBLE EXPENSES

Eligible expenses include:

(1) Veterinary costs – Reimbursement may be requested for veterinary expenditures incurred for the assessment, diagnostic and triage evaluation, medical treatment, minor surgical treatment, medications, first aid and minor medical supplies, vaccinations, parasite control/treatment, or euthanasia of animals housed at the shelter at the time of the event or impounded during the interim or transition period.

(2)   Sanitation costs – Reimbursement may be requested for expenditures related to sanitation of the affected shelter, including detergent/disinfectant supplies, cleaning supplies, labor costs for the sanitation of the shelter, and waste and carcass disposal costs.

(3)   Animal sustenance and supplies – Reimbursement may be requested for expenditures for animal food, provision of water to the shelter, and food and water bowls or buckets, as well as labor costs for the feeding and watering of the shelter animals.

(4)   Temporary housing and sheltering of animals – Reimbursement may be requested for expenditures for animal cages and kennels, animal transport carriers, fencing panels for runs, tarps, fencing, dog or cat houses and other construction supplies, as well as labor costs or equipment or facility leasing expenses incurred during the construction or repair of temporary animal housing.

02 NCAC 52J .0902   APPLICATION GUIDELINES

(a) A local government applying for reimbursement from the Fund shall submit the request for reimbursement to the Animal Welfare Section (AWS) of the North Carolina Department of Agriculture and Consumer Services.

(b) The request shall:

(1)   be received by AWS by mail, email, or fax within 60 days of the date the eligible expense was incurred;

(2)   include a completed "Animal Shelter Support Fund Reimbursement Application" with the county name, tier of county, facility name, facility license number, and contact information. This application can be found on the AWS website (http://www.ncagr.gov/vet/AWS/);

(3)   include an itemized listing of eligible expenses for which reimbursement is sought;

(4)   include proof that matching funds have been provided; and

(5)   include proof of payment of the eligible expense. If the payment of expense occurs after the application was submitted, proof of payment shall be submitted to AWS within 30 days of payment of the expense.

Chapter 8

Service Animals in Public Places

Some individuals with disabilities use service animals to help them carry out their daily activities. An animal may be trained, for example, to guide a person with a visual impairment, open doors for a person with a physical disability, or remind a person to take his or her medication, as well as many other important support functions.

- Bethe Bennett's miniature schnauzer nudged her back to consciousness after a fall. The trained service dog also retrieved an emergency phone list so that Bennett could call neighbors for assistance.
- A pooch named Mr. Gibbs totes Alida Knobloch's oxygen tank so the 2-year-old can dash around with other children. Mr. Gibbs even braves playground slides with Alida. Sandra Leavitt relies on a service dog to help battle her rare seizure disorder. Nikki, a 4-year-old pit bull, was trained to detect scent changes in Leavitt's blood and provide warning signs up to two hours before seizures occur.*

---

*Morieka Johnson, *5 Things You Don't Know About Service Dogs*, CNN.COM (June 15, 2012), http://www.cnn.com/2012/06/15/living/service-dogs-mnn/. *See also* 28 C.F.R. § 36.104 (federal regulations' definition of "service animal" includes the following examples of work or tasks the animal may be trained to perform: "assisting individuals who are blind or have low vision with navigation and other tasks, alerting individuals who are deaf or hard of hearing to the presence of people or sounds, providing non-violent protection or rescue work, pulling a wheelchair, assisting an individual during a seizure, alerting individuals to the presence of allergens, retrieving items such as medicine or the telephone, providing physical support and assistance with balance and stability to individuals with mobility disabilities, and helping persons with psychiatric and neurological disabilities by preventing or interrupting impulsive or destructive behaviors"); JACQUIE BRENNAN & VINH NGUYEN, ADA NAT'L NETWORK, SERVICE ANIMALS AND EMOTIONAL SUPPORT ANIMALS: WHERE ARE THEY ALLOWED AND UNDER WHAT CONDITIONS? (2014), https://adata.org/publication/service-animals-booklet (describing different kinds of service animals and the types of training they receive).

Individuals with disabilities who rely on service animals have various legal protections at both the federal and state levels. At the state level, Chapter 168 of the North Carolina General Statutes (hereinafter G.S.) grants a person with a disability the right to be accompanied by a service animal in certain places and the right to keep a service animal on certain premises.[1] Chapter 168 provides a criminal penalty for depriving a person of those rights,[2] and G.S. Chapter 168A, the North Carolina Persons With Disabilities Protection Act, provides that a person with a disability may bring a civil action to enforce his or her rights.[3]

At the federal level, the Americans with Disabilities Act of 1990 (ADA)[4] and its implementing regulations prohibit discrimination against persons on the basis of disability and require that public[5] and private[6] entities modify their policies, practices, or

---

1. *See* Chapter 168, Section 4.2 of the North Carolina General Statutes (hereinafter G.S.).
2. G.S. 168-4.5.
3. G.S. 168A-11.
4. 42 U.S.C. §§ 12101–12189.
5. 28 C.F.R. § 35.104.
6. 28 C.F.R. § 36.104.

procedures to permit the use of service animals.[7] A person may file a complaint with the U.S. Department of Justice and bring a private civil action in federal court to remedy violations of the ADA.[8] While the state and federal laws regarding service animals are largely independent from a legal perspective, they do overlap and have common features as a practical matter. For a local official, one important common feature of the federal and state laws is that the obligations imposed with respect to permitting the use of service animals apply to both local governments and private entities. That is, a local government must modify its policies, practices, or procedures in order to permit the use of service animals in appropriate situations, as must private businesses and organizations.

Some individuals have emotional support or comfort animals that are not considered service animals and are therefore not entitled to all of the same legal protections granted to service animals.

Members of the public often rely on local animal services officials to help them interpret and apply the laws, particularly as they relate to public places.[9] This chapter is intended to provide a brief overview of this area of the law so that local officials will have a general understanding of the rights of individuals who rely on service animals as well as the duties of the individuals and organizations that interact with them.

Animal Terminology

Several terms are used in this area of the law to refer to animals that provide assistance to people. Some of these terms overlap or are occasionally used interchangeably. As a result, there can be confusion when trying to decide whether an individual's animal is entitled to legal protection. Below are explanations of the terms that are used in this chapter.

Service Animal

The term "service animal" is used in both federal and state law. At the federal level, a detailed definition is found in the regulations implementing the Americans with Dis-

---

7. *See generally* U.S. Dep't Just., Civil Rights Div., Disability Rights Sec., *Frequently Asked Questions about Service Animals and the ADA* (July 20, 2015), https://www.ada.gov/regs2010/service_animal_qa.pdf.

8. *Id.*

9. For purposes of this chapter, the phrase "public place" refers to public facilities (as defined by Title II of the ADA) and places of public accommodation (as defined by Title III of the ADA).

abilities Act of 1990 (ADA). The definition, which was revised in 2010, includes several key components.

- A service animal is "any dog that is individually trained to do work or perform tasks for the benefit of an individual with a disability, including a physical, sensory, psychiatric, intellectual, or other mental disability."[10] Note that the ADA definition does *not* extend to service animals in training.
- "The work or tasks performed by a service animal must be directly related to the individual's disability."[11]
- "The crime deterrent effects of an animal's presence and the provision of emotional support, well-being, comfort, or companionship do not constitute work or tasks for the purposes of [the] definition."[12]

Prior to the recent revisions, the definition of "service animal" was more expansive and included animals other than dogs. The 2010 revisions clearly narrowed the scope of the definition by limiting it to dogs.[13] The regulations do, however, include separate subsections that apply the service animal requirements to miniature horses in some circumstances. If a horse is "individually trained to do work or perform tasks for the benefit of the individual with a disability," then "reasonable modifications" in policies, practices, or procedures must be made so that the miniature horse may accompany an individual with a disability.[14]

---

10. While there are two bodies of ADA regulations that define "service animal," the definitions are identical in each. 28 C.F.R. § 35.104 (governing state and local governments); § 36.104 (governing places of public accommodation).

11. When the regulations were amended in 2010, there was a mistake in the definition of "service animal." It required that the work or tasks performed by the animal be directly related to the "handler's" disability. The language was amended a few months later to clarify that the work or tasks must be directly related to the "individual's" disability, because, in some instances, the handler of the animal will be a person other than the individual who has a disability. 76 Fed. Reg. 13,285, 13,285 (Mar. 11, 2011).

12. 28 C.F.R. § 35.104; § 36.104.

13. *Id.* Prior to the 2010 revisions, the law allowed other species to be recognized as service animals. As a result, some individuals worked with animals such as monkeys, pigs, and reptiles. In the analysis accompanying the final regulation, the United States Department of Justice explained its rationale for limiting the scope to dogs: "The Department agrees with commenters' views that limiting the number and types of species recognized as service animals will provide greater predictability for State and local government entities as well as added assurance of access for individuals with disabilities who use dogs as service animals. As a consequence, the Department has decided to limit this rule's coverage of service animals to dogs, which are the most common service animals used by individuals with disabilities." 75 Fed. Reg. 56,164, 56,193 (Sept. 15, 2010); *id.* at 56,236, 56,267.

14. 28 C.F.R. § 35.136(i); § 36.302(c)(9). Because the regulations take a somewhat convoluted approach to including miniature horses within the scope of the regulation, they are technically not included in the legal definition of "service animal." But because the regulations

Evaluating whether a dog meets the definition of "service animal" under the ADA involves examining the question of the dog's training.[15] At the summary judgment stage of litigation, where the issue before the court is whether triable issues of material fact exist such that the case should proceed towards trial, courts have "set a low bar for demonstrating" that a dog has been trained to work or perform tasks on behalf of a disabled individual.[16] They have not required documentation of training[17] or evidence that the training was conducted by a "certified trainer."[18] Furthermore, courts have held that "[t]here are no requirements as to the amount or type of training that a service animal must undergo, nor the type of work or assistance that a service animal must provide . . . ."[19] As one court explained, "[t]his is not a taxing requirement, . . . and there are no federally-mandated animal training standards."[20]

Examining the work or tasks that a dog has been trained to perform for a disabled individual is a key factor in determining whether the animal is a service animal under federal law. If evidence is presented showing that the work or tasks are closely related

---

extend similar requirements to miniature horses that have been appropriately trained, they are effectively working as service animals and must be recognized as such. The regulations list certain "assessment factors" to be used in determining whether it is possible to make reasonable modifications to accommodate the presence of a miniature horse. Among the factors are the size and weight of the horse and whether the presence of a miniature horse would compromise the safe operation of the facility at issue. *Id.* For a recent case discussing a city's potential obligation to make reasonable modifications to its policies, practices, or procedures to allow an individual with a disability to keep a miniature horse at her residence despite a city ordinance prohibiting the keeping of farm animals within the city, see *Anderson v. City of Blue Ash*, 798 F.3d 338 (6th Cir. 2015).

15. *See, e.g.,* Prindable v. Ass'n of Apartment Owners of 2987 Kalakaua, 304 F. Supp. 2d 1245 (D. Haw. 2003) (inquiring into the issue of a dog's training when determining whether it was a service animal under the ADA definition in a Fair Housing Act case), *aff'd on other grounds,* 453 F.3d 1175 (9th Cir. 2006); Baugher v. City of Ellensburg, No. CV-06-3026-RHW, 2007 WL 858627, at *6 (E.D. Wash. Mar. 19, 2007) (unpublished) (rejecting plaintiff's claim under the ADA that her dog was a service animal where there was no evidence that the dog was trained to perform specific tasks or work for the plaintiff's benefit).

16. Cordoves v. Miami-Dade Cty., 92 F. Supp. 3d 1221, 1230 (S.D. Fla. 2015).

17. *See Baugher,* 2007 WL 858627, at *5.

18. Green v. Hous. Auth. of Clackamas Cty., 994 F. Supp. 1253, 1256 (D. Or. 1998).

19. Rose v. Springfield–Greene Cty. Health Dep't, 668 F. Supp. 2d 1206, 1214–15 (W.D. Mo. 2009), *aff'd per curiam,* 377 F. App'x 573 (8th Cir. 2010) (unpublished).

20. *Prindable,* 304 F. Supp. 2d at 1256. *See also* Davis v. Ma, 848 F. Supp. 2d 1105, 1116 (C.D. Cal. 2012) ("The ADA does not create unlimited license for disabled customers to enter facilities of public accommodation with their pets. The federal regulations limit protected entry to trained service animals that help ameliorate their owner's qualifying disability. 28 C.F.R. § 36.104. As Plaintiff fails to present any evidence creating a triable issue of fact as to whether Plaintiff's puppy was a trained service dog, the Court finds Plaintiff cannot—as a matter of law—prove the elements of his ADA claim."), *aff'd on other grounds,* 568 F. App'x 488 (9th Cir. 2014) (unpublished).

to the individual's disability, it is more likely that the animal will qualify as a service animal.[21]

At the state level, the term "service animal" is used in the context of several laws that allow persons with disabilities to be accompanied by service animals or service animals in training.[22] The term "service animal" is not, however, defined in state law. The law simply requires that one of the following two requirements be satisfied:

- the animal must have a service animal tag issued by the North Carolina Department of Health and Human Services (DHHS) or
- the person with a disability (or, presumably, the animal's handler) must show that the animal is being trained or is trained as a service animal.[23]

In the absence of a narrower definition (like the one found in the revised ADA regulations), it may be reasonable to assume that any type of animal may be considered a service animal under North Carolina law if one of these two requirements is satisfied. Therefore, if an individual with a disability is accompanied by a service animal other than a dog or miniature horse, it may be a violation of state discrimination laws to deny the person a service or access.

Assistance Animal

The term "assistance animal" is used in the context of a North Carolina law that imposes criminal penalties for harming such animals. The term is defined as "an animal that is trained and may be used to assist a 'person with a disability.'" The definition specifically states that it applies to any type of animal, not just dogs.[24] Given the overlapping concepts and definitions, it appears that any dog considered to be a service animal under the ADA will also be considered an assistance animal under state law.

Emotional Support or Comfort Animal

Some individuals may have animals they rely on for emotional support or comfort in certain situations. There is often confusion surrounding this class of animals for two reasons. First, the U.S. Department of Justice (DOJ) takes the position that an emotional

---

21. *Compare Cordoves*, 92 F. Supp. 3d at 1231–32 (jury could find dog to be service animal where there was evidence that dog would "alert" and summon assistance when owner was about to have a panic attack; there was also evidence that "alert" behavior lessened severity of the panic attacks), *with Davis*, 848 F. Supp. 2d at 1115–16 (plaintiff failed to present any evidence that would prove that a puppy was a trained service animal where plaintiff, who suffered from a degenerative back disability, admitted at deposition that puppy could not assist him in walking or balancing).

22. *See* G.S. Chapter 168, Article 1. The term "person with a disability" is defined in G.S. 168A-3(7a).

23. G.S. 168-4.2.

24. G.S. 14-163.1(a)(1).

support animal is not a service animal under the law but that an animal trained to provide assistance for emotional issues may be classified as a "psychiatric service animal."[25] Guidance from the DOJ explains that

> [t]he ADA makes a distinction between psychiatric service animals and emotional support animals. If the dog has been trained to sense that an anxiety attack is about to happen and take a specific action to help avoid the attack or lessen its impact, that would qualify as a [psychiatric] service animal. However, if the dog's mere presence provides comfort, that would not be considered a service animal under the ADA.[26]

Therefore, the issue for ADA purposes is not whether the individual refers to the animal as a service animal or an emotional support animal. The key question is whether the animal has been trained to assist the individual by performing work or tasks directly related to the individual's disability. Because state law governing service animals also refers to training requirements, it would be reasonable to assume that a similar analysis would apply when interpreting and applying state law to this class of animals.

The second area of confusion regarding emotional support and comfort animals stems from the fact that federal laws *other than* the ADA, such as those related to housing and air travel, extend protections to this class of animals in some circumstances. These laws are discussed briefly at the end of this chapter.

Access to Public Places and Services

For local government officials, the topic of service animals typically arises when a citizen has a question about whether a service animal must be allowed to accompany a person in a public place or whether a person with a service animal is allowed to access certain accommodations or services available to the public at large. Below is a brief overview of both the federal and state law in this area.

Government Places, Services, and Programs

The general rule under Title II of the Americans with Disabilities Act of 1990 (ADA) is that public entities are required to modify their policies, practices, and procedures to allow a person with a disability to be accompanied by a service animal wherever members of the public, invitees, or program participants are allowed to go.[27] This general rule stems from a foundational requirement of the ADA:

---

25. U.S. Dep't of Just., *supra* note 7.
26. *Id.*
27. 28 C.F.R. § 35.136 ("Generally, a public entity shall modify its policies, practices, or procedures to permit the use of a service animal by an individual with a disability.").

No qualified individual with a disability shall, on the basis of disability, be excluded from participation in or be denied the benefits of the services, programs, or activities of a public entity, or be subjected to discrimination by any public entity.[28]

The ADA's general rule is consistent with state laws extending protections to individuals with disabilities.[29] The ADA also prohibits several other specific types of discrimination, including several that are directly relevant to service animals, such as

- a prohibition on selecting the location of a facility that has the effect of excluding individuals with disabilities or substantially impairing their ability to participate;[30]
- a requirement that individuals with disabilities have an equal opportunity to participate in or benefit from any aid, benefit, or service provided by the entity;[31] and
- a prohibition on imposing a surcharge to cover the costs of measures required to provide for nondiscriminatory treatment.[32]

The term "public entity" is defined broadly in federal regulations to include (1) any state or local government; (2) any department, agency, special purpose district, or other instrumentality of a state or local government; and (3) AMTRAK and any commuter authority.[33] Note that this definition encompasses not only cities and counties, but also local government entities such as public schools and public authorities.[34]

---

28. 28 C.F.R. § 35.130(a).

29. *See* G.S. 168-2 ("Persons with disabilities have the same right as persons without disabilities to the full and free use of the streets, highways, sidewalks, walkways, public buildings, public facilities, and all other buildings and facilities, both publicly and privately owned, which serve the public.").

30. 28 C.F.R. § 35.130(b)(4).

31. 28 C.F.R. § 35.130(b)(1).

32. 28 C.F.R. § 35.130(f).

33. 28 C.F.R. § 35.104. The term "commuter authority" is defined as "any state, local, regional authority, corporation, or other entity established for purposes of providing commuter rail transportation (including, but not necessarily limited to, the New York Metropolitan Transportation Authority, the Connecticut Department of Transportation, the Maryland Department of Transportation, the Southeastern Pennsylvania Transportation Authority, the New Jersey Transit Corporation, the Massachusetts Bay Transportation Authority, the Port Authority Trans-Hudson Corporation, and any successor agencies) and any entity created by one or more such agencies for the purposes of operating, or contracting for the operation of, commuter rail transportation." 49 C.F.R. § 37.3.

34. Service animals in schools have been the subject of much litigation over the years. *See, e.g.*, Tara A. Waterlander, *Canines in the Classroom: When Schools Must Allow a Service Dog to Accompany a Child with Autism into the Classroom under Federal and State Laws*, 22 Geo. Mason U. Civ. Rts. L. J. 337 (2012) (reviewing service animal cases specifically related to children with autism); Sarah Allison L. Wieselthier, *Grooming Dogs for the Educational*

A public entity may refuse to permit a service animal to accompany a disabled individual if it can demonstrate that allowing the animal would require the entity to "fundamentally alter the nature of [a] service, program, or activity" provided to the public.[35] The U.S. Department of Justice has explained that, "[i]n most settings, the presence of a service animal will not result in a fundamental alteration."[36] It offered examples of the types of exceptional situations that may rise to the level of a fundamental alteration, such as excluding a service animal from an area of a zoo "where the presence of a dog would be disruptive, causing the displayed animals to behave aggressively or become agitated."[37] In this example, the agency emphasized that the service animal must be allowed in all other areas of the zoo.[38] Based on this guidance, it is clear that the "fundamental alteration" language is intended to be interpreted quite narrowly.

In situations where a public entity must permit the use of a service animal as a general matter because doing so would not require a fundamental alteration, the entity may nonetheless ask that a particular service animal be removed from the premises if (1) the animal is out of control and its handler does not take effective action to control it or (2) the animal is not housebroken.[39]

As previously mentioned, the ADA requires that a public entity make "reasonable modifications in policies, practices, or procedures" in order to permit the use of a miniature horse by a person with a disability, though miniature horses are not technically service animals under federal law. In the case of a miniature horse, the public entity must consider certain "assessment factors" in determining whether a "reasonable modification" can be made such that the horse may be allowed into a facility. Specifically, the entity must consider (1) the type, size, and weight of the horse and whether the facility can accommodate it; (2) whether the handler has sufficient control of the horse; (3) whether the horse is housebroken; and (4) whether the horse's presence "compromises legitimate safety requirements that are necessary for safe operation[s]."[40]

A service animal must be under control at all times, which typically means that it must be on a harness, leash, or other tether unless the person's disability prevents this

---

Setting: The "IDEIA" Behind Service Dogs in the Public Schools, 39 HOFSTRA L. REV. 757 (2011) (reviewing service animal cases involving students with a range of disabilities).

35. 28 C.F.R. § 35.130(b)(7). The federal Department of Justice has stated that it would be unusual for this exception to apply. U.S. Dep't of Just., *supra* note 7.

36. U.S. Dep't of Just., *supra* note 7, at Q26.

37. *Id.*

38. *Id.* Another example provided by the Justice Department was "at a boarding school, service animals could be restricted from a specific area of a dormitory reserved specifically for students with allergies to dog dander." *Id.*

39. 28 C.F.R. § 35.136(b).

40. 28 C.F.R. § 35.136(i).

or if it would interfere with the animal's work.[41] In those instances, the person must be able to control the animal with voice, signals, or other means.[42]

State law regarding access to public services and places aligns with ADA provisions on this topic in most respects. There is one body of law that establishes rights for individuals with disabilities, including the right to have access to and use of public places. In this law, public places include "streets, highways, sidewalks, walkways, public buildings, public facilities, and all other buildings and facilities, both publicly and privately owned, which serve the public."[43] Another body of North Carolina law prohibits government entities from discriminating against an individual with a disability.[44] It states that entities must not exclude a person "from participation in or deny [that person] the benefits of services, programs, or activities because of a disability or . . . refuse to provide reasonable accommodations . . . provided that the accommodations do not impose an undue hardship on the entity involved."[45] Both bodies of law—the individual rights provisions and the prohibitions on discrimination—are applicable to situations involving individuals accompanied by service animals.

Public Accommodations

Title III of the ADA is very similar to Title II, but it applies to places of public accommodation rather than to public entities. It requires, as set out in federal regulations, places of public accommodation to modify policies, practices, and procedures to allow an individual with a disability to be accompanied by a service animal, subject to limited exceptions.[46] Like the mandate in Title II, this requirement is based upon a foundational requirement that is tied to a prohibition on discrimination:

> No individual shall be discriminated against on the basis of disability in the full and equal enjoyment of the goods, services, facilities, privileges, advantages, or accommodations of any place of public accommodation by any private entity who owns, leases (or leases to), or operates a place of public accommodation.[47]

---

41. 28 C.F.R. § 35.136(d).

42. *Id.*

43. G.S. 168-2. This section of the General Statutes was briefly repealed in 2015. S.L. 2015-241, § 12F.17. It was restored shortly thereafter in a revised form, which retained the substantive right of access to public places but deleted language that required the state to produce, print, promote, and distribute a publication entitled "ACCESS NORTH CAROLINA." S.L. 2015-264, §§ 87(a), (b).

44. G.S. 168A-7. This section extends protections to "a qualified person with a disability." In this context, that term means "a person with a disability who meets prerequisites for participation that are uniformly applied to all participants, such as income or residence, and that do not have the effect of discriminating against persons with a disability." *Id.* § 168A-3(9).

45. G.S. 168A-7(a).

46. 28 C.F.R. § 36.302(c).

47. 28 C.F.R. § 36.201.

The term "place of public accommodation" is defined broadly in the ADA regulations to mean a private entity that falls within one of the following categories:

- lodging facilities (hotels, inns, etc.), subject to limited exceptions;
- food or drink establishments (restaurants, bars, etc.);
- places of exhibition or entertainment (theaters, stadiums, etc.);
- places of public gathering (auditoriums, theaters, convention centers, etc.);
- sales or rental establishments (grocery stores, shopping centers, etc.);
- service establishments (banks, gas stations, accountants' offices, pharmacies, hospitals, etc.);
- public transportation stations;
- places of public display or collection (museums, libraries, etc.);
- places of recreation (parks, zoos, amusement parks, etc.);
- private places of education;
- social services locations (senior citizen centers, homeless shelters, food banks, etc.); and
- places of exercise or recreation (spas, golf courses, etc.).[48]

The term does not include private clubs, religious entities, or public entities.[49]

The same exceptions that apply in Title II also extend to Title III. A place of public accommodation does not have to permit the use of service animals if it can demonstrate that doing so "would fundamentally alter the nature of the goods, services, facilities, privileges, advantages, or accommodations" it provides.[50] In addition, in situations where a place of public accommodation must permit the use of service animals as a general matter, a person with a service animal may be asked to remove a particular animal from the premises if (1) it is out of control and the handler does not take effective action to control it or (2) the animal is not housebroken.[51]

The provisions in Title III of the ADA are consistent with the protections afforded under state law. As discussed above, there are two bodies of law that address this issue—the individual rights provisions[52] and (2) the prohibitions on discrimination.[53] Both bodies of law address public accommodations. The first—which covers individual rights—describes (but does not define) the concept of public accommodations as "hotels,

---

48. 28 C.F.R. § 36.104.

49. 28 C.F.R. § 36.102(e) ("This part does not apply to any private club (except to the extent that the facilities of the private club are made available to customers or patrons of a place of public accommodation), or to any religious entity or public entity."). Note that public entities are subject to Title II of the ADA.

50. 28 C.F.R. § 36.302(a). Recall that, as discussed above, the U.S. Department of Justice has indicated that the application of this exception would be rare.

51. 28 C.F.R. § 36.302(c).

52. Article 1 of G.S. Chapter 168.

53. G.S. Chapter 168A.

lodging places, places of public accommodation, amusement or resort to which the general public is invited."[54] This body of law specifically provides that individuals have the right to be accompanied by service animals in places of public accommodation.[55] This right also extends to modes of public transportation, including buses, boats, and trains.[56]

The second body of state law—the prohibitions on discrimination—defines the term "place of public accommodations" to include (but not to be limited to) "any place, facility, store, other establishment, hotel, or motel, which supplies goods or services on the premises to the public or which solicits or accepts the patronage or trade of any person."[57] This body of law imposes a general prohibition:

> It is a discriminatory practice for a person to deny a qualified person with a disability the full and equal enjoyment of the goods, services, facilities, privileges, advantages, and accommodations of a place of public accommodation on the basis of a disabling condition.[58]

While this body of law does not specifically address service animals, it seems reasonable to infer that an individual with a disability who is accompanied by a service animal is subject to its protections.

Verification

When someone comes into a public place accompanied by an animal, the person in charge of the place may have questions about whether the animal is a service animal or a companion animal. Because of the legal landscape and the gravity of the individual rights involved, it is important to be cautious when asking questions or otherwise evaluating the status of the animal.

If the role of an animal assisting an individual with a disability is not obvious (such as pulling a wheelchair or guiding someone who appears to be visually impaired), the person in charge of the public place may ask two narrowly tailored questions.[59] The questions are focused on identifying the animal's connection to the individual (i.e., does a disability make the animal's presence necessary?) and the work or tasks the animal has been trained to perform.

---

54. G.S. 168-3.
55. G.S. 168-4.2.
56. G.S. 168-3.
57. G.S. 168A-3(8). This definition is consistent with the more detailed definition used in the ADA. *See* 28 C.F.R. § 36.104.
58. G.S. 168A-6.
59. *See* U.S. Dep't of Just., *supra* note 7.

Acceptable Conduct by Person in Charge of Public Place	Unacceptable Conduct
• Visually assess the situation and allow the animal entry without asking any questions • Ask if the animal is required because of a disability • Ask what work or task the animal has been trained to perform	• Ask for specific information about the individual's disability • Require that the animal demonstrate the work or task(s) it is trained to do • Request written proof of training • Require that the animal have a tag, certificate, or vest

The first permissible question is fairly straightforward: Is the animal required because of a disability? Note that the question does not solicit specific information about the individual's disability. This is an important point because it not only preserves the individual's privacy, it also supports the philosophical foundation for the expansive definition of disability in the ADA regulations. The revised regulations emphasize that "the definition of 'disability' . . . shall be construed broadly in favor of expansive coverage to the maximum extent permitted by the terms of the ADA."[60] The regulations further explain that the primary focus should be on whether entities have discriminated, not on whether an "individual meets the definition of 'disability.'"[61] In the context of service animals, the focus should not be on whether the individual has a disability but on whether a service animal should be allowed to accompany the individual.[62]

If the individual states that the animal is required because of a disability and is able to explain the work or tasks the animal has been trained to perform (i.e., the individual can answer the second question), the person in charge of the public place should not probe any further and should make every effort to accommodate the individual and the animal. As discussed above, the individual and the animal should not be denied access or a service unless (1) a fundamental alteration would be required to accommodate the animal, (2) the animal is out of control, or (3) the animal is not housebroken.

---

60. 28 C.F.R. § 36.101(b) (describing the purpose of the 2008 amendments to the ADA and concluding that "[t]he question of whether an individual meets the definition of 'disability' under this part should not demand extensive analysis."); § 36.105(a)(2)(i) ("The definition of 'disability' shall be construed broadly in favor of expansive coverage, to the maximum extent permitted by the terms of the ADA."). *But see* Sande Buhai, *Preventing the Abuse of Service Animal Regulations*, 19 N.Y.U. J. LEGIS. & PUB. POL'Y 771, 793–94 (2016) (arguing that the "deliberately vague" questions have "the effect of creating a large loophole that pet owners can abuse. If pet owners answer the permitted questions 'correctly,' the manager of a business cannot do anything for the fear of violating the ADA.").

61. 28 C.F.R. § 36.101(b).

62. The term "disability" has a complex definition that is included in both the Title II and Title III regulations. *See* 28 C.F.R. § 35.108; § 36.105. Because the term should not be the focus of an inquiry related to service animals, it is not addressed in detail in this chapter.

In North Carolina, an individual with a disability may register a service animal with the state and receive a special tag for the animal.[63] If an animal has such a tag, a person in charge of a public place can be assured that the state reviewed the application for registration and concluded that the animal has received or is receiving training as a service animal. When an animal is wearing such a tag, it is important to remember that both the animal and the individual are protected under state law, regardless of the applicability of the ADA. For example, if a service animal is a monkey and is wearing a state tag, the ADA would not apply (because it is not a dog or horse) but state law would. In such cases, the person in charge of the public place or service should make every effort to accommodate the individual with the monkey.

A local government may not require individuals to register their service animals or otherwise verify that an animal is a service animal.[64] A local government may, however, create a voluntary registry of service animals. These types of registries may be helpful in the event emergency responders are called to a disabled individual's home or need to transport the individual in an ambulance.

Several private organizations operate voluntary registries and sell identification cards, patches, vests, and certificates. These registrations and identification tools, just like the state registration process, are entirely optional.[65] A person in charge of a public place should not require an individual with a service animal to provide any such identification or certification. Regardless of whether there is a certificate or badge, the person in charge of the public place may always ask the second key question: What work or task has the animal been trained to perform? The answer to this question, in combination with the response to the first question, should guide whether the service animal is allowed in the place and how it may behave once it enters.

Service Animals in Training

The protections in the ADA do not extend to service animals in training, but those found in state law do. Trainers may be accompanied by animals in training in all of the places service animals are allowed to enter under state law, including public facilities

---

63. G.S. 168-4.2 (tag); 168-4.3 (registration). Each tag will say "NORTH CAROLINA SERVICE ANIMAL PERMANENT REGISTRATION" and will include a registration number. The application for registration is available online at the following website: https://www.ncdhhs.gov/service-animals-people-disabilities. The state may not charge a fee for registration. G.S. 168-4.3.

64. *See* Buhai, *supra* note 60, at 791–93 (discussing whether state and local laws requiring licensure or registration of service animals are preempted).

65. One author expressed concern about how the presence of these organizations contributes to the abuse of legal protections for service animals. *Id*. at 793–94 ("If a pet owner wants to pass his or her pet off as a service animal, retailers now make it easy. With $20–$300, he or she can order a service animal vest, certification of a trained service animal, and other materials that 'prove' that a pet is a service animal.").

and public accommodations. The animal must wear a leash, harness, or cape identifying it as a service animal in training.[66]

Related Laws

This chapter does not provide a comprehensive review of laws that govern the use of service animals by individuals with disabilities. There are other federal laws that apply in certain contexts.

- **Section 504 of the Rehabilitation Act of 1973.** Section 504 is an expansive federal law that prohibits discrimination against individuals with disabilities by federal agencies and programs and by others who receive federal funding.[67] Federal agencies have adopted agency-specific regulations implementing Section 504 and are responsible for enforcement of those regulations.[68]
- **Fair Housing Act (FHA).** This law prohibits discrimination in housing on the basis of disability. It requires "reasonable accommodations," which are changes that are necessary for a person with a disability to have an equal opportunity to use and enjoy a dwelling.[69] A reasonable accommodation may include establishing an exception to a "no pets" policy to allow an animal to occupy a dwelling with an individual who has a disability. There are many similarities between the ADA and the FHA, but there are also differences. Two issues that are litigated frequently are (1) whether the FHA requires an animal to be specifically trained to provide assistance and (2) whether the FHA requires accommodations not only for service animals but also for emotional support animals.[70]

---

66. G.S. 168-4.2(b).

67. 29 U.S.C. §§ 701 *et seq.*

68. *See, e.g.*, 45 C.F.R. pt. 84 (regulations adopted by the U.S. Department of Health and Human Services (U.S. DHHS) implementing Section 504); 45 C.F.R. pt. 85 (delegating enforcement authority for the U.S. DHHS Section 504 regulations to the U.S. DHHS Office for Civil Rights); 49 C.F.R. pt. 27 (regulations adopted by the U.S. Department of Transportation (U.S. DOT) implementing Section 504).

69. 42 U.S.C. §§ 3601–3619; 24 C.F.R. § 100.204. *See also* U.S. Dep't of Just., Civ. Rts. Div., & U.S. Hous. & Urb. Dev., Off. of Fair Hous. & Equal Opportunity, Joint Statement of the Department of Housing and Urban Development and the Department of Justice: Reasonable Modifications under the Fair Housing Act (2008), https://www.justice.gov/sites/default/files/crt/legacy/2010/12/15/reasonable_modifications_mar08.pdf.

70. *See, e.g.*, Overlook Mut. Homes, Inc. v. Spencer, 666 F. Supp. 2d 850, 861 (S.D. Ohio 2009) ("In sum, this Court concludes that the types of animals that can qualify as reasonable accommodations under the FHA include emotional support animals, which need not be individually trained."); Fair Hous. of the Dakotas, Inc. v. Goldmark Prop. Mgmt., Inc., 778 F. Supp. 2d 1028, 1036 (D.N.D. 2011) ("Upon a careful review of the other judicial opinions in this area, the [Department of Justice]'s explanations of its interpretation of the FHA and corresponding ADA, and after giving deference to [the Department of Housing and Urban Development]'s

- **Air Carrier Access Act (ACAA).** Airlines are required to allow service animals to accompany individuals with disabilities on flights.[71] The ADA does not apply on air carriers but will typically apply to areas in U.S. airports (1) where individuals board carriers and (2) that meet the definition of public accommodations, such as restaurants.[72] Therefore, both statutes are relevant in the context of air travel and, for the most part, are consistent with one another. One noteworthy difference is that the ACAA allows an individual to be accompanied by an emotional support animal or a psychiatric service animal with written documentation from a mental health professional.[73] Therefore, it is reasonable for an airport to allow an individual with a disability to bring an emotional support animal into public accommodations at the airport even though the ADA does not require it.[74]

- **Other Types of Transportation.** There is some overlap between the ADA and laws that apply to modes of transportation other than air carriers. For example, public entities that provide public transportation services, such as AMTRAK (trains), will be subject to both Title II of the ADA and any discrimination-related statutes or regulations enforced by the U.S. Department of Transportation (U.S. DOT).[75] With respect to private entities, Title III of the ADA will apply if the transportation entity is also a public accommodation, such as a vessel operated by a private entity primarily engaged in the business of transporting people (e.g., a passenger ferry, a cruise ship traveling from one place to another). These types of vessels will be subject to both the ADA and

---

regulations regarding the meaning of the FHA, the Court finds the FHA encompasses all types of assistance animals regardless of training, including those that ameliorate a physical disability and those that ameliorate a mental disability.").

71. 49 U.S.C. § 41705; 14 C.F.R. § 382.117 (specific regulation related to service animals).

72. 75 Fed. Reg. 56,236, 56,239–40 (Sept. 15, 2010).

73. 14 C.F.R. § 382.117(e). The documentation must be recent and must explain that (1) the passenger has a mental or emotional disability, (2) the passenger needs the animal as an accommodation for air travel and/or for activity at the destination, and (3) the person providing the documentation is a licensed mental health professional and the passenger is under his or her care. Details regarding the mental health professional's licensure must also be provided.

74. 75 Fed. Reg. 56,240 (Sept. 15, 2010) ("If a particular animal is a service animal for purposes of the ACAA and is thus allowed on an airplane, but is not a service animal for purposes of the ADA, nothing in the ADA prohibits an airport restaurant from allowing a ticketed passenger with a disability who is traveling with a service animal that meets the ACAA's definition of service animal to bring that animal into the facility even though under the ADA's definition of service animal the animal lawfully could be excluded.")

75. *See, e.g.*, 49 C.F.R. pts. 37 and 39 (federal regulations implementing the ADA and Section 504 of the Rehabilitation Act of 1973 with respect to transportation services and passenger vessels).

the U.S. DOT regulations.[76] The U.S. DOT regulations may include additional requirements that are specific to transportation, but a regulated entity should be able to comply with both bodies of law.[77]

- **Individuals with Disabilities Education Act (IDEA).** This federal law specifically addresses discrimination in schools for children with disabilities. The protections of the IDEA, in conjunction with the ADA and Section 504 of the Rehabilitation Act, have been the subject of significant litigation over the years.[78] One of the main issues addressed in service animal cases involving schools is whether the child or the child's representative must exhaust administrative remedies available under the IDEA before seeking redress under other laws related to discrimination.[79]

Local governments should evaluate all potentially applicable laws when developing policies related to service animals. If there is a conflict or area of overlap, it would be prudent to comply with the law that provides the most generous rights of access to individuals accompanied by service animals.

Enforcement

If a government entity or place of public accommodation refuses an individual with a service animal access in violation of federal law, there are several potential consequences that could follow.

---

76. *See* 49 C.F.R. pt. 39. If the private entity is not primarily engaged in the business of transporting people (such as boat tours that begin and end in the same location), only the ADA regulations will apply and not the U.S. DOT regulations. *See* 75 Fed. Reg. 56,236, 56,238 (Sept. 15, 2010).

77. In the analysis accompanying the ADA regulations implementing Title II, the Department of Justice explains:

> The Department recognizes that DOT has its own independent regulatory responsibilities under subtitle B of title II of the ADA. To the extent that the public transportation services, programs, and activities of public entities are covered by subtitle B of title II of the ADA, they are subject to the DOT regulations at 49 CFR parts 37 and 39. Matters covered by subtitle A are covered by this rule. However, this rule should not be read to prohibit DOT from elaborating on the provisions of this rule in its own ADA rules in the specific regulatory contexts for which it is responsible, after appropriate consultation with the Department. . . . While DOT may establish transportation-specific requirements that are more stringent or expansive than those set forth in this rule, any such requirements cannot reduce the protections and requirements set forth in this rule.

75 Fed. Reg. 56,164, 56,167 (Sept. 15, 2010).

78. *See, e.g.,* Waterlander, *supra* note 34 (reviewing service animal cases specifically related to children with autism); Wieselthier, *supra* note 34 (reviewing service animal cases involving students with a range of disabilities).

79. See articles cited *supra* note 78.

- The individual could file a private, civil action alleging a violation of the ADA, Section 504 of the Rehabilitation Act, or other applicable laws.[80]
- The individual could file a complaint with the federal government. If the complaint relates to a place of public accommodation, the U.S. Department of Justice will be responsible for the investigation. If the complaint relates to a public entity, other federal agencies (such as the U.S. Department of Health and Human Services or the Department of Transportation) will have responsibility for investigating, depending upon the nature of the entity involved.[81]
- A federal agency could initiate a compliance review.[82]
- A federal agency could initiate a civil action seeking injunctive relief or civil penalties.[83]
- A federal agency could withhold federal funding.[84]

The individual could also bring a civil action under state law.[85]

North Carolina has several criminal penalties related to service and assistance animals. First, it is a Class 3 misdemeanor to deprive a person with a disability of rights granted under state law, including the right to be accompanied by a service animal.[86] Second, it is a misdemeanor to disguise an animal as a service animal or a service animal in training.[87] Finally, as discussed in detail in chapter 2, it is a crime for a person to hurt or interfere with an animal knowing that it is an assistance animal.

---

80. *See, e.g.*, Green v. Hous. Auth. of Clackamas Cty., 994 F. Supp. 1253, 1256 (D. Or. 1998) (plaintiff asserted violations of the ADA, the FHA, and Section 504 of the Rehabilitation Act after housing authority attempted to evict plaintiff for having a hearing assistance dog).

81. 28 C.F.R. § 35.190 (delegating responsibility for enforcement of ADA Title II to various federal agencies). The regulations implementing the ADA include general provisions related to filing complaints. *See, e.g.*, 28 C.F.R. pt. 35, subpt. F (describing compliance procedures related to violations of Title II); 28 C.F.R. pt. 36, subpt. E (describing enforcement procedures related to violations of ADA Title III). Individual agency regulations will also include provisions related to complaints or grievances. *See, e.g.*, 14 C.F.R. pt. 382, subpt. K (describing complaint and enforcement procedures for air carriers).

82. *See* 28 C.F.R. § 35.172 (authorizing compliance reviews related to public entities); § 36.502 (authorizing compliance reviews related to places of public accommodation).

83. *See, e.g.*, 28 C.F.R. § 36.503 (authorizing U.S. Attorney General to bring civil action related to violation of ADA Title III in certain circumstances).

84. *See, e.g.*, 49 C.F.R. § 27.125 (authorizing the U.S. DOT to refuse federal financial assistance in some circumstances).

85. *See, e.g.*, Stroud v. Harrison, 131 N.C. App. 480 (1998).

86. G.S. 168-4.5.

87. *Id.*

Appendix A. Relevant Sections of the North Carolina General Statutes (G.S.)

Article 1 [of G.S. Chapter 168].
Rights.

§ 168-1. Purpose and definition.

The State shall encourage and enable persons with disabilities to participate fully in the social and economic life of the State and to engage in remunerative employment. For purposes of this Article, the term "person with a disability" shall have the same meaning as set forth in G.S. 168A-3(7a).

§ 168-2. Right of access to and use of public places.

Persons with disabilities have the same right as persons without disabilities to the full and free use of the streets, highways, sidewalks, walkways, public buildings, public facilities, and all other buildings and facilities, both publicly and privately owned, which serve the public.

§ 168-3. Right to use of public conveyances, accommodations, etc.

Persons with disabilities are entitled to accommodations, advantages, facilities, and privileges of all common carriers, airplanes, motor vehicles, railroad trains, motor buses, streetcars, boats, or any other public conveyances or modes of transportation; hotels, lodging places, places of public accommodation, amusement or resort to which the general public is invited, subject only to the conditions and limitations established by law and applicable alike to all persons.

· · ·

§ 168-4.2. May be accompanied by service animal.

(a) Every person with a disability has the right to be accompanied by a service animal trained to assist the person with his or her specific disability in any of the places listed in G.S. 168-3, and has the right to keep the service animal on any premises the person leases, rents, or uses. The person qualifies for these rights upon the showing of a tag, issued by the Department of Health and Human Services, under G.S. 168-4.3, stamped "NORTH CAROLINA SERVICE ANIMAL PERMANENT REGISTRATION" and stamped with a registration number, or upon a showing that the animal is being trained or has been trained as a service animal. The service animal may accompany a person in any of the places listed in G.S. 168-3.

(b) An animal in training to become a service animal may be taken into any of the places listed in G.S. 168-3 for the purpose of training when the animal is accompanied by a person who is training the service animal and the animal wears a collar and leash, harness, or cape that identifies the animal as a service animal in training. The trainer shall be liable for any damage caused by the animal while using a public conveyance or on the premises of a public facility or other place listed in G.S. 168-3.

§ 168-4.3. Training and registration of service animal.

The Department of Health and Human Services, shall adopt rules for the registration of service animals and shall issue registrations to a person with a disability who makes application for registration of an animal that serves as a service animal or to a person who is training an animal as a service animal.

The rules adopted regarding registration shall require that the animal be trained or be in training as a service animal. The rules shall provide that the certification and registration need not be renewed while the animal is serving or training with the person applying for the registration. No fee may be charged the person for the application, registration, tag, or replacement in the event the original is lost. The Department of Health and Human Services may, by rule, issue a certification or accept the certification issued by the appropriate training facilities.

§ 168-4.4. Responsibility for service animal.

Neither a person with a disability who is accompanied by a service animal, nor a person who is training a service animal, may be required to pay any extra compensation for the animal. The person has all the responsibilities and liabilities placed on any person by any applicable law when that person owns or uses any animal, including liability for any damage done by the animal.

§ 168-4.5. Penalty.

It is unlawful to disguise an animal as a service animal or service animal in training. It is unlawful to deprive a person with a disability or a person training a service animal of any rights granted the person pursuant to G.S. 168-4.2 through G.S. 168-4.4, or of any rights or privileges granted the general public with respect to being accompanied by animals or to charge any fee for the use of the service animal. Violation of this section shall be a Class 3 misdemeanor.

• • •

[G.S.] Chapter 168A.
Persons With Disabilities Protection Act.

§ 168A-1. Title.

This Chapter may be cited as the North Carolina Persons With Disabilities Protection Act.

§ 168A-2. Statement of purpose.

(a) The purpose of this Chapter is to ensure equality of opportunity, to promote independent living, self-determination, and economic self-sufficiency, and to encourage and enable all persons with disabilities to participate fully to the maximum extent of their abilities in the social and economic life of the State, to engage in remunerative employment, to use available public accommodations and public services, and to otherwise pursue their rights and privileges as inhabitants of this State.

(b) The General Assembly finds that: the practice of discrimination based upon a disabling condition is contrary to the public interest and to the principles of freedom and equality of opportunity; the practice of discrimination on the basis of a disabling condition threatens the rights and proper privileges of the inhabitants of this State; and such discrimination results in a failure to realize the productive capacity of individuals to their fullest extent.

§ 168A-3. Definitions.

As used in this Chapter, unless the context otherwise requires:

(1) "Covered governmental entity" means any State department, institution, agency, or any political subdivision of the State or any person that contracts with a State department, institution, agency, or political subdivision of the State for the delivery of public services, including, but not limited to, education, health, social services, recreation, and rehabilitation.

(1a)   "Disabling condition" means any condition or characteristic that renders a person a person with a disability.

(1b)   "Discriminatory practice" means any practice prohibited by this Chapter.

(2)   "Employer" means any person employing 15 or more full-time employees within the State, but excluding a person whose only employees are hired to work as domestic or farm workers at that person's home or farm.

(3)   "Employment agency" means a person regularly undertaking with or without compensation to procure for employees opportunities to work for an employer and includes an agent of such a person.

(4)   Recodified as G.S. 168A-3(7a).

(4a)   "Information technology" has the same meaning as in G.S. 143B-1320. The term also specifically includes information transaction machines.

(5)   Recodified as G.S. 168A-3(1).

(6)   "Labor organization" means an organization of any kind, an agency or employee representation committee, a group association, or a plan, in which employees participate and which exists for the purpose, in whole or in part, of dealing with employers concerning grievances, labor disputes, wages, rates of pay, hours, or other terms or conditions of employment.

(7)   "Person" includes any individual, partnership, association, corporation, labor organization, legal representative, trustee, receiver, and the State and its departments, agencies, and political subdivisions.

(7a)   "Person with a disability" means any person who (i) has a physical or mental impairment which substantially limits one or more major life activities; (ii) has a record of such an impairment; or (iii) is regarded as having such an impairment. As used in this subdivision, the term:

    a.   "Physical or mental impairment" means (i) any physiological disorder or abnormal condition, cosmetic disfigurement, or anatomical loss, caused by bodily injury, birth defect or illness, affecting a body system, including, but not limited to, neurological; musculoskeletal; special sense organs; respiratory, including speech organs; cardiovascular; reproductive; digestive; genitourinary; hemic and lymphatic; skin; and endocrine; or (ii) any mental disorder, such as mental retardation, organic brain syndrome, mental illness, specific learning disabilities, and other developmental disabilities, but (iii) excludes (A) sexual preferences; (B) active alcoholism or drug addiction or abuse; and (C) any disorder, condition or disfigurement which is temporary in nature, lasting six months or fewer, and leaving no residual impairment. A disorder, condition, or disfigurement that is episodic or in remission is a physical or mental impairment if it would substantially limit a major life activity when active.

    b.   "Major life activities" means functions, including, but not limited to, caring for one's self, performing manual tasks, walking, seeing, hearing, speaking, eating, sleeping, lifting, bending, standing, breathing, learning, reading, concentrating, thinking, communicating, and working. A major life activity also includes the operation of a major bodily function, including, but not limited to, functions of the immune system, normal cell growth, and digestive, bowel, bladder, neurological, brain, respiratory, circulatory, endocrine, and reproductive functions.

    c.   "Has a record of such an impairment" means has a history of, or has been misclassified as having, a mental or physical impairment that substantially limits major life activities.

    d.   "Is regarded as having an impairment" means (i) has a physical or mental impairment that does not substantially limit major life activities but that is treated as constituting such a limitation; (ii) has a physical or mental impairment that substantially limits major life activities because of the attitudes of others; or (iii) has none of the impairments defined in paragraph a. of this subdivision but is treated as having such an impairment.

The determination of whether an impairment substantially limits a major life activity shall be made without regard to the ameliorative effects of mitigating measures, such as (i) medication, medical supplies, equipment, or appliances, low-vision devices, which do not include ordinary eyeglasses or contact lenses, prosthetics, including limbs and devices, hearing aids and cochlear implants or other implantable hearing devices, mobility devices, or oxygen therapy equipment and supplies; (ii) use of assistive technology; (iii) reasonable accommodations or auxiliary aids or services; or (iv) learned behavioral or adaptive neurological modifications.

(8) "Place of public accommodations" includes, but is not limited to, any place, facility, store, other establishment, hotel, or motel, which supplies goods or services on the premises to the public or which solicits or accepts the patronage or trade of any person.

(9) "Qualified person with a disability" means:

   a. With regard to employment, a person with a disability who can satisfactorily perform the duties of the job in question, with or without reasonable accommodation, (i) provided that the person with a disability shall not be held to standards of performance different from other employees similarly employed, and (ii) further provided that the disabling condition does not create an unreasonable risk to the safety or health of the person with a disability, other employees, the employer's customers, or the public;

   b. With regard to places of public accommodation a person with a disability who can benefit from the goods or services provided by the place of public accommodation; and

   c. With regard to public services and public transportation a person with a disability who meets prerequisites for participation that are uniformly applied to all participants, such as income or residence, and that do not have the effect of discriminating against persons with a disability.

(10) "Reasonable accommodations" means:

   a. With regard to employment, making reasonable physical changes in the workplace, including, but not limited to, making facilities accessible, modifying equipment and providing mechanical aids to assist in operating equipment, or making reasonable changes in the duties of the job in question that would accommodate the known disabling conditions of the person with a disability seeking the job in question by enabling him or her to satisfactorily perform the duties of that job; provided that "reasonable accommodation" does not require that an employer:

      1. Hire one or more employees, other than the person with a disability, for the purpose, in whole or in part, of enabling the person with a disability to be employed; or

      2. Reassign duties of the job in question to other employees without assigning to the employee with a disability duties that would compensate for those reassigned; or

      3. Reassign duties of the job in question to one or more other employees where such reassignment would increase the skill, effort or responsibility required of such other employee or employees from that required prior to the change in duties; or

      4. Alter, modify, change or deviate from bona fide seniority policies or practices; or

      5. Provide accommodations of a personal nature, including, but not limited to, eyeglasses, hearing aids, or prostheses, except under the same terms and conditions as such items are provided to the employer's employees generally; or

        6.   Repealed by Session Laws 2002-163, s. 2, effective January 1, 2003.

        7.   Make any changes that would impose on the employer an undue hardship.

   b.   With regard to a place of public accommodations and a covered governmental entity, making reasonable efforts to accommodate the disabling conditions of a person with a disability, including, but not limited to, making facilities accessible to and usable by persons with a disability, redesigning equipment, providing auxiliary aids and services needed to make aurally and visually delivered materials available, as needed, to individuals with hearing or sight impairments, providing mechanical aids or other assistance, or using alternative accessible locations, provided that reasonable accommodations does not require efforts which would impose an undue hardship on the entity involved.

(11) "Undue hardship" means a significant difficulty or expense. The following factors shall be considered in determining whether an accommodation would impose an undue hardship:

   a.   The nature and cost of the accommodations needed under this Chapter.

   b.   The overall financial resources of the particular facility or facilities involved in the provision of the accommodation, the number of persons employed at the facility, the effect on expenses and resources at the facility, and any other impact on the operation of the facility.

   c.   The overall effect on the financial resources of the covered entity, the number of persons employed by the covered entity, and the number, type, and location of the covered entity's facilities.

   d.   The type of operations of the covered entity, including the composition, structure, and functions of the workforce of the entity, the geographic separateness of the particular facility to the covered entity, and the administrative or fiscal relationship of the particular facility to the covered entity.

§ 168A-4. Reasonable accommodation duties.

(a)   A qualified person with a disability requesting a reasonable accommodation must apprise the employer, employment agency, labor organization, place of public accommodation, or covered governmental entity of his or her disabling condition, submit any necessary medical documentation, make suggestions for such possible accommodations as are known to such person with a disability, and cooperate in any ensuing discussion and evaluation aimed at determining possible or feasible accommodations.

(b)   Once a qualified person with a disability has requested an accommodation, or if a potential accommodation is obvious in the circumstances, an employer, employment agency, labor organization, place of public accommodation, or covered governmental entity shall investigate whether there are reasonable accommodations that can be made and make reasonable accommodations as defined in G.S. 168A-3(10).

· · ·

Appendix B. Relevant Sections of the Code of Federal Regulations (C.F.R.)

[C.F.R.] Title 28. Judicial Administration
Chapter I. Department of Justice

Part 35. Nondiscrimination on the Basis of Disability
in State and Local Government Services

. . .

28 C.F.R. § 35.101. Purpose and broad coverage.

(a) Purpose. The purpose of this part is to implement subtitle A of title II of the Americans with Disabilities Act of 1990 (42 U.S.C. 12131–12134), as amended by the ADA Amendments Act of 2008 (ADA Amendments Act) (Pub. L. 110–325, 122 Stat. 3553 (2008)), which prohibits discrimination on the basis of disability by public entities.

(b) Broad coverage. The primary purpose of the ADA Amendments Act is to make it easier for people with disabilities to obtain protection under the ADA. Consistent with the ADA Amendments Act's purpose of reinstating a broad scope of protection under the ADA, the definition of "disability" in this part shall be construed broadly in favor of expansive coverage to the maximum extent permitted by the terms of the ADA. The primary object of attention in cases brought under the ADA should be whether entities covered under the ADA have complied with their obligations and whether discrimination has occurred, not whether the individual meets the definition of "disability." The question of whether an individual meets the definition of "disability" under this part should not demand extensive analysis.

. . .

28 C.F.R. § 35.104. Definitions.

For purposes of this part, the term—

. . .

Public entity means—
(1) Any State or local government;
(2) Any department, agency, special purpose district, or other instrumentality of a State or States or local government; and
(3) The National Railroad Passenger Corporation, and any commuter authority (as defined in section 103(8) of the Rail Passenger Service Act).

Qualified individual with a disability means an individual with a disability who, with or without reasonable modifications to rules, policies, or practices, the removal of architectural, communication, or transportation barriers, or the provision of auxiliary aids and services, meets the essential eligibility requirements for the receipt of services or the participation in programs or activities provided by a public entity.

. . .

Service animal means any dog that is individually trained to do work or perform tasks for the benefit of an individual with a disability, including a physical, sensory, psychiatric, intellectual, or other mental disability. Other species of animals, whether wild or domestic, trained or untrained, are not service animals for the purposes of this definition. The work or tasks performed by a service animal must be directly related to the individual's disability. Examples of work or tasks include, but are not limited to, assisting individuals who are blind or have low vision with navigation and other tasks, alerting individuals who are deaf or hard of hearing to the presence of people or sounds, providing non-violent protection or rescue work, pulling a wheelchair, assisting an individual during a seizure, alerting individuals to the presence of allergens, retrieving items such as medicine or the telephone, providing physical support and assistance with balance and stability to individuals with mobility disabilities, and helping persons with psychiatric and neurological disabilities by preventing or interrupting impulsive or destructive behaviors. The crime deterrent effects of an animal's presence and the provision of emotional support, well-being, comfort, or companionship do not constitute work or tasks for the purposes of this definition.

· · ·

28 C.F.R. § 35.130. General prohibitions against discrimination.

(a) No qualified individual with a disability shall, on the basis of disability, be excluded from participation in or be denied the benefits of the services, programs, or activities of a public entity, or be subjected to discrimination by any public entity.

(b) (1) A public entity, in providing any aid, benefit, or service, may not, directly or through contractual, licensing, or other arrangements, on the basis of disability—

(i) Deny a qualified individual with a disability the opportunity to participate in or benefit from the aid, benefit, or service;

(ii) Afford a qualified individual with a disability an opportunity to participate in or benefit from the aid, benefit, or service that is not equal to that afforded others;

(iii) Provide a qualified individual with a disability with an aid, benefit, or service that is not as effective in affording equal opportunity to obtain the same result, to gain the same benefit, or to reach the same level of achievement as that provided to others;

(iv) Provide different or separate aids, benefits, or services to individuals with disabilities or to any class of individuals with disabilities than is provided to others unless such action is necessary to provide qualified individuals with disabilities with aids, benefits, or services that are as effective as those provided to others;

(v) Aid or perpetuate discrimination against a qualified individual with a disability by providing significant assistance to an agency, organization, or person that discriminates on the basis of disability in providing any aid, benefit, or service to beneficiaries of the public entity's program;

(vi) Deny a qualified individual with a disability the opportunity to participate as a member of planning or advisory boards;

(vii) Otherwise limit a qualified individual with a disability in the enjoyment of any right, privilege, advantage, or opportunity enjoyed by others receiving the aid, benefit, or service.

(2) A public entity may not deny a qualified individual with a disability the opportunity to participate in services, programs, or activities that are not separate or different, despite the existence of permissibly separate or different programs or activities.

· · ·

(4) A public entity may not, in determining the site or location of a facility, make selections—

(i)   That have the effect of excluding individuals with disabilities from, denying them the benefits of, or otherwise subjecting them to discrimination; or

(ii) That have the purpose or effect of defeating or substantially impairing the accomplishment of the objectives of the service, program, or activity with respect to individuals with disabilities.

. . .

(7) (i)   A public entity shall make reasonable modifications in policies, practices, or procedures when the modifications are necessary to avoid discrimination on the basis of disability, unless the public entity can demonstrate that making the modifications would fundamentally alter the nature of the service, program, or activity.

. . .

28 C.F.R. § 35.136. Service animals.

(a) General. Generally, a public entity shall modify its policies, practices, or procedures to permit the use of a service animal by an individual with a disability.

(b) Exceptions. A public entity may ask an individual with a disability to remove a service animal from the premises if—

(1) The animal is out of control and the animal's handler does not take effective action to control it; or

(2) The animal is not housebroken.

(c) If an animal is properly excluded. If a public entity properly excludes a service animal under § 35.136(b), it shall give the individual with a disability the opportunity to participate in the service, program, or activity without having the service animal on the premises.

(d) Animal under handler's control. A service animal shall be under the control of its handler. A service animal shall have a harness, leash, or other tether, unless either the handler is unable because of a disability to use a harness, leash, or other tether, or the use of a harness, leash, or other tether would interfere with the service animal's safe, effective performance of work or tasks, in which case the service animal must be otherwise under the handler's control (e.g., voice control, signals, or other effective means).

(e) Care or supervision. A public entity is not responsible for the care or supervision of a service animal.

(f) Inquiries. A public entity shall not ask about the nature or extent of a person's disability, but may make two inquiries to determine whether an animal qualifies as a service animal. A public entity may ask if the animal is required because of a disability and what work or task the animal has been trained to perform. A public entity shall not require documentation, such as proof that the animal has been certified, trained, or licensed as a service animal. Generally, a public entity may not make these inquiries about a service animal when it is readily apparent that an animal is trained to do work or perform tasks for an individual with a disability (e.g., the dog is observed guiding an individual who is blind or has low vision, pulling a person's wheelchair, or providing assistance with stability or balance to an individual with an observable mobility disability).

(g) Access to areas of a public entity. Individuals with disabilities shall be permitted to be accompanied by their service animals in all areas of a public entity's facilities where members of the public, participants in services, programs or activities, or invitees, as relevant, are allowed to go.

(h) Surcharges. A public entity shall not ask or require an individual with a disability to pay a surcharge, even if people accompanied by pets are required to pay fees, or to comply with other requirements generally not applicable to people without pets. If a public entity normally charges individuals for the damage they cause, an individual with a disability may be charged for damage caused by his or her service animal.

   (i)   Miniature horses.

      (1)   Reasonable modifications. A public entity shall make reasonable modifications in policies, practices, or procedures to permit the use of a miniature horse by an individual with a disability if the miniature horse has been individually trained to do work or perform tasks for the benefit of the individual with a disability.

      (2)   Assessment factors. In determining whether reasonable modifications in policies, practices, or procedures can be made to allow a miniature horse into a specific facility, a public entity shall consider—

         (i)   The type, size, and weight of the miniature horse and whether the facility can accommodate these features;

         (ii)   Whether the handler has sufficient control of the miniature horse;

         (iii)   Whether the miniature horse is housebroken; and

         (iv)   Whether the miniature horse's presence in a specific facility compromises legitimate safety requirements that are necessary for safe operation.

      (3)   Other requirements. Paragraphs 35.136(c) through (h) of this section, which apply to service animals, shall also apply to miniature horses.

[C.F.R.] Title 28. Judicial Administration
Chapter I. Department of Justice.

28 C.F.R. § 36.101. Purpose and broad coverage.

   (a)   Purpose. The purpose of this part is to implement subtitle A of title III of the Americans with Disabilities Act of 1990 (42 U.S.C. 12181–12189), as amended by the ADA Amendments Act of 2008 (ADA Amendments Act) (Pub. L. 110–325, 122 Stat. 3553 (2008)), which prohibits discrimination on the basis of disability by covered public accommodations and requires places of public accommodation and commercial facilities to be designed, constructed, and altered in compliance with the accessibility standards established by this part.

   (b)   Broad coverage. The primary purpose of the ADA Amendments Act is to make it easier for people with disabilities to obtain protection under the ADA. Consistent with the ADA Amendments Act's purpose of reinstating a broad scope of protection under the ADA, the definition of "disability" in this part shall be construed broadly in favor of expansive coverage to the maximum extent permitted by the terms of the ADA. The primary object of attention in cases brought under the ADA should be whether entities covered under the ADA have complied with their obligations and whether discrimination has occurred, not whether the individual meets the definition of "disability." The question of whether an individual meets the definition of "disability" under this part should not demand extensive analysis.

. . .

28 C.F.R. § 36.104. Definitions.

For purposes of this part, the term—

. . .

Place of public accommodation means a facility operated by a private entity whose operations affect commerce and fall within at least one of the following categories—

(1) Place of lodging, except for an establishment located within a facility that contains not more than five rooms for rent or hire and that actually is occupied by the proprietor of the establishment as the residence of the proprietor. For purposes of this part, a facility is a "place of lodging" if it is—

    (i) An inn, hotel, or motel; or

    (ii) A facility that—

        (A) Provides guest rooms for sleeping for stays that primarily are short-term in nature (generally 30 days or less) where the occupant does not have the right to return to a specific room or unit after the conclusion of his or her stay; and

        (B) Provides guest rooms under conditions and with amenities similar to a hotel, motel, or inn, including the following—

            (1) On- or off-site management and reservations service;

            (2) Rooms available on a walk-up or call-in basis;

            (3) Availability of housekeeping or linen service; and

            (4) Acceptance of reservations for a guest room type without guaranteeing a particular unit or room until check-in, and without a prior lease or security deposit.

(2) A restaurant, bar, or other establishment serving food or drink;

(3) A motion picture house, theater, concert hall, stadium, or other place of exhibition or entertainment;

(4) An auditorium, convention center, lecture hall, or other place of public gathering;

(5) A bakery, grocery store, clothing store, hardware store, shopping center, or other sales or rental establishment;

(6) A laundromat, dry-cleaner, bank, barber shop, beauty shop, travel service, shoe repair service, funeral parlor, gas station, office of an accountant or lawyer, pharmacy, insurance office, professional office of a health care provider, hospital, or other service establishment;

(7) A terminal, depot, or other station used for specified public transportation;

(8) A museum, library, gallery, or other place of public display or collection;

(9) A park, zoo, amusement park, or other place of recreation;

(10) A nursery, elementary, secondary, undergraduate, or postgraduate private school, or other place of education;

(11) A day care center, senior citizen center, homeless shelter, food bank, adoption agency, or other social service center establishment; and

(12) A gymnasium, health spa, bowling alley, golf course, or other place of exercise or recreation.

. . .

Service animal means any dog that is individually trained to do work or perform tasks for the benefit of an individual with a disability, including a physical, sensory, psychiatric, intellectual, or other mental disability. Other species of animals, whether wild or domestic, trained or untrained, are not service animals for the purposes of this definition. The work or tasks performed by a service animal must be directly related to the individual's disability. Examples of work or tasks include, but are not limited to, assisting individuals who are blind or have low vision with navigation and other tasks, alerting individuals who are deaf or hard of hearing to the presence of people or sounds, providing non-violent protection or rescue work, pulling a wheelchair, assisting an individual during a seizure, alerting individuals to the presence of allergens, retrieving items such as medicine or the telephone, providing physical support and assistance with balance and stability to individuals with mobility disabilities, and helping persons with psychiatric and neurological disabilities by preventing or interrupting impulsive or destructive behaviors. The crime deterrent effects of an animal's presence and the provision of emotional support, well-being, comfort, or companionship do not constitute work or tasks for the purposes of this definition.

. . .

28 C.F.R. § 36.201. General.

(a) Prohibition of discrimination. No individual shall be discriminated against on the basis of disability in the full and equal enjoyment of the goods, services, facilities, privileges, advantages, or accommodations of any place of public accommodation by any private entity who owns, leases (or leases to), or operates a place of public accommodation.

(b) Landlord and tenant responsibilities. Both the landlord who owns the building that houses a place of public accommodation and the tenant who owns or operates the place of public accommodation are public accommodations subject to the requirements of this part. As between the parties, allocation of responsibility for complying with the obligations of this part may be determined by lease or other contract.

(c) Claims of no disability. Nothing in this part shall provide the basis for a claim that an individual without a disability was subject to discrimination because of a lack of disability, including a claim that an individual with a disability was granted a reasonable modification that was denied to an individual without a disability.

. . .

28 C.F.R. § 36.302. Modifications in policies, practices, or procedures.

(a) General. A public accommodation shall make reasonable modifications in policies, practices, or procedures, when the modifications are necessary to afford goods, services, facilities, privileges, advantages, or accommodations to individuals with disabilities, unless the public accommodation can demonstrate that making the modifications would fundamentally alter the nature of the goods, services, facilities, privileges, advantages, or accommodations.

. . .

(c) Service animals—

   (1) General. Generally, a public accommodation shall modify policies, practices, or procedures to permit the use of a service animal by an individual with a disability.

   (2) Exceptions. A public accommodation may ask an individual with a disability to remove a service animal from the premises if:
     (i) The animal is out of control and the animal's handler does not take effective action to control it; or
     (ii) The animal is not housebroken.

   (3) If an animal is properly excluded. If a public accommodation properly excludes a service animal under § 36.302(c)(2), it shall give the individual with a disability the opportunity to obtain goods, services, and accommodations without having the service animal on the premises.

   (4) Animal under handler's control. A service animal shall be under the control of its handler. A service animal shall have a harness, leash, or other tether, unless either the handler is unable because of a disability to use a harness, leash, or other tether, or the use of a harness, leash, or other tether would interfere with the service animal's safe, effective performance of work or tasks, in which case the service animal must be otherwise under the handler's control (e.g., voice control, signals, or other effective means).

   (5) Care or supervision. A public accommodation is not responsible for the care or supervision of a service animal.

   (6) Inquiries. A public accommodation shall not ask about the nature or extent of a person's disability, but may make two inquiries to determine whether an animal qualifies as a service animal. A public accommodation may ask if the animal is required

because of a disability and what work or task the animal has been trained to perform. A public accommodation shall not require documentation, such as proof that the animal has been certified, trained, or licensed as a service animal. Generally, a public accommodation may not make these inquiries about a service animal when it is readily apparent that an animal is trained to do work or perform tasks for an individual with a disability (e.g., the dog is observed guiding an individual who is blind or has low vision, pulling a person's wheelchair, or providing assistance with stability or balance to an individual with an observable mobility disability).

(7)   Access to areas of a public accommodation. Individuals with disabilities shall be permitted to be accompanied by their service animals in all areas of a place of public accommodation where members of the public, program participants, clients, customers, patrons, or invitees, as relevant, are allowed to go.

(8)   Surcharges. A public accommodation shall not ask or require an individual with a disability to pay a surcharge, even if people accompanied by pets are required to pay fees, or to comply with other requirements generally not applicable to people without pets. If a public accommodation normally charges individuals for the damage they cause, an individual with a disability may be charged for damage caused by his or her service animal.

(9)   Miniature horses.

(i)   A public accommodation shall make reasonable modifications in policies, practices, or procedures to permit the use of a miniature horse by an individual with a disability if the miniature horse has been individually trained to do work or perform tasks for the benefit of the individual with a disability.

(ii)   Assessment factors. In determining whether reasonable modifications in policies, practices, or procedures can be made to allow a miniature horse into a specific facility, a public accommodation shall consider—

(A)   The type, size, and weight of the miniature horse and whether the facility can accommodate these features;

(B)   Whether the handler has sufficient control of the miniature horse;

(C)   Whether the miniature horse is housebroken; and

(D)   Whether the miniature horse's presence in a specific facility compromises legitimate safety requirements that are necessary for safe operation.

(iii)   Other requirements. Sections 36.302(c)(3) through (c)(8), which apply to service animals, shall also apply to miniature horses.

• • •

Chapter 9
Exotic Animals

In North Carolina, private ownership or keeping of inherently dangerous, non-native, or exotic animals (referred to in this chapter by the general term "exotic animals") is regulated primarily by local governments. This chapter briefly reviews the arguments for and against such regulation, summarizes the limited provisions that address exotic animals in federal and state law, and analyzes some of the ordinances adopted by the state's cities and counties.

At the outset, it is important to note that human interactions with exotic animals take a variety of forms. A person may be compelled by kindness to begin caring for a wild animal in distress that he or she has discovered by chance, a person may seek out an exotic pet because he or she believes that caring for such a pet will be exciting and rewarding, or a person may be involved with a rescue or rehabilitation effort focused on exotic animals. The primary concern of this chapter is a discussion of regulations having to do with private, individual ownership of exotic animals as, for lack of better descriptions, a recreational pursuit or a matter of liberty. Administering veterinary care to exotic animals or exhibiting exotic animals to the public, to name just two examples, are among the countless activities that raise legal issues that go beyond mere ownership or possession and, consequently, are beyond the scope of this chapter.

Background

Private ownership of exotic animals, like many animal-related issues, is quite controversial. Proponents of exotic animal regulation typically focus on challenges related to public safety, public health, the environment, and animal welfare.[1] First, they argue that exotic species can present a risk to public safety. North Carolina examples include

- a ten-year-old Wilkes County boy killed by his aunt's pet tiger,[2]
- a fourteen-year-old girl in Surry County attacked by one of her family's four pet tigers,[3]
- two people in Catawba County bit by a macaque monkey,[4]

---

1. Martha Drouet, Mich. State Univ. Animal Legal & Historical Ctr., *Detailed Discussion of Exotic Pet Law Update* (2014), https://www.animallaw.info/article/detailed-discussion-exotic-pet-laws-update.

2. *See* Dennis Rogers, *Time for a Ban on Big Cats*, News & Observer (Raleigh), Feb. 14, 2004.

3. *Id.*

4. *See* Evan Matsumoto, *Monkey Off Their Back: Catawba County Board of Commissioners Wants Animals Banned*, Hickory Record (Oct. 7, 2014), http://www.hickoryrecord.com/news/monkey-off-their-back-catawba-county-board-of-commissioners-wants/article_76885ef0-4e3c-11e4-878f-0017a43b2370.html.

- a worker at a hospital In Mecklenburg County attacked by a Capuchin monkey,[5] and

- an Orange County man bitten by his pet cobra.[6]

Outside of the state, in 2011 an Ohio man caused panic in his community by releasing dozens of exotic animals he had been keeping in and around his home, including lions, tigers, bears, and wolves; many of the animals were killed during efforts by authorities to recapture them and protect the public.[7]

Second, say proponents of regulation, exotic animals can create threats to both the public health and the environment.[8] Examples of such risks include the 2003 outbreak of monkeypox in humans attributed to pet prairie dogs[9] and the escape and proliferation of Burmese pythons in the Florida Everglades.[10] Finally, proponents argue, exotic animals often suffer when owned privately because their keepers are neither trained nor equipped to provide appropriate care.[11]

Opponents argue that regulation interferes with the educational benefits associated with private zoos and traveling animal exhibitions. Others contend that private owners can help prevent the extinction of many species through captive breeding programs.

---

5. *See* Trish Williford, *Monkey Captured After Escaping from Hospital Parking Lot*, WSOCTV.COM (Mar. 26, 2015), https://www.wsoctv.com/news/local/report-monkey-bites-guard-escapes-capture-universi/52166155.

6. *See* Tammy Grub & Mark Schultz, *King Cobra Bite Leaves Orange County Man in Critical Condition*, NEWS & OBSERVER (Raleigh) (May 5, 2016), http://www.newsobserver.com/news/local/community/chapel-hill-news/article75323972.html; Shea Denning, *Is it Legal to Keep a King Cobra as a Pet?*, N.C. CRIM. L., UNC SCH. OF GOV'T BLOG (May 11, 2016), https://nccriminallaw.sog.unc.edu/legal-keep-king-cobra-pet/.

7. Greg Bishop & Timothy Williams, *Police Kill Dozens of Animals Freed on Ohio Reserve*, N.Y. TIMES (Oct. 19, 2011), http://www.nytimes.com/2011/10/20/us/police-kill-dozens-of-animals-freed-from-ohio-preserve.html.

8. *See, e.g., Importation of Exotic Species and the Impact on Public Health and Safety: Hearing Before the Sen. Comm. on* Environment and Public Works, 108th Congress (July 17, 2003) (testimony of Robert A. Cook on behalf of the Wildlife Conservation Society and the American Zoo and Aquarium Association; testimony of Gabriela Chavarria on behalf of the National Environmental Coalition on Invasive Species), https://www.epw.senate.gov/public/index.cfm/2003/7/full-committee-hearing-importation-of-exotic-species-and-the-impact-on-public-health-and-safety.

9. Ctrs. for Disease Control & Prevention, *Update: Multistate Outbreak of Monkeypox— Illinois, Indiana, Kansas, Missouri, Ohio, and Wisconsin, 2003*, 52 MORTALITY & MORBIDITY WKLY. REP. 629, 642–46 (July 11, 2003), www.cdc.gov/mmwr/PDF/wk/mm5227.pdf.

10. *See* Robert Brown, *Note: Exotic Pets Invade United States Ecosystems: Legislative Failure and a Proposed Solution*, 81 IND. L. J. 713 (2006).

11. *See* Christopher M. Lucca, *Keeping Lions, Tigers, and Bears (Oh My!) in Check: The State of Exotic Pet Regulation in the Wake of the Zanesville, Ohio Massacre*, 24 VILL. ENVTL. L. J. 125, 127 (2013) (noting this argument).

Finally, some disagree with the public health and safety arguments put forward by proponents and argue that government regulation unnecessarily infringes individuals' property rights to own such animals and earn a living through private enterprises.[12]

Federal Law

Generally speaking, there is very little federal law directly regulating the private ownership of exotic animals.[13] Because of constitutional limitations on the powers of Congress, federal law deals primarily with issues related to commercial activities involving exotic animals or activities that involve bringing exotic animals into the country from abroad. As a result, federal law has some indirect influence on private ownership as a practical matter, but ownership, as an issue itself, largely is unregulated at the federal level.[14]

Pursuant to authority granted under the Public Health Service Act,[15] the Food and Drug Administration (FDA) in the U.S. Department of Health and Human Services has regulations in place that (1) prohibit the sale of turtles (with shells less than four inches long) and turtle eggs[16] and (2) restrict interstate transport of psittacine birds such as parrots, cockatoos, and parakeets.[17] These regulations are intended to minimize the transmission of salmonellosis (from turtles) and psittacosis (from birds) to humans. Following the 2003 monkeypox outbreak mentioned above, the FDA and the Centers for Disease Control and Prevention adopted regulations prohibiting the import of African rodents (or products from such rodents) and the capture, sale, transport, or release of several animals with known potential for transmitting the monkeypox virus to humans; the prohibited animals include prairie dogs, Gambian rats, and certain squirrels and porcupines.[18] Both sets of monkeypox regulations provide for limited exceptions to the prohibitions.

Some federal laws are not based on public health concerns but, rather, speak more directly to the issue of exotic animals. The three federal laws most commonly encountered in the area of exotic animal law are the Animal Welfare Act,[19] the Endangered

---

12. *See generally*, Alice Miller & Anuj Shah, *Invented Cages: The Plight of Wild Animals in Captivity*, 1 J. ANIMAL L. 23 (2005) (noting these arguments advanced in favor of permitting private ownership of wild or exotic animals).

13. Drouet, *supra* note 1.

14. *Id.*

15. 42 U.S.C. ch. 6A.

16. 21 C.F.R. § 1240.62.

17. 21 C.F.R. § 1240.65.

18. 21 C.F.R. § 1240.63 (FDA regulation); 42 C.F.R. § 71.56.

19. 7 U.S.C. §§ 2131 *et seq.*

Species Act,[20] and the Lacey Act.[21] Broadly speaking, the Animal Welfare Act regulates the transportation of, breeding for sale of, exhibition of, and biomedical research on animals (exotic or not); the Endangered Species Act regulates the import and sale of endangered species; and the Lacey Act regulates interstate and foreign commerce of certain animals, including exotic big cats.[22] As examples of the activities regulated under these laws, it is generally unlawful under the Lacey Act to

- import certain animals and fish deemed "injurious" to people or agricultural interests;[23]
- import, export, transport, sell, receive, acquire, or purchase fish, wildlife, or plants that are taken, possessed, transported, or sold in violation of any law (including foreign, federal, and state laws);[24] and
- import, export, transport, sell, receive, acquire, or purchase live lions, tigers, leopards, snow leopards, clouded leopards, cheetahs, jaguars, or cougars, or any hybrid combination of these species.[25]

While it may appear upon first glance that the federal laws would, at least as a practical matter, impose significant limitations upon the ownership of exotic animals, the reality is that federal law primarily regulates *activity* involving exotic animals and does not directly regulate private *ownership* as a stand-alone matter.[26] In addition, it is not uncommon for those involved in exotic animal commerce to take advantage of exceptions or loopholes in the laws, leading to imports or sales of exotic animals that do not technically violate federal law. Thus, state and local laws are the primary source of restrictions on ownership or possession of exotic animals.

---

20. 16 U.S.C. §§ 1531 *et seq.*
21. 16 U.S.C. §§ 3371 *et seq.*
22. *See generally* Miller & Shah, *supra* note 12 (discussing these federal laws).
23. 18 U.S.C. § 42.
24. 16 U.S.C. §§ 3371–3378.
25. 16 U.S.C. §§ 3371–3372. The provisions of the law addressing large cats are known collectively as the Captive Wildlife Safety Act, Pub. L. No. 108-191, 117 Stat. 2871, *amending* the Lacey Act, 16 U.S.C. §§ 3371–3372.
26. *See generally* Drouet, *supra* note 1.

State Law

North Carolina does not have a general statewide law regulating the ownership or possession of exotic animals.[27] The General Assembly has considered legislation several times, most recently in 2015, but has not acted.[28] According to researchers at Michigan State University, twenty states have adopted relatively comprehensive state laws prohibiting ownership of exotic animals, thirteen states have adopted partial bans, and fourteen states allow ownership of exotic pets under a licensure or permit system.[29] North Carolina remains one of four states that has no such legal framework in place.[30]

North Carolina, though lacking a general statewide law, does have some specific laws that regulate native wildlife as well as the ownership, possession, or keeping of certain exotic or dangerous animals. The Wildlife Resources Commission (WRC) is the state agency that regulates North Carolina's wildlife resources and, among other things,

---

27. Interestingly, one state statute included in the conservation and wildlife laws appears on its face to create a prohibition:

> Except as specifically permitted in this Subchapter or in rules made under the authority of this Subchapter, no person may take, possess, buy, sell, or transport any wildlife – whether dead or alive, in whole or in part. Nor may any person take, possess, buy, sell, or transport any nests or eggs of wild birds except as so permitted. No person may take, possess, buy, sell, or transport any wildlife resources in violation of the rules of the Wildlife Resources Commission.

Chapter 113, Section 291 of the North Carolina General Statutes (hereinafter G.S.).

The term "wildlife" is defined broadly enough in G.S. 113-129 to arguably encompass exotic animals: "Wild animals; wild birds; all fish found in inland fishing waters; and inland game fish. Unless the context clearly requires otherwise, the definitions of wildlife, wildlife resources, wild animals, wild birds, fish, and the like are deemed to include species normally wild, or indistinguishable from wild species, which are raised or kept in captivity." G.S. 113-129(16). But because this statute is integrated into a larger statutory context related to conservation which focuses the authority of the state agencies and commissions on primarily *native* species, it appears that this statute has not been interpreted to extend to exotic or non-native species. *See, e.g.,* G.S. 113-131 (addressing the jurisdiction of the Wildlife Resources Commission); N.C. Dep't of Cultural Res. & N.C. Wildlife Res. Comm'n, Joint Final Report to the Environmental Review Commission, Article 55 Study 8 (Dec. 31, 2017), https://www.ncleg.net/documentsites/committees/ERC/ERC%20Reports%20Received/2017/Dept%20Natural%20Cultural%20Resources/2017-Dec%20DNCR-WRC%20jt%20rpt.pdf (discussing how the scope of the Wildlife Resources Commission's authority is limited to native species).

28. *See e.g.,* S.L. 2006-248, §§ 32.1 through 32.3 (requiring a study regarding inherently dangerous animals); S. 1477/H. 1614, 2007–2008 Gen. Assemb., Reg. Sess. (N.C. 2007) (proposed legislation to regulate inherently dangerous animals); H. 554, 2015–2016 Gen. Assemb., Reg. Sess. (N.C. 2015) (proposed legislation to regulate dangerous animals).

29. Mich. State Univ. Animal Legal & Historical Ctr., *Map of Private Exotic Pet Ownership Laws* (2018), https://www.animallaw.info/content/map-private-exotic-pet-ownership-laws.

30. The other three states are Alabama, Nevada, and Wisconsin. *Id.*

enforces the state's fishing, hunting, trapping, and boating laws.[31] In addition, the WRC has the authority to regulate the "acquisition, importation, possession, transportation, disposition, or release into public or private waters or the environment of zoological or botanical species or specimens that may threaten the introduction of epizootic disease or may create a danger to or an imbalance in the environment inimical to the conservation of wildlife resources."[32] This WRC regulatory authority is limited, however, to species or specimens that may have a negative environmental impact. It does not appear to extend to the regulation of animals that some perceive as dangerous for other reasons, such as tigers. The Commission for Public Health has regulatory authority with respect to control measures for communicable diseases, and some regulations adopted pursuant to that authority involve animals.[33]

As a non-exhaustive list of examples, the state has statutes and administrative regulations that

- regulate the ownership, use, and handling of venomous reptiles, large constricting snakes, and crocodilians;[34]
- prohibit the commercial raising of American alligators without a proper license;[35]
- prohibit the release of exotic species of wild animals or wild birds into an area for the purpose of stocking an area for hunting or trapping;[36] and
- regulate certain sales of turtles.[37]

In addition, local public health directors have independent authority to declare "vicious and a menace to the public health" any animal that makes an unprovoked attack on a person causing bodily harm.[38] Once an animal has been declared vicious, it must be confined to its owner's property, except when (1) accompanied by a responsible adult and (2) restrained on a leash.[39]

---

31. *See* Article 24 of G.S. Chapter 143 (establishing the WRC); G.S. Chapter 113 (including various statutes governing the jurisdiction and activities of the WRC).

32. G.S. 113-292(d).

33. *See* G.S. 130A-144(g); *infra* note 37.

34. G.S. 14-416 *et seq.*

35. G.S. 106-763.1.

36. G.S. 113-292(e).

37. Title 10A, Chapter 41A, § .0302 of the North Carolina Administrative Code (hereinafter N.C.A.C.). This regulation is intended to "prevent the spread of salmonellosis from pet turtles to humans." The prohibition does not apply to sales of turtles used for scientific, educational, or food purposes. *Id.*

38. G.S. 130A-200. The animal must not have been "teased, molested, provoked, beaten, tortured, or otherwise harmed."

39. *Id.*

Local Ordinances

Many North Carolina local governments have adopted local exotic animal ordinances. As discussed in Chapter 1, cities and counties interested in adopting such ordinances may rely upon two different sources of statutory authority:

- general ordinance-making authority to protect citizens' health, safety, and welfare[40] and
- specific authority to regulate animals that are dangerous to persons or property.[41]

General ordinance-making authority, often referred to as "police power," is broad in scope and can be the basis for various types of exotic animal regulations, including those that completely ban private ownership. The second source of authority, which allows for the regulation of dangerous animals, may be interpreted either narrowly or broadly. A narrow interpretation of the term *dangerous* would limit regulation to animals that might injure people (e.g., tigers, venomous reptiles). A wider interpretation could permit regulation of animals—such as prairie dogs—that are not necessarily threats to physical safety but may introduce diseases dangerous to humans or domestic animals.

The scope and content of local regulation of exotic animals vary across the state. Based on a sample of ordinances, it appears that local governments considering regulation in this area must answer two closely related policy questions:[42]

- What is the local government trying to achieve by adopting an exotic animals ordinance?
- What types of animals does the jurisdiction want to regulate?

Local governments across the state have answered these questions differently.

What Is the Local Government's Objective in Adopting an Exotic Animals Ordinance?

North Carolina local governments take a variety of approaches to regulating exotic animals within their jurisdictions. The most common tactic appears to be a ban on private ownership; the ordinance excerpts below serve as examples.

- "No person, firm, or corporation shall keep, maintain, possess or have within the county any venomous reptile or any other wild or exotic animal."[43]

---

40. G.S. 153A-121 (counties); 160A-174 (cities).
41. G.S. 153A 131 (counties); 160A-187 (cities).
42. This section is based on a review of ordinances available on www.municode.com and on the individual websites of some jurisdictions.
43. BUNCOMBE COUNTY, N.C., CODE OF ORDINANCES § 6-61; *see also* CITY OF CHARLOTTE, N.C., CODE OF ORDINANCES § 3-73(a) (using similar language); CURRITUCK COUNTY, N.C., CODE OF ORDINANCES § 3-88 (similar).

- "It is unlawful to keep, harbor, breed, sell or trade any wild or exotic animal for any purpose, except as may be licensed by the state wildlife resources commission under its regulations pertaining to wildlife rehabilitators."[44]

Ordinances that bar private ownership of exotic animals often include at least one exception to the ban. Common exceptions cover circuses, carnivals, zoos, pet shops, animal transport vehicles passing through the jurisdiction, scientific research laboratories, veterinary clinics, and wildlife rehabilitators.

Some jurisdictions do not adopt bans on private ownership of exotic animals but decide instead to take alternative regulatory approaches.

- **Reporting requirements.** Owners of exotic animals in Cary or Smithfield must comply with several reporting requirements. They must notify animal control officials of (1) their exotic animal's arrival; (2) any injuries to persons, other animals, or property caused by the animal; and (3) if the animal is required to be confined, any incident in which it escapes or roams at large.[45]
- **Permitting requirements.** Wilmington requires owners of livestock and wild animals to obtain permits, but it appears to limit wild animal permits to people who hold licenses or permits from the North Carolina Wildlife Resources Commission, such as wildlife captivity licenses or wildlife rehabilitation permits.[46]
- **Bonding requirements**. If a person wants to temporarily exhibit a wild or non-domesticated animal within the city of Henderson, he or she must post a $10,000 bond and have a $1 million insurance policy in place insuring against any damage or injury caused by the animal.[47]

Which Types of Animals Does the Local Government Want to Regulate?

Ordinances address and define a variety of different categories of animals, including those that are wild, exotic, or inherently dangerous. Some define a category by listing common names or species of the animals that fall within the category, while others define a category much more broadly. The ordinance excerpts below serve as examples.

- "***Exotic animals*:** Exotic animals are animals other than domestic animals, farm animals, and wild animals which are not native to North Carolina."[48]
- "***Wild animal*** means an animal that (i) typically is found in a non-domesticated state and that, because of its size or vicious propensity or because it is poisonous

---

44. Cumberland County, N.C., Code of Ordinances § 3-17(b).
45. Town of Cary, N.C., Code of Ordinances § 6-63; Town of Smithfield, N.C., Code of Ordinances § 4-63.
46. City of Wilmington, N.C., Code of Ordinances § 6-2.
47. City of Henderson, N.C., Code of Ordinances § 6-10.
48. Town of Chapel Hill, N.C., Code of Ordinances § 4-1(k) (emphasis added).

or for any other substantial reason, poses a potential danger to persons, other animals or property, or (ii) is classified as a wild animal by the North Carolina Wildlife Resources Commission (WRC) so that any person wishing to possess the same is required by state law to obtain a permit from WRC."[49]

- "An ***exotic or wild animal*** is an animal that would ordinarily be confined to a zoo, or one that would ordinarily be found in the wilderness of this or any other country or one that is a species of animal not indigenous to the United States or North America, or one that otherwise is likely to cause a reasonable person to be fearful of significant destruction of property or of bodily harm and the latter includes but is not limited to: coyotes, monkeys, raccoons, squirrels, ocelots, bobcats, wolves, hybrid wolves, venomous reptiles, and other such animals. Such animals are further defined as those mammals or non-venomous reptiles weighing over fifty (50) pounds at maturity, which are known at law as ferae naturae. Exotic or wild animals specifically do not include animals of a species customarily used in North Carolina as ordinary household pets, animals of a species customarily used in North Carolina as domestic farm animals, fish confined in an aquarium other than piranha, birds, or insects. However, this shall not apply to animals in a municipal zoo."[50]

- "**(1)** ***Wild animals dangerous to humans and property.*** Wild animals are any animals not normally domesticated. For purposes of this chapter, wild animals are deemed inherently dangerous. They are deemed as such because of their vicious propensities and capabilities, the likely gravity of harm inflicted by their attack and unpredictability despite attempts at domestication. The category of wild animals includes but is not limited to:

    a. Members of the Canidae family such as wolves (Canis lupus) and coyotes (Canis latrans) and wolf-dog or coyote-dog hybrids.

    b. Members of the Ursidae family that includes any member of the bear family or hybrids thereof.

    c. Members of the Felidae family such as wild cats, cougars, mountain lions, or panthers.

- **(2)** ***Exotic animals dangerous to humans and property.*** Exotic animals are also considered to be inherently dangerous for purposes of this chapter. Like wild animals, exotic animals are dangerous because of their vicious propensities and capabilities, the gravity of harm inflicted by their attack, and

---

49. City of Wilmington, N.C., Code of Ordinances § 6-2(a)(5) (emphasis added).

50. City of Lexington, N.C., Code of Ordinances § 8-57 (emphasis added). Similar definitions are used in other jurisdictions. *See, e.g.,* City of Charlotte, N.C., Code of Ordinances § 3-3; Town of Davidson, N.C., Code of Ordinances § 10-3, Town of Holly Springs, N.C., Code of Ordinances § 12-61.

unpredictability despite attempts at domestication. The category of exotic animals includes, but is not limited to:

    a. Reptiles or amphibians which are venomous or constricting reptiles more than eight (8) feet in length.

    b. Nonhuman primates (all).

    c. Members of the feline family other than domestic house cats, including, but not limited to lions, tigers, leopards, and hybrid cats.

    d. Reptiles that are members of the crocodile family, including, but not limited to alligators and crocodiles.

- **(3) *Wild and exotic animals do not include*:**

    a. Foreign rodents such as guinea pigs, hamsters, ferrets, and chinchillas.

    b. Members of the reptile and amphibian family not specifically mentioned above such as small lizards and iguanas, salamanders, turtles, and frogs.

    c. Vietnamese potbellied pigs, and other members of the Suidae family, except wild boar and peccary.

    d. Horses and other members of the Equidae family.

    e. Cows and other members of the Bovidae family.

    f. Deer and other members of the Cervidae family.

    g. Domestic dogs and cats.

These animals do not have dangerous propensities and pose no serious threat to the safety of persons and property within Iredell County."[51]

One of the most controversial issues in recent years has been whether and how to define or categorize hybrid animals, particularly wolf-dog hybrids. Members of a state study commission that examined this issue in 2007 could not reach consensus on whether these animals were "inherently dangerous."[52] For the most part, North Carolina localities that regulate exotic animals have included wolf-dog hybrids within the scope of their ordinances, and several local governments have specifically included hybrids of other animals (such as bears and cats) as well.[53]

---

51. Iredell County Code of Ordinances, § 3-1.

52. Inherently Dangerous Exotic Animals in North Carolina: Recommendations of the Study Committee (May 2007) (on file with author).

53. *See, e.g.,* Town of Smithfield, N.C., Code of Ordinances, § 4-3 ("A hybrid of any [exotic or wild animal], regardless of genetic percentages, shall be deemed exotic or wild."); Cumberland County, N.C., Code of Ordinances, § 3-17 ("Hybrids or cross-breeds of any wild or exotic animals shall also be considered as wild or exotic animals.").

Conclusion

Taken together, state and federal laws and local ordinances create a patchwork of regulation governing some aspects of private ownership of wild and exotic animals. Given the national trend toward statewide regulation and the General Assembly's recent discussion about inherently dangerous animals, it would not be surprising if North Carolina implemented more comprehensive legislation in coming years.

Appendix. Relevant Sections of the North Carolina General Statutes (G.S.)

Article 55 [of G.S. Chapter 14].
Regulation of Certain Reptiles.

§ 14-416. Mishandling of poisonous reptiles declared public nuisance and criminal offense.

The intentional or negligent exposure of other human beings to unsafe contact with venomous reptiles, large constricting snakes, or crocodilians is essentially dangerous and injurious and detrimental to public health, safety and welfare, and is therefore declared to be a public nuisance and a criminal offense, to be abated and punished as provided in this Article.

§ 14-417. Regulation of ownership or use of venomous reptiles.

(a) It shall be unlawful for any person to own, possess, use, transport, or traffic in any venomous reptile that is not housed in a sturdy and secure enclosure. Permanent enclosures shall be designed to be escape-proof, bite-proof, and have an operable lock. Transport containers shall be designed to be escape-proof and bite-proof.

(b) Each enclosure shall be clearly and visibly labeled "Venomous Reptile Inside" with scientific name, common name, appropriate antivenin, and owner's identifying information noted on the container. A written bite protocol that includes emergency contact information, local animal control office, the name and location of suitable antivenin, first aid procedures, and treatment guidelines, as well as an escape recovery plan must be within sight of permanent housing, and a copy must accompany the transport of any venomous reptile.

(c) In the event of an escape of a venomous reptile, the owner or possessor of the venomous reptile shall immediately notify local law enforcement.

§ 14-417.1. Regulation of ownership or use of large constricting snakes.

(a) As used in this Article, large constricting snakes shall mean: Reticulated Python, Python reticulatus; Burmese Python, Python molurus; African Rock Python, Python sebae; Amethystine Python, Morelia amethistina; and Green Anaconda, Eunectes murinus; or any of their subspecies or hybrids.

(b) It shall be unlawful for any person to own, possess, use, transport, or traffic in any of the large constricting snakes that are not housed in a sturdy and secure enclosure. Permanent enclosures shall be designed to be escape-proof and shall have an operable lock. Transport containers shall be designed to be escape-proof.

(c) Each enclosure shall be labeled clearly and visibly with the scientific name, common name, number of specimens, and owner's identifying information. A written safety protocol and escape recovery plan shall be within sight of permanent housing, and a copy shall accompany the transport of any of the large constricting snakes. The safety protocol shall include emergency contact information, identification of the local animal control office, and first aid procedures.

(d) In the event of an escape of a large constricting snake, the owner or possessor shall immediately notify local law enforcement.

§ 14-417.2. Regulation of ownership or use of crocodilians.

(a) All crocodilians, excluding the American alligator, shall be regulated under this Article. It shall be unlawful for any person to own, possess, use, transport, or traffic in any crocodilian that is not housed in a sturdy and secure enclosure. Permanent enclosures shall be designed to be escape-proof and have a fence of sufficient strength to prevent contact between an observer and the crocodilian and shall have an operable lock. Transport containers shall be designed to be escape-proof.

(b) A written safety protocol and escape recovery plan shall be within sight of permanent housing, and a copy must accompany the transport of any crocodilian.

(c) In the event of the escape of a crocodilian, the owner or possessor shall immediately notify local law enforcement.

§ 14-418. Prohibited handling of reptiles or suggesting or inducing others to handle.

(a) It shall be unlawful for any person to handle any reptile regulated under this Article in a manner that intentionally or negligently exposes another person to unsafe contact with the reptile.

(b) It shall be unlawful for any person to intentionally or negligently suggest, entice, invite, challenge, intimidate, exhort or otherwise induce or aid any person to handle or expose himself in an unsafe manner to any reptile regulated under this Article.

(c) Safe and responsible handling of reptiles for purposes of animal husbandry, exhibition, training, transport, and education is permitted under this section.

§ 14-419. Investigation of suspected violations; seizure and examination of reptiles; disposition of reptiles.

(a) In any case in which any law-enforcement officer or animal control officer has probable cause to believe that any of the provisions of this Article have been or are about to be violated, it shall be the duty of the officer and the officer is authorized, empowered, and directed to immediately investigate the violation or impending violation and to consult with representatives of the North Carolina Museum of Natural Sciences or the North Carolina Zoological Park or a designated representative of either the Museum or Zoological Park to identify appropriate and safe methods to seize the reptile or reptiles involved, to seize the reptile or reptiles involved, and the officer is authorized and directed to deliver: (i) a reptile believed to be venomous to the North Carolina State Museum of Natural Sciences or to its designated representative for examination for the purpose of ascertaining whether the reptile is regulated under this Article; and, (ii) a reptile believed to be a large constricting snake or crocodilian to the North Carolina Zoological Park or to its designated representative for the purpose of ascertaining whether the reptile is regulated under this Article. In any case in which a law enforcement officer or animal control officer determines that there is an immediate risk to public safety, the officer shall not be required to consult with representatives of the North Carolina Museum of Natural Sciences or the North Carolina Zoological Park as provided by this subsection and may kill the reptile.

(b) If the Museum or the Zoological Park or their designated representatives find that a seized reptile is a venomous reptile, large constricting snake, or crocodilian regulated under this Article, the Museum or the Zoological Park or their designated representative shall determine an interim disposition of the reptile in a manner consistent with the safety of the public, until a final disposition is determined by a court of competent jurisdiction. In the case of a venomous reptile for which antivenin approved by the United States Food and Drug Administration is not readily available, the reptile may be euthanized unless the species is protected under the federal Endangered Species Act of 1973. Where the Museum or the Zoological Park or their designated representative determines euthanasia to be the appropriate interim disposition, or where a reptile seized pursuant to this Article dies of natural or unintended causes, the Museum, the Zoological Park, or their designated representatives shall not be liable to the reptile's owner.

(b1) Upon conviction of any offense contained in this Article, the court shall order a final disposition of the confiscated venomous reptiles, large constricting snakes, or crocodilians, which may include the transfer of title to the State of North Carolina and reimbursement for the necessary expenses incurred in the seizure, delivery, and storage thereof.

(c) If the Museum or the Zoological Park or their designated representatives find that the reptile is not a venomous reptile, large constricting snake, or crocodilian regulated under this Article, and either no criminal warrants or indictments are initiated in connection with the reptile within 10 days of initial seizure, or a court of law determines that the reptile is not being owned, possessed, used, transported, or trafficked in violation of this Article, then it shall be the duty of the law enforcement officer to return the reptile or reptiles to the person from whom they were seized within 15 days.

§ 14-420. Arrest of persons violating provisions of Article.

If an examination made by the North Carolina State Museum of Natural Sciences or the North Carolina Zoological Park or their designated representatives conducted pursuant to this Article shows that the reptile is a venomous reptile, large constricting snake, or crocodilian subject to this Article, it shall be the duty of the officer making the seizure with probable cause to believe that the reptile is being owned, possessed, used, transported, or trafficked in violation of this Article, to arrest all persons violating any of the provisions of this Article.

§ 14-421. Exemptions from provisions of Article.

This Article shall not apply to the possession, exhibition, or handling of reptiles by employees or agents of duly constituted veterinarians, zoos, serpentariums, museums, laboratories, educational or scientific institutions, public and private, in the course of their educational or scientific work, or Wildlife Damage Control Agents in the course of the work for which they are approved by the Wildlife Resources Commission.

§ 14-422. Criminal penalties and civil remedies for violation.

(a) Any person violating any of the provisions of this Article shall be guilty of a Class 2 misdemeanor.

(b) If any person, other than the owner of a venomous reptile, large constricting snake, or crocodilian, the owner's agent, employee, or a member of the owner's immediate family, suffers a life threatening injury or is killed as the result of a violation of this Article, the owner of the reptile shall be guilty of a Class A1 misdemeanor. This subsection shall not apply to violations that result from incidents that could not have been prevented or avoided by the owner's exercise of due care or foresight, such as natural disasters or other acts of God, or in the case of thefts of the reptile from the owner.

(c) Any person intentionally releasing into the wild a nonnative venomous reptile, a large constricting snake, or a crocodilian shall be guilty of a Class A1 misdemeanor.

(d) Violations of this Article as set forth in subsections (b) or (c) of this section shall constitute wanton conduct within the meaning of G.S. 1D-5(7) and subject the violator to punitive damages in any civil action that may be filed as a result of the violator's actions.

Miscellaneous Provisions

§ 106-763.1. Propagation and production of American alligators.

(a) License Required. – A person who intends to raise American alligators commercially must first obtain an Aquaculture Propagation and Production Facility License from the Department. The Board of Agriculture may regulate a facility that raises American alligators to the same extent that it can regulate any other facility licensed under this Article.

(b) Requirements. – A facility that raises American alligators commercially must comply with all of the following requirements:

  (1) Before a facility begins operation, it must prepare and implement a confinement plan. After a facility begins operation, it must adhere to the confinement plan. A confinement plan must comply with guidelines developed and adopted by the Wildlife Resources Commission. The Department may inspect a facility to determine if the facility is complying with the confinement plan. As used in this subdivision, "confinement" includes production within a building or similar structure and a perimeter fence.

  (2) A facility can possess only hatchlings that have been permanently tagged and have an export permit from their state of origin. The facility must keep records of all hatchlings it receives and must make these records available for inspection by the Wildlife Resources Commission and the Department upon request.

  (3) If the facility uses swine, poultry, or other livestock for feed, it must have a disease management plan that has been approved by the State Veterinarian, and it must comply with the plan.

  (4) The activities of the facility must comply with the Endangered Species Act and the Convention on International Trade in Endangered Species. The Department is the State agency responsible for the administration of this program for farm-raised alligators.

(c) Sanctions. – The operator of a facility that possesses an untagged or undocumented alligator commits a Class H felony if the operator knows the alligator is untagged or undocumented. Conviction of an operator of a facility under this section revokes the license of the facility for five years beginning on the date of the conviction. An operator convicted under this section may not be the operator of any other facility required to be licensed under this Article for five years beginning on the date of the conviction.

§ 113-292. Authority of the Wildlife Resources Commission in regulation of inland fishing and the introduction of exotic species.

(a) The Wildlife Resources Commission is authorized to authorize, license, regulate, prohibit, prescribe, or restrict all fishing in inland fishing waters, and the taking of inland game fish in coastal fishing waters, with respect to:

  (1) Time, place, character, or dimensions of any methods or equipment that may be employed in taking fish;

  (2) Seasons for taking fish;

  (3) Size limits on and maximum quantities of fish that may be taken, possessed, bailed to another, transported, bought, sold, or given away.

(b) The Wildlife Resources Commission is authorized to authorize, license, regulate, prohibit, prescribe, or restrict:

  (1) The opening and closing of inland fishing waters, whether entirely or only as to the taking of particular classes of fish, use of particular equipment, or as to other activities within the jurisdiction of the Wildlife Resources Commission; and

(2) The possession, cultivation, transportation, importation, exportation, sale, purchase, acquisition, and disposition of all inland fisheries resources and all related equipment, implements, vessels, and conveyances as necessary to implement the work of the Wildlife Resources Commission in carrying out its duties.

To the extent not in conflict with provisions enforced by the Department, the Wildlife Resources Commission may exercise the powers conferred in this subsection in coastal fishing waters pursuant to its rule of inland game fish in such waters.

(c) The Wildlife Resources Commission is authorized to make such rules pertaining to the acquisition, disposition, transportation, and possession of fish in connection with private ponds as may be necessary in carrying out the provisions of this Subchapter and the overall objectives of the conservation of wildlife resources.

(c1) The Wildlife Resources Commission is authorized to issue proclamations suspending or extending the hook-and-line season for striped bass in the inland and joint waters of coastal rivers and their tributaries, and the Commission may delegate this authority to the Executive Director. Each proclamation shall state the hour and date upon which it becomes effective, and shall be issued at least 48 hours prior to the effective date and time. A permanent file of the text of all proclamations shall be maintained in the office of the Executive Director. Certified copies of proclamations are entitled to judicial notice in any civil or criminal proceeding.

　　The Executive Director shall make reasonable effort to give notice of the terms of any proclamation to persons who may be affected by it. This effort shall include press releases to communications media, posting of notices at boating access areas and other places where persons affected may gather, personal communication by agents of the Wildlife Resources Commission, and other measures designed to reach persons who may be affected. Proclamations under this subsection shall remain in force until rescinded following the same procedure established for enactment.

(d) The Wildlife Resources Commission is authorized to authorize, license, regulate, prohibit, prescribe, or restrict anywhere in the State the acquisition, importation, possession, transportation, disposition, or release into public or private waters or the environment of zoological or botanical species or specimens that may threaten the introduction of epizootic disease or may create a danger to or an imbalance in the environment inimical to the conservation of wildlife resources. This subsection is not intended to give the Wildlife Resources Commission the authority to supplant, enact any conflicting rules, or otherwise take any action inconsistent with that of any other State agency acting within its jurisdiction.

(e) It is unlawful for any person to:
　(1) Release or place exotic species of wild animals or wild birds in an area for the purpose of stocking the area for hunting or trapping;
　(2) Release or place species of wild animals or wild birds not indigenous to that area in an area for the purpose of stocking the area for hunting or trapping;
　(3) Take by hunting or trapping any animal or bird released or placed in an area in contravention of subdivisions (1) and (2) of this subsection, except under a permit to hunt or trap which may be issued by the Wildlife Resources Commission for the purpose of eradicating or controlling the population of any species of wildlife that has been so released or placed in the area.

§ 130A-200. Confinement or leashing of vicious animals.

A local health director may declare an animal to be vicious and a menace to the public health when the animal has attacked a person causing bodily harm without being teased, molested, provoked, beaten, tortured or otherwise harmed. When an animal has been declared to be vicious and a menace to the public health, the local health director shall order the animal to be confined to its owner's property. However, the animal may be permitted to leave its owner's property when accompanied by a responsible adult and restrained on a leash.

§ 153A-121. General ordinance-making power.

(a) A county may by ordinance define, regulate, prohibit, or abate acts, omissions, or conditions detrimental to the health, safety, or welfare of its citizens and the peace and dignity of the county; and may define and abate nuisances.

(b) This section does not authorize a county to regulate or control vehicular or pedestrian traffic on a street or highway under the control of the Board of Transportation, nor to regulate or control any right-of-way or right-of-passage belonging to a public utility, electric or telephone membership corporation, or public agency of the State. In addition, no county ordinance may regulate or control a highway right-of-way in a manner inconsistent with State law or an ordinance of the Board of Transportation.

(c) This section does not impair the authority of local boards of health to adopt rules and regulations to protect and promote public health.

§ 153A-131. Possession or harboring of dangerous animals.

A county may by ordinance regulate, restrict, or prohibit the possession or harboring of animals which are dangerous to persons or property. No such ordinance shall have the effect of permitting any activity or condition with respect to a wild animal which is prohibited or more severely restricted by regulations of the Wildlife Resources Commission.

§ 160A-174. General ordinance-making power.

(a) A city may by ordinance define, prohibit, regulate, or abate acts, omissions, or conditions, detrimental to the health, safety, or welfare of its citizens and the peace and dignity of the city, and may define and abate nuisances.

(b) A city ordinance shall be consistent with the Constitution and laws of North Carolina and of the United States. An ordinance is not consistent with State or federal law when:
  (1) The ordinance infringes a liberty guaranteed to the people by the State or federal Constitution;
  (2) The ordinance makes unlawful an act, omission or condition which is expressly made lawful by State or federal law;
  (3) The ordinance makes lawful an act, omission, or condition which is expressly made unlawful by State or federal law;
  (4) The ordinance purports to regulate a subject that cities are expressly forbidden to regulate by State or federal law;
  (5) The ordinance purports to regulate a field for which a State or federal statute clearly shows a legislative intent to provide a complete and integrated regulatory scheme to the exclusion of local regulation;
  (6) The elements of an offense defined by a city ordinance are identical to the elements of an offense defined by State or federal law.

The fact that a State or federal law, standing alone, makes a given act, omission, or condition unlawful shall not preclude city ordinances requiring a higher standard of conduct or condition.

§ 160A-187. Possession or harboring of dangerous animals.

A city may by ordinance regulate, restrict, or prohibit the possession or harboring within the city of animals which are dangerous to persons or property. No such ordinance shall have the effect of permitting any activity or condition with respect to a wild animal which is prohibited or more severely restricted by regulations of the Wildlife Resources Commission.

Chapter 10
Miscellaneous Issues

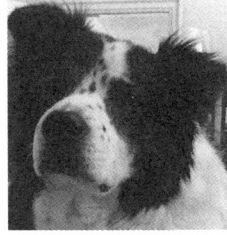

This chapter discusses miscellaneous issues that did not warrant individual treatment in stand-alone chapters. The fact that the topics did not merit coverage in other chapters should not be interpreted to mean that they are unimportant; many of the issues discussed here are frequent and significant challenges for local governments across the state.

North Carolina's Spay/Neuter Program

According to the American Veterinary Medical Association (AVMA), the "population of dogs and cats in the United States currently exceeds the capacity of our society to care and provide homes for them as companion animals" and, therefore, population control for these animals is "a primary welfare concern of our society."[1] The AVMA, animal welfare organizations, and others have long encouraged state and local governments to take an active role in controlling pet populations.[2] Finding that "unacceptable numbers" of unwanted dogs and cats in North Carolina constituted a public nuisance and a public health hazard, caused the animals themselves to suffer, and burdened local governments with significant expenses, the North Carolina General Assembly established a spay/neuter program intended to reduce the number of unwanted dogs and cats in the state. In addition to the statewide spay/neuter program, some local governments have adopted a comprehensive approach to this issue. Moore County, for example, implemented a strategic plan specifically focused on pet overpopulation.[3]

The statewide spay/neuter program, codified in Article 5 of Chapter 19A of the North Carolina General Statutes, has two components: (1) a statewide public education campaign and (2) direct reimbursement to local governments for certain sterilization procedures.[4] When the program was initially established, administrative responsibility was assigned to the Division of Public Health in the N.C. Department of Health and Human

1. Am. Veterinary Med. Ass'n, *Policy Statement: Dog and Cat Population Control* (2018), https://www.avma.org/KB/Policies/Pages/Dog-And-Cat-Population-Control.aspx.

2. *Id.* (recommending that state and local governments provide more funding for animal control, prohibit the sale or adoption of intact animals by animal control and humane organizations, and promote sterilization); *see also* Am. Soc'y for the Prevention of Cruelty to Animals, *Position Statement on Mandatory Spay/Neuter Laws* (2018), https://www.aspca.org/position statement-mandatory-spayneuter-laws ; Jean McNeil & Elisabeth Constandy, *Addressing the Problem of Pet Overpopulation: The Experience of New Hanover County Animal Control Services*, 12 J. Pub. Health Mgmt. & Prac. 452 (2006).

3. Animal Operations Advisory Bd., Managing Pet Overpopulation: A Strategic Plan for Moore County, NC (2015), https://www.moorecountync.gov/images/departments/animal-operations/AOAB_Strategic_Plan_July62015.pdf.

4. Chapter 19A, Section 61 of the North Carolina General Statutes (hereinafter G.S.).

Services.[5] In 2010, the General Assembly shifted responsibility to the Department of Agriculture and Consumer Services.[6]

The program has two primary sources of funding: state appropriations and a $20 surcharge on every special "Animal Lovers" license plate purchased in the state.[7] In calendar year 2017, appropriations totaled $250,000 and license plate revenue provided $155,180.[8] Funds may be allocated as follows:

- up to 20 percent for program administration,
- up to 20 percent for a statewide public education campaign, and
- the remainder for reimbursements to local governments.[9]

The statewide spay/neuter program provides financial assistance to local governments that offer reduced-cost spay/neuter services to low-income persons. The term "low-income person" is defined by statute to mean "[a]n individual who qualifies for one or more of the programs of public assistance administered by the Department of Health and Human Services . . . or whose annual household income is lower than one hundred percent (100%) of the federal poverty level guidelines."[10] The financial assistance provided to local governments comes in the form of reimbursement for the direct costs of spay/neuter surgical procedures for dogs or cats owned by low-income persons. In order to be eligible to receive reimbursement, the local government must offer one of the following programs on a year-round basis to low-income persons who are seeking sterilization of their pets:

- a spay/neuter clinic operated by the local government,
- a spay/neuter clinic operated by a non-profit organization under contract with the local government,
- reduced-cost spay/neuter procedures offered by one or more veterinarians under contract with the local government,

---

5. S.L. 2000-163.

6. S.L. 2010-31.

7. G.S. 19A-62.

8. Memorandum from N.C. Department of Agriculture & Consumer Services to Animal Shelters in Receipt of State/Local Funds, *Requirement to Report Shelter Data; Notification of Funding; Maximum Amount Allowed for Procedure Type (Estimates)* (Dec. 30, 2017), http://www.ncagr.gov/vet/aws/Fix/documents/WebsiteYearlyShelterReportMemo12-20-17.pdf.

9. G.S. 19A-62.

10. G.S. 19A-63(b)(2). In 2018, the federal poverty guideline for an individual was $12,140; it was $20,780 for a family of three. 83 Fed. Reg. 2642-01 (Jan. 18, 2018). The definition of "low-income person" changed in 2015, significantly narrowing the scope of the eligible population. The income threshold was reduced from 300 percent of the federal poverty guideline to 100 percent. S.L. 2015-241, § 13.7(a). 2015 revisions also severed the tie between eligibility for spay/neuter reimbursement and eligibility for other public assistance programs. *Id.* Legislation in 2016 restored the eligibility connection but maintained the income threshold at 100 percent of the federal poverty guidelines. S.L. 2016-94, § 13.1(b).

- a program that allows low-income pet owners to use vouchers or other mechanisms to access discounted spay/neuter procedures from participating veterinarians, or
- a program that reduces the cost of a spay/neuter procedure for a pet that is adopted from an animal shelter operated by or under contract with the local government.[11]

Every county seeking reimbursement must (1) provide proof that all local veterinarians[12] had an opportunity to participate in the program[13] and (2) make rules or publish guidelines that designate what proof a person must submit to establish that he or she is a "low-income person" as that term is defined under statute.[14] In addition, in order to be eligible for reimbursement, the local government program must require that, at the time of the procedure, each animal's owner either (1) provide proof of rabies vaccination or (2) obtain a vaccination for the animal.[15]

Eligible cities and counties may be reimbursed for the direct costs of each surgical procedure, including anesthesia, medications, and veterinary services.[16] Capital expenditures and administrative costs are not eligible for reimbursement.[17] Applications for reimbursement must be submitted quarterly.[18] If there are not enough funds available to reimburse all applicants, G.S. 19A-64 specifies how the funds should be allocated. Specifically, the statute requires that 50 percent of the available funds be distributed to the most economically distressed counties.[19] The amount of funding available to

---

11. G.S. 19A-63(a).

12. Note that the term "local" is interpreted to extend beyond the county to adjacent counties if no licensed veterinarian practices within the county. G.S. 19A-63(b)(1).

13. G.S. 19A-63(d).

14. G.S. 19A-63(c). As an example, one multi-county program requires that a person submit one of the following forms of proof to establish that he or she is a low-income person: a Medicaid card; a Women, Infants, and Children program voucher; proof that his or her only source of income is from Social Security benefits; an EBT (food stamp) card; or an IRS Form 1040 showing a qualifying income level. Spay-Neuter Assistance Program of N.C. (SNAP-NC), *Prevent Another Litter Subsidy Program for Low Income Families* (2018), http://www.snap-nc.org/Pals.asp#app (covering Johnston, Lee, Wake, Wayne, and Wilson counties). *See also* Paws for Life Animal Rescue, *Spay & Neuter in Franklin County (SNIF)*, http://pawsforlifenc.org/programs/spay-neuter-in-franklin-county/ (last visited Apr. 18, 2018) (stating similar requirements); Animal Kind, *The $20 Fix* (2018), http://animalkind.org/programs/20-fix/ (same; Orange and Alamance counties).

15. G.S. 19A-62(b)(4).

16. G.S. 19A-64(a).

17. *Id.*

18. Applications and other information related to the application process are available here: N.C. Dep't of Agriculture & Consumer Services, Veterinary Div., Animal Welfare, *Spay/Neuter Program*, http://ncagr.gov/vet/aws/fix/ (last visited Apr. 18, 2018).

19. G.S. 19A-64(c)(1). The North Carolina Department of Commerce evaluates the financial condition of all 100 counties on an annual basis and places each county into one of three

each county also depends on the proportion of dogs and cats vaccinated.[20] In 2017, thirty-one counties and three municipalities received funding through the program;[21] the average reimbursement was approximately $4,573 for Tier 1 counties and $3,141 for Tier 2 and Tier 3 counties.[22] Some jurisdictions, such as Haywood, McDowell, and Robeson counties, have clearly made this program a priority, resulting in more than $20,000 in reimbursements for each county in 2017.[23]

Feral Cats

Feral cats are a challenge in jurisdictions across the United States, including many counties and cities in North Carolina.[24] Generally speaking, a feral cat is a free-roaming cat that has adapted to living outdoors and that has little, if any, contact with humans.[25] Feral cats can disrupt ecosystems, pose threats to public health, and burden the resources of local governments.[26] Some animal welfare organizations are attempting to control the population of feral cats through "Trap-Neuter-Return" programs (sometimes called "Trap-Neuter-Release" programs), and some North Carolina jurisdictions have enacted ordinances regulating such programs.[27] The typical Trap-Neuter-Return program involves a citizen trapping a feral cat in a humane manner and transporting the cat to be neutered or spayed at a participating clinic, often at a reduced cost.

Because Trap-Neuter-Return programs typically involve a citizen taking some measure of responsibility for a cat, even if only temporarily, there arguably is some tension

---

development tiers, with tier one being the most economically distressed and tier three being the least distressed. G.S. 143B-437.08; *see also* N.C. Dep't of Commerce, *2018 County Tier Designations* (2018), https://www.nccommerce.com/research-publications/incentive-reports/county-tier-designations.

20. G.S. 19A-64(c)(2)–(3).

21. Reports about reimbursements are accessible on the website cited *supra* note 18. A report for 2017 is available here: http://ncagr.gov/vet/aws/Fix/documents/2017Q4WebsiteBreakdown.pdf.

22. N.C. Dep't of Agric. & Consumer Servs., *2017 Spay and Neuter Reimbursement Program Summary*, http://ncagr.gov/vet/aws/Fix/documents/2017Q4WebsiteBreakdown.pdf.

23. *Id.* (McDowell ($22,263), Haywood ($24,140), Robeson ($57,869)).

24. *See, e.g.*, Caroline McMillan, *Feral Cat Problem Difficult to Control*, Charlotte Observer (Oct. 9, 2012), http://www.charlotteobserver.com/news/local/community/university-city/article9084221.html (stating that there were "tens of thousands of feral and stray cats in Mecklenburg County" at the time the article was written).

25. *Cf.* G.S. 130A-184(4a) (defining the term "feral" for purposes of state rabies control law to mean "[a]n animal that is not socialized").

26. *See generally* Am. Veterinary Med. Ass'n, *Free-Roaming Abandoned and Feral Cats* (2018), https://www.avma.org/KB/Policies/Pages/Free-roaming-Abandoned-and-Feral-Cats.aspx.

27. *See, e.g.*, City of Greenville, N.C., Code of Ordinances § 12-2-37 (regulating Trap-Neuter-Return programs); Wake County, N.C., Code of Ordinances § 91.41 (same).

between such programs and the state's rabies control laws which, as discussed in detail in chapter 5, generally require owners of cats to have their animals regularly vaccinated and require vaccinated animals to wear tags. Some jurisdictions in North Carolina have addressed this issue by requiring that Trap-Neuter-Return cats be vaccinated for rabies when they are brought in to be spayed or neutered.[28]

Pet Licensing

As discussed in chapter 1, local governments have specific authority to require that citizens obtain licenses and pay taxes on their domestic pets.[29] Several jurisdictions in North Carolina have adopted ordinances imposing such licensing requirements. Their form and purpose varies according to the given city or county's desire to promote other policy goals, such as encouraging owners to sterilize or vaccinate their animals or expanding the authority to impound stray animals.

New Hanover County, for example, requires that dogs, cats, and ferrets be registered in the county and charges a fee for the registration.[30] The New Hanover fee varies depending on the animal's age and whether it has been spayed or neutered, with the fee being lower if the animal has been spayed or neutered.[31] At the time of publication, the county offered both one- and three-year licenses. The City of Asheville takes a slightly different approach, charging a one-year licensing fee of $10 for all animals but requiring animal owners who have not had their pets sterilized to apply for an "unaltered animal permit" and pay a one-time $100 fee.[32] A study by a University of North Carolina graduate student in public administration looked at jurisdictions that linked licensing with rabies vaccination requirements, a current practice in both New Hanover County and the City of Asheville.[33] The author concluded that linking the two requirements

---

28. For example, the Greenville and Wake ordinances cited immediately above each require that Trap-Neuter-Return cats be vaccinated.

29. G.S. 153A-153 (counties); 160A-212 (cities).

30. *See* NEW HANOVER COUNTY, N.C., CODE OF ORDINANCES § 5-5; New Hanover Cty. Sheriff's Off., *Animal Services Unit: Pay Pet Registration Online!*, https://www.newhanoversheriff.com/animal-services-unit/ (last visited Apr. 18, 2018).

31. *See* New Hanover Cty. Sheriff's Off., *supra* note 30.

32. CITY OF ASHEVILLE, N.C., CODE OF ORDINANCES § 3-5; City of Asheville, *Animal Services*, http://www.ashevillenc.gov/departments/police/policing_services/animal.htm (last visited Nov. 2, 2017).

33. *See* NEW HANOVER COUNTY, N.C., CODE OF ORDINANCES § 5-5; CITY OF ASHEVILLE, N.C., CODE OF ORDINANCES § 3-5.

not only increased the local vaccination rates and improved enforcement of licensure requirements, but could also significantly increase the number of animals licensed.[34]

A local government that is considering adopting a domestic pet licensing scheme must balance the benefits associated with licensing, such as the potential for increased revenue and increased vaccination rates, against the associated costs, such as the potential political ramifications of a new tax and administrative burdens related to collecting the tax.[35]

Public Records

As a general rule, records generated by local government animal services programs are public records, and state law guarantees the public a right of access to some of those records. Below are some brief highlights from the public records law as it applies to animal services.[36]

- Many of the records maintained by animal services programs will be considered public records.[37] Some information in records may be subject to an exception, such as information related to a criminal investigation and information that identifies a person who has or may have rabies (see discussion below).
- The law requires the "custodian" of public records to provide access to the records.[38] While the head of a given agency responsible for animal services programs is likely the "custodian" of a program's records, everyone involved

34. Catherine M. Clark, *The Truth about Cats and Dogs: Vaccinations, Licenses, Service, Revenue*, 67 POPULAR GOV'T 40 (Winter 2002).

35. For details about collecting local taxes, including animal taxes or license fees, see Christopher B. McLaughlin, *Beyond the Property Tax: Collecting Other Taxes and Fees*, PROP. TAX BULL. No. 162 (Feb. 2011), https://www.sog.unc.edu/sites/www.sog.unc.edu/files/reports/ptb162.pdf; Kara A. Millonzi, *Revenues*, in COUNTY AND MUNICIPAL GOVERNMENT IN NORTH CAROLINA 273, 279 (UNC School of Government, Frayda S. Bluestein ed., 2d ed. 2014), https://www.sog.unc.edu/publications/book-chapters/revenues.

36. For a comprehensive review of this body of law, see DAVID M. LAWRENCE, PUBLIC RECORDS LAW FOR NORTH CAROLINA LOCAL GOVERNMENTS (UNC School of Government, 2d ed. 2010); Frayda S. Bluestein, *Public Records*, in COUNTY AND MUNICIPAL GOVERNMENT IN NORTH CAROLINA (UNC School of Government, Frayda S. Bluestein ed., 2d ed. 2014), https://www.sog.unc.edu/publications/book-chapters/public-records.

37. Frayda Bluestein, *Is This a Public Record? A Framework for Answering Questions About Public Records Requests*, COATES' CANONS: N.C. LOC. GOV'T L. blog (June 9, 2010), https://canons.sog.unc.edu/is-this-a-public-record-a-framework-for-answering-questions-about-public-records-requests/.

38. Frayda Bluestein, *Custodians of Public Records*, COATES' CANONS: NC LOC. GOV'T L. blog (Dec. 19, 2014), https://canons.sog.unc.edu/custodians-of-public-records/.

with the program has an obligation to manage and retain records in order to preserve the right of public access.

- Any person can request public records.[39] The requester is not required to be a resident of the state or of the specific jurisdiction involved.
- Records related to public employees are confidential, but some personnel information is public.[40]
- A private entity that has an integrated relationship with a government entity, such as an animal shelter, may be subject to public records laws in some circumstances.[41]

Exceptions

As mentioned above, there are many exceptions to the state public records law. Exceptions tend to fall into one of two categories: (1) *mandatory* exceptions, under which records are considered confidential and the government must not provide access to them, and (2) *discretionary* exceptions, under which the government may choose whether to provide access.[42] Three exceptions require special attention in the animal services arena: criminal investigation records, communicable disease information, and controlled substances records. The controlled substances and communicable disease exceptions are mandatory and the criminal investigation exception is discretionary.[43]

---

39. Frayda Bluestein, *Who Can Request Public Records?* Coates' Canons: NC Loc. Gov't L. blog (May 10, 2013), https://canons.sog.unc.edu/who-can-request-public-records/.

40. Parallel statutes for cities (G.S. 160A-168) and counties (G.S. 153A-98) require the release of a given employee's name, age, position, salary, and title, as well as limited information about disciplinary actions and promotions, demotions, separations, and other changes of position related to the employee.

41. Frayda Bluestein, *When Do Government Transparency Laws Apply to Private Entities?*, Coates' Canons: NC Loc. Gov't L. blog (June 1, 2011). https://canons.sog.unc.edu/when-do-government-transparency-laws-apply-to-private-entities/.

42. Bluestein, *supra* note 37.

43. In 2018, the state legislature established an exception to the public records law that applies only in Guilford County. S.L. 2018-105 (enacting G.S. 132-1.15 and stating that the statute applies to Guilford County only). This provision allows (but does not require) the county animal services agency to withhold "personally identifiable information" about any individual who has
- voluntarily surrendered ownership of an animal to an animal shelter,
- adopted an animal from an animal shelter, or
- received a foster animal from an animal shelter.
Note that this exception applies only when the animal has gone to an individual. It does not apply when an animal shelter places an animal with a rescue organization. G.S. 132-1.15(b).

Criminal Investigation Records

The criminal investigation exception allows public law enforcement agencies to withhold some information that is included in investigation records. The term "public law enforcement agency" is defined broadly enough to include most, if not all, animal services programs because it encompasses not only traditional law enforcement agencies, such as police and sheriffs' departments, but also "any State or local agency, force, department, or unit responsible for investigating, preventing, or solving violations of the law."[44] The records governed by this exception include "all records or any information that pertains to a person or group of persons that is compiled by public law enforcement agencies for the purpose of attempting to prevent or solve violations of the law, including information derived from witnesses, laboratory tests, surveillance, investigators, confidential informants, photographs, and measurements."[45]

Communicable Disease Information

The communicable disease information exception is based on the state's general law, G.S. 130A-143, which makes certain health information confidential. In short, any information that identifies a person who has or may have a reportable communicable disease or condition—including human rabies—is "strictly confidential" and may be disclosed only under limited circumstances. When an animal services program receives a report that an animal has bitten a human and either the animal is unvaccinated or the animal's vaccination status is unknown, the program must treat information about the bite victim as confidential pursuant to this state law. As a result, if the program receives a public records request during the time the person's rabies status is unclear (i.e., when the person "may have" a reportable communicable disease), it must not release information that identifies the person without the person's consent or a court order.

Once it is clear that the person does *not* have rabies, this confidentiality law no longer applies. If the public records request is submitted to an animal services department or other program that is not subject to other confidentiality laws, the program may release information that identifies the victim. If, however, the public records request is submitted to a component of local government that is subject to other confidentiality laws, disclosure may still be prohibited. For example:

- Communicable disease or health services units in local health departments may maintain records that identify bite victims. Those units are subject to several confidentiality laws that still protect this information even after the communicable disease confidentiality law, G.S. 130A-143, no longer applies.[46]

---

44. G.S. 132-1.4(b)(3).
45. G.S. 132-1.4(b)(1).
46. G.S. 130A-12; Health Insurance Portability and Accountability Act of 1996 (HIPAA), 42 U.S.C. §§ 1320d-1 to 1320d-8; 45 C.F.R. pts. 160, 164 (HIPAA Privacy Rule).

They should disclose information that identifies bite victims only when authorized by other applicable laws.

- A police department may maintain a bite record that identifies a bite victim. If no other confidentiality laws or public records exceptions apply, the department would be authorized to disclose the identity of the victim once it is clear that he or she does not have and is not at risk of developing rabies.

If an animal services program is part of a local health department, the confidentiality questions can become more complicated because other confidentiality laws will likely apply. Specifically, directors of such departments will need to pay careful attention to how their internal policies address applicability of the HIPAA Privacy Rule to animal services.[47]

Controlled Substances Records

Most animal shelters use controlled substances to euthanize animals. Strict state and federal laws govern the use of the drugs and require the shelters to maintain certain types of records related to the drugs. State and federal laws provide that those records are confidential,[48] and therefore shelters may not release them in response to a public records request.

Restrictions on Ownership

As mentioned in chapter 1, local governments, as a general matter, have the authority to pass ordinances that place restrictions on the ownership or keeping of animals, and North Carolina courts have upheld some of these ordinances in the face of challenges to their constitutionality. For example, in *Town of Atlantic Beach v. Young*, the North Carolina Supreme Court concluded that the town had the power to enact an ordinance that prohibited keeping animals other than housepets within city limits and further concluded that the ordinance was constitutional.[49] In *State v. Maynard*, the North Carolina Court of Appeals upheld an ordinance that limited the number of dogs that could be kept on property inside Nashville's city limits.[50]

---

47. Entities, such as counties, that are required to comply with HIPAA may decide to exclude some parts of the entity from HIPAA compliance. For more information about this option, see Aimee N. Wall, *Should a Local Government Be a HIPAA Hybrid Entity?*, COATES' CANONS: NC LOC. GOV'T L. blog (Apr. 28, 2015), https://canons.sog.unc.edu/should-a-local-government-be-a-hipaa-hybrid-entity/.

48. G.S. 90-113.74 (providing that prescription information is not a public record and may be disclosed only as provided in state law).

49. 307 N.C. 422 (1983).

50. 195 N.C. App. 757 (2009).

As discussed in Chapter 4, several local governments in North Carolina have considered adopting ordinances that would restrict or prohibit the ownership of certain breeds of dogs, such as pit bulls. Though no breed-specific prohibition on ownership has been enacted in the state, local governments probably do have the power to pass such bans, and courts in other states have upheld these kinds of ordinances in certain circumstances.[51]

While no local government has prohibited the ownership of particular breeds of dogs, some local governments have enacted ordinances that prohibit the ownership of certain other types of animals. For example, a Durham County ordinance generally prohibits the ownership or keeping of "inherently dangerous animals."[52] That term is defined to include nonhuman primates, wolves, crocodiles, and several other animals.[53] Nash County also generally prohibits the keeping of inherently dangerous animals,[54] though the definition of the term "inherently dangerous animal" differs substantially from the Durham County definition.[55] In Nash County, any "non-domestic mammal which is dangerous to persons or property or which has the reasonable potential of being dangerous to persons or property" is an "inherently dangerous animal."[56] Many local governments regulate the keeping of chickens on single-family properties, a pursuit that has become increasingly popular in recent years.[57] It is common for ordinances of this type to prohibit the keeping of roosters and to have specific requirements for the manner of keeping chickens.[58]

Local governments sometimes regulate the ownership or keeping of animals through zoning ordinances. For example, the Town of Cary regulates the keeping of chickens in the backyards of single-family properties through the town's land development ordinance.[59] As the discussion in this section illustrates, local governments have significant authority to regulate the ownership and keeping of animals, and a wide variety of ordinances imposing regulations have been enacted across the state.

---

51. Jeanette Cox, *Ordinances Targeting Pit Bull Dogs Must Be Drafted Carefully*, Loc. Gov't L. Bull. No 106 (Nov. 2004), http://www.sog.unc.edu/sites/www.sog.unc.edu/files/reports/lglb106_0.pdf.

52. Durham County, N.C., Code of Ordinances § 4-323.

53. *Id.* § 4-321.

54. Nash County, N.C., Code of Ordinances § 4-11.

55. *Id.* § 4-1.

56. *Id.*

57. *See, e.g.*, City of Asheville, N.C., Code of Ordinances Ch. 3, Art. IV (regulating the keeping of fowl within the city).

58. *Id.* (generally prohibiting the keeping of roosters and specifying requirements for chicken enclosures); *see also* Town of Cary, *Backyard Chickens FAQ*, http://www.townofcary.org/connect-engage/town-departments-offices/planning-department/faq/backyard-chickens-faq (last visited Apr. 18, 2018) (noting that the keeping of roosters is prohibited and explaining requirements for enclosures for chickens).

59. *See generally* Town of Cary, *supra* note 58.

Petting Zoos

In the fall of 2004, more than 100 people—mostly children under the age of 6—contracted a communicable E. coli infection after visiting the petting zoo at the North Carolina State Fair.[60] At the time, North Carolina had no state laws regulating sanitation at petting zoos. In response to the E. coli outbreak, the North Carolina Department of Agriculture and Consumer Services (Department)—which oversees the state fair—instituted new restrictions covering the fair's animal exhibitions.[61] In addition, the General Assembly passed legislation directing the commissioner of agriculture to establish a permitting system for animal exhibitions.[62]

The General Statutes define "animal exhibitions" as agricultural fairs where animals are displayed on the exhibition grounds for physical contact with humans.[63] The term "fair" is a specialized term that refers to exhibitions designed to promote agriculture and other industries by offering premiums and awards.[64] Such fairs were already required to obtain licenses from the Department; the sanitation requirements related to animal exhibitions added a new layer of regulation.[65] The regulations, which went into effect in September 2006, require exhibitions to, among other things,

- provide fencing to minimize contact between the public and the manure or bedding of the animals;
- provide hand-washing stations (which should include soap and running water, not hand sanitizers and hand wipes);
- post signs regarding the health risks related to animal contact and identifying the location of hand-washing stations; and
- maintain health certificates for animals included in the exhibition.[66]

Periodically, the National Association of State Public Health Veterinarians (NASPHV) releases a report recommending measures for preventing disease associated with animals

---

60. *See* Ctrs. for Disease Control & Prevention, *Outbreaks of Escherichia coli 0157:H7 Associated with Petting Zoos—North Carolina, Florida, and Arizona, 2004 and 2005*, Morbidity & Mortality Wkly. Rep. 1277–80 (Dec. 23, 2005), https://www.cdc.gov/mmwr/preview/mmwrhtml/mm5450a1.htm; Lisa Hoppenjans, *As Girl Copes, Legacy May Protect Others*, News & Observer (Raleigh), July 26, 2005, at 1A.

61. *See* Ctrs. for Disease Control & Prevention, *supra* note 60, at 1280.

62. G.S. 106-520.3A.

63. G.S. 106-520.3A(b)(2).

64. G.S. 106-520.1. The term "fair" does not encompass "noncommercial community fairs." *Id.* § 106-520.3.

65. G.S. 106-520.3A.

66. *See* Title 2, Chapter 52, Subchapter K, §§ .0101–.0702 of the North Carolina Administrative Code (hereinafter N.C.A.C.) (establishing standards for animal exhibitions at agricultural fairs; the list of requirements in the text is not comprehensive).

in public settings.[67] The report's recommendations are largely consistent with the state regulations, emphasizing the importance of fencing, signage, and hand-washing stations.

If an exhibition is in violation of the regulations, the Department may deny, suspend, or revoke its permit and may also assess a civil monetary penalty of up to $5,000.[68] In addition, private individuals who are harmed at such exhibitions may consider bringing civil lawsuits against the exhibition operators to recover money damages. In 2007, however, the General Assembly made clear that a statutory limitation on civil liability with regard to agritourism activity applied to animal exhibitions.[69] In general terms, the law provides that, subject to limited exceptions, the operator of an exhibition will not be liable for "injury to or death of a participant resulting from the inherent risks" related to the exhibition's activity.[70] To take advantage of this limitation on liability, the operator must post a sign warning the public about the "inherent risks" related to the animal exhibition.[71]

Disposal of Dead Animals

When an animal, either domestic or wild, dies, questions often arise about what is required with respect to disposing of the animal. In certain circumstances, state law imposes specific duties on animal owners, owners of property where dead animals are found, cities and counties, and on the North Carolina Department of Transportation (NCDOT).

Under G.S. 106-403, if a domesticated animal dies, the animal's owner or the person who owns or operates the property where the animal died must dispose of it within

---

67. *See* NASPHV, Animal Contact Compendium Comm., *Compendium of Measures to Prevent Disease Associated with Animals in Public Settings, 2017*, 251 J. Am. Veterinary Med. Ass'n 1268 (2017), http://www.nasphv.org/Documents/AnimalContactCompendium2017.pdf.

68. G.S. 106-520.3A(f).

69. S.L. 2007-171 (amending G.S. 99E-30(1) to explicitly provide that the limitation on agritourism activity liability described in Article 4 of G.S. Chapter 99E applies to animal exhibitions).

70. G.S. 99E-31(a). The exceptions may apply if the operator (1) commits an act or omission that constitutes willful or wanton disregard for the safety of the participant or (2) has actual knowledge or reasonably should have known of an existing dangerous condition. *Id.* § 99E-31(b).

71. G.S. 99E-32. The sign must include the following language: "WARNING. Under North Carolina law, there is no liability for an injury to or death of a participant in an agritourism activity conducted at this agritourism location if such injury or death results from the inherent risks of the agritourism activity. Inherent risks of agritourism activities include, among others, risks of injury inherent to land, equipment, and animals, as well as the potential for you to act in a negligent manner that may contribute to your injury or death. You are assuming the risk of participating in this agritourism activity." *Id.*

twenty-four hours of learning of its death.[72] The term *domesticated animal* is not defined in the law but typically is used to refer to animals that are socialized.[73] In other words, animals that have adapted to live closely with or alongside humans, such as pet dogs, cats, and rabbits. Though the term is not otherwise defined, *poultry* may be considered "domesticated animals" according to this statute.

The approved disposal methods under this law are

- burying the animal at least 3 feet underground and no less than 300 feet from any flowing stream or public body of water;
- rendering the animal at a licensed rendering plant;
- completely incinerating the animal;
- for poultry, placing in a disposal pit as authorized by law; and
- any other method approved by the State Veterinarian at the North Carolina Department of Agriculture and Consumer Services.[74]

A willful violation of this law is a Class 2 misdemeanor.[75]

Cities and counties are required to designate a person to arrange for the removal of dead animals whose owners cannot be identified. Cities are responsible for animals within city limits, and counties are responsible for all areas outside the limits of any municipality.[76] Some jurisdictions, such as Winston-Salem and Asheville, have sanitation services available to pick up dead animals from their owners and dispose of them.[77]

NCDOT is charged with removing and disposing of dead animals from primary and secondary roads. If someone notices a dead animal on the road, he or she can contact NCDOT through an online portal or by phone.[78] If it finds some evidence about the ownership of a dog found dead, NCDOT must take "reasonable steps" to notify the

72. G.S. 106-403.

73. *Cf.* G.S. 130A-184 (defining "feral" in the context of state rabies control law to mean an animal that is not socialized).

74. G.S. 106-403; 2 N.C.A.C. 52C, § .0102.

75. G.S. 106-405.

76. G.S. 106-403.

77. *See* City of Winston-Salem, Sanitation Div., *Collections* (2018), http://www.cityofws.org/departments/sanitation/collections#Dead%20Animal%20Removal ("The City provides dead animal collection Monday through Friday from 8:00 am to 2:00 pm and on Saturdays from 8:00 am to 12:00 pm. Animals are collected from the streets. No collections are made on private property. Residents should place animals in a bag and place by the curb."); City of Asheville, Sanitation Services, *Bulky Item Collection*, http://www.ashevillenc.gov/departments/sanitation/bulky_item_collection.htm ("Small dead animals, such as a cat, dog or other small, household pet, must be wrapped in a plastic bag and placed at the curb.") (last visited Apr. 18, 2018).

78. NCDOT, *Report a Debris Problem* (last updated July 17, 2018), https://www.ncdot.gov/contact/Pages/form.aspx?UnitName=debris&sourceUrl=/contact/.

owner.[79] Municipalities may also be involved with removing dead animals from the roads maintained by the municipality.[80]

Emergency Preparedness

In 2006, Congress passed federal legislation addressing care for animals during natural disasters and emergencies.[81] The federal law made three policy changes. First, it requires state and local government emergency preparedness plans to "take into account the needs of individuals with household pets and service animals prior to, during, and following a major disaster or emergency."[82] These plans are important because the Federal Emergency Management Agency (FEMA) may rely on them when allocating and distributing certain federal preparedness funds to states and other governmental entities.[83] The second change specifically allows FEMA to provide funding to state and local authorities for animal emergency preparedness purposes.[84] Finally, the act authorizes FEMA to provide assistance and funding to state and local governments involved with the "provision of rescue, care, shelter, and essential needs" to people who have household pets and service animals.[85] In October 2007, FEMA released guidance outlining the parameters of the new policy.[86] In summary, the guidance

- defines key terms, including "household pet" and "service animal";
- identifies entities that are eligible for reimbursement; and
- lists the types of activities and services that are reimbursable, including certain costs incurred for labor, facilities, supplies, equipment, veterinary services, transportation, and removal and disposal of dead animals.

---

79. G.S. 136-18(21).

80. *See* G.S. 136-66.1 (defining the maintenance responsibilities for streets and highways inside municipalities). For example, the City of Durham's Street Maintenance Division will collect and dispose of dead animals found on streets within the city right-of-way. City of Durham, *Street Maintenance Division*, https://durhamnc.gov/979/Street-Maintenance-Division (last visited Apr. 18, 2018).

81. Pets Evacuation and Transportation Standards Act of 2006 (PETS Act), Pub. L. No. 109-308, 120 Stat. 1,725 (2006).

82. 42 U.S.C. § 5196b(g).

83. 42 U.S.C. §§ 5196b(a), (f).

84. 42 U.S.C. § 5196(j)(2).

85. 42 U.S.C. § 5170b(a)(3).

86. FEMA, FEMA Disaster Assistance Policy No. 9523.19, *Eligible Costs Related to Pet Evacuation and Sheltering* (Oct. 24, 2007), https://www.hsdl.org/?abstract&did=769097.

Bird Sanctuaries

North Carolina cities have the authority to adopt ordinances establishing bird sanctuaries within their jurisdictions.[87] If a city establishes a sanctuary, it may restrict the hunting, killing, and trapping of birds within city limits. The restrictions will not extend, however, to birds that are considered pests under state law. For example, the North Carolina Pesticide Board has declared the red-winged blackbird a pest and has authorized the use of pesticides on the birds in certain circumstances.[88] Use of such pesticides would be allowed within a bird sanctuary. Below is an example of a sanctuary ordinance.

(a) *Town designated as sanctuary.* The area within the corporate limits of the town and all land owned or leased by the town outside the corporate limits is hereby designated as a bird sanctuary, as authorized by G.S. 160A-188.

(b) *Unlawful to trap, etc.* It shall be unlawful intentionally to trap, hunt, shoot, or otherwise kill, within the sanctuary hereby established, any native wild bird, except those birds classified as a pest under article 22A of chapter 113 of the General Statutes (G.S. 113-300.1 et seq.) and the Structural Pest Control Act of North Carolina of 1955 (G.S. 106-55.22 et seq.) or the North Carolina Pesticide Law of 1971 (G.S. 143-434 et seq.), pursuant to an appropriate permit issued by the North Carolina Wildlife Commission.[89]

Pets in Food and Lodging Establishments

Food and lodging establishments may allow companion animals[90] to accompany their owners in certain circumstances. Note that service animals are subject to several other bodies of law, discussed in chapter 8.

Operators of inns and hotels may establish policies allowing guests to bring pets into sleeping rooms and adjoining rooms.[91] Hotels that allow pets must (1) post a notice of that fact in the registration area, (2) post a sign in any sleeping room where pets are allowed, and (3) prohibit pets in at least 10 percent of the sleeping rooms. An operator may be charged with a Class 3 misdemeanor for failing to comply with these

---

87. G.S. 160A-188.

88. 2 N.C.A.C. 09L, § .0706 ("Pesticides registered for use to control the red-winged blackbird may be used when it is committing or about to commit depredations upon ornamental or shade trees, agricultural crops, livestock, or wildlife, or when concentrated in such numbers or manner as to constitute a health hazard or other nuisance.").

89. Town of Smithfield, N.C., Code of Ordinances § 4-60.

90. See Chapter 8 for a discussion of service or assistance animals.

91. G.S. 72-7.1.

requirements. In addition, a person who brings a pet into a room where pets are prohibited may be charged with a Class 3 misdemeanor.

Regulated food establishments may allow dogs and cats in outdoor dining areas, but only if the animal is physically restrained; does not pass through indoor areas of the establishment; and does not come into physical contact with food, food service items (e.g., dishes, utensils), or employees engaged in the preparation or handling of food.[92]

Abandoned Livestock

A recent change in the law allows for disposition of livestock that is left in the paid care of another and then subsequently abandoned by the owner.[93] This amended law would apply, for example, if a horse owner boards a horse at a farm but stops paying the boarding fee after a few months. Specifically, livestock will be considered "abandoned" under this provision if

- The animal was placed in the custody of another person for treatment, boarding, or care;
- The owner of the animal does not retake custody within two months of the owner's last payment; and
- The custodian of the animal has made reasonable efforts to collect payment during those two months.[94]

After the two months since the last payment have passed, the custodian may sell or transfer the animal. At the time of the sale or transfer, the custodian must execute an affidavit certifying that the requirements of this law have been satisfied and identifying the buyer or transferee. If the custodian is unable to sell or transfer the animal, the custodian may humanely dispose of it, though the custodian is not required to do so. Note that custodians are required at the time the animal is delivered to provide owners with written notice of this law and the consequences of abandonment.[95]

---

92. 15A N.C.A.C. 18A, § .2656 (incorporating by reference the U.S. Food and Drug Administration's 2009 U.S. Food Code, ch. 6, subpt. 501, §115, available at https://www.fda.gov/Food/GuidanceRegulation/RetailFoodProtection/FoodCode/ucm2019396.htm).

93. G.S. 68-17 (as amended by S.L. 2017-108).

94. G.S. 68-17(b).

95. *Id.*

Electronic Dog Collars

It is a crime to intentionally remove or destroy an electronic dog collar or other electronic device placed on a dog by its owner to maintain control of the dog.[96] The first violation is a Class 3 misdemeanor, and subsequent convictions are Class 2 misdemeanors.

---

96. G.S. 14-401.17.

Appendix. Relevant Sections of the North Carolina General Statutes (G.S.)

Article 5 [of G.S. Chapter 19A].
Spay/Neuter Program.

§ 19A-60. Legislative findings.

The General Assembly finds that the uncontrolled breeding of cats and dogs in the State has led to unacceptable numbers of unwanted dogs, puppies and cats and kittens. These unwanted animals become strays and constitute a public nuisance and a public health hazard. The animals themselves suffer privation and death, are impounded, and most are destroyed at great expense to local governments. It is the intention of the General Assembly to provide a voluntary means of funding a spay/neuter program to provide financial assistance to local governments offering low-income persons reduced-cost spay/neuter services for their dogs and cats and to provide a statewide education program on the benefits of spaying and neutering pets.

§ 19A-61. Spay/Neuter Program established.

There is established in the Department of Agriculture and Consumer Services a voluntary statewide program to foster the spaying and neutering of dogs and cats for the purpose of reducing the population of unwanted animals in the State. The program shall consist of the following components:

  (1) Education Program. – The Department shall establish a statewide program to educate the public about the benefits of having cats and dogs spayed and neutered. The Department may work cooperatively on the program with the North Carolina School of Veterinary Medicine, other State agencies and departments, county and city health departments and animal control agencies, and statewide and local humane organizations. The Department may employ outside consultants to assist with the education program.

  (2) Local Spay/Neuter Assistance Program. – The Department shall administer the Spay/Neuter Account established in G.S. 19A-62. Monies deposited in the account shall be available to reimburse eligible counties and cities for the direct costs of spay/neuter surgeries for cats and dogs made available to low-income persons.

§ 19A-62. Spay/Neuter Account established.

  (a) Creation. – The Spay/Neuter Account is established as a nonreverting special revenue account in the Department of Agriculture and Consumer Services. The Account consists of the following:

   (1) [Repealed by S.L. 2010-31, § 11.4(c), effective October 1, 2010.]

   (2) Twenty dollars ($20.00) of the additional fee imposed by G.S. 20-79.7 for an Animal Lovers special license plate.

   (3) Any other funds available from appropriations by the General Assembly or from contributions and grants from public or private sources.

  (b) Use. – The revenue in the Account shall be used by the Department of Agriculture and Consumer Services as follows:

   (1) [Repealed by S.L. 2010-31, § 11.4(c), effective October 1, 2010.]

   (2) Up to twenty percent (20%) may be used to develop and implement the statewide education program component of the Spay/Neuter Program established in G.S. 19A-61(1).

(3) Up to twenty percent (20%) of the money in the Account may be used to defray the costs of administering the Spay/Neuter Program established in this Article.

(4) Funds remaining after deductions for the education program and administrative expenses shall be distributed quarterly to eligible counties and cities seeking reimbursement for reduced-cost spay/neuter surgeries performed during the previous calendar year. A county or city is ineligible to receive funds under this subdivision unless it requires the owner to show proof of rabies vaccination at the time of the procedure or, if none, require vaccination at the time of the procedure.

(c) Report. – In March of each year, the Department must report to the Joint Legislative Commission on Governmental Operations and the Fiscal Research Division. The report must contain information regarding all revenues and expenditures of the Spay/Neuter Account.

§ 19A-63. Eligibility for distributions from Spay/Neuter Account; Definitions.

(a) A county or city is eligible for reimbursement from the Spay/Neuter Account if it meets the following condition:

(1) The county or city offers one or more of the following programs to low-income persons on a year-round basis for the purpose of reducing the cost of spaying and neutering procedures for dogs and cats:

    a. A spay/neuter clinic operated by the county or city.

    b. A spay/neuter clinic operated by a non-profit organization under contract or other arrangement with the county or city.

    c. A contract or contracts with one or more veterinarians, whether or not located within the county, to provide reduced-cost spaying and neutering procedures.

    d. Subvention of the spaying and neutering costs incurred by low-income pet owners through the use of vouchers or other procedure that provides a discount of the cost of the spaying or neutering procedure fixed by a participating veterinarian.

    e. Subvention of the spaying and neutering costs incurred by persons who adopt a pet from an animal shelter operated by or under contract with the county or city.

(2) Reserved for future codification purposes.

(b) The following definitions apply in this Article:

(1) Local veterinarian. – A veterinarian licensed by the North Carolina Veterinary Medical Board under Article 11 of Chapter 90 of the General Statutes and practicing within the county where the services are provided. If no licensed veterinarian practices within that county, then a local veterinarian is a licensed veterinarian practicing in a county adjacent to the county where the services are provided. For purposes of this definition, "practicing" means engaging in the practice of veterinary medicine, as defined in Article 11 of Chapter 90 of the General Statutes.

(2) Low-income person. – An individual who qualifies for one or more of the programs of public assistance administered by the Department of Health and Human Services pursuant to Chapter 108A of the General Statutes or whose annual household income is lower than one hundred percent (100%) of the federal poverty level guidelines published by the United States Department of Health and Human Services.

(c) Each county shall make rules or publish guidelines that designate what proof a low-income person must submit to establish that the person has an annual household income lower than one hundred percent (100%) of the federal poverty level guidelines published by the United States Department of Health and Human Services.

(d)   Each county shall provide the opportunity to participate in the program created by this Article to all local veterinarians. Proof of the provision of this opportunity shall be included in the first reimbursement request of each calendar year.

§ 19A-64. Distributions to counties and cities from Spay/Neuter Account.

(a)   Reimbursable Costs. – Counties and cities eligible for distributions from the Spay/Neuter Account may receive reimbursement for the direct costs of a spay/neuter surgical procedure for a dog or cat owned by a low-income person as defined in G.S. 19A-63(b). Reimbursable costs shall include anesthesia, medication, and veterinary services. Counties and cities shall not be reimbursed for the administrative costs of providing reduced-cost spay/neuter services or capital expenditures for facilities and equipment associated with the provision of such services. The reimbursement amount for each surgical procedure for a female dog or cat shall be no more than one hundred fifty percent (150%) of the average reimbursement allowed for surgical procedures for female dogs and cats by the Spay/Neuter Program during the prior calendar year. The reimbursement amount for each surgical procedure for a male dog or cat shall be no more than one hundred fifty percent (150%) of the average reimbursement allowed for surgical procedures for male dogs and cats by the Spay/Neuter Program during the prior calendar year.

(b)   Application. – A county or city eligible for reimbursement of spaying and neutering costs from the Spay/Neuter Account shall apply to the Department of Agriculture and Consumer Services by the last day of January, April, July, and October of each year to receive a distribution from the Account for that quarter. The application shall be submitted in the form required by the Department and shall include an itemized listing of the costs for which reimbursement is sought.

(c)   Distribution. – The Department shall make payments from the Spay/Neuter Account to eligible counties and cities who have made timely application for reimbursement within 30 days of the closing date for receipt of applications for that quarter. In the event that total requests for reimbursement exceed the amounts available in the Spay/neuter Account for distribution, the monies available will be distributed as follows:

   (1)   Fifty percent (50%) of the monies available in the Spay/Neuter Account shall be reserved for reimbursement for eligible applicants within development tier one areas as defined in G.S. 143B-437.08. The remaining fifty percent (50%) of the funds shall be used to fund reimbursement requests from eligible applicants in development tier two and three areas as defined in G.S. 143B-437.08.

   (2)   Among the eligible counties and cities in development tier one areas, reimbursement shall be made to each eligible county or city in the proportion that the rate of spays and neuters per one thousand persons in that city or county compares to the total rate of spays and neuters per one thousand persons within the total tier one area. Population data shall be obtained from the most recent decennial census.

   (3)   Among the eligible counties and cities in development tier two and three areas, reimbursement shall be made to each eligible county or city in the proportion that the rate of spays and neuters per one thousand persons in that city or county compares to the total rate of spays and neuters per one thousand persons within the total tier two and three area. Population data shall be obtained from the most recent decennial census.

   (4)   Should funds remain available from the fifty percent (50%) of the Spay/Neuter Account designated for development tier one areas after reimbursement of all claims by eligible applicants in those areas, the remaining funds shall be made available to reimburse eligible applicants in development tier two and three areas.

§ 19A-65. Annual Report Required From Every Animal Shelter in Receipt of State or Local Funding.

Every county or city animal shelter, or animal shelter operated under contract with a county or city or otherwise in receipt of State or local funding shall prepare an annual report in the form required by the Department of Agriculture and Consumer Services setting forth the numbers, by species, of animals received into the shelter, the number adopted out, the number returned to owner, and the number destroyed. The report shall also contain the total operating expenses of the shelter and the cost per animal handled. The report shall be filed with the Department of Agriculture and Consumer Services by March 1 of each year. A city or county that does not timely file the report required by this section is not eligible to receive reimbursement payments under G.S. 19A-64 during the calendar year in which the report was to be filed.

§ 19A-66. Notification of available funding.

Prior to January 1 of each year, the Department of Agriculture and Consumer Services shall notify counties and cities that have, prior to that notification deadline, established eligibility for distribution of funds from the Spay/Neuter Account pursuant to G.S. 19A-63, of the following:

(1) The amount of funding in the Spay/Neuter Account that the Department will have available for distribution to each county or city receiving notification to pay reimbursement requests submitted by the county or city during the calendar year following the notification deadline; and

(2) The amount of additional funding, if any, the Department estimates, but does not guarantee, may be available to pay reimbursement requests submitted by the notified county or city to the Department during the calendar year following the notification deadline.

(3) The maximum amount that may be reimbursed for each surgical procedure for a female dog or cat during the upcoming calendar year.

(4) The maximum amount that may be reimbursed for each surgical procedure for a male dog or cat during the upcoming calendar year.

Article 7 [of G.S. Chapter 153A].
Taxation.

. . .

§ 153A-153. Animal tax.

A county may levy an annual license tax on the privilege of keeping dogs and other pets within the county.

. . .

Article 9 [of G.S. Chapter 160A].
Taxation.

. . .

§ 160A-212. Animal taxes.

A city shall have power to levy an annual license tax on the privilege of keeping any domestic animal, including dogs and cats, within the city. This section shall not limit the city's authority to enact ordinances under G.S. 160A-186.

. . .

Article 8 [of G.S. Chapter 160A].
Delegation and Exercise of the General Police Power.

. . .

§ 160A-188. Bird sanctuaries.

A city may by ordinance create and establish a bird sanctuary within the city limits. The ordinance may not protect any birds classed as a pest under Article 22A of Chapter 113 of the General Statutes and the Structural Pest Control Act of North Carolina of 1955 or the North Carolina Pesticide Law of 1971. When a bird sanctuary has been established, it shall be unlawful for any person to hunt, kill, trap, or otherwise take any protected birds within the city limits except pursuant to a permit issued by the North Carolina Wildlife Resources Commission under G.S. 113-274(c) (1a) or under any other license or permit of the Wildlife Resources Commission specifically made valid for use in taking birds within city limits.

. . .

Article 4 [of G.S. Chapter 99E].
Agritourism Activity Liability.

§ 99E-30. Definitions.

As used in this Article, the following terms mean:
   (1)   Agritourism activity. – Any activity carried out on a farm or ranch that allows members of the general public, for recreational, entertainment, or educational purposes, to view or enjoy rural activities, including farming, ranching, historic, cultural, harvest-your-own activities, or natural activities and attractions. An activity is an agritourism activity whether or not the participant paid to participate in the activity. "Agritourism activity" includes an activity involving any animal exhibition at an agricultural fair licensed by the Commissioner of Agriculture pursuant to G.S. 106-520.3.
   (2)   Agritourism professional. – Any person who is engaged in the business of providing one or more agritourism activities, whether or not for compensation.
   (3)   Inherent risks of agritourism activity. – Those dangers or conditions that are an integral part of an agritourism activity including certain hazards, including surface and subsurface conditions, natural conditions of land, vegetation, and waters, the behavior of wild or domestic animals, and ordinary dangers of structures or equipment ordinarily used in farming and ranching operations. Inherent risks of agritourism activity also include the potential of a participant to act in a negligent manner that may contribute to injury to the participant or others, including failing to follow instructions given by the agritourism professional or failing to exercise reasonable caution while engaging in the agritourism activity.
   (4)   Participant. – Any person, other than the agritourism professional, who engages in an agritourism activity.
   (5)   Person. – An individual, fiduciary, firm, association, partnership, limited liability company, corporation, unit of government, or any other group acting as a unit.

§ 99E-31. Liability.

   (a)   Except as provided in subsection (b) of this section, an agritourism professional is not liable for injury to or death of a participant resulting from the inherent risks of agritourism activities, so long as the warning contained in G.S. 99E-32 is posted as required and, except as provided in subsection (b) of this section, no participant or participant's representative can maintain an action against or recover from an agritourism professional for injury, loss, damage, or death of the participant resulting exclusively from any of the inherent risks of agritourism activities. In any action for damages against an agritourism professional for agritourism activity, the agritourism professional must plead the affirmative defense of assumption of the risk of agritourism activity by the participant.

(b) Nothing in subsection (a) of this section prevents or limits the liability of an agritourism professional if the agritourism professional does any one or more of the following:

  (1) Commits an act or omission that constitutes willful or wanton disregard for the safety of the participant, and that act or omission proximately causes injury, damage, or death to the participant.

  (2) Has actual knowledge or reasonably should have known of an existing dangerous condition on the land, facilities, or equipment used in the activity or the dangerous propensity of a particular animal used in such activity and does not make the danger known to the participant, and the danger proximately causes injury, damage, or death to the participant.

(c) Nothing in subsection (a) of this section prevents or limits the liability of an agritourism professional under liability provisions as set forth in Chapter 99B of the General Statutes.

(d) Any limitation on legal liability afforded by this section to an agritourism professional is in addition to any other limitations of legal liability otherwise provided by law.

§ 99E-32. Warning required.

(a) Every agritourism professional must post and maintain signs that contain the warning notice specified in subsection (b) of this section. The sign must be placed in a clearly visible location at the entrance to the agritourism location and at the site of the agritourism activity. The warning notice must consist of a sign in black letters, with each letter to be a minimum of one inch in height. Every written contract entered into by an agritourism professional for the providing of professional services, instruction, or the rental of equipment to a participant, whether or not the contract involves agritourism activities on or off the location or at the site of the agritourism activity, must contain in clearly readable print the warning notice specified in subsection (b) of this section.

(b) The signs and contracts described in subsection (a) of this section must contain the following notice of warning:

"WARNING

Under North Carolina law, there is no liability for an injury to or death of a participant in an agritourism activity conducted at this agritourism location if such injury or death results from the inherent risks of the agritourism activity. Inherent risks of agritourism activities include, among others, risks of injury inherent to land, equipment, and animals, as well as the potential for you to act in a negligent manner that may contribute to your injury or death. You are assuming the risk of participating in this agritourism activity."

(c) Failure to comply with the requirements concerning warning signs and notices provided in this subsection will prevent an agritourism professional from invoking the privileges of immunity provided by this Article.

Article 45 [of G.S. Chapter 106].
Agricultural Societies and Fairs.

. . .

§ 106-520.3A. Animal exhibition regulation; permit required; civil penalties.

(a) Title. – This section may be referred to as "Aedin's Law". This section provides for the regulation of animal exhibitions as they may affect the public health and safety.

(b) Definitions. – As used in this section, unless the context clearly requires otherwise:

    (1) "Animal" means only those animals that may transmit infectious diseases.

    (2) "Animal exhibition" means any sanctioned agricultural fair where animals are displayed on the exhibition grounds for physical contact with humans.

(c) Permit Required. – No animal exhibition may be operated for use by the general public unless the owner or operator has obtained an operation permit issued by the Commissioner. The Commissioner may issue an operation permit only after physical inspection of the animal exhibition and a determination that the animal exhibition meets the requirements of this section and rules adopted pursuant to this section. The Commissioner may deny, suspend, or revoke a permit on the basis that the exhibition does not comply with this section or rules adopted pursuant to this section.

(d) Rules. – For the protection of the public health and safety, the Commissioner of Agriculture, with the advice and approval of the State Board of Agriculture, and in consultation with the Division of Public Health of the Department of Health and Human Services, shall adopt rules concerning the operation of and issuance of permits for animal exhibitions. The rules shall include requirements for:

    (1) Education and signage to inform the public of health and safety issues.

    (2) Animal areas.

    (3) Animal care and management.

    (4) Transition and nonanimal areas.

    (5) Hand-washing facilities.

    (6) Other requirements necessary for the protection of the public health and safety.

(e) Educational Outreach. – The Department shall continue its consultative and educational efforts to inform agricultural fair operators, exhibitors, agritourism business operators, and the general public about the health risks associated with diseases transmitted by physical contact with animals.

(f) Civil Penalty. – In addition to the denial, suspension, or revocation of an operation permit, the Commissioner may assess a civil penalty of not more than five thousand dollars ($5,000) against any person who violates a provision of this section or a rule adopted pursuant to this section. In determining the amount of the penalty, the Commissioner shall consider the degree and extent of harm caused by the violation.

    The clear proceeds of civil penalties assessed pursuant to this section shall be remitted to the Civil Penalty and Forfeiture Fund in accordance with G.S. 115C-457.2.

(g) Legal Representation by Attorney General. – It shall be the duty of the Attorney General to represent the Department of Agriculture and Consumer Services or designate a member of the Attorney General's staff to represent the Department in all actions or proceedings in connection with this section.

. . .

Article 34 [of G.S. Chapter 106].
Animal Diseases.

• • •

§ 106-403. Disposition of dead domesticated animals.

It is the duty of the owner of domesticated animals that die from any cause and the owner or operator of the premises upon which any domesticated animals die, to bury the animals to a depth of at least three feet beneath the surface of the ground within 24 hours after knowledge of the death of the domesticated animals, or to otherwise dispose of the domesticated animals in a manner approved by the State Veterinarian. It is a violation of this section to bury any dead domesticated animal closer than 300 feet to any flowing stream or public body of water. It is unlawful for any person to remove the carcasses of dead domesticated animals from the person's premises to the premises of any other person without the written permission of the person having charge of the other premises and without burying the carcasses as provided under this section. The governing body of each municipality shall designate some appropriate person whose duty it shall be to provide for the removal and disposal, according to the provisions of this section, of any dead domesticated animals located within the limits of the municipality when the owner of the animals cannot be determined. The board of commissioners of each county shall designate some appropriate person whose duty it shall be to provide for the removal and disposal under this section, of any dead domesticated animals located within the limits of the county, but without the limits of any municipality, when the owner of the animals cannot be determined. All costs incurred by a municipality or county in the removal of dead domesticated animals shall be recoverable from the owner of the animals upon admission of ownership or conviction. "Domesticated animal" as used in this section includes poultry.

• • •

Article 2 [of G.S. Chapter 136].
Powers and Duties of Department and Board of Transportation.

• • •

§ 136-18. Powers of Department of Transportation.

The said Department of Transportation is vested with the following powers:

• • •

(21) The Department of Transportation is hereby authorized and directed to remove all dead animals from the traveled portion and rights-of-way of all primary and secondary roads and to dispose of such animals by burial or otherwise. In cases where there is evidence of ownership upon the body of any dead dog, the Department of Transportation shall take reasonable steps to notify the owner thereof by mail or other means.

• • •

Article 1 [of G.S. Chapter 72].
Innkeepers.
. . .

§ 72-7.1. Admittance of pets to hotel rooms.

(a)   Innkeepers may permit pets in rooms used for sleeping purposes and in adjoining rooms. Persons bringing pets into a room in which they are not permitted are in violation of this section and punishable according to subsection (d) of this section.

(b)   Innkeepers allowing pets must post a sign measuring not less than five inches by seven inches at the place where guests register informing them pets are permitted in sleeping rooms and in adjoining rooms. If certain pets are permitted or prohibited, the sign must so state. If any pets are permitted, the innkeeper must maintain a minimum of ten percent (10%) of the sleeping rooms in the inn or hotel as rooms where pets are not permitted and the sign required by this subsection must also state that such rooms are available.

(c)   All sleeping rooms in which the innkeeper permits pets must contain a sign measuring not less than five inches by seven inches, posted in a prominent place in the room, which shall be separate from the sign required by G.S. 72-6, stating that pets are permitted in the room, or whether certain pets are prohibited or permitted in the room, and stating that bringing pets into a room in which they are not permitted is a Class 3 misdemeanor.

(d)   Any person violating the provisions of this section shall be guilty of a Class 3 misdemeanor.

(e)   The provisions of this section are not applicable to assistance dogs admitted to sleeping rooms and adjoining rooms under the provisions of Chapter 168 of the General Statutes.

Article 52 [of G.S. Chapter 14].
Miscellaneous Police Regulations.
. . .

§ 14-401.17. Unlawful removal or destruction of electronic dog collars.

(a)   It is unlawful to intentionally remove or destroy an electronic collar or other electronic device placed on a dog by its owner to maintain control of the dog.

(b)   A first conviction for a violation of this section is a Class 3 misdemeanor. A second or subsequent conviction for a violation of this section is a Class 2 misdemeanor.

(c)   This act is enforceable by officers of the Wildlife Resources Commission, by sheriffs and deputy sheriffs, and peace officers with general subject matter jurisdiction.

(d)   [Repealed by S.L. 2005-94, § 1, effective December 1, 2005, and applicable to offenses committed on or after that date.]